Photographs by

Franz Lanting
Ralph Buchsbaum
Catherine Cardwell
and others.

The Natural History
of
AÑO NUEVO

EDITED
BY

Burney J. Le Boeuf
and

Stephanie Kaza

CONTRIBUTORS:

Kenneth T. Briggs
Judith E. Hansen
Stephanie Kaza

Burney J. Le Boeuf
John S. Pearse
W. Breck Tyler

Gerald E. Weber

THE BOXWOOD PRESS

Distributed by:

The Boxwood Press
P.O. Box 444
Pacific Grove, CA 93950

408—375-9110

Library of Congress Cataloging in Publication Data

The Natural History of Año Nuevo.

  Bibliography: p.

  Includes index.

  1. Natural history—California—Año Nuevo Island.
  2. Año Nuevo Island (Calif.)

  I. Le Boeuf, Burney J.
  II. Kaza, Stephanie.
  III. Briggs, Kenneth.

  QH105.C2N37   508.794'69   81-65545

  ISBN 0-910286-77-9   AACR2

Printed in U.S.A.

PREFACE

THE Año Nuevo region is an eminent part of the central California coastline 30 km north of Santa Cruz and 67 km south of San Francisco. The land is rugged, spacious, varied in terrain, sparsely inhabited, and reminiscent of an earlier time. Stands of Monterey pine and cypress dot a wild, windy coastline that projects out into the Pacific Ocean. Steep seacliffs rise from sandy beaches and extensive rocky intertidal reefs. High forested mountains drop down to rolling pastures and cultivated artichoke, flower, and brussels sprouts fields.

The idea for a book about Año Nuevo arose because several of us from the University of California at Santa Cruz were conducting research in the region during the period 1967 to 1980. Although we worked in the same area at the same time, we represented several different fields of study. We discussed bringing our independent endeavors together as a book. Our feeling was that a whole story would emerge which would be more than the sum of our individual studies. We discussed teaching a new course, *The Natural History of the Año Nuevo Region,* which would facilitate the exchange of information and encourage us to formalize our respective contributions.

When elephant seals began to frequent the mainland at Año Nuevo State Reserve in 1974, the need for such a course became critical. The seals attracted thousands of tourists to the area overnight, making it impossible for the small, existing staff of rangers to protect the seals from people and people from the seals. Roger Werts, Parks and Recreation area manager for the reserve, had the idea that student interns might act as guides, leading people on tours to see the seals. They would need to acquire relevant background information which might be conveyed in a preparation course taught by the research scientists working at Año Nuevo. With this proposal, a safe, high quality tour experience could be provided for the public without the need for additional state money or staff, which even if it could be obtained, would not be forthcoming for several years.

The plan worked, to the astonishment of many of us, and continues to work. Since 1975, the Año Nuevo course has been taught each fall, and 40 to 70 students have acted as guides each winter when the seals and seal-watchers arrive. This cooperative program provides an unusual opportunity for students to work closely with a variety of public visitor groups, and for reserve visitors to gain detailed information about the

v

area through the refreshing enthusiasm of the volunteer student guides.

This book should serve as an introduction to the natural history of the Año Nuevo region. Our primary aim is to provide an overview of the area with details about the main attraction, the elephant seals, as well as the plants, the other animals, the geology, the climate, and the history of the area. We attempt to present a picture of Año Nuevo as a whole system rather than a collection of isolated parts. The multidisciplinary approach and the original research in each chapter should interest students of ecology, biology, geology, and natural history. The book is written for a broad, general audience but contains information that will be useful to specialists.

Our emphasis is deliberately biased in several respects. We concentrate on Año Nuevo Island, the coastline from Pigeon Point south to Waddell Creek, and the lowlands south of Pescadero to Point Año Nuevo. We give short shrift to the northern reaches of the old rancho between Butano and Pescadero. We focus on the most accessible, or to us, the most fascinating aspects of the area. This book is a summary of research to date and reflects the specific interests of the investigators. There are notable omissions. We do not treat fishes, reptiles, amphibians, insects, and non-vascular land plants for the simple reason that little is known about them in this area.

We are grateful to many people and institutions for making this book and the underlying research possible. We thank Roger Werts, San Mateo District of the California State Department of Parks and Recreation, for his constant encouragement and support. Año Nuevo rangers Lisa Beutler, Mike Bradeen, Nina Gordon, George Gray, Candace Ward, Walter Ward, and others were helpful in coordinating field work. Jenny Anderson supervised the internship program in its formative years and helped in innumerable ways.

Many people helped with various aspects of the book. We thank Roy Gordon, John Hansen, Laurie Kiguchi, and Julie Packard for assistance with research on marine and terrestrial plants; Dane Hardin, Bill Kennedy, and Chris Tarp for for help with intertidal invertebrates; Robert Gisiner, Mark Pierson, Joanne Reiter, and Marianne Riedman and many others who contributed to the research efforts on marine mammals; Hulda McLean for information on Rancho del Oso and Paul Mobley for access to U.S. Coast Guard logbooks on Año Nuevo Island. Several people offered helpful comments and advice on various drafts of chapter manuscripts, especially Ralph and Mildred Buchsbaum, Ellen Chu, William Doyle, Leo Ortiz, and Vicki Pearse.

Undergraduate student research in the Año Nuevo course contributed substantially to the collection of information about the Año Nuevo region. Scores of students pursued numerous facets of Año Nuevo, filling in the nooks and crannies of larger research efforts. We drew on work by Elliot Burch, Sabrina Chalmers, Fran Ciesla, Michael Dashe, Hannah Good, Carol Hamilton, Tom Hawke, Janna Heath, Laurie Herlich, Anne Hoover, Martha Imler, Cynthia Lance, Ralph Mitchell, Jr., Patrick Murphy, John Peterson, Nancy Rosner, Russ Rosner, Irene Reti, Charles Salmen, Susan Saylor, John Selby, Ricky Smith, Eddy Szyjewicz, and Jane Thomson.

Many people provided technical support and assistance. We thank Ann Cascarano and Annette Whelan for geology figures, Fran Ciesla for land plant drawings, Terry Brown and Lynn Campbell for bird illustrations, Julie Packard and Cathy Short for drawings of the marine algae, and Sharon Hobson for intertidal invertebrate drawings. Stan Stevens and Annette Whelan provided maps and map representations. Dotty Hollinger provided fast and efficient typing.

Financial support for earlier versions of this book was provided by three minigrants from the Committee on Instructional Improvement, University of California, Santa Cruz. Much of the geological research was funded by the U.S. Geological Survey, initially through Dr. Kenneth R. Lajoie's ongoing study of Pacific Coast marine terraces and recent tectonics, and recently through the U.S.G.S. Earthquakes Hazards Reduction Program Contract No. 14-08-0001-16822 to G. E. Weber and W.R. Cotton. Marine plant research was supported in part by NOAA Sea Grants R/A-17-A and R/A-34 to W.T. Doyle and J.E. Hansen, and intertidal invertebrates by Sea Grant No. USDC 04-3-158-22 and by the Janss Foundation, both to W.T. Doyle and J.S. Pearse. Elephant seal research was supported in part by National Science Foundation grants GB-16321, GB-36288, 41487, and DEB 77-17063 to B.J. Le Boeuf. Logistics to Año Nuevo Island were provided by the Center for Coastal Marine Studies.

Permission to carry out research on Año Nuevo State Reserve was granted by the California State Department of Parks and Recreation. The National Marine Fisheries Service provided permits for tagging and marking elephant seals and the U.S. Fish and Wildlife Service and California State Department of Fish and Game permitted the marking of seabirds and the collection of intertidal specimens.

For their inspiration, goldmine of readily given firsthand information, and direct physical support we are especially thankful to some native Año Nuevans and longtime guardians of the area. Betty and

Hank Bradley of Coastways ranch have been watching the island from the house on the former Osman Steele ranch since 1945. So have the McCrary brothers, owners of Big Creek Lumber Company, near Waddell Creek. These people possess a vast knowledge of the area and its natural dangers and they monitor it constantly. They have initiated or have been the principals in numerous rescue operations. Hank Bradley has rowed his dory into a windy channel to tow in a raft of exhausted student researchers in distress and Lud McCrary has rappelled down precipitous coastal cliffs to lift to safety someone trapped by the incoming tide. Mrs. Bradley has met shivering, wet, frightened people on the beach with blankets, brandy, and coffee. No change within their purview is overlooked. When the Año Nuevo buoy twice broke from its mooring, on 9 February 1960 and 28 October 1974, the Bradleys put in both reports. "We miss our buoy when its not buoying," said Mrs. Bradley. Another time when fishermen in distress spent the night in an open boat tied to the buoy, it was Lud McCrary who spotted them with his high-powered telescope and called for help. For a personal picture of past times at Año Nuevo, we thank Mrs. Catherine B. Steele, a former teacher and California historian who lived at Green Oaks ranch most of her life and is imbued with the spirit of the place. She remembers the unrecorded past: the unbearable "no-see-'ums" (gnats) which abounded in the sand dunes on a still day before insecticides; the "boy with the soft brown eyes"—who tried to negotiate Green Oaks ranch for a government missile tracking station (no deal), and the sound of the rum-runner's boats doing their business on Año Nuevo Bay during prohibition.

Lastly, all of us are grateful and better for our experience with this special place. We are fortunate to have had the opportunity to observe, to learn, and to be touched by the incredible beauty and mysterious complexity of this stretch of land.

Burney J. Le Boeuf
Stephanie Kaza

Santa Cruz, California
February 1, 1981

CONTENTS

LIST OF AUTHORS

Kenneth T. Briggs
Assistant Research Biologist, Center for Coastal Marine Studies
University of California, Santa Cruz, CA 95064

Judith E. Hansen
Research Associate, Hopkins Marine Station of Stanford University
Pacific Grove, CA 93950

Stephanie Kaza
Research Associate, Center for Coastal Marine Studies
University of California, Santa Cruz, CA 95064

Burney J. Le Boeuf
Professor of Biology, Crown College
University of California, Santa Cruz, CA 95064

John S. Pearse
Professor of Biology, College Eight
University of California, Santa Cruz, CA 95064

W. Breck Tyler
Assistant Marine Specialist, Center for Coastal Marine Studies
University of California, Santa Cruz, CA 95064

Gerald E. Weber
Geologic Consultant
Weber and Associates
1729 Seabright Ave., Santa Cruz, CA 95062

1

HISTORY

Burney J. Le Boeuf

Traveler near Pescadero asking directions from an old
Indian (Evans, 1874):
"And how far is it to Point Año Nuevo?"
"Oh, señor, it must be a very long way! I think it is in the
neighborhood of the other world!"

S EVENTEEN YEARS before the pilgrims landed at Plymouth
Rock, two Spanish ships sailed past a low, jutting point which
the commander of the expedition, Sebastián Vizcaino, took to be
the north end of the Bay of Monterey. It was January 3, 1603, and
Father Antonio de la Ascensión, diarist and chaplain of the expedition, wrote on his map, "Punta de Año Nuevo." The cape, for that is
what it was then, was named, the name stuck, and it still holds today
(Wagner, 1929).

Other explorers like Sir Francis Drake and Juan Rodríguez Cabrillo
had passed this way more than a half a century earlier but they did not
make a record of it. In 1584, Francisco de Gali, returning from the
Philippines, sailed in close enough to make note of the numerous seals
which abounded in the area (Wagner, 1929). Some speculate that
oriental sailors may have set eyes on this place long before the European
explorers since numerous oriental junks were found derelict or washed
ashore from Mexico to the Aleutian chain during early California
history (Denis, 1927).

The Spanish explorers of the 16th and 17th centuries must have
witnessed a profusion of animal life as they sailed along the California
coast. The wholesale slaughter and exploitation of marine mammals
that came later had not yet begun and coastal waters were no doubt
teeming with various whales and porpoises, two kinds of fur seals, two
species of sea lions, elephant seals, harbor seals, sea otters, and perhaps

1

even an occasional sea cow strayed from its home in the Aleutians. The fur seals alone probably numbered in the millions. With few exceptions, there is but scant mention of the marine creatures in the ship logs of the European mariners. This may have been because sailing along the rocky and often foggy, uncharted coast was dangerous, and sightseeing was less important than safety. Wise captains probably stayed well clear of the coast and its unknown hazards. Indeed, even before Punta del Año Nuevo was named, Spanish galleons were ordered to stay far out to sea when they reached this latitude for it already had a reputation for treacherous waters. Maybe the Spanish sailors were simply not interested in these curious mammals or didn't see the value in them, or they refused to be distracted from their primary mission. In the 18th century some explorers who ventured closer to shore were impressed by the numbers of whales in Monterey Bay. For example, one French explorer wrote, "It is impossible to describe either the number of whales with which we were surrounded, or their familiarity. They blowed every half minute within half a pistol shot from our frigates" (La Pérouse, J.F.G. de, 1798, vol. 2, p. 178).

Spain was a mighty nation in the 16th century, and her navy contained more vessels than that of any other country in the world. Spanish galleons explored the edges of the world unknown to western civilization and Spain had interests in places as widely separated as Turkey, South America, the Philippines, and New Spain (Mexico and California). But paradoxically, there was internal disorganization, political infighting, and near bankruptcy at home. Resources for the incessant wars during the reign of Philip II (1556-1598) were sought in part from the gold and silver mines of America. But there was nothing left to compare with the treasures that Cortés and Pizarro had plundered from the Aztecs and Incas in Mexico and Peru during the early part of the century. Protestant rulers, threatened by the imperialism of Roman Catholic Spain, began competing in trade and commerce. Spanish galleons were intercepted and pirated by the English, French, and Dutch (Wright, 1970). In 1585, near the height of Spanish power, open war began with England. Two years later, Drake burned a large part of the huge Spanish armada. By 1598, when Phillip III ascended to the throne, Spain was still at war with England as well as the Netherlands. For several decades, well into the 17th century, Spanish rule was characterized by decadent leaders and political and financial turmoil. The empire had started to crumble.

In New Spain there was a need for a port of refuge to rehabilitate the exhausted, scurvy-weakened sailors after their difficult return from

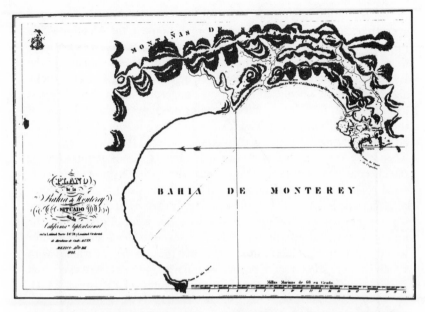

A chart of Monterey Bay drawn by Admiral Jean Francois Galaup de La Pérouse, captain of the frigate *La Boussole* and commander-in chief of a voyage destined to circumnavigate the world, during his three-week visit in 1786. This edition was published in Mexico City in 1825. Note that Punta de Año Nuevo was charted as the northernmost point on Monterey Bay.

Manila (Schurz, 1959), as well as to provide a place of escape from pirates. Luís de Velasco, the King's viceroy in Mexico City, ordered Sebastián Rodríguez Cermeño to survey the coast on his return voyage from the Philippines. Cermeño started his survey at Point Reyes (Drake's Bay) in 1595 but no sooner had he set forth when disaster struck. A southeast gale destroyed his ship and its entire precious cargo from the Orient. Although he made a courageous attempt to complete the survey in an open launch by sailing from one headland to another, he could only record in a sketchy way the general contour of the coast. He no doubt saw Cape Año Nuevo but made no specific mention of it (Wagner, 1929; Stanger, 1966).

The new viceroy, the Count of Monte-Rey, made the decision to send an exploring expedition directly north from Acapulco, and he picked Sebastián Vizcaíno as his commander, equipping him with two ships and a small frigate for close-in sailing. Vizcaíno saw nothing promising until he reached Monterey, which impressed him so much that he anchored and spent two weeks studying the area. He concluded that this location would be suitable and named it Monte-Rey after the viceroy.

3

A map of Monterey Bay done in 1793, by Francisco Eliza or Juan Martinez y
Zayas, captains of Spanish ships that sailed up the coast of Alta California in
1793. The Santa Cruz Mission had been established only two years earlier. Note
that the map shows an island off Punta de Año Nuevo.

He prepared a glowing report and dispatched it south with one of his
largest ships, while he continued his reconnaissance up the coast.

Punta del Año Nuevo was named as he passed by on his way northward to Point Reyes. Vizcaíno makes no mention of San Francisco Bay
or the Farallones in his journal. Perhaps he played it safe by passing the
latter to seaward. Whatever the reason, the narrow entrance to San
Francisco Bay was overlooked, and this great harbor remained
unknown to Spain and the outside world for another 150 years
(Stanger, 1966).

The Portolá Expedition

There is no record of European contact with Punta del Año Nuevo region, or with any of Alta California for that matter, until 166 years later when Gaspar de Portolá and his overland party passed by on their northward expedition which led to the discovery of San Francisco Bay. Vizcaíno's rosy report had been received, but the Spanish empire had more pressing problems and Alta California was ignored. The galleons continued to make yearly voyages to the Philippines, and returning, sailed down the coast within sight of land. But no harbor of refuge was established nor was an attempt made to colonize the country until Spain's possession was threatened by British and Russian interests. The Russians had crossed the Bering Sea and established themselves on the Alaska coast, and their hunters were beginning to pursue the sea otter into more southern waters. England had obtained Canada from France and was starting to eye Spanish possessions. In 1768 the Spanish king decided to defend the territory by occupying it.

The man sent to do the job was Gaspar de Portolá. He was appointed Governor of "The Californias" and Commander of the military; Fray Junípero Serra and several other priests accompanied him with the charge of founding missions. Portolá left San Diego on July 14, 1769 with 64 men, most of whom were leather-jacketed soldiers, and 200 animals in the pack train. It took them two months of hard marching through the wilderness to reach Monterey, which turned out to be a great disappointment to Portolá. His view from the land did not fit the glowing report Vizcaíno had made while anchored in the harbor near Point Pinos. Portolá and his men assembled to discuss the possibility that a mistake had been made in calculating the latitude. The meeting ended with his officers voting unanimously to continue north despite the hardships, excessive labor, shortage of provisions and disease (17 men were already half crippled with scurvy and could do no work).

The party moved slowly northward, keeping close to the coast. They camped at Soquel Creek, San Lorenzo River, Coja Creek, and Scott Creek. On 20 October they reached Waddell Creek and the autumn rains caught up with them. The men were drenched and forced to remain here for two more days—wet, sick, and miserable. To compound their discomfort, the entire party was attacked by diarrhea, a condition which may have been induced from eating too many blackberries, which one diarist noted were plentiful in the area. In the end, the gastric ailment was worth it, for the vitamin C in the berries apparently counteracted the dread scurvy, so that when the storm ended, all the men felt better, even the very sick, and the area was named "La Cañada de la Salud." As they broke camp on 23 October, Punta del Año Nuevo could be seen about one league (approximately 4.2 kilometers) to the north. Like many early mariners, they took it to be the northernmost point on Monterey Bay.

The expedition followed the beach as they departed La Cañada de la Salud, probably because the crumbling "Sierra Blanca" north of the creek thwarted their passage overland and they had to wait for low tide in order to pass. The following night the party camped at Whitehouse Creek where they visited the Indian village, and according to Fray Crespi's log (Bolton, 1927), were welcomed with "demonstrations of pleasure." The Indians were given beads in exchange, a commodity the Spanish had been using in trade with natives of the New World since the expeditions of Columbus. Fray Crespi thought the region offered a good arroyo of water, much pasture, and an abundance of firewood. On their return trip from San Francisco Bay they found the village deserted and made camp on Año Nuevo Creek on 19 November 1769 (Bolton, 1927).

The Ohlones

The aborigines began occupying coastal California at least 10,000 years ago (Meighan, 1965). The early Spanish settlers called the Indians they encountered between San Francisco Bay and the area a few miles below Monterey, "Costeños" or coast people, but later the name was corrupted to "Costaños" or "Costanoans" (Stanger, 1966). Descendants of these people call themselves "Ohlones."

The Ohlones were not a unified tribe of people like the Sioux or Navajo. There were approximately 40 different groups of people, each with their own territory and chief, in the coastal area between Point Sur and San Francisco Bay. The average size of a group was about 250 people. This was the densest population of aborigines north of Mexico. Eight to twelve different languages were spoken. Some groups living only 20 miles apart had difficult understanding each other (Margolin, 1978). Lorenzo Venancio, an Indian born and raised at Mission Santa Cruz, was quoted as saying "These tribes nearest to the mission, such as up the coast a way, and as far south as Aptos, could understand each other, but those from a few miles farther off did not" (Torchiana, 1933).

One of the largest Indian communities in the Monterey Bay region was in the Año Nuevo area. The other large population center was on the Monterey Peninsula. In Portolá's time there were villages on Año

Nuevo Creek and Whitehouse Creek.

We know little about these people and how they lived because their culture did not last long after contact with the Europeans. Diseases to which they had never been exposed and to which they had built up no immunity, decimated their numbers within a few decades. Whooping cough and measles may have been responsible for many deaths, as was the case with other California Indians. Those Indians that did not succumb to disease were driven away from their food supply or the resource itself was destroyed as Europeans settled in the area (Cook, 1943). It is estimated that there were perhaps 4,000 Costanoans living in the Monterey Bay area when the first Europeans arrived. In 1920, there were only 56 survivors.

Another reason for our ignorance about this culture is that the Spanish missionaries did not attempt to record all native customs, especially those which were in opposition to their own. With few exceptions, "the official attitude, imposed by both state and church, was that all pagan practices were of the Devil and must be stamped out with all possible vigor" (Stanger, 1966).

Our knowledge of Ohlone culture comes from the observations of early travelers, from mission records, and from artifacts found at village sites. Miguel Costanso, a member of the Portolá expedition, described the first contact with Año Nuevo Indians in 1769 (Teggart, 1911):

Monday October 23. We moved the camp a distance of two leagues [about 10 km] from the *Cañada de la Salud* [Waddell Creek], and camped near an Indian village, discovered by the scouts, situated in a pleasant and attractive spot at the foot of a mountain range and in front of a ravine covered with pine and savin, among which descended a stream from which the natives obtained water. The land appeared pleasant; it was covered with pasture, and was not without firewood. We traveled part of the way along the beach; the rest, from the point of rocks previously mentioned, to the village, over high, level land with plenty of water standing in ponds of greater or less extent.

The Indians, advised by the scouts of our coming to their lands, received us with great affability and kindness, and, furthermore, presented us with seeds kneaded into thick pats. They also offered us some cakes of a certain sweet paste, which some of our men said was the honey of wasps; they brought it carefully wrapped in the leaves of *carrizo* cane, and its taste was not all bad.

In the middle of the village there was a large house, spherical in form and very roomy; the other small houses, built in the form of a pyramid, had very little room, and were built of split pine wood. As the large house so much surpassed the others, the village was named after it.

According to Stanger (1966), this Village of the Casa Grande was on Whitehouse Creek, about a mile and a half east of Highway No. 1, where the "girl-scout-camp-road" first comes down into the valley of the creek.

On the following day, Costanso writes:

Tuesday, October 24. The Indians of La Casa Grande furnished us with guides to go forward. We traveled to the north over high hills, not far from the shore. We encountered a number of slopes which were rather troublesome, and we had to put them in condition for travel—as also the crossing of two streams thickly grown with brush [Gazos and Pescaderos Creeks]—before we arrived at an Indian village, two leagues from the place from which we started. This we found to be without inhabitants, who were out at the time getting seeds. We saw six or seven of them at work, and they informed us that a little farther on there was another and more populous village, and that the inhabitants of it would make us presents and aid us in whatever we needed. We believed them, and although it was somewhat late we passed on and proceeded for two leagues more over rolling country until we reached the village. The road, while difficult, over hills and canyons, was attractive. To us, the land seemed rich and of good quality; the watering places were frequent; and the natives of the best disposition and temper that so far we had seen.

The village stood within a valley surrounded by high hills, and the ocean could be seen through an entrance to the west-north-west. There was in the valley [San Gregorio] a stream of running water, and the land, though burned in the vicinity of the village, was not without pasture on the hillsides.

The Village of the Casa Grande was deserted on 19 November 1769 when the Portolá expedition returned on its trek south. Five years later, Captain Fernando Rivera's expedition found only "vestiges of a deserted village" in the same area (Bolton, 1927). Stanger (1966) believes that the Casa Grande was no ordinary sweat house but rather had a ceremonial function. He reports that nothing like it appears anywhere else in central California and that it doesn't resemble Indian construction in more distant regions.

Another early description of Indian culture is by Pedro Fages, also a member of the Portolá expedition. He wrote specifically of the Indians in the Año Nuevo region (Priestly, 1937):

The Indians who live in the direction of the Punta del Año Nuevo, eight leagues inland and about twelve leagues from this royal presidio [Monterey], are of good features, their skin is not so dark, and they wear long moustaches. They are very clever at going out to fish embarked on rafts of reeds, and they succeed, during good weather, in getting their provisions from the sea, especially since the land also provides them with abundance of seeds and fruits which have been mentioned a little above, although the harvesting of them and their enjoyment is disputed with bow and arrow among these natives and their neighbors, who live almost constantly at war with each other.

Much of what we know of how Ohlones made a living is inferred from examination of old habitation sites. These are located today by shellmounds or kitchen-midden deposits which accumulated in the villages. The largest of these Indian refuse heaps north of the Monterey Peninsula is on the dunes of Año Nuevo Point. In fact, this midden area extends to Gazos Greek, as far northward as the dunes themselves. More than a dozen shellmounds are located on the dunes of Año Nuevo Point alone. Proximity to an intertidal zone where shellfish and the like were abundant (e.g., areas of reefs and gradually sloping rock areas) and closeness to fresh water creeks were no doubt important factors in the selection of habitation sites (Gordon, 1974).

Ohlones ate various forms of shorelife. Gordon (1974) found remains of the following animals at the surface of one shellmound on Año Nuevo Point: shells of the California mussel, black turban, shell limpet, littleneck clam, purple-hinged scallop, olivella, red abalone, barnacles, and some large sea snails such as the red turban; gumboot chiton plates, purple sea urchin tests, and crab claws; and fish, bird, and mammal bones. In these mounds, as well as others in the area, the mussel predominates. Along with the shells and other animal remains, Gordon recorded large quantities of chipped chert and flint, smooth flat stones (about the size of a fist) used in boiling water, and small amounts of obsidian.

Ohlones cooked their food by dropping heated stones into tightly woven baskets filled with water. When the water reached the boiling point food was added. Since shells found in the middens are usually unbroken, they may have been boiled whole for soups. This method of food preparation would help to explain the small size of many of the shells found in the middens (Gordon, 1974).

Most of the bones identified in the mounds belong to marine mammals. This has been documented in the Monterey Bay area, where Edna Fisher (quoted in Gordon, 1974) found that seal, sea lion, and sea otter bones were more numerous than terrestial mammal bones. Marine mammal material in the mounds on Año Nuevo Point has not been analyzed in detail but it is likely that similar results would be found, for pinnipeds have long been associated with this area. Indeed, archeological evidence indicates that sea mammals were an important source of food for Indians along the entire California coast; the early Spanish explorers made no mention of this habit.

A basket containing boiling stones, a mortar and pestle, and a winnowing basket with arrowheads made from chipped chert, photographed on a kitchen midden at Año Nuevo Point. (F. Lanting)

Another important food source for California Indian populations was acorns and buckeyes which, like the shellfish, were collected by women. Both seeds contain bitter, unpalatable tannin which was removed by crushing and leaching before the meal was dried and stored or eaten. Buckeyes are still strung out along Año Nuevo Creek, between Highway 1 and the Año Nuevo State Preserve parking lot, where a principle Ohlone village was located. These trees also grow near shell-mounds on Scott and Laguna Creeks (Gordon, 1974).

The Indians also ate grass seeds (Bolton, 1930), and they gathered other fibrous plants such as hemp and milkweed for use in their baske-try. To facilitate grass-growing and to aid in capturing small game, the Indians practiced extensive burning. Fire was a principle tool of land management. Burning was done with considerable skill and foresight, and the successional consequences of burning were well understood (Gordon, 1974). This practice was a continual source of mystery and annoyance to the first Spanish settlers who condemned this "bad habit of the heathens" (Rivera y Moncada, 1774). Indian burning was still going strong after several years of Spanish rule and settlement. This angered the cattlemen who pressured the missions to put a stop to it. Mission Santa Cruz was one of the missions that was given warning. The Año Nuevo region was in this jurisdiction, and burning in the area had long been practiced.

Another aspect of Ohlone existence in the Año Nuevo area was stoneworking and the making of arrowpoints. Among the sand dunes on the point, where no early traveler seems to have gone, was what Stanger (1966) calls "a primitive industrial center." In this location was a large outcrop of siliceous shale, a quarry essentially, from which the Ohlone chipped their arrow points and other stone articles. Stanger writes, "The black, siliceous shale, which is exposed in a low bluff along the rocky beach, is marked by streaks of white porcelaneous material which may well have been the trademark of the weapon makers here." Wandering among the dunes, one can find numerous quantities of chipped chert fragments. However, complete arrowpoints are surpris-ingly rare. One explanation for this paradox is that only preliminary flaking was done here and the task completed elsewhere (Heizer and Treganza, 1944).

In 1925, Theodore J. Hoover, brother of the President, conducted an archaeological study of the "Indian workshops" and "kitchen middens" but the findings were never published. The uniqueness of this material warrants further study.

Varieties of siliceous shale *(below)* **found on Año Nuevo Point used by the Ohlone for making arrowheads** *(above).* (F. Lanting)

In a recent book, Margolin (1978) gives a quite different interpretation to Ohlone culture than the one we get from simply cataloging archeological finds or from reading the diaries and travelogues of the European observers. He stresses the conflict between the European and Indian cultures and argues that the image we have of the central California "digger" Indians is the misleading legacy of the biased Spanish observers. The Ohlones were a wandering people, a lifestyle that well adapted them to the environment in which they lived. Throughout the year, they made a series of treks from one harvest to another: to the seashore for shellfish, to rivers for salmon, to marshes for ducks and geese, to oak groves for acorns, and to hills and meadows for seeds, roots and grasses. They lived in an extremely bountiful land that was very different from the one we know today. Water was everywhere; rivers overflowed, and salt and freshwater marshes covered enormous expanses. Tall, shoulder-high strands of native bunchgrasses covered meadowland and savannahs. Hillsides were thick with forests of oak, bay laurel, and redwood. Wildlife proliferated on land and in the ocean. There was no need to develop agricultural methods as the Europeans had done. It was easy to make a living by simply moving from one natural harvest to the next.

The wandering life style of the Ohlones led to personal habits which were odious and incomprehensible to early European travelers, given their different cultural heritage. Indian gluttony and indolence is reported time and time again as traits repulsive to the observers. However, the Europeans failed to understand that much of the Indian food, e.g., duck eggs, berries, whales, became available only for a few weeks of each year. "Get it while you can" was necessary, energetically and economically. Similarly, in the rich habitat of the Ohlone, hard work was done in spurts, e.g., during the deer hunt or acorn or salmon harvests. When the work was over there was little else to do. The Spanish thought the Indians were poor because they did not build permanent structures and they did not accumulate goods like people who lead settled lives. There was good reason for this. Moving and transience dictated their architecture. They could erect a tule house or boat in a few hours wherever and whenever they needed them. Baskets were preferred to pottery for the same reason.

Status, prerogative, and generosity were more important to the Ohlone than material wealth, a preference that befuddled the Spanish. Seating place in a sweat-house was more important than gold; what you gave away was more important than what you had. In the eyes of the Europeans, Ohlones were miserable failures because they were poor. Nothing could be further from the truth according to Margolin (1978, p. 57), "... the Ohlones did not practice agriculture or develop a rich material culture ... because they succeeded so well in the most ancient of all ways of life." Margolin finds it quite ironic that the things thay many of us strive to attain today in our own culture, the Ohlones, and many Stone-Age people the world over, had: "a balanced (rather than exploitive) relationship with the environment; an economic system based on sharing rather than competing; a strong sense of family and community; social moderation and restraint; the opportunity for widespread artistic creativity; a way of governing that serves without oppressing; a deeply spiritual sense of the world" (p. 170).

The Mission period

After Portolá's time, an inland route to San Francisco Bay through what is now Gilroy was found by Pedro Fages. The natives of the Año Nuevo region were left alone until the Santa Cruz mission was founded in 1791. Being off the main route, several other missions were constructed along El Camino Real before *Misión La Exaltación de la Santa Cruz* was completed on May 10, 1794. It was located near the site where a replica of the original adobe now stands. The mission's task was to convert Indians to Christianity and to graze cattle. The mission's domain was described as three leagues [about 15 km] wide and 11 leagues long [50 km], extending from Aptos to San Gregorio (Torchiana, 1933). The Santa Cruz mission was small compared to other California missions. It claimed 523 Indian converts or neophytes in 1796 but in subsequent years the number declined because of a high mortality rate among the Indians.

With the coming of the mission, Indian life in the Año Nuevo region changed drastically. According to Spanish or Franciscan logic, the land became the property of the mission. The Indians became "slaves of the priests" and the produce of their labor was for the priesthood (Craven, 1846). This was a refinement of the rationale used earlier by the Renaissance explorers who reasoned that enslavement of heathens was all right if, in exchange, you converted them to Christianity and taught them how to save their souls. What you did to a non-Christian's life was of no consequence, since it was the afterlife that was important. This logic condoned a multitude of cruelties perpetrated on the Indians, atrocities which came to be known as the "black legend" (Wright, 1970). Mission padres induced, seduced or coerced all converts to abandon their villages, or *rancherias* as the Spanish called them, and come to live in the mission. There, they were indoctrinated into the ways of the church and were taught to tend cattle and work crops. Instead of hunting and fishing, they labored from dawn to dusk in the mission vegetable garden, located where downtown Santa Cruz is today (Koch, 1973). Most converts ate, slept, worked, and died in the mission where all "necessities" were provided. Infractions of the rules were punished by the lash. The most trusted of the neophytes watched over the grazing herds and lived as far away as Punta Año Nuevo or Aptos (Stanger, 1966).

Mission activities in the Año Nuevo region increased during the late 1790's when the Spanish viceroy in Mexico City, the Marquis of Branciforte, decided to stimulate life in Alta California by founding pueblas of ordinary settlers—men and their families from Mexico who would make their living from the soil and who could be organized as a militia when the need arose. The Governor of California, Diego de Borica, liked the idea and selected three sites: Los Angeles, San José, and Santa Cruz. The latter was called Villa de Branciforte, named after the viceroy, and was located just across the San Lorenzo River from the Santa Cruz mission.

Naturally, this proposal horrified the mission fathers who objected to such a development so close to their missions and in the middle of their best grazing land. Through their superiors, they suggested instead a site at Punta del Año Nuevo or even farther north. But the astute governor knew these sites to be unfeasible because of their remoteness, and to prove his point he ordered his engineer to make a survey of the area. Meanwhile, he followed his original plan to locate the settlement "temporarily" where he'd always wanted it.

Because of this episode, we have a map of the coast made in 1798, showing various place names. More important, this episode stimulated interest in the area and prompted the mission fathers to move their most important cattle and sheep herding activities to the Año Nuevo region (Stanger, 1966). Perhaps the move was precipitated by the glowing report of the governor's engineer, Sgt. Pedro Amador, who decribed the rich soil and abundant water in the San Gregorio Valley and in the Punta del Año Nuevo region. Perhaps it was necessary to relocate their herds to the north after losing the Branciforte grazing land. Whatever the reason, there were 2,900 head of mission cattle at Punta Año Nuevo by 1814 (Torchiana, 1933). The "point" where the cattle grazed had the most general meaning. The actual grazing land lay between the sand dunes and the mountains and so far northward as the cattle cared to go, usually somewhere in the Butano-Pescadero area, but at times as far north as South San Francisco (Stanger, 1966).

The mission fathers did not soon forget the Branciforte intrusion; the proximity of the villa and its spirited citizens provided a constant reminder. The villa's first settlers were eight convicted criminals from Mexico, followed by a second contingent of retired soldiers and their families. Perched on the hill, the mission padres could look across the river and witness the diversions popular with the Spanish Dons: horse racing, gambling, fandangoes, and bear and bull fights (Koch, 1973). To accomodate this boisterous settlement, the church had to give up its best grazing land and extend its operations northward. The padres complained that the Indians tending their outposts in the "frigid northern mountains" couldn't attend mass except once every two weeks (Stanger, 1966).

Despite these complaints, the bulk of the mission's herding continued to be north of Punta del Año Nuevo. In 1825, 16 men and a woman were stationed there to take care of the cattle. Eighteen men and 8 women herded sheep in the San Gregorio Valley. Mission property was inventoried in 1835 and the total value of the livestock at Punta del Año Nuevo was given as $10,302 and at all other places $7,279 (Anonymous, 1935).

The missions went into decline after Mexico got its independence from Spain in 1822, and the end came in 1834 when the missions were "secularized." The rationale was that the work of converting heathens was finished and the missions should now become parish churches. The Indians had become converted indeed, if not from "paganism" to Christianity, then from the living to the dead. With secularization, the natives were released from mission control, but by now their numbers were severely depleted.

For the surviving Ohlone, the damage done during the 64-year mission period was irrevocable. Basketmaking and other crafts were lost; rituals and dances were confused and forgotten; native languages were dropped in favor of Spanish. The once familiar networks of support and sharing disintegrated. Margolin (1978, p. 164) writes, "Confidence in the permanence and validity of the old ways was destroyed, and hopelessness took its place."

The Foreign Invasion

In addition to the Spanish missionaries and soldiers, some of the first visitors to California and some of its earliest settlers were trappers, sailors, sealers, skinners, flensers, and marksmen. They came from various corners of the world. What attracted them to California, and put them in contact with the Año Nuevo region in particular, was the luxuriant fur of sea otters and fur seals and the abundant fat store of the numerous great whales, sea elephants, and sea lions. Fur and oil were valuable commodities at this time.

The sea otter was hunted first because its pelts commanded the highest price. In the 18th century, this animal ranged in an unbroken line from Japan across the North Pacific down to Baja California. It was abundant along the entire Alta California coast, especially in San Francisco Bay and near seal rookeries like Año Nuevo and the Channel Islands. Russian fur traders started the sea otter industry on islands in the Bering Sea in 1740. They hired fearless Aleuts to hunt for them in two-man seal-skin boats with spear, hook, and club, reimbursing them with trinkets and vodka (Ogden, 1941).

By 1774, the Russians had progressed across the Aleutians and were working down the North American coast. The Spanish, feeling that their claim in Alta California was threatened, dispatched the *Santiago* from Baja California to investigate. From this voyage, plus reports from Portolá's overland expedition to San Francisco Bay a few years earlier, the Spanish learned of the value of otter pelts and the ease of obtaining them. The Indians offered their finest otter furs for iridescent abalone shells which the Spanish sailors had picked up along the beaches at Monterey. On subsequent voyages, beads, knives, and old clothes were traded for skins, and the otter trade in California began.

For a few years, Spanish missionaries and soldiers continued to barter for pelts with the Ohlone. The pelts were shipped to Acapulco and subsequently to Manila, where they were traded. This Spanish monopoly was short-lived. Captain Cook, returning from the Pacific, extolled the potential riches of the California otter trade in a manuscript published in 1784. The race for the otter fields was on.

A woodcut showing Aleut Indians hunting sea otters in a two-man seal-skin boat) (From Scammon, 1874)

By the turn of the century, English, American, and Russian vessels were competing furiously with each other for otter pelts along the California coast, all the while avoiding the Spanish. Customary business practices were trading, smuggling, hunting, theft, and trickery of all sorts. The Spanish retaliated with harsher regulations and the seizure of ships and men, but controlling the otter fields was a difficult and futile endeavor.

The year of the highest yield was 1811 when 9,356 pelts were taken. The following year, the Russians established their southern sea ottering base at Fort Ross, and hunted as far south as the Channel Islands. Ten years later, when Mexico got its independence from Spain, there were few animals left. Under the loose controls of the new government, most of the remaining animals were soon finished and so was the otter industry. It is estimated that in 50 years about 356,000 to 1,000,000 sea otters were killed (Ogden, 1941).

The sea otter fur trade of California was the first commercial enterprise, as well as one of the most profitable, to attract merchants to the Pacific Coast. During the same period, thousands of fur seals were killed and great whales, elephant seals, and sea lions were hunted for their blubber. Hunting whales was almost exclusively a Yankee enterprise.

The reason for emphasizing the commercial exploitation of these marine mammals off the California coast is that many of the men who came to California to make their fortune in the fur and oil business stayed here, became the first Californians, and influenced the development of places like Año Nuevo. A cursory inspection of the tombstones in Evergreen Cemetery in Santa Cruz attests to the multi-national heritage of this area. On a larger scale, these commercial enterprises brought American products and American citizens into California during the Spanish and Mexican periods. This "... spread over the land influences and interests which determined to a great extent the ultimate political destiny of that segment of the Pacific littoral" (Ogden, 1941, p. v). By 1846, the fur hunters and sealers had lost their livelihood and most of them had joined Fremont's army. Two years later, they moved to the mountains and became gold miners.

Early owners of Año Nuevo

When the missions were secularized, the extentivė mission grazing lands were granted as *ranchos* to private individuals. *Rancho Punta del Año Nuevo* was granted to the uncle of the Governor of California, El Señor don José Simeón de Nepomuceno Castro, a prominent resident of Monterey. Don Castro already was the owner of a 35,000 acre grant on the Salinas River. Nevertheless, he did what was required of a gentleman of his station, and in 1840 he "occupied" the rancho by putting 400 head of cattle on the place and constructing a house for the herdsmen. By 1842, the rancho was running cattle and producing the usual hides and tallow as well as crops of wheat, corn, melons, and potatoes. Don Castro's grant was signed as law by the governor on 27 May 1842 (Stanger, 1966).

The rancho contained 17,753 acres and extended from Año Nuevo Point northward to Butano Creek and ostensibly from the coast to the top of the mountains, but in actuality only to the present line between San Mateo and Santa Cruz counties. It was a medium-sized grant.

Don Castro died in 1842 and his family in Monterey inherited *Rancho Punta del Año Nuevo*. They showed little concern for this far off place. The Mexican war was fought in 1846–1848, and in the treaty that

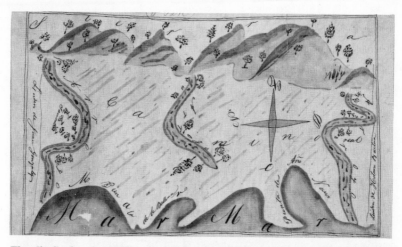

The diseño for the California rancho, Punta del Año Nuevo, was character-istically abstract as were all the other diseños. The three points in the foreground are Pigeon Point (then called Punta de la Ballena), Franklin Point, and Año Nuevo Point.

ended it, the United States agreed to honor land titles granted under previous Mexican laws. Many land grants in California passed into American hands at this time by fair or foul means—*Rancho Punta del Año Nuevo* was one of the last. In 1851, Castro's heirs sold the rancho at a sheriff's sale to the famous frontiersman and mountain man, Isaac Graham, for $18,000.

Graham was a very rugged hombre, one of the first Americans in California history, and a legend in his own time. His life served as a model for the western frontiersman myth which became so popular (see Farnham, 1859). A native of Kentucky and cousin of Daniel Boone, he left his family and headed west earning his livelihood as a trapper. After several narrow escapes from hostile Indians, he arrived in California around 1833, attracted here, no doubt, by the lucrative sea otter and fur seal trade. When the fur trade began to wane he moved on to other things. He constructed a distillery, a sawmill, and grist mill, acquired two ranchos and another wife and family, spearheaded a revolution which deposed a California governor, and gave his name to a *cause célebre* which helped to justify the occupancy of California by the United States (Nunis, 1967).

After the death of Governor José Figueroa in 1835, the Mexican territory of Alta California entered a period of political upheaval. Four

The boundaries of the original Mexican land grant of 1842 called Rancho Punta del Año Nuevo.

governors came and went in 16 months; the last one was deposed in a native revolution. In 1836, the secretary of the Territorial Deputation, Juan B. Alvarado, forced out the incumbent governor with the aid of foreigner Graham and his volunteer *Americanos*. Graham had recruited a company of *rifleros* from the vagabond foreigners that congregated around his distillery in Natividad, east of Salinas, and they marched to Monterey on the third of November. The revolution was an easy success, in large part because of the muscle provided by Graham's band of "dead shot" riflemen. Graham, then reputed to be a "wild and reckless fellow," and his band of bearded roughnecks, made up mostly of deserters from Yankee ships and a sprinkling of fur trappers, simply demanded the surrender of the government.

A reputedly bogus portrait of Isaac Graham which appeared in an 1859 reprint-ing of Thomas Jefferson Farnham's *Early Days in California.* According to Nunis (1967): "By 1859 the dime novels were busy creating the myth of the frontiersman and 'Old Graham The Hunter' was elevated to that august assembly."

An oil portrait of Isaac Graham in his later years. (California State Library, Sacramento)

After two days of parleying and councils, Graham grew tired "a waitin' on them baars" and sent a flag to the Presidio with the notice that the Governor and his officers would be given two hours to surrender. Precisely two hours later a four-pound brass cannonball crashed through the roof of the Governor's house, and the Governor packed off to Mexico pronto (Anonymous, 1883; Fink, 1972). After this, Graham's name and reputation were well known in California.

In exchange for their support, Alvarado had promised to reward Graham and his crew of foreigners with citizenship and large land grants (Nunis, 1967). Graham and his men pressed these claims on the new governor, but the latter failed to honor his pledge. Cognizant of the revolt against Mexico in Texas, Alvarado began to view the foreigners with increasing fear and suspicion. In 1840, he turned on the *Americanos* and had Graham and 30 others arrested for treason. They were held prisoners for over a year in Tepic near San Blas, Mexico. This episode, "the Graham affair," became a kind of rallying cry similar to "Remember the Alamo." It was an affront to the testy United States at the height of its sense of "manifest destiny." The Graham affair was used to justify U.S. penetration and eventual conquest of California (Nunis, 1967).

Isaac Graham had this house constructed on Whitehouse Creek shortly after he purchased Rancho Punta del Año Nuevo. He never lived in it. The house was being used by migrant workers when this photograph was taken in 1977. The house burned down in 1978. (B. Le Boeuf)

Upon his release from prison, Graham returned to California and with a friend, purchased Rancho Zayante. Here, he ran a successful and innovative sawmill and did some cattle ranching. It wasn't until 1851, during his retiring years, that he purchased *Rancho Punta del Año Nuevo,* a place he probably encountered earlier while trapping sea otters along the coast. He had a house constructed near the main road on Whitehouse Creek, but there is no record of how much time he spent there. Soon after he acquired the rancho, Graham leased it to his son, Isaac Wayne, who used it for farming and grazing operations. But a dispute arose between father and son and by 1853 the question of ownership and management had to be determined in court. The elder Graham won and the son left for Texas, forever estranged from his father.

Although Graham had prospered financially during the gold rush days, in the late 1850s he guessed wrong about silver ore on his Zayante ranch and ended up heavily in debt. This gamble forced him to sell his Año Nuevo Rancho. As usual, he put up a fight. He secured a court injunction giving him an additional 60 days to raise approximately $24,000 before foreclosure. But he couldn't do it, and on 31 March 1862 the rancho was sold at public auction to John H. Baird, who offered the

Colburn's folly, the grand hotel with accompanying stables constructed at Pebble Beach near Pescadero was a financial disaster.

highest bid, $20,000. Graham died a year later and is buried in Santa Cruz at Evergreen Cemetery (Stanger, 1966). Without doubt, he was one of the most colorful men in early California history.

After holding the property for only five months, Baird sold it to Loren Coburn and his brother-in-law, Jeremiah Clarke, for a handsome profit of $10,000. Later, the partners purchased the Butano ranch to the north and a boundary dispute that went back to Spanish times was finally settled. Coburn later bought out his partner and became sole owner of both ranches.

Loren Coburn was a paradox. He was shy and inoffensive in manner but underneath this deceptive exterior was a tough, unscrupulous and shrewd businessman. He made a fortune during gold rush times and at his death in 1918, "He counted his acreages, not by the acre but by the square mile, and the figure was in the neighborhood of fifty" (Stanger, 1966).

When Coburn purchased the Año Nuevo property he had already worked out a profitable lease agreement with an interested dairy group, the Steele brothers. They would pay him $6,000 per year for ten years plus all taxes on the whole rancho. There was also a clause stipulating an option to buy the 7,000 acres (2,800 hectares) south of Gazos Creek when the lease expired. The deal closed on 12 September 1862 and was signed less than 30 days later. Coburn made a neat 20% per year on his investment. Two pieces of land were notably excepted from the lease: Año Nuevo Island and Pigeon Point. There had been a few shipwrecks in this area and Coburn saw an opportunity to make a bundle selling this land to the Federal government for a lighthouse (Stanger, 1966).

Coburn's personal dealing with people won him the reputation of an ogre. The following episode indicates why he had few friends. Pebble Beach is a small cove on *Rancho Punta del Año Nuevo,* 4.8 km south of Pescadero. In Coburn's day, many semi-precious stones were found among the smoothed and sand-polished rocks: carnelian, ruby, amethyst, emerald, garnet, amber, and opal. In summer, tourists from San Francisco flocked to Pescadero and the diversion provided by rock hunting at Pebble Beach. Since access to the beach was through Coburn's property, he attempted to monopolize the resource. He closed his private road, opened another one, and began construction of a large hotel on the beach. Citizens of Pescadero were outraged, and physical and legal altercations ensued. The county declared the road public and the state did the same for the beach. This didn't stop Coburn. He brought suit in the United States Circuit Court. During litigation, Coburn put up barriers to close the old road and these were immediately sawed or chopped away. He dug a ditch and it was filled. He dug another and filled it himself with a dead horse. The public simply went around the smelly carcass on their way to the beach.

Eventually, Coburn won in court, but the prize disappeared. The beach lost its popularity when cut off from the town. An economic depression reduced the summer trade and the automobile began taking people farther down the coast. Coburn's grand hotel, nicknamed "Coburn's folly," stood empty and alone for many years after his death. It finally burned down and its remains were flattened to make way for the modern Cabrillo highway (Stanger, 1966).

The Steele Era

Coburn's lessees, the Steele brothers, were an enterprising clan who began a dairy industry in Sonoma in 1857. Later in the year, the three brothers, Edgar, George, and Isaac, and a cousin, Rensselaer, moved their cattle to cold, windswept Point Reyes despite advice to the contrary that coast lands were unsuitable for raising good stock. This venture was so successful that they were soon searching for additional grazing land. In 1861, Isaac Steele rented a horse from Loren Coburn's stable in San Francisco and rode south to look over the lands of *Rancho Punta del Año Nuevo,* which he knew were for lease and which were similar to the coastal lands in Marin County. Isaac was impressed with what he saw, proclaimed the area another "cow heaven," and arranged a ten year lease with an option to buy the southern portion of the rancho. It must have been love at first sight, for there was never any question that the Steeles would take up the option to buy. Isaac immediately began building his home at Green Oaks Creek and Rensselaer built on Cascade Creek. Both homes are still standing (Steele, 1941).

The Steeles purchased 1,100 head of cattle for the new rancho at an average of 15 dollars a piece, and Indian laborers were brought down

J. C. Steele

Isaac Chapman Steele, pioneer and successful dairyman in the Año Nuevo area, was born in New York on August 14, 1820, and died at Green Oaks on February 25, 1903.

The house that Isaac Steele built at Green Oaks Ranch in 1862. (H. Rommel)

from Point Reyes to work. With butter selling at a dollar a pound and cheese at 27 cents a pound, business prospered.

During the Civil War, in which one brother, Frederick, was a Union general, the Steeles received much national publicity because of a giant wheel of cheese which they made and donated to the Sanitary Commission, a forerunner of today's Red Cross. A supply of milk collected over several days was hauled from the dairies on Punta del Año Nuevo to Green Oaks by oxen teams, and there a mammoth cheese weighing 3,850 pounds was created. "A gigantic hoop and press were made for the purpose, and novel appliances were required to handle the great weight and safely transport it to San Francisco, it being over twenty feet (6 m) in circumference and eighteen inches (46 cm) thick, thoroughly made, and of the richest quality" (Anonymous, 1883). The big cheese was auctioned at a dollar a pound at the Mechanic's Fair and pieces of it were sent to President Lincoln, General Grant, and General Frederick Steele (Steele, 1941).

As the business grew, other members joined the clan, and the Steeles rose quickly to a position of leadership in the state's dairy industry. By 1867, the Steeles were operating 11 dairies in three counties: Marin, San Mateo, and San Luis Obispo.

But during the 1870s valuable land was coveted by many, and the Steeles became involved in expensive litigation which ultimately forced them to sell much of their holdings. Isaac continued to look after his property on Punta del Año Nuevo and took an active part in the growth

Rennselaer Steele's house on Cascade Creek.

of the state in education and agriculture. When he ran for political office in San Mateo County, he found that instead of being a respected pioneer he was considered a "land monopolist, an ogre who sat on the veranda of his great rancho while hundreds of coolies slaved for him" (Steele, 1941). The changing conditions bewildered him and he returned more and more to the land he loved.

When the Steeles took up their option and purchased the land lying south of Gazos Creek, Coburn retained the northern portion of the rancho. This was the second time that the original Mexican land grant was divided, the first being when Coburn excluded Año Nuevo Island and Pigeon Point from the lease arrangement with the Steele brothers. With the passing of the pioneer Steele brothers, their dairy land was fractionated again and again. The land was passed on to sons and daughters and relatives by marriage and some of it was purchased by the state.

Isaac's Green Oaks ranch remained in the family until 1965 when his heirs sold most of it to wholesale florists, Leon and Paul Gregoire. When Leon died, half of the beach frontage was sold to State Beaches and Parks and the other half to Janet Bickford. Other portions of the ranch east of Highway 1 were sold to flower growers from Mountain View and to Drs. Margaret and John Kosek. The original Rensselaer Steele home and Cascade ranch was encumbered by Rensselaer Steele, Jr., and subsequently acquired by Humphrey Estates, Inc.

Part of nephew Charley Steele's ranch on Gazos Creek, where Pin-

Cattle have grazed in the pastures of Año Nuevo since the arrival of the Spanish in the mid 18th century. This photograph was taken during the early part of this century when dairy ranching was still practiced by the Steele family.

ky's Tavern is now located, passed to a Portuguese man called Bennett. The Osman Steele II ranch was sold to David Atkins and Mary DeFremery Atkins. This ranch, called "Coastways," is located between Año Nuevo Creek and Wilson Gulch. Fitch Point was named after Colonel Roger Fitch, commandant of Fort Ord during World War II, who owned 20 acres of Coastways for a short time.

South of Green Oaks Ranch, in the center of Año Nuevo Point, is the place which belonged to George H. Steele, the son and heir of Isaac Chapman Steele. It is now owned by Capitola Berry Farms, Inc. A house and several white buildings are lined up on the west side of Highway 1 in front of the ranch, which is called "Rancho Año Nuevo."

Headquarters of the Año Nuevo State Reserve are located on the former Flora Dickerman Steele ranch on the southern portion of the point. Flora Steele was the adopted daughter of Edwin Dickerman who married Effie Steele, daughter of Isaac Chapman Steele. Flora married Jay Steele, son of Frank Steele. Before she died, she deeded the beach frontage of her ranch to State Beaches and Parks, and the remainder of her ranch was acquired by the State after her death. The old house and ranch faces Año Nuevo Bay and commands a superb view. Mission headquarters in the area are believed to have been located near Flora Steele's house.

It was also on this ranch that a 210 m wharf called New Year's Landing was constructed in 1864. Soon after coming to the area, the Steeles gave W.W. Waddell, who lived in the canyon south of Point

Ranch hands on a Steele dairy farm at Año Nuevo shortly after the turn of the century.

Año Nuevo, the right-of-way across the south edge of their property and a site for a landing. Waddell built a sawmill in the canyon which now bears his name and a wooden railroad down to the beach. Hard bedrock thwarted his attempt to build a wharf at the canyon mouth, so he extended his railroad about 4 km up the coast. Waddell's wharf was located 450 m west of Año Nuevo Creek where the water was deep, there were no dangerous reefs, and the bluff was lowest. Four-horse teams hauled timbers in flat cars over the wooden rails. There was a warehouse, stacks of lumber, and a small residence at the wharf which served Waddell's mill, the Steele mill, and the nearby region for 13 years. It handled 2 million feet of lumber a year. W.W. Waddell died from wounds inflicted by a grizzly bear in 1875 (Stanger, 1966).

During the time of the Waddell wharf, Santa Cruz County gave away part of the original rancho because of the crumbling cliffs north of Waddell Creek. Residents in the area had long complained that the mountains made it difficult for them to reach the county seat in Santa Cruz. Mud and rock avalanches buried the road from time to time. In 1868, the injustice was rectified and part of the rancho was included in 30 square miles of territory that was transferred to the adjacent county to the north, San Mateo.

Of the Steeles' once extensive dairy operation on *Rancho Punta del Año Nuevo,* only 14 acres remain in the hands of a Steele. Two other members of the family have reserved life estate interests: Bernice Steele Taylor on the Capitola Berry Farms, and Catherine B. Steele on Green

The Flora Dickerman Steele house overlooking Año Nuevo Bay. This house now serves as a ranger residence near the entrance to Año Nuevo State Reserve.

A weathered barn on the former Flora Dickerman Steele ranch stands near the entrance to Año Nuevo State Reserve. (F. Lanting)

The mud road north of Waddell Creek *(above)* was often buried by an avalanche of rocks and mud from the crumbling cliffs or washed out by high surf *(below)*. This made it difficult for Año Nuevo residents to get to Santa Cruz so in 1868 the area north of the crumbling cliffs was transferred to San Mateo County.

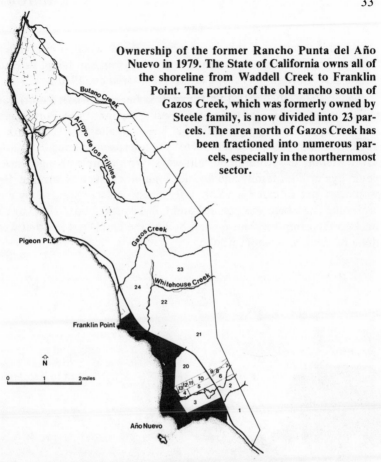

Ownership of the former Rancho Punta del Año Nuevo in 1979. The State of California owns all of the shoreline from Waddell Creek to Franklin Point. The portion of the old rancho south of Gazos Creek, which was formerly owned by Steele family, is now divided into 23 parcels. The area north of Gazos Creek has been fractioned into numerous parcels, especially in the northernmost sector.

Oaks Ranch Historical Site. The latter, a 13-site lying along Green Oaks Creek and fronting on Cabrillo Highway, was deeded as a gift to San Mateo county by Catherine B. Steele in 1967. County management did little to preserve either the heritage of this pioneering California family or the house and its artifacts. The property was reclaimed and returned to Mrs. Steele in 1977.

Shore Whaling

Another group of people who inhabited part of the original rancho during the latter half of the 19th century were Portuguese shore whalers from the Azores. Shore whaling was practiced at the same time as the more common technique using whaling ships. Captain John Davenport, an American from New England, and Captain Joseph Clark

(Machado) a native of the Azores, began the practice around 1850. Twelve shore stations were soon in operation from San Diego to Half Moon Bay (Scammon, 1874; Clarke, 1954; Orlando, 1960).

Pigeon Point, then called La Punta de la Ballena (Whale Point) was the location of one of these shore whaling stations. The Portuguese whalers erected 12 cottages there and began whaling in 1862 (Starks, 1923; Orlando, 1960; Hoover, 1966). The approach differed from off-shore whaling in several important ways. With shore whaling, a man could live with his family and do additional work, such as farming. He would set out to catch a whale only when one was spotted by the look-out. The whale was pursued and killed by small boat, then towed back to the camp for flensing and boiling the blubber, a job that was done on deck in offshore whaling.

PIGEON POINT.

Portuguese whalers at Pigeon Point in pursuit of passing whales. Woodcut from Evans (1874).

By 1871, the Portuguese whaling crew numbered 17 and everyone owned a share in the company. There were two boats, each manned by six whalers. Four men stayed on shore as lookouts and to render the oil. The 17th member was a cook and housekeeper for whalers with family (*Alta California,* 16 June 1871).

Colonel Albert Evans, riding a horse down the coast from San Francisco in 1869, noted that the lookout's responsibility was to spot the whale with "sea glasses," keep an eye on the whaling boats, and signal the progress of the hunt to coworkers on the beach. He remembers that the translation of the hunt was animated and laced with curses "in good Portuguese, honestly and squarely for fifteen minutes, and I felt may respect for him rising almost to the point of admiration" (Evans, 1874).

The whalers sailed after a whale if there was a wind. The killing operation was strictly by hand and always dangerous. Once the harpoon was set, a "Nantucket sleighride" lasting several hours might follow until the "whale's life" was reached with additional lancing. When the whale died, a flag was attached if they were to return for the

TRYING OUT.

Portuguese whalers flensing and trying out whales at Pigeon Point during the later part of the 19th century. (Woodcut from Evans, 1874)

whale after decomposition gases built up to assist in flotation. Otherwise, a towing strap was attached and towing began immediately.

This was grueling work after several hours of grappling with a gray or a humpback, the most frequent quarry. It often required 12 or more hours to row the 30-foot whales back to shore. The lookout assisted by lighting a fire of boiled whale blubber on top of his perch to serve as a beacon in the fading light.

On shore, the blubber was flensed and placed in very large try-pots and boiled. The boiling temperature had to be just right and it was tested by spitting into the vat. If the oil cracked, more blubber was added. If the oil got too hot, the vat boiled over because of the large amount of water in the tissue. As the boiling went on through the night, hungry whalers threw popcorn, chicken or fish directly into the boiling vat of whale oil for a deep-fried treat.

As the whales became scarce and harder to catch, greater distances had to be traveled and the explosive lances costing $4 apiece proved too expensive for whalers already living a marginal existence. Most shore whaling stations were defunct by 1880 (Brown, 1944). The Pigeon Point Station was abandoned in 1895 (Starks, 1923).

The Hazardous Coastline

While numerous changes were taking place on the mainland, the treacherous coastline of *Rancho Punta del Año Nuevo* was developing its own notorious reputation. Año Nuevo Island, Franklin Point, and Pigeon Point present a low profile of rocky projections into the sea which reach out to almost the same longitude as the Golden Gate. When seamen navigated by the sun and stars, this area was given a wide berth. Even as early as the sixteenth century, the Spanish sailors respected this latitude. There is no telling how many ships were lost in the area during those times. With the gold rush, ship traffic along the California coast increased tremendously, and the shoreline between Año Nuevo Island and Pigeon Point was the scene of numerous shipwrecks.

The following excerpt from the *Pacific Coast Pilot* by George Davidson (1889) gives a mariner's description of the treacherous Point Año Nuevo area:

This point lies eighteen and a half miles from Point Santa Cruz, and is formed by rolling hills of shifting sand, varying from twenty to one hundred feet in elevation, while behind them rises the Santa Cruz range of mountains, attaining a height of fifteen hundred feet in four or five miles.

A quarter of a mile outside the point lies a black, jagged islet, about thirty feet high, consisting of a sloping ledge of rocks covered with a stratum of yellow clay, about four feet thick, and this again covered with sand (1853). But in 1869-70-71 the covering of sand did not exist and very slight signs remained of the patches of clay. This rocky ledge is one of the most dangerous on the coast in its relation to the large amount of coast trade. In thick weather a vessel coming from the westward is close upon it before seeing it, the more especially as the land to the eastward retreats one and a half miles, is quite low, and frequently cannot be made out. The islet sends off a ledge for half a mile to the east-southeast (ESE) that serves to break the swell before reaching the cove, but increasing the danger to vessels approaching from the southeastward around to northwest.

Two breakers are reported off the islet; the first lies about one-quarter of a mile south-southwest (SSW) from it, and the second about one-third of a mile south. With a large swell these breakers are very heavy.

A depth of five fathoms of water is found just inside the islet, and the ten-fathom line is less than two-thirds of a mile from the point itself, and about one-third of a mile outside the fog-whistle. At two miles, the depth of water is thirty fathoms over green sand and mud; at four and a half miles, it is fifty fathoms over green mud; at eleven miles, it is one hundred fathoms over fine green sand; thence the slope to the one-thousand-fathom line is sharp.

Hidden Danger. — In the approaches from the northwest a large body of kelp stretches northwest by west (NW by W) one and one-third miles from the islet; and inside this field, one mile northwest one quarter west (NW ¼ W) from the fog-whistle and a half a mile from shore, is a rock with seventeen feet of water. The three fathom curve lies about half-way between this rock and the shore ... .

Col. Albert Evans (1874) described the area more succinctly: "It is a place where black reefs of rock rear their ugly fangs, like wild beasts waiting for their prey."

A major shipwreck was the *Carrier Pigeon,* a brand new clipper ship which ran aground at La Punta de la Ballena. The magnitude of the disaster prompted the name change to Pigeon Point. Clippers were the fastest sailing ships built and they made news in gold-rush times as they raced between New York or Boston and San Francisco. The *Carrier Pigeon* was a three-masted medium clipper with a long narrow hull and a cutting bow. It left Boston on its maiden voyage on 28 January 1853 with 1,300 tons of cargo in its hold. On June 6, 129 days out, Captain Azariah Doane believed he was near the Farallon Islands when he hit the rocks. There was no loss of life but the beautiful new ship was split in two and gradually beaten to pieces, and its entire cargo was lost.

Scarcely twelve years later another clipper, the *Sir John Franklin,* went down near a round cape between Pigeon Point and Año Nuevo Island. Bound for San Francisco, the ship got lost in a dense fog on 17 January 1865. The Captain thought he was far out at sea but when the fog lifted, the ship could not be brought about in time and it drifted into the breakers and broke up on the rocks. Members of the crew tried to reach shore through the mountainous surf. The first, second, and third mates made it, but the Captain and 12 seamen were lost. The location of this tragedy is now called Franklin's Point.

The wreck of the *Coya* was even more disastrous. This British bark had cleared Sydney, Australia, on 24 September 1866, bound for San Francisco. On 24 November the California coast was in view in early evening, but soon the fog came in, obscuring the shore from view. At 7:30 pm breakers were seen at a safe distance ahead and the order was given to veer, but in the process the ship hit a hidden reef, turned broadside, and in the heavy seas, broke up quickly. Made of iron and loaded with coal, the ship keeled over quickly and sank in deep water. It carried 20 passengers and a crew of 10, including the Captain's wife and child. Only three persons survived: the first mate, a young member of the crew, and a passenger. The survivors somehow managed to swim to shore and avoided being mangled to death on the rocky coast.

The coroner was called to investigate the disaster and the jury's report was sent to various authorities and congressmen. It reads:

The undersigned jurors, summoned to hold an inquest on the bodies of the unfortunate crew and passengers of the bark *Coya,* wrecked on the coast near New Year's Point, on the 24th of November, 1866, would respectfully represent to the proper authorities that the coast near New Year's Point is a very dangerous one, on account of the peculiar location, climate and currents—the best illustration of which is the fact that only two years since the *Sir John Franklin* was wrecked on the same coast, within one fourth of a mile of the site of the present disaster, and some nine years since, the *Carrier Pigeon* was wrecked at a point on the coast only two miles distant from the site of the before-mentioned disaster.

It appears in evidence that the bark *Coya,* on the night of the 24th of November, was supposed by her officers to be in the neighborhood of the Farallone Islands, and were under easy sail to make out the light. The weather had been so foggy that for two days they had had no observation, and they were running by dead reckoning. Their course was northeast half east, direct for the head light, from the position they supposed themselves to be, but on account of having no observation, the true position of the bark could not be ascertained, and she was wrecked as before mentioned, on the night of the 24th of November, at half-past seven.

When the above-mentioned facts are considered, it seems to be very evident that it is the duty of the proper authorities to put a light on Point New Years.

Four years later, in May 1870, the Federal government purchased Año Nuevo Island and Pigeon Point from Loren Coburn for $10,000. Congress had passed a bill of appropriations for miscellaneous government expenses on 20 July 1868 which included " ... a first-order lighthouse at Point Año Nuevo, or vicinity, California, ninety thousand dollars."

An aerial photograph of the southern portion of Año Nuevo Island taken in 1934 when the island was still being maintained by the U.S. Coast Guard as a lighthouse station. At the top of the picture, going from left to right, one sees the foghorn house, a gasoline storage building, and the lighthouse tower behind an octagonal-shaped building of unknown usage. The sloping cement structure to the left of the tower is a cachement basin for collecting water. A boat storage shed is to the right of the picture and the lighthouse keeper's house is in the foreground. The animals in the picture are California sea lions. Note the widespread and lush vegetation.

The wreck of another vessel, the *Hellespont,* at Pigeon Point on 21 November 1868 helped pave the way for the purchase and construction of warning signals which began almost immediately. This American sailing ship, headed for San Francisco with coal from Australia, crashed on the rocks near Pigeon Point in the darkness shortly before dawn. Only 7 of the 18 men on board survived. The Portuguese whalers living at the point took the survivors to Pescadero in a farmer's wagon.

When construction of the safety devices began, two disasters had occurred at Pigeon Point, one at Franklin Point, and the *Coya* near Año Nuevo Island. Early reports were vague about where the *Coya* went down but George Davidson, author of *Coast Pilot,* placed it correctly at about a mile from the island (*Santa Cruz Sentinel,* 1 December 1866). Accoordingly, a light was put on Pigeon Point first. Its revolving beam was first lit on 15 November 1872. The tower was constructed on a 40-foot bluff at the tip of the point. Earlier in the year a "twelve-inch steam fog-whistle" was installed on Año Nuevo Island.

An aerial photograph of Año Nuevo Island taken in 1934 from the seaward or western side of the island. A few Steller sea lions are visible on the rocks in the foreground.

When its first blast sounded on 29 May all the dairy cows in the vicinity stampeded down to the beach. A resident Steele remarked that they must have thought there was a wonderful bull down there! Eight years later another 12-inch whistle with boiler and engine was installed. The annual energy requirement for the station was approximately 50 tons of coal delivered by supply ship. This kept the whistle working an average of 800 hours per year. An early problem, which persisted through the years up to the present, was the undermining of foundation structures by the shifting sands (*The Half Moon Bay Review*, 20 February 1969).

During the early years, the two keepers and their families lived in a 36 x 28 foot, one-story building. In 1904, a large, double, substantial house was constructed which included 8 rooms and a bath for the keeper and 7 rooms and bath for the assistant. The residence was renovated in 1911. Legend has it that some materials were hauled out to the island by horse and wagon at low tide when much of the channel to the mainland was exposed.

Life on the island presented some unusual problems. A catchment basin for rainwater and a 90,000 gallon cistern had to be constructed to provide fresh water. Although the water was good and adequate, the mammoth containers had to be cleaned annually. Indeed, general cleaning and maintenance had to be done constantly. In the salt air environment, wood structures needed numerous and repeated applications of paint, and metal needed continual oiling. The houses and gardens had to be surrounded by fences to keep the seals out, and attempts to plant grass to keep the sand from blowing were unsuccessful. In 1918, Becker, the lighthouse keeper, made an official complaint to the department that young pups of the fast-growing sea lion rookery were becoming so numerous that they were over-running his house. He claimed that on one occasion, a killer whale had stirred up the seals so much that they forced their way into every room of his house (*San Francisco Chronicle*, 16 July, 1918).

Going for groceries was no picnic either, for the channel crossing to the mainland was very dangerous. Even so, there were compensations, as the wife of one keeper testified. She enjoyed the relief of knowing that her children were not exposed to the dangers of traffic—horse and buggy traffic. According to her, the sea posed little threat since the youngsters had discovered early that the water was very cold and so they avoided it. There is no mention of the panoramic view from the island, the innumerable, full sky multicolor sunsets, the fresh air, the birds and the seals. These private pleasures seem to have been taken for granted. During winter tempests it must have been a secure feeling to sit near a hissing coal fire, listening to the wind howl and the ocean roar. Año Nuevo Island is a place of extremes: fresh, clean, vibrant and vital, or cold, dank, depressing and dangerous.

In 1914, a bigger and better lens was installed on a square skeleton steel tower. The top of the lantern was 22 m above the water and could be seen for 22 km at sea (*The Half Moon Bay Review*, 20 February 1969). The low level of the light at Año Nuevo Island, relative to the light at Pigeon Point, was intentional. An exhaustive study of the area had revealed that fog in the area often rested on a blanket of warm air, keeping it about 30 m above the sea. Thus, the Pigeon Point light, at 42 m above sea level, would beam out above the fog and the Año Nuevo light beneath it (Stanger, 1966).

During the 1930s, the Canadian-developed diaphone, the low-frequency, two-toned, airpowered horn whose bellow is familiar to all fogbound harbor residents, replaced former sound systems in light-houses all over the country. A diaphone was installed on Año Nuevo Island in 1939, along with a siren just in case the diaphone failed to work.

As the character of marine traffic began changing after the end of World War II, it was evident that the operation of the Año Nuevo Island station was getting to be more trouble than it was worth. It was difficult, dangerous, and expensive to keep the island installation supplied and maintained, and automation was beginning to prove feasible. On 15 May 1948, the United States Coast Guard ordered the station discontinued and a 400-candlepower marker buoy with automatic light, sound and radar reflector, took over the job. The buoy is anchored by a 100 m chain to a 2,700 kg concrete sinker located 1,485 m south of the island in 25 m of water. Every 700 days a coast guard vessel comes by to change the batteries. Installation of safety signals on Año Nuevo Island and Pigeon Point never put a complete stop to shipwrecks, and maritime problems along this part of the coast have continued to the present.

The Channel

While the reefs off this part of the coast posed a constant threat to large shipping vessels, the 0.8 km channel separating Año Nuevo Island from the mainland was no less dangerous to those trying to get to the island in small craft. These people included lighthouse keepers, coast guardsmen, fishermen, scuba divers, and scientists.

Elsewhere, (Le Boeuf, 1974) I said that the channel crossing was like playing a tough hole on a professional golf course. The channel is roughest and most treacherous in winter. Large swells break on both sides of the island and come to meet on the landward side near the center of the channel. Small boat access through the channel is made difficult by the surf, the chop created by the refraction of waves meeting waves, and the fact that the middleground is shallow and numerous rocks are exposed at low tides of approximately +0.3 m and below. The danger is compounded by a strong current which flows through the channel with an ebbing tide. The direction and force of the current is unpredictable. Because of these conditions, the position and orientation of boats crossing the channel is critical. On a typical winter day the safest part of the "fairway" to the island may be no more than 12-15 m wide near midchannel. If the craft gets too far to the right (going out), it runs the risk of being swamped by 1-3 m breakers from the northwest. Being out of position on the left exposes the boat to "rooster-tails"—the shifting area where the waves from both sides meet. Motorcraft may lose power by shearing pins or propellers on submerged rocks, then they are at the mercy of wind and current. The greatest danger lies in drifting out of the channel to the south and northwest in the vicinity of the huge (4-6 m and higher) breakers. Recent history attests to the severe penalty of being in this rough area.

The first recorded tragedy in the channel involved the lighthouse

An aerial photograph of Año Nuevo Point, Año Nuevo Island and the channel separating the two. This picture was taken on March 3, 1941, and shows the typical dangerous winter wave pattern in the middle of the channel. Approach to the island from the mainland by small boat is made through a narrow zone between the white water on both sides of the channel.

keeper, his assistant and two friends. The circumstances surrounding the accident were described by the *San Mateo County Gazette* on 14 April 1883:

One of the most appalling accidents that ever occurred on this coast, happened at Año Nuevo Island, twelve miles south of Pescadero, Sunday afternoon, April 8th, resulting in the death by drowning of four young men—Henry W. Colburn, Bernard A. Ashley, Clayton A. and Frank L. Pratt. The Pratt brothers, who lived with their parents at the White House ranch, were in the habit of visiting their island friends Sundays, when the weather permitted. Sunday morning last, after having completed their work, the two brothers started for the island. It was a very rough crossing, but they reached the shore

An aerial photograph of the summer channel separating Año Nuevo Island from the mainland. This picture was taken on July 22, 1974, a time when the sea is typically smooth. Nevertheless, wave convection around the island is apparent. (F. McCrary, Jr.)

without accident. Having spent the day pleasantly with their friends, at 2:30 pm, they started on the return trip to the mainland. Instead of taking the usual course—by the "beacon stake"—they started on what is known as the "straight cut." The distance across in an air line is something more than half a mile. When about half the distance over, a heavy breaker partially filled the boat. Three of the occupants commenced bailing out the water, but before they had completed their task, another still heavier breaker swamped the boat, filling it with water. At this time all four of the men were sitting in the boat, which continued drifting out to sea until a heavy breaker rolled over them, and they disappeared from sight, which was the last ever seen of them. During all this time, Mrs. Colburn and Mrs. Ashley were witnesses to the horrible fate of their husbands and friends. With a presence of mind rarely equalled, these two brave ladies rushed to the boat house and tried to launch the remaining life-boat. Finding it too heavy to move, they directed their attention to the boat which was yet to be seen with the occupants when they sighted a steamer. Immediately, a flag was hoisted at half mast, Union down. They then hurried to the fog signal, started a fire and soon had up steam. The steamer proved to be the *Los Angeles,* coming up from the southern coast. Hearing the fog horn, and seeing the signal of distress, she changed her course; lowered a boat which pulled for the island. On learning of the disaster, the boat's crew cruised about for half an hour, but failed to find any of the bodies, or traces of the boat. The *Los Angeles* then steamed down the coast six miles in hopes of recovering some of the bodies, but the search proved fruitless.

Many accidents have occurred in the channel since the above episode and numerous lives have been lost. Although no one has ever compiled the grisly statistic of total lives lost, the number would be staggering. One indication of the danger of the area is that nine people drowned in the surf near Año Nuevo Island in two accidents six days apart (*San Francisco Chronicle*, 22 July 1957)!

A few headlines which have appeared in local papers such as the *San Francisco Chronicle* and the *Santa Cruz Sentinel,* underscore the hazards of the area:

**A WATERY GRAVE—FEARFUL ENDING FOR FOUR
YOUNG LIVES NEAR PESCADERO
FLYER DIES OFF SAN MATEO COAST
3 SAVED ON ISLE
FIVE RISK SEA IN SMALL BOAT—DIE
COAST GUARD RESCUES FOUR OFF AÑO NUEVO ISLAND
SENTINEL WRITER ABOARD CRAFT WHICH OVERTURNS
BOAT CAPSIZES AT AÑO NUEVO POINT
12 SKINDIVERS STRANDED OFF AÑO NUEVO POINT
SMALL BOAT OVERTURNS: 5 DROWN
FIVE MEN PLUCKED FROM RAGING SURF
2 SEA RESCUES IN HEAVY STORM**

Some accidents could have been avoided, like the one which involved five fisherman that capsized in a 5 m lake boat, the *Pen-Jay*. A resident who helped them launch remembered: "They didn't know too much about what they were doing. ... They've been here before a dozen times. Lots of folks warned them that they shouldn't take a boat out to those islands ... they talked about how calm it was. It looks calm ashore but it can get rough right away. I guess their luck ran out" (*San Francisco Chronicle*, 22 July 1957). Others were ironic. Three Air Force personnel were set adrift from Pigeon Point in a rubber raft as part of a survival test. The craft was swamped by high surf in the Año Nuevo channel, and one of the crew drowned (*San Francisco Chronicle*, 29 March 1956).

Many incidents involved horripilating rescues. In 1943 a boat containing two men and a woman overturned in the channel. One man tried to tie the boat to a telephone pole then located near midchannel, but a large wave capsized the boat completely, leaving him clinging to the pole, his wife in the water, and his friend riding the overturned boat. The woman reached the boat and clung to it until she was exhausted and let go. The man on the boat grabbed her by the hair and pulled her back. The overturned boat swept south 1 km before the Coast Guard came to the rescue (U.S. Coast Guard News Release, 29 October 1952).

Even experienced seamen with considerable local knowledge have had close calls in the channel. The most recent episode, part of which I witnessed in abject terror, occurred on 22 May 1975 and involved an associate of mine, who had piloted Avon dinghies to the island hundreds of times before, often in rough seas and under marginal conditions. On this day, he launched the inflatable raft from the point at 11:30 am. On board was a new employee (being shown how to pilot across the channel!), a ranger from the State Parks and Recreation department, and two officials from Calfornia State Fish and Game. The officials intended to observe the extent of abalone predation by divers on the first day of the season. The seas were high around the point and there was a heavy ground swell coming in from the northwest. The tide was ebbing and the fairway through midchannel was quite flat except for a few occasional breakers. Near mid-channel, a combination of large waves and a strong current forced the craft out of position. A 3 m wave curled and broke over the stern of the boat, overturning it and spilling everyone into the water. The boat could not be righted and everyone climbed aboard the overturned raft.

The overturned raft drifted south for approximately two hours, miraculously avoiding the dangerous rocks and huge breakers. The state officials were without wetsuits and one of them could not swim. By now the craft was edging dangerously close to the huge breakers forming approximately a half km out from the mainland at Fitch Point. An army helicopter and a volunteer marine rescue team arrived, but the aircraft winch wasn't working and they were powerless to rescue the men. At last, two Navy helicopters arrived from Monterey at approximately 2:00 pm and the men were hoisted to safety one by one. Less than

Air-sea rescue by the U.S. Coast Guard off Fitch Point on 25 March 1975. Five men were plucked from the overturned rubber raft *(barely visible below the nose of the helicopter)* **minutes before the raft was torn apart by huge breakers on Waddell Beach.** (B. Le Boeuf)

an hour later the raft washed up on Waddell Beach and was completely torn apart in its brief, violent contact with the mighty surf.

A few daring people were lucky in their dealings with the channel. One winter day in 1974, I watched in open-mouthed wonder as a Chris Craft-type powerboat cut across the channel headed north without so much as slowing down. There was only about one-half meter of water in some places in the middle of the channel! A fishing boat captain tried this trick in the mid-1950's, whether by design or accident I do not know, and his vessel ran aground and became a permanent part of the scenery on the sandy island beach facing the channel until a winter storm tore it apart in 1978. Several one-time visitors such as newspapermen and photographers out for a story have been dumped into the surf and stranded on the island (*San Francisco Examiner,* 16 March 1958; *Santa Cruz Sentinel,* 8 November 1961). There have been many other narrow escapes, but most of these didn't make the newspapers. Those who know this patch of the Pacific, like the long-time residents on the point, respect it. The one predictable thing about crossing the channel is that it is unpredictable.

**Aerial view of the southern portion of Año Nuevo Island taken during the
winter of 1972. Compare this picture to the one taken in 1934. Several buildings
have been destroyed, the elaborate catwalk system is gone, part of the cement
cachement basin has broken off, and this part of the island is devoid of
vegetation. However, this has not prevented the elephant seals from thriving.
(B. Le Boeuf)**

The Island in Transition

During their 76 years on Año Nuevo Island, the Lighthouse Service and
the Coast Guard maintained the structures and houses in typically
spotless and orderly military fashion. When the island was abandoned
in 1948, the structures began to weather and deteriorate rapidly. For the
next 20 years the Federal government ignored its possession and made
no attempt to restrict its use. Fishermen, abalone divers, and the curious
were the only visitors. The buildings were used and abused. Windows
were broken, fixtures removed, and doors were left open or stolen.
When the vandals left, the seals, sea lions, and gulls reclaimed the
island. Sea lions blundered into the stately residence of the former
lighthouse keepers. In time they occupied every room and left their
unmistakable imprint—feces and molted fur piled high on the ground
floor, and several dead bodies. One animal died in the second floor
bathtub. In the space of a few years, the house became transformed into
a sea lion "comfort station," completely uninhabitable to humans. It is
only a shell of a house today, which repels entry by the powerful stench
of ammonia left by its current tenants.

    During this period many of the lesser structures were destroyed or
burned as firewood by campers or men who had the ill luck to be
stranded there. Three military men who washed up on the island in

1956, burned down the boat shed and set the grass on fire to call attention to their distress. The wind and rain began eroding the foundations of the cement catchment basin, aided by rabbits that devoured the vegetation. The cement cracked and finally broke up into fragments which now litter much of the top of the island. The wind, rain, and seas gradually and inexorably demolished the intricate catwalk system and boat launching area. The metal structures, such as the lighthouse tower, began to rust.

By August, 1955 the Federal government was anxious to get rid of the island and agreed to sell it to the state of California at half the market value, $18,094. But the State Division of Beaches and Parks, who wanted the spectacular little island as a park, couldn't raise the purchase price (San Francisco Chronicle, 2 March 1958). The state stalled for time.

Two years later, the Federal government could wait no longer and Año Nuevo Island was declared "excess" property. The General Services Administration, with the aid of the Ross Mercantile Company, advertised a public auction sale to be held in San Francisco at 2 pm on 19 March 1958 (Half Moon Bay Review, 6 April 1958). GSA intended to sell the island to the highest bidder, and most people felt that it would go to private interests. California claimed it had a "sales agreement" to buy the rocky island, but the Federal government declared it was going ahead with the auction anyway. Governor Goodwin J. Knight wired Washington and requested postponement of the auction sale to give time for the state to enact legislation to purchase the island (Half Moon Bay Review, 6 April 1958). Within a few days the federal agency agreed to give the state 60 more days and determined to hold the auction on a conditional basis. This meant that the highest bidder would not get the island if the state came up with the money in accordance with the previous agreement.

The upcoming sale was given a lot of press so that by auction time, some 400 excited bidders and onlookers showed up and the auction had to be moved to a larger room. Diverse interests were represented. Mrs. Perc S. Brown, described as a stylish East Bay socialite, wanted the island for "sentimental" reasons. Ray Spafford of Los Gatos, who had inspected the island by kayak, wanted it for a private sporting club. Mrs. Margaret Whitestone Taylor, who flew in from Tucson, thought the island would be a nice change from the dry Arizona climate. "I've always wanted an island for a summer home .. a place to hang a hat and give clambakes for my relatives and friends," she said. Mrs. Catherine

Steele and Mr. and Mrs. Henry Bradley, of Coastways Ranch, were interested spectators.

In the carnival-like atmosphere, auctioneer Henry Ross banged his gavel and called for order. He opened the bidding at $5,000 and then went into his sing-song selling chant. In a few minutes, the bidding had climbed to $40,000 and all but two bidders were eliminated. They were attorney John V. Lewis, representing the Whittell Realty Company, and Max Walden, bidding for his business associate, Frank Spenger, 68-year-old owner of Spenger's Fish Grotto in Berkeley. The opponents matched each other with $5,000 increments until the bidding reached $85,000, at which point Walden boomed, "100,000!"

Spenger immediately divulged his plan to build a causeway across the channel and make the island into a combination recreation resort for the public and a base for commercial fishermen. He had seen the island only once previously—that was two weeks before the auction and from a boat at a distance of two miles away. He gave his reason for buying the island: "I've been a fisherman since I was 9 years old. I like the water. And I just like to do things. I would have paid $120,000 for it," he added, smiling. Later on television he said that the first thing he was going to do was to get rid of all the sea lions.

Spenger had good reason to be enthusiastic. The waters around Año Nuevo had long been a delight to fishermen. Nearly every species of rock cod was caught around the island and they were twice the size of fish caught near Monterey. Before the local sardine population declined drastically, the fleet was most successful in the vicinity of the island. Several decades ago, Stagnaro boats out of Santa Cruz began making two sport fishing trips a week to "New Year's Island." Indeed, the fishing in this area was so good that Monterey Bay fishermen set up a tremendous clamor in 1948 when the Coast Guard replaced the beacon with a buoy. They maintained that the change would endanger small-boat fishermen around the island.

As it turned out, Spenger didn't get the island. The state acquired the property before the 6-day extension period expired, largely through the efforts of State Senator Richard J. Dolwig of San Mateo County. But Spenger's bid was a measure of the market value of the property and the state had to ante up $52,000—half the market value, plus costs, as the two parties had previously agreed.

Things didn't change much with the transfer of ownership. The Division of Parks and Recreation had a limited budget and was unable to maintain the Coast Guard installations on the island, let alone make the area available to the public. The seals and sea lions continued their re-invasion of the deserted island. Meanwhile, the state concentrated on acquiring more acreage in the area. The Flora E. Steele ranch, 129 acres of the southern half of the point facing Año Nuevo Bay, was acquired at about the same time as the island. Other portions of the point acquired subsequently were 165 acres from Evadna L. Currie et al. in 1968, 126 acres from Capitola Berry Farms, Inc. in the same year, and 52 acres from Elise Gregoire et al. in 1969. The state continued to purchase land in this area during the 1970s. By 1979, the state owned a large part of the coastline on what was once *Rancho Punta del Año Nuevo.*

Research on Año Nuevo Island

On 11 May 1962, the Division of Parks and Recreation granted a temporary permit to the Stanford Research Institute to use Año Nuevo Island as an outdoor research laboratory for studying the seals and sea lions which frequented the island. This permit was consistent with state plans to retain the island as part of a marine reserve (Hanson, 1962).

The man who engineered the permit was Dr. Thomas C. Poulter, the Scientific Director and Manager of Physical and Life Sciences at Stanford Research Institute. Poulter was an eminent scientist with an imposing list of credentials covering his research in chemistry, physics, geophysics, and high explosive and shock pulse phenomena. He was the author of over 100 articles, a couple of books, and he held more than 75 patents in various countries around the world. He had made his reputation early as senior scientist, second in command of the 1933-1935 Byrd Antarctic Expedition, an expedition in which he saved Byrd's life. In 1961, Poulter was interested in weather missiles and was looking for a place to put the project when he happened across Año Nuevo Island. He became so fascinated with the seals that he "sort of forgot about the missiles" (*San Francisco Chronicle,* 2 July 1962). He developed a particular interest in whether sea lions, like bats, use a sonar ranging system to feed and to avoid obstacles, a system in which the animal locates an object in its path by the sounds the object makes or which bounce off it. Poulter subsequently published several papers on this topic (Poulter, 1963a, 1963b; Poulter, 1966; Shaver and Poulter, 1967).

Shortly after obtaining permission to use Año Nuevo Island and to collect specimens there for his research, Poulter applied to the National Science Foundation for $325,000 to construct specialized facilities and to rehabilitate Año Nuevo Island and convert it into a marine biological research facility to be known as Año Nuevo Marine Biological Park

(Orr and Poulter, 1962). Poulter (undated grant proposal) argued that the Año Nuevo site was unique in that six marine mammal species visited the island. The location of the island made it accessible for studying the pinnipeds, and it was isolated enough to be free of human disturbance. Poulter had grandiose plans for installing special electronic equipment for tracking the sea mammals and a design for a system of barricades and blinds for observing the seals at close range.

The laboratory was to be located on a mainland site which Stanford Research Institute had arranged to lease from the owner, Capitola Berry Farms. There was to be a permanent staff of 30. The public was to have access to the island via a landing craft donated by the U.S. Navy. The buildings were to be refurbished, the corrosion stopped, and the wind and water erosion checked. Poulter began erecting blinds for observing the shy sea lions. One of them was an engineering masterpiece, with sliding panels and built-in, one-way glass windows, perched on sloping shale in the middle of a rookery. But, alas! This grand dream, like that of Spenger's, never came to fruition. The National Science Foundation rejected the proposal.

Aided by several colleagues, Poulter continued to observe the pinnipeds on Año Nuevo Island, but his field operation, without funding, never approached the magnitude of the original plan. He concentrated on projects such as marking and tagging elephant seals for studying their movements, the cause of Steller sea lion pup mortality, and husbandry of pinnipeds in captivity. Young pups were transported from Año Nuevo Island to the Biological Sonar Laboratory at Coyote Hills (a department of SRI), where Poulter maintained the animals in large holding tanks and studied their sonar capacities. He and Dr. Robert T. Orr, Curator of Birds and Mammals at the California Academy of Sciences, collaborated on papers dealing with the habits of sea lions and seals and their number and composition on Año Nuevo Island (Orr and Poulter, 1965; Orr and Poulter, 1967).

In 1967, Dr. Richard S. Peterson and his students began studying the pinnipeds of Año Nuevo Island under the state permit to the Stanford Research Institute. Peterson, a new member of the University of California at Santa Cruz faculty, was a specialist on the behavior of sea lions and fur seals. He, Poulter, Orr, and others shared the view that the island should be set aside as a reserve to protect the unique marine life. They communicated their point of view to the Director of Parks and Recreation. On 29 June 1967, Año Nuevo Island was declared prohibited to the public (Closure Order No. 67-6).

The problem of whether to continue the prohibition was taken up at a public hearing of the State Park Commission in Santa Cruz on 21 October 1967. At the hearing, several scientists presented their ideas on the uniqueness of the island. We argued that there were few comparable pinniped (seal and sea lion) rookeries outside the Arctic and Antarctic where individuals representing as many as five different species came ashore. Marine life on the island was fragile, and great disturbance was created by an unknowing public. It was pointed out that one person walking the crest of the island in view of hundreds of sea lions could frighten the animals so that they would plunge headlong *en masse* down high enbankments in their rush to reach the security of the water. Stampedes resulted in great loss of life, particularly to newborns during the breeding season. There was the danger that repeated disturbance by humans would cause the sea lions to forsake the rookery.

After hearing testimony on both sides, the commission moved to restrict public access to the island and classify it as a scientific reserve. One resolution said: "The management of scientific reserves (such as Año Nuevo) must be predicated on the principle of special use rather than multiple use. The public, whenever possible, should be permitted to share the particular values of such reserves through an interpretive program carried on outside the fragile area" (*Santa Cruz Sentinel,* 22 October 1967).

By the end of the year, the Stanford Research Institute project was drawing to a close, and Peterson requested a use permit for the University of California at Santa Cruz. On 1 July 1968 the University, through its Natural Land and Water Reserves System, was granted a 10-year lease to conduct research on the island fauna and develop observation facilities. At about the same time, a breakwater was proposed for the area to provide a small harbor for boats seeking refuge in Año Nuevo Bay. This plan, like many previous ones, was never realized.

The face of the island didn't change much when the University took over as "concessioner." The buildings continued to fall apart, the metal kept corroding, and the wind, rain, and rabbits kept eating away at the island, making it smaller every day. The University's budget for the operation was small and sufficient to make habitable only the living and eating quarters of the scientists. These were constructed by Peterson and graduate student, Roger Gentry, in late 1967. They weren't located in the elegant house one sees from the mainland, for it was too late to save it and the cost would have been exorbitant. Instead, the former Coast Guard gasoline storage building, a cement blockhouse with walls 30 cm thick, was selected. This one-room stronghold was outfitted with a stove, refrigerator and lights—all run on propane—and cabinets, a desk, and three bunks. A little later, a classic outdoor privy was constructed nearby and wooden snowfencing was erected on the perimeter of the island to shield the humans from the seals. All materials were transported across the channel in a small boat.

Having shelter and a place to cook enabled Peterson, Gentry, and I (I entered the picture in the fall of 1967) to initiate several long-term projects on the behavior and biology of seals and sea lions. For much of the year, we worked in two shifts. One group of 2-3 observers spent 3-4 days on the island and was then relieved by another crew. In this way we could observe the animals continuously during the daylight hours throughout their 3-month breeding season. No other pinniped rookery in the world is as conveniently located and as accessible to "civilization" as Año Nuevo Island. In less than an hour, one can drive from Santa Cruz, launch a rubber dinghy at the point, and be on the island changed into dry clothes. This convenience enabled us to continue studying these animals from year to year for over a decade. Some of our findings are discussed in chapters 7 and 8.

Año Nuevo today

What are the island and the point like today, in 1980? What grandiose plans for their use are being incubated?

University studies on the island continue. Funds have been raised for minor repairs and restoration of buildings. The old foghorn house has been re-roofed and the windows replaced, and for the last few years it has been a bedroom for scientists and their students. The blockhouse proved to be a poor place to sleep because of its location near a small and steep-sided rocky cove. In winter, subadult male elephant seals practiced their bellowing in this echochamber, and as many of us learned, the racket is amplified in the blockhouse and the result is like trying to sleep inside a gigantic speaker. The stately old house which dominates the silhouette of the island at sunset continues to fall apart.

The island is losing ground at a rapid rate. The sea continues to pound the southwest side, visibly enlarging the coves every year. Unchecked erosion undercut the lighthouse tower foundation, and the tower began listing precipitously in 1972. On 26 July 1976, this rusty landmark came crashing down, flattening out the once familiar silhouette of the island. The wind is removing sand from the top of the island at an astonishing rate. In some places a depth of 1.5 m of sand has

The former lighthouse keeper's house is slowly deteriorating. (B. Le Boeuf)

The southern portion of Año Nuevo Island in 1978 showing the old Foghorn house, the fallen tower, and the sparse vegetation on the top of the island. (F. Lanting)

been uncovered in the space of 8 years. At this rate, the island may be no more than a jumble of jagged rocks by the year 2000.

The waters off the island are still a great place to fish. The Stagnaro sport fishing boats come up the coast and fish in approximately the same place every weekend. The good fishing, it seems, is due to the *presence* of the seals and sea lions. The latter fertilize the surrounding waters, enriching the marine plants and small animals on which fish feed (see chapter 4).

The most dramatic change that has taken place in the Año Nuevo area during the last decade has been the conversion of the mainland point from a lonely windswept dunefield frequented primarily by local residents, bird watchers, and an occasional hiker, to an exceedingly popular tourist site. This abrupt change was precipitated by an increase in the elephant seal population on the island (see chapter 8). Crowded conditions on the island during the winter breeding season forced some seals to start using nearby mainland beaches. At first, only residents in the area knew about the few gigantic animals sleeping on the beach. Año Nuevo Point is about a 45-minute walk from the highway and attracted few visitors. However, the number of seals resting on the mainland increased annually and they were officially discovered in December, 1973, when *Sunset* magazine published an article calling attention to them.

The elephant seals resting on Año Nuevo Point were discovered in December 1973. Tourists flocked to the area to view them up close before restrictions on approaching the dangerous animals were put into effect. (B. Le Boeuf)

The publicity had an immediate and explosive effect; thousands of interested people flocked to the isolated point to view the rare spectacle of these huge, lethargic, improbable-looking marine mammals. Over 60,000 people visited the area between January and March of 1974, and over 140,000 the following winter. Despite the tourists, the seals established a firm beachhead on the mainland by starting to breed there in 1975. It is most unusual for elephant seals to breed on mainland beaches near human habitation. This made the place even more attractive to tourists.

Unrestricted human access to the area was potentially dangerous to human life, disturbing to the animals, and injurious to the fragile dune habitat. In 1976, the Department of Parks and Recreation reduced these hazards by instituting a tour reservation system which has accomodated approximately 50,000 tourists each winter. Students from the University of California at Santa Cruz act as tour guides, leading groups of 20 people on a 1½ hour tour through the elephant seal breeding area. Guides are trained in interpretive techniques and take a course in the Natural History of Año Nuevo (using this book and taught by the chapter authors). Over 2,300 tours were conducted in 1979; approximately one-fourth of them were organized school groups from central California.

Accomodating this large number of tourists brought about some physical changes in the area. The Flora Steele house at the entrance to the park was improved to provide a home for a resident ranger. Park signs were posted near the entrance; a parking lot and restrooms were constructed; a staging area for tours was set up on a path to the point; and temporary rope and stake paths were made in the dunes near the seals. Care has been taken to keep the area as natural as possible and, at the same time, give visitors a high quality experience.

Increased human traffic did not inhibit use of the area by the seals. The colony grew from a single pup born in 1975 to 147 born in 1980 and from a total of 96 animals present on the mainland in 1975 to over 800 present in 1980.

Tomorrow

Will the elephant seal population increase to thousands in the next few years? Will the seal spectacle grow even larger with concessions selling seal memorabilia? Will there be oil drilling and derricks a few kilometers offshore? An atomic energy plant in the area? A major shipwreck? An earthquake? Is there a modern day Graham or Coburn

Tour group viewing a breeding aggregation of elephant seals at Año Nuevo Point. (F. Lanting)

scheming to buy a large part of the old rancho to use it for who knows what? What will happen to Pigeon Point now that the lighthouse has been automated? How many more years will the island endure the pounding surf of winter storms? How will state ownership of a large portion of the coast change human and other animal land use in the area? Whatever happens, it seems clear that this unique, special, bitter-sweet place will continue to change and touch those who are fortunate enough to get to know and experience it.

References

Anonymous 1835. *Archivo de California,* State Papers, Missions, vol. 5, p. 54, Diciembre 1, 1835, Inventario de Santa Cruz. Bancroft Library, University of California, Berkeley.
Anonymous 1883. *History of San Luis Obispo County, California, with Illustrations and Biographical Sketches of Its Prominent Men and Pioneers.* Thompson and West, Oakland, California.
Bolton, H. E. 1927. *Fray Juan Crespi, Missionary Explorer on the Pacific Coast, 1769-1774.* University of California Press, Berkeley, California.
Bolton, H.E. 1930. *Anza's California Expedition.* Vols. II and IV. University of California Press, Berkeley, California.
Brown, W.J. 1944. Portuguese in California. A thesis submitted to the University of Southern California.

Clarke, R. 1954. Open boat whaling in the Azores: the history and present methods of a relict industry. *Discovery reports,* 26.

Cooke, S.F. 1943. The conflict between the California Indians and the white civilization. Pt. 1: *The Indian Versus the Spanish Missions.* Ibero-Americana No. 21, Berkeley.

Craven, T.A.M. 1846. Naval Conquest in the Pacific: The Journal of Lieutenant Tunis Augustus Macdonough Craven, U.S.N., during a Cruise to the Pacific in the Sloop of War Dale, 1846-49. J.R. Kemble (Ed.) in *Calif. Hist. Soc. Quart.,* 1941, 20, 193-234.

Davidson, G. 1889. *Pacific Coast Pilot.* U.S. Government Printing Office, Washington, D.C.

Denis, A. J. 1927. *Spanish Alta California.* The Macmillan Company, N. Y.

Evans, Col. A. S. 1874. *A La California: Sketches of Life in the Golden State.* A.L. Bancroft and Co., San Francisco.

Farnham, J.T., Esq. 1859. *Early Days of California.* John E. Potter, Philadelphia, Penn.

Fink, A. 1972. *Monterey: The Presence of the Past,* Chronicle Books, San Francisco.

Gordon, B.L. 1974. *Monterey Bay Area: Natural History and Cultural Imprints.* The Boxwood Press, Pacific Grove, California.

Hanson, E.P. 1962. Letter to Hon. Joseph P. Houghtelling, Chairman and member, California State Park Commission, 11 May.

Heizer, R.E., and Treganza, A. 1944. California Indian Mines and Quarries. *California Journal of Mines and Geology* 40, 3, 291-359.

Hoover, M. 1966. *Historic Spots in California.* Manuscript in Special Collections, McHenry Library, University of California, Santa Cruz.

Koch, M. 1973. *Santa Cruz County: Parade of the Past.* Valley Publishers, Fresno, California.

La Pérouse, Jean Francois de Galaup De (1798) *A Voyage Round the World, in the Years 1785, 1786, 1787, and 1788.* Edited by Louis Marie Antoine Destouff, Baron de Milet de Mureau, and translated from the French. 3 vols. London.

Le Boeuf, B.J. 1974. An island perspective. In: *In the Ocean Wind.* C. Wayburn and P. Scott (eds.), Glenwood Press, Felton, California.

Margolin, M. 1978. *The Ohlone Way.* Heyday Books, Berkeley, California.

Meighan, C.W. 1965. Pacific Coast Archaeology. *The Quarternary of the United States,* H.E. Wright and D.C. Frey (eds.), Princeton.

Nunis, D.B.,Jr. 1967. *The Trials of Isaac Graham.* Dawson's Book Shop, Los Angeles.

Ogden, A. 1941. *The California Sea Otter Trade, 1784-1848.* University of California Press, Berkeley, California.

Orlando, A. 1960. History of Davenport, California. Manuscript in Special Collections, McHenry Library, University of California, Santa Cruz.

Orr, R.T. and Poulter, T.C. 1962. Año Nuevo Marine Biological Park. *Pacific Discovery,* 15, 13-19.

Orr, R.T., and Poulter, T.C. 1965. The pinniped population of Año Nuevo Island. *Proc. Calif. Acad. Sci.* 32, 377-404.

Orr, R.T. and Poulter, T.C. 1967. Some observations on reproduction, growth, and social behavior in the Steller sea lion. *Proc. Calif. Acad. Sci.* 35, 193-226.

Poulter, T.C. 1963a. Sonar signals of the sea lion. *Science* 139, 735-755.

Poulter, T.C. 1963b. The sonar of the sea lion. *IEEE Trans. on Ultrasonics Engineering,* UE,10, 109-111.

Poulter, T.C. 1966. The use of active sonar by the California sea lion. *J. Aud. Res.* 6, 165-173.

Priestly, H.I. 1937. *A Historical, Political and Natural Description of California by Pedro Fages, Soldier of Spain, Dutifully Made for the Viceroy in the year 1775.*. University of California Press, Berkeley.

Rivera y Moncada, F. 1774. Diario del Captain Comandante Fernando de Rivera y Moncada. (ed. by E.J. Burrus), In *Collección Chimalistac,* 24, 2 vols., J. Porrua Turanzas, Madrid, 1967.

Scammon, C.M. 1874. *The Marine Mammals of the Northwestern Coast of North America.* John Carmany and Sons, San Francisco.

Schurz, W.L. 1959. *The Manilla Galleon.* E.P. Dutton Co., Inc., New York.

Shaver, H.N. and Poulter, T.C. 1967. Sea lion echo ranging. *J. Acoust. Soc. of America* 42, 428-437.

Stanger, F.M. 1966. *A History of Point Año Nuevo in San Mateo County, California.* Prepared for the State Division of Beaches and Parks, January.

Starks, E. 1923. A history of California shore whaling. *State of California Fish and Game Commission Bulletin,* 6.

Steele, C.B. 1941. The Steele brothers: Pioneers in California's great dairy industry. *Calif. Hist. Soc. Quart.* 20, 259-273.

Teggart, F.J. (ed.) 1911. *Diary of Miguel Costanso, the Portolá Expedition of 1769-1770.* University of California, Berkeley.

Torchiana, H.A.V. 1933. *Story of the Mission Santa Cruz.* p. Elder and Co., San Francisco.

Wagner, H.R. 1929. *Spanish Voyages to the Northwest Coast of America in the Sixteenth Century.* San Francisco, California Historical Society.

Wright, L.B. 1970. *Gold, Glory and the Gospel,* Atheneum, New York.

2

PHYSICAL ENVIRONMENT

Gerald E. Weber

STRETCHING out from the edge of the Coast Range, Punta del Año Nuevo is a striking feature of the central California coastline. A small rocky island lies about 600 m offshore from the low headland which juts out 2 km into the Pacific Ocean from the general north-northwest trend of the coastline. The headland is formed in a wide, gently sloping marine terrace. Except for the high cliffs along the south shore, the coastline at Point Año Nuevo grades gently into the sea.

The headland consists of a broad, rounded northern point separated from the sharp southern point by a symmetrical bight. The island lies directly off the southern point and is connected by a rocky reef which is almost completely exposed at low tide. Año Nuevo Point and Franklin Point, the next point north, are unique as the sites of the only active coastal dunes between San Francisco and the mouth of the Salinas River in Monterey Bay.

Oblique aerial photograph of Point Año Nuevo looking north. Coastways and Frijoles faults lie in a broad linear depression, lying west of the tree-covered Santa Cruz Mountains. Franklin and Pigeon Points lie north of Año Nuevo. (G. Weber)

61

Año Nuevo is the approximate dividing line between two physio-graphic provinces. North from Santa Cruz the coastal landscape con-sists of broad marine terraces, or benchlands, separated by distinctly steeper slopes rising in stairlike formation up the flanks of the Santa Cruz Mountains. High, vertical sea cliffs are present along this entire coastal strip except at the mouths of recent stream valleys. The sea cliffs become progressively higher from south to north, increasing from 5 to 7 m near Santa Cruz to greater than 35 m near Greyhound Rock and as high as 110 m north of Waddell Creek. At Año Nuevo the terrain changes and maintains its regional character north to the mouth of Pescadero Creek. The terrain is still dominated by marine terraces but these are not well defined and lack the distinctive stair-step shape, giving the area a gentle rolling appearance.

These two physiographic regions are separated by a major fault, the San Gregorio fault zone. Slow continual movement along this fault zone during the past 18 million years has juxtaposed different rock types with different histories of formation, deformation, and resistance to erosonal processes. The striking differences in the landscape and vegetation found on opposite sides of the fault are directly related to differences in rock types and their erosional characteristics.

Point Año Nuevo and the surrounding region are in many respects unique along the central California coastline. The area contains geo-logic features indicative of the immense changes that have occurred here during the last several million years. A record of the continuing move-ment along a great active fault zone is clearly exposed in the sea cliffs. The marine terraces record the complex history of continental uplift and sea level fluctuations that accompanied the climatic oscillations of the Pleistocene epoch, when immense ice sheets advanced and retreated at least 4 times across most of North America. The geologic record preserved at Point Año Nuevo presents a window in time through which we can look back and reconstruct events that occurred during the evolution of this small area as well as much of the central California coastline.

In addition to preserving a record of past geologic changes, Año Nuevo is an area of ongoing change. The processes in operation today are identical to those that molded the landscape for millions of years. Surf, wind, rain, streams, and more recently people, continue to change the landscape in the same slow fashion. Most of these changes take place slowly and intermittently, while others are only temporary or seasonal lying within the dynamic equilibrium or natural variability of geological processes. Some natural changes and some changes initiated

by humans are rapid and irreversible. Within this system of continual
change due to the uniformity of process, a biota has developed which is
dependent upon both the nature of the underlying earth materials and
the oceanic, atmospheric, and geologic processes operating with the
environment.

CLIMATE AND WEATHER

Oceanic and Atmospheric Variables

The climate at Año Nuevo and most of the central California coast is
characterized by year-round moderate temperatures, high incidence of
fog, and seasonal rainfall. The regional climate patterns are determined
by the development and movement of hemispheric air masses and the
circulation of the North Pacific Ocean. These patterns, in turn, are
modified by the local physiography of the Coast Ranges, resulting in a
variety of microclimates in the Santa Cruz Mountains and along the
coast from San Francisco to Monterey Bay. The circulation patterns in
the atmosphere and the oceans that control weather and climate are
directly related to variations in insolation (absorption of solar radiation), reradiation of solar heat, and the shape of the continental land
masses and the ocean basins. The atmospheric and oceanic circulation
patterns do not act separately but form complex interactions as circulation within one body affects and modifies movements within the
other.

North Pacific High. The regional weather patterns at Point Año
Nuevo are most strongly determined by the large-scale circulation of air
masses over the Pacific Ocean. The movements and behavior of one
single cool air mass, the North Pacific High, determine seasonal variations in temperature and rainfall for all of central coastal California.
The North Pacific High is formed as air warmed by the sun at the
equator rises and moves northward toward the Arctic. Some of this air
cools off in the upper atmosphere and sinks toward the ocean surface,
forming a large column of cool dense air several thousand km north of
the equator. This air mass forms an area characterized by high atmospheric pressure at the ocean's surface.

    The North Pacific High is a dynamic air mass, moving seasonally
according to variation in heating patterns determined by the apparent
motion of the sun. The North Pacific High has a yearly north-south
migration roughly similar to the sun's apparent movement between the
Tropics of Cancer and Capricorn. During the winter, as the area of

maximum heating (nadir point for the sun) moves south, the High also moves south, locating near or below the latitude of the Hawaiian Islands (20°N). In the spring and early summer the High migrates slowly northward and eventually positions itself near the latitude of San Francisco (38°N).

As the High moves north in the spring, it "strengthens," or increases in both size and relative atmospheric pressure. In the fall, as the apparent movement of the sun starts to the south and the days shorten, the High starts to weaken and moves south with the sun. The yearly cycle follows this overall pattern of north-south movement, strengthening and weakening, but the precise behavior of the North Pacific High is erratic and unpredictable. Sometimes the High is weak, sometimes it is strong. Some years it does not move as far north as usual. Some years it moves well north of its normal position. The High also moves in an east-west direction, sometimes lying far offshore and sometimes moving in over the North American continent. The seasonal changes in California's coastal climate and the regional weather patterns are closely linked to the yearly migration and development of the North Pacific High, while the day-to-day fluctuations in weather are caused by erratic or abnormal movements of the High.

The position of this high pressure system determines the direction from which cyclonic storms and associated frontal precipitation approach the coast, and whether the air masses reaching central California are maritime or continental. The summer climate of the coastal areas is controlled by the strength and position of the High; the high pressure area either dissipates the large cyclonic storms moving east from the western Pacific or deflects them far to the north so they completely miss the California coast. For this reason precipitation is slight during summer months and occurs only if the North Pacific High moves sufficiently far south or weakens enough to allow storms to move into the area.

During winter months, when the High weakens and moves far to the south, the coast is no longer protected and large cyclonic storms formed in the western Pacific Ocean impinge directly upon the coast. However, if the High neither weakens nor moves far enough to the south, it will continue to dissipate and deflect all but the largest storm systems, resulting in a season of below average rainfall and drought conditions.

From late spring into early fall, when the North Pacific High lies offshore, a seasonal low pressure area lies over the inland areas of California, particularly over the Great Valley. The inland areas are effectively isolated from the cool maritime air masses by the Coast

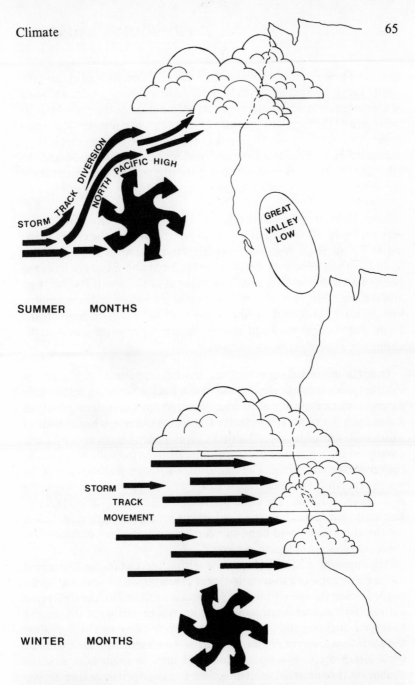

Relative strength and position of the North Pacific High during summer and winter months. The high is larger in the summer and is capable of either dissipating large storms or deflecting them to the north. The Great Valley Low is absent during the winter.

Ranges. These mountains prevent the easterly flow of cool air into the inland areas. Consequently, these inland areas absorb greater amounts of solar radiation during the summer, accounting for their hot summer climates and the large low pressure trough. This low pressure area lying directly inland from the High out in the Pacific Ocean creates a large seasonal temperature and pressure gradient between the coast and the inland areas. It is this gradient that is the primary driving force for the movement of maritime air masses, fogs, and onshore winds to the continent.

Since air masses flow from regions of high pressure to regions of low pressure, winds flow out radially in all directions from the center of the North Pacific High. Because of the effect of the earth's rotation (Coriolis force), these winds are deflected to the right and spiral out from the High in a clockwise direction. The strength of the North Pacific High and the size of the pressure gradient between the High and surrounding low pressure areas controls the intensity of the winds coming off the High. The stronger the High and the steeper the pressure gradient, the stronger the winds emanating from it.

The California Current. The circulation pattern of the North Pacific Ocean is dominated by the North Pacific Gyre, several oceanic currents which flow in a clockwise direction around the margin of the north Pacific. The gyre includes the California Current, a broad body of water (640 km wide at 32°N) that moves sluggishly southeast nearly parallel to the west coast of North America from the Gulf of Alaska to the tip of Baja California. The California Current is an extension of the warm Kuroshio Current (Japan Current) that flows north-northeast near Japan. However, the water has been cooled by its journey through northerly latitudes. Thus, the California Current is largely responsible for the abnormally cold band of nearshore water which characterizes the western coast of North America.

Although the major surface flow within the California Current is southward nearshore water movement exhibits distinct seasonal variations. During the winter months (November to March), the California Current migrates offshore causing the nearshore portion of the current to reverse direction and flow north. This forms a counter current called the Davidson Current, which appears to be a semipermanent eddy or gyre within the California Current and may be related to seasonal changes in the dominant wind direction. During April there is an abrupt reversal. The California Current migrates back inshore, eliminating the Davidson Current; and for the rest of the year all of the surface currents

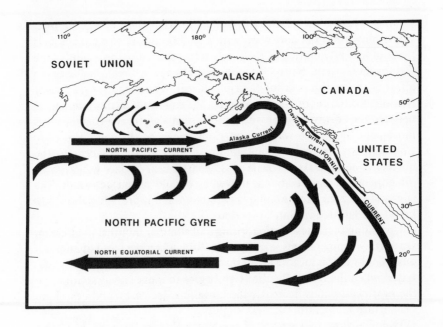

System of surface currents in the North Pacific Ocean.

generally flow south. From late spring through the summer, surface water also flows offshore as a result of upwelling. These general patterns may show occasional reversals that are probably due to eddies and gyres within the California Current. The speed of these surface currents is variable, but minimum speeds range from 1 km/day to about 12 km/day. However, maximum speeds of 16 km/day have been measured for extended periods of time.

Upwelling. The cold California Current flows off the west coast in proximity to nearshore waters that have anomalously low temperatures. In mid-summer, a narrow band of water lying immediately offshore along northern and central California is the coldest surface water along the entire west coast of the United States. These low temperatures are due to the upwelling of cold water from depths of 200 to 300 m near the edge of the continental shelf.

Upwelling is the result of a complex interplay between the movement of the California Current and the northwest winds of spring and summer which blow off the North Pacific High. The strong, summer winds blow from the northwest with a slight onshore component, and the southeasterly motion of the winds is transferred to the waters of the California Current, but with a clockwise change in direction due to the effect of the earth's rotation (Coriolis force). Although the exact water motion at different depths is complex, the end result of this interaction between the northwest wind and the California Current is that the mass movement of surface waters is at right angles to the wind direction. Consequently, in areas of maximum winds directly adjacent to the northern and central California coast, coastal near-surface water moves offshore and is replaced by the upwelling of cold subsurface water. The width of the zone of upwelling is variable, but it is probably about 130 km at the latitude of San Francisco.

Upwelling is greatest during spring and summer months. Its effect on sea surface temperatures is greatest in July, when the band of anomalously cold water is located farthest south, just north of the Golden Gate. Later, when the North Pacific High begins to move slowly southward, the northwest winds decrease, the upwelling decreases, and nearshore sea surface temperatures warm slightly.

In conclusion, movements of the North Pacific High, as well as its fluctuating strength, exert a strong influence on the development of northwest winds, and these in turn control the amount of upwelling in the coastal waters and the temperature of the nearshore portions of the California Current. These water movements also affect the development of the Davidson Current and help determine seasonal differences in the incidence of rain and fog in coastal California.

Regional and Seasonal Weather Patterns

Distinct seasons are weakly developed along the central California coast. The most noticeable variation is in the temporal pattern of rainfall and fog. Temperatures are mild, a general characteristic of maritime climates, and the winds are generally onshore or along shore, only rarely blowing offshore. Deviations from this pattern are correlated with variations in physiography along the shoreline. At Point Año Nuevo, the climate is influenced most by the presence of a low peninsula that juts out from the base of a steep mountain front. Although systematic weather records are not available for Point Año Nuevo, the area appears to have a distinct microclimate, differing significantly from the weather recorded at nearby stations at Pigeon Point, Pescadero, and Half Moon Bay.

West coast of United States taken September 11, 1974 (NOAA-3 Satellite infrared image). Dark tonal areas are warmer than light tonal areas. Note the low temperature of the fog bank south of Monterey Bay, cloud covered areas, and the forested Cascade Range in Oregon, Washington, and Northern California. Note the shape, width, and relatively low temperature of the nearshore waters lying directly off the coast that shows up as a light-colored band. This band of cold nearshore water is the result of upwelling.

Precipitation. Variation in regional rainfall is indicated on the isohyetal map. The general pattern indicates that rainfall increases with elevation and increases as one proceeds from south to north. The low-lying coastal areas have far less rainfall than the adjacent mountains. Año Nuevo, with an average yearly rainfall of approximately 50 cm (20 inches), has an average rainfall that is more similar to that of cities along southern San Francisco Bay than to that of nearby towns in the Santa Cruz Mountains.

Monthly figures for rainfall in central California and along San Francisco Bay indicate its seasonal nature. All stations indicate less than 2.5 cm (1 inch) of rainfall per month for the 5 summer months (May-September), while more than 2/3 of the annual rainfall occurs during the four months from December through March, a time when the North Pacific High moves south. In July and August, when the North Pacific High is strongest, rainfall averages less than 2.5 mm per month.

The rainfall averages tell only part of the story. Averaging the annual rainfall obscures the considerable variation in rainfall from year to year, a factor of great importance to the biota. At Locatelli Ranch near Boulder Creek in the Santa Cruz Mountains, the average rainfall is 127 cm (50 inches), but it has fluctuated from a high of 315 cm (124 in.) in 1889-90 to a low of 51 cm (20 in.) in 1923-24. The greatest variation in rainfall between consecutive years occurred between 1939 and 1940: 249 cm (98 in.) or 196% of average. Yearly fluctuations in rainfall of 75 to 115 cm, (30 to 45 in.) about 60 to 90% of average, are common at this station.

Snow almost never falls at Año Nuevo or along the coast, for it is generally restricted to higher elevations. Coastal snowfalls, if present, are usually very light and stay on the ground only a short time.

Temperature. The moderating effect of the ocean in combination with local physiography determines the temperature in coastal areas. Stations such as the Farallon Islands and San Francisco, which are surrounded or nearly surrounded by water, show the smallest seasonal and monthly variations in temperature. Coastal communities like Half Moon Bay, Santa Cruz, and Monterey, which have less interface with the water, show greater temperature variations.

Although weather records are lacking for Año Nuevo, the exposed location suggests that the average temperatures and temperature variations should be similar to those recorded at the Pigeon Point and Half Moon Bay stations and unlike those at Santa Cruz, which lies in the lee

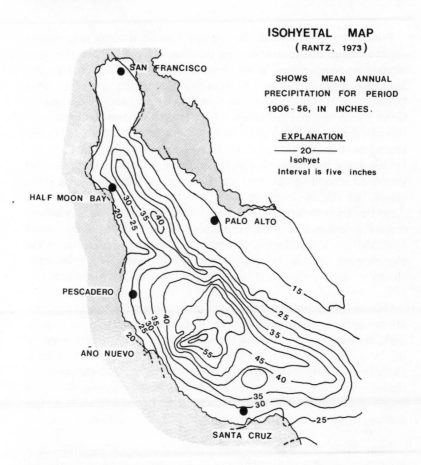

ISOHYETAL   MAP
(RANTZ, 1973)

SHOWS   MEAN ANNUAL
PRECIPITATION FOR PERIOD
1906 - 56, IN INCHES.

EXPLANATION
——— 20 ———
Isohyet
Interval is five inches

Average annual rainfall (isohyetal) map of Santa Cruz Mountains.

of Point Santa Cruz and is protected from the dominant northwesterlies
and much of the storm weather. Located on the south-facing slope of
Ben Lomond Mountain, Santa Cruz also benefits from increased exposure to the sun. Nevertheless, personal observations of weather patterns
along the Santa Cruz-San Mateo County coastlines, observations of
long-time local residents, and studies by research scientists indicate that
the situation is complicated. A distinct microclimate exists in the vicinity of Point Año Nuevo; the area is considerably warmer and has
significantly more sunshine and fog-free days than coastal areas lying
either directly to the north or to the south. Consequently, average
temperatures may be closer to those of the Santa Cruz station than to
those of the Half Moon Bay Station.

Winds. The North Pacific High plays an important role in determining the nature of the winds along the Pacific Coast. From March to September, winds spiraling out from the North Pacific High are dominantly west-northwest to northwesterly. Wind strength depends upon the offshore pressure gradient between the North Pacific High and the Great Valley thermal low pressure area that exists over California and Nevada during the summer months. Variations in this pattern are related to shifts in the position of the North Pacific High. As the North Pacific High moves south during the fall and winter, extra-tropical storms generated in the West Pacific follow a more southerly route across the Pacific, bringing them into the Pacific Coast of North America. The winds related to these cyclonic storms are highly variable in both direction and intensity, but high intensity winds usually come from the south, southwest, or southeast. At Point Año Nuevo the alignment of sand dunes in the dune field (40° west of north) indicates clearly the predominant wind direction during the spring, summer, and fall.

During spring and summer, and at other times when cyclonic storms are not present, the winds have a distinct diurnal variation. During the night and early morning hours, the winds are generally absent or of low intensity. The warming of the air mass over the continent during daylight hours decreases the atmospheric pressure and increases the onshore pressure gradient. Consequently, winds increase slowly in intensity during the late morning, and they do not subside until late evening or until the fog bank moves in over the mainland.

Fog. Most of the central California coast is characterized by a seasonal development of fog during spring and summer and the absence of fog during fall and winter. Daily, weekly, and seasonal patterns of fog movement occur predictably, based on the strength and movements of the North Pacific High and the size and extent of the pressure gradient between the High and the inland Great Valley Low.

The word "fog" refers to condensation near the ground that reduces horizontal visibility. The term "stratus" refers to condensation at a relatively low level that reduces only vertical visibility. Fog or stratus form when an air mass cools until it reaches dewpoint. Cooling of an air mass to create fog can occur in several different ways. The formation of summer stratus and fog in coastal California is caused by the movement of water-saturated air across the cold ocean surface. The cold surface is caused by the upwelling of water from the ocean depths. During their course across the Pacific Ocean, the predominant westerlies coming off the North Pacific High absorb great quantities of moisture from the ocean's surface. When these winds approach the coast, the relatively warm, water-saturated air mass comes in contact with cold upwelled waters, and the air mass is cooled below dew point. This causes moisture to condense and form a surface fog on the water. The great fog bank that hangs along the California coast intermittently during late spring and summer ranges in width from 100 m to more than 160 km and may vary in height from 30 m to almost 1000 m (Gilliam, 1962).

These spring and summer surface fogs are "advection fogs" because they are formed by horizontal movement of air masses. Depending on the degree of upwelling, the ocean is sometimes not cold enough and the moisture content of the air is not high enough to allow a surface fog to form on the water. Under these conditions a low-lying bank of stratus may form, creating the gray overcast typical of many summer days along the coast. This low-lying deck of stratus is formed by convection, the vertical movement of air. Although a fog does not form on the ocean surface, the onshore winds push the mass of cold saturated air against the hills, forcing the air to rise. As it rises, it expands and cools, causing vapor to condense. Thus, stratus forms against the hills, with the base of the cloud bank situated well above the ocean surface.

The movement of air masses during the formation of fog and stratus leads to a "temperature inversion," a phenomenon common in coastal California but abnormal in the atmosphere. The normal temperature gradient in the atmosphere ranges from warm at the earth's surface to cooler temperatures at higher elevations. This condition is unstable, as the warm air tends to move up and the cold air down. The result is a continual state of vertical circulation or convection within the atmosphere. Along the coast the cool heavy ocean air, including the fog or stratus, moves horizontally on shore and slides underneath the warmer air mass which normally overlies the land. A warm, light layer of air sitting on a cool, dense layer of air forms an inversion layer or temperature inversion. These two layers are stable in their relative positions, and unless conditions change, there is no tendency for the air masses to mix or the inversion layer to break up. The position of the air masses encourages a perpetuation of the inversion and the formation of fog and stratus. Once the inversion forms in the summer it is long-lasting, only rising and falling, or moving onshore and offshore.

During a temperature inversion, air masses are stable and thunder and lightning storms are relatively rare. Because of this, and despite low levels of rainfall and dry conditions on land, forest fires caused by lightning storms occur infrequently in the Santa Cruz Mountains.

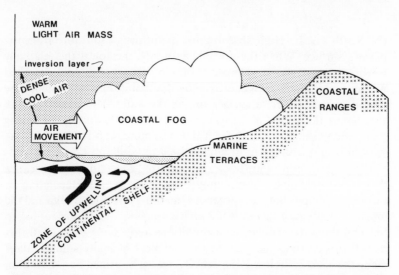

Formation of fog. Horizontal movement of warm water saturated air mass across the cold upwelled nearshore waters results in the condensation of fog on the ocean surface.

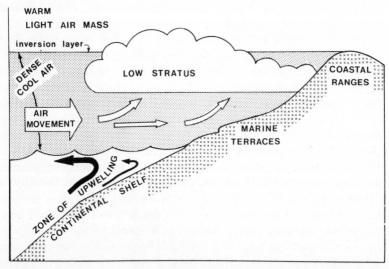

Formation of low stratus. If the horizontally moving air mass does not cool to dew point while crossing cold upwelled waters, a surface fog will not form. Winds push the air mass into coast ranges causing air to rise. As the water saturated air rises it expands and cools (adiabatic cooling) eventually reaching dew point and forming a low lying deck of stratus.

    In both instances the cool dense layer of air lying below the less dense warmer air forms a stable non-convective condition in the atmosphere—temperature inversion.

Along the central coast, lightning storms associated with strong atmospheric convection occur most frequently in winter, when forest fire hazard is low from cool temperatures and wet conditions.

Although the summer climate at Año Nuevo is characterized by atmospheric stability, there is day-to-day variation in weather. Summer is not one long fog-enshrouded period. Some days are hot and clear with little trace of fog or stratus, while other days are characterized by morning fogs which "burn off" by mid-day or early afternoon. Interspersed with these fog-free days are consecutive days during which much of the coastline is continually overlain by fog or stratus.

Fog and stratus along the coast normally ebb and flow in three distinct cyclical patterns. The most obvious pattern of fog movement is the daily cycle or diurnal variation. In late afternoons and at night, the stratus or fog spreads slowly inland and thickens downward. Along the coast, a surface fog does not usually form but instead a low deck of stratus forms with its base at about 180 m elevation. In the morning the sun begins to warm the atmosphere, and by 10 to 11 am the stratus begins to thin and eventually break up as it is burned off. In the evening, the cycle starts over again as the stratus or fog thickens and moves inland. Occasionally, the stratus is so thick that it never burns off and the area remains fog-enshrouded all day. Observations in the San Francisco Bay area indicate that the maximum distribution of stratus is at 4:30 am, while the minimum is at 4:30 pm.

The weekly cycle is highly variable, and can range from 3 to 14 days depending on the existence of the onshore temperature gradient. The winds which create the stratus and fog and push it on land result from the onshore temperature and pressure gradients. If these gradients are weakened or disappear, the fog-forming system is temporarily destroyed.

Over a period of days, the onshore temperature and pressure gradient draws cool maritime air masses into the inland valleys, where the cool air replaces the rising warm air masses and the area is covered with fog or stratus. Eventually, the cool air masses lower the temperature in the valleys, and this decreases and eventually eliminates the large masses of rising warm air. Without these warm air masses to draw the cool air in off the Pacific, the onshore temperature gradient is reduced, the winds decrease, and the fog-producing system breaks down. The stratus layer is burned off and the coastline is fog-free for a few days. However, the process may start over again as the valley air warms and the onshore temperature and pressure gradients are reestablished. The westerlies increase in force and duration and fog is once again formed along the coast and driven inland.

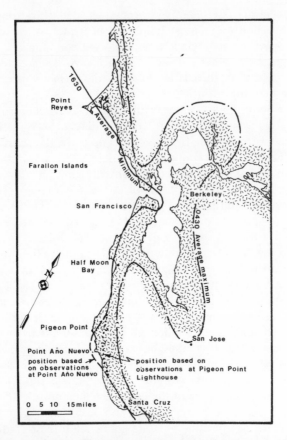

Daily movement of the fog bank in the San Francisco Bay area. The average daily maximum extent of the fog bank occurs around 4:30 am, while the average daily minimum occurs about 4:30 pm. A diurnal variation of this magnitude occurs approximately 30% of the time from June through August. Larger magnitudes of movement occur less frequently.

   The seasonal cycle is relatively simple and is merely superimposed upon the "weekly" cycle and the diurnal cycle. As the North Pacific High moves toward its northernmost position in early spring and summer, the stratus penetrates farther inland, becomes thicker, and remains longer with each weekly and daily cycle. As the North Pacific High moves south and begins to weaken in late summer and fall, the fog and stratus become progressively thinner and penetrate less distance inland with each daily and weekly cycle.

The Año Nuevo Microclimate

Although seasonal variation and climatic fluctuations recorded along the central California coast are generally applicable to the Año Nuevo region, the climate here differs significantly from that of nearby areas. As already mentioned, observations of numerous long-time residents of the area indicate that the climate at Año Nuevo is considerably milder, with more sunshine and less fog than that of the rest of the San Mateo County coastline. On many spring and summer days, the great fog bank is driven back several hundred meters or more seaward of Point Año Nuevo, with the front of the fog bank intersecting the coast just south of the Pigeon Point lighthouse. The lighthouse itself is often invisible, surrounded by a thick fog or overlain by low-lying stratus, while Año Nuevo lies in bright sunshine.

Don Garibaldi, flower farmer at Rancho Año Nuevo, says that there are 30 to 40 more days of sunshine per year at Point Año Nuevo than at Pescadero, 16 km north and slightly inland. The Año Nuevo region is sometimes clear and sunny while the northern coastal areas of Santa Cruz County are blanketed by fog or low-lying stratus. Overall, the climate of Año Nuevo is probably most closely comparable to that of Santa Cruz.

Specific reasons for this variation in climate are not completely known. It seems that the geographic location of Point Año Nuevo, where the steep and high mountain front lies directly adjacent to the coastline, may be an important factor. North of Año Nuevo, the high mountain front is farther and farther inland, and low rolling hills lie directly adjacent to the coastline. South of the point, the steep, high Waddell Bluffs and the low terraces of Ben Lomond Mountain form the shoreline. The eastern edge of the fog bank lies closest to the coastline at Point Año Nuevo, so each day as the fog burns off or draws back to the west, there is less fog to burn off or a shorter distance for the fog to retreat before Año Nuevo is exposed.

The presence of this unusual microclimate has attracted farmers and tourists to the area despite the strong spring and summer winds that often blow across the point. This complex climate, the geologic environment, and the dynamic coastal processes determine the foundations and conditions for life in the area.

GEOLOGY

The landscape of Point Año Nuevo reflects the geologic processes and forces that have shaped the central California coastline over the past 65 million years. Erosion and deposition, major changes in sea level, slow inexorable movement of huge continental plates, and the uplift of the continental margin, have all left their marks on Año Nuevo. Some of these processes, such as fault movement and the continuing continental uplift, operate slowly and intermittently and are discernible only in the geologic record. Other processes, such as marine erosion, sand dune formation, and beach movement occur rapidly and are observable on a yearly, monthly, or even daily basis.

The Año Nuevo region offers a unique opportunity to view these varied and continuing geologic processes. Although it may not be obvious to the human observer, geologic change is continual. We tend to relate to the earth as a solid, stable, unchanging foundation, and we generally react with astonishment when shaken by earthquakes or other "natural disasters," such as floods or the recent eruption of Mount St. Helens. Our concept of geologic permanence is the result of our short human-lifetime scale of reference. The landforms, shoreline, and rocks are continually undergoing modification. Rates of change are highly variable and range from the hourly variation in sand volume on the beaches, to the seasonal effects of storm erosion along the cliffs, to the episodic fault movements and earthquakes along the San Gregorio fault zone, to the great global climatic changes that have lowered the sea level as much as 120 m once every 150,000 to 400,000 years for the past 2 to 3 million years.

Marine Terraces

The most obvious physical feature of Point Año Nuevo is the low, double-pointed headland extending from the foot of the Santa Cruz Mountains to the ocean. This broad flatland or bench is the youngest and most prominent of a sequence of marine terraces that were formed along the coast during the Pleistocene epoch. A marine terrace is a previous ocean floor formed in the surf zone of an ancient sea by wave erosion and subsequently uplifted by earth movements to its present position above sea level. All marine terraces are exceedingly uniform in general shape. They are almost planar and slope gently seaward at an angle of approximately one degree.

At least five marine terraces are visible along the Santa Cruz and San Mateo county coastlines. The highest terrace is the oldest and each succeeding lower terrace is younger. The stair-step pattern of these coastal marine terraces is a direct reflection of past worldwide climatic fluctuations and striking evidence of the slow continuous uplifting of the coastline with respect to the sea.

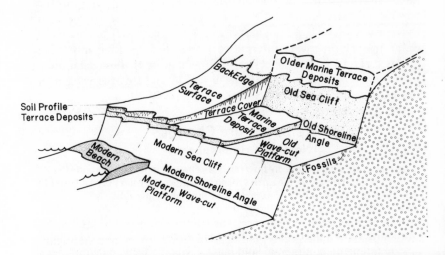

The relationships of the major elements of a marine terrace: the wave-cut platforms and the various terrace deposits. (K.R. Lajoie)

The extent to which a terrace has eroded gives an indication of its age. The youngest terrace is usually the largest and best preserved, for stream erosion has not had time to dissect the terrace into numerous small remnants. Higher and older terraces are not as readily identifiable as the younger terraces; they appear as successively smaller flat areas in the foothills and mountains. The steep slopes or risers between the terraces are modified sea cliffs. Originally, these were vertical sea cliffs eroded on a yearly basis by storm waves. Once sea level dropped or the land was uplifted, these cliffs were no longer affected by wave action. Subsequent erosion by streams and running water cut back, lowered, and rounded off the top of the old sea cliff, causing rock debris and sediment to accumulate at the base of the cliff. The cliff face gradually changed from its original vertical profile to the moderately steep slopes that we see today. These slopes get lower and flatter with increasing age.

The marine terraces along the central California coastline were all formed during the Pleistocene epoch in which there were at least four major, worldwide periods and numerous smaller episodes of glaciation. The periods of glacial advance (ice ages) were the result of a decrease in global air temperature of about 3 to 6°C. This temperature change had

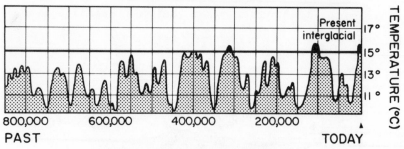

Air Temperature Changes
(Northern Hemisphere)

Changes in air temperature are inferred from changes in ice volume and O^{16}/O^{18} isotope ratios. Obviously the earth's mean air temperature has been consistently less than it is today with the exception of three short periods.

a major effect on the climate and on the pattern and amount of precipitation falling on continental land masses. Geologic and paleobotanical evidence suggest that precipitation in coastal California was several times greater then than now. These wet climates were prevalent as recently as 10,000 to 15,000 years ago. Precipitation was also higher in mountainous areas and in the polar and subpolar regions, where most precipitation fell as snow. With increased snowfall, mountain glaciers and polar ice caps increased in size and thickness. At the glacial maxima, continental ice sheets covered almost all of Canada and large parts of northern United States, Europe, and Asia with ice sheets several kilometers thick. Because of the increase in the volume of water trapped in the expanding ice sheets, the amount of water returned to the ocean by continental runoff was reduced. Consequently, sea level fell worldwide during the glacial advances, with some drops as great as 120 m. The California coast at that time was near the present edge of the continental shelf. As recently as 10,000 years ago, the shoreline at Point Año Nuevo was approximately 5 to 6 km west of the present point. What are now the Farallon Islands were merely small hills on a broad coastal plain 15,000 years ago; and 10,000 years ago, they were still accessible by foot along the peninsula that connected them to the mainland.

When each glacial advance came to an end, the ensuing warming trend resulted in the slow melting and retreat of the glaciers and the return of glacial water to the ocean basins. Sea level rose to former levels. These periods of maximum glacial retreat, warm air tempera-

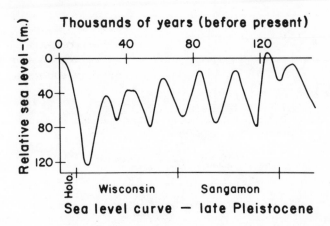

Sea level curve — late Pleistocene

Sea level for the Wisconsin glacial and Sangamon interglacial periods (the last 130,000 years). The greatest depression of sea level was between 15,000 and 20,000 years ago. Sea level has risen rapidly during the last 10,000 years reaching its present level about 3,000 to 5,000 years ago.

tures, and high stands of sea level are referred to as the interglacial periods. Geologic evidence suggests that there is sufficient water in the ice sheets of Antarctica and Greenland to raise sea level 120 to 150 m higher than at present, if the ice sheets were to be completely melted. However, it appears that this never happened during the Pleistocene, since sea level was never much greater than 9 m above present sea level.

Interglacial periods are abnormally warm and fair compared to the average climate of the earth. We are currently living during one of these periods. The present interglacial is only one of four periods of time in the past 850,000 years that the air temperature has been as warm as it is at present. Each period of abnormally high temperature has lasted no more than 10,000 to 15,000 years. It is no wonder that the development of agriculture and civilization occurred during the past 5,000 years or more as world climate moved into a relatively warm and dry period and sea level stabilized at its present position.

The wave-cut platform of each of the marine terraces at Año Nuevo was formed by wave erosion when sea level was slowly rising, culminating in the high stand of sea level. Marine terraces appear to have been formed only during major rises in sea level following glacial maxima, but minor fluctuations in sea level occasionally cut small steps into the broad wave-cut platforms.

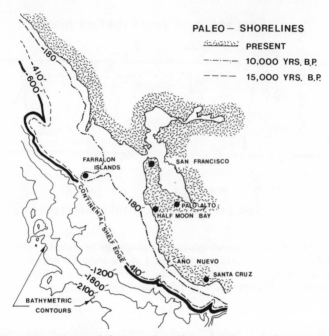

Approximate locations of former shorelines on the continental shelf. Approximately 15,000 years ago the shore line lay near the edge of the continental shelf, about 125 m lower than at present.

The marine terrace that forms Point Año Nuevo is known as the Santa Cruz Terrace. Although apparently quite uniform in shape, it has a complex history. We can be fairly certain that the wave-cut platform of the terrace was initially formed by wave erosion during the rise in sea level that began about 135,000 years ago and ended 125,000 years ago. At that time sea level was approximately 7 to 8 m higher than it is today. This high sea level period of warm interglacial climate was relatively brief, and sea level dropped over the next 10,000 years, leaving the terrace that forms Año Nuevo stranded high and dry 60 to 70 m above the sea.

During the next 10,000 years (between 115,000 and 105,000 years before the present [B.P.]) sea level rose again in response to a warming of world climate. The sea, however, did not rise as much as during the previous high stand, and sea level 105,000 years ago was about 12 to 15 m lower than at present. This 105,000-year-old high stand in sea level, lying 20 m lower than the 125,000 B.P. high stand sea level that initially formed the Santa Cruz Terrace, covered the older, wave-cut platform.

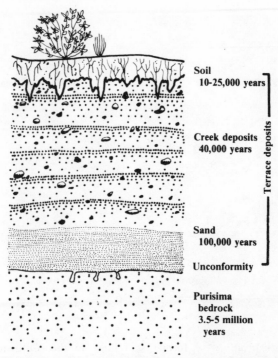

Soil
10-25,000 years

Creek deposits
40,000 years

Terrace deposits

Sand
100,000 years

Unconformity

Purisima
bedrock
3.5-5 million
years

Diagrammatic representation of the marine terrace deposits visible in the sea cliff along the south shore of Point Año Nuevo.

For this to occur, the land surface of present-day Point Año Nuevo must have been slowly lowered 18 to 21 m by earth movements between 125,000 and 105,000 years ago.

An exceptionally well-exposed layer of fossils that overlies the uniformly flat wave-cut platform along the entire south shore of Point Año Nuevo provides evidence for this movement. The layer of fossil marine organisms, containing mostly molluscs and a few scattered corals, is typical of the shallow water marine environment in which the terrace was formed. Rock-boring clams of the family Pholadidae can be found in the rock burrows they formed in this former ocean floor when a receding sea covered them with a thick layer of sand about 105,000 years ago. In the sea cliff these former beaches can be seen as a ½ to 2½ m thick bed of fine to medium-grained and light gray to tan sand that overlies the relatively thin layer of fossil shell debris. Samples collected from this site (one of only three marine fossil localities between Point Conception and San Francisco Bay) have been dated as being approximately 105,000 years old. The new dating technique, amino acid racemi-

105,000-year-old wave-cut platform of the Santa Cruz terrace. Nearshore marine and beach sands overlie platform. Fossil mollusc shells are visible along platform. (G. Weber)

Contact between the fine-grained beach sand deposits *(lower portion of picture)* and the stream deposits composed largely of mudstone pebbles and cobbles. (G. Weber)

zation, is based on the time-dependent breakdown of the amino acid leucine, which is present in the mollusc shell.

Following this high stand of sea level, Point Año Nuevo has been subjected to slow but continuing uplift while sea level has continued to fluctuate, rising to its present position only within the past 3,000 to 5,000 years. Since the lowering of sea level 100,000 years ago, Año Nuevo has been continually above sea level.

As the sea level slowly fell to its lowest point during the last glacial maximum, a broad coastal plain (the former ocean floor) lay at the foot of the Santa Cruz Mountains. This plain extended for about 16 km southwest of Año Nuevo and was initially covered only with a series of abandoned beach ridges and sand dunes. At the same time that sea level was receding, the climate became wetter. Heavy rainfall in the Santa Cruz Mountains caused extensive erosion as the coastal streams flowed at high levels, carrying vast amounts of sand, silt, clay, and gravel. These heavy flows from the streams deposited large amounts of sediment upon this large coastal plain, creating thick, extensive sheets of stream deposits overlying the beach deposits. Such coastal stream deposits are easily identified by an abundance of pebbles and clay and a lack of sand.

Recent soils developed on these stream deposits are characterized by a dark gray, sandy surface overlying a dark gray to dark red-brown clay rich subsoil. The soils are easily distinguished in the sea cliff by their color and uppermost position. They represent the cumulative effect of weathering processes and soil-forming processes occurring over a period of 15,000 to 30,000 years.

Since the last glacial maxima about 15,000 to 20,000 years ago, when sea level was 120 m lower than today, sea level rose rapidly and reached its present position about 5,000 years ago. After sea level stabilized, continuing wave action, oceanic currents, littoral drift, and streams all contributed to the slow modification of Point Año Nuevo into what it is today.

Bedrock Geology

Although the Santa Cruz Terrace is the most prominent geologic and geographic feature at Año Nuevo, it represents only a small portion of the complex geologic history of the area. The older rocks lying below the terrace deposits indicate a history of continental plates moving along a large active fault zone and of deposition of sediments in ancient seas that once covered the area. Terrace formation took less than one

percent of the total geologic time represented by the rocks visible at
Point Año Nuevo.

Vaqueros Formation. The oldest rocks exposed at Point Año
Nuevo are a group of interbedded, dusky, yellowish-brown, medium-to
fine-grained sandstones and phosphatic mudstones that directly overlie
a group of deeply weathered and chemically altered volcanic rocks. This
heterogeneous group of rocks is known as the Vaqueros Formation. It
lies about 360 m east of Point Año Nuevo and forms the core of a small
anticlinal fold. The volcanic rocks are exposed near a small headland
and form a distinct yellowish to yellowish-brown rock mass cut by
numerous fractures that give the rocks a broken appearance. This
volcanic breccia (rock composed of coarse angular fragments) is broken
by numerous fractures which have been filled with veins of calcite,
dolomite, opaline quartz, and iron pyrite. The intense fracturing of the
rock is the result of numerous episodes of movement on small faults that
are related to the Año Nuevo thrust fault that lies directly east of the
outcrop of the Vaqueros Formation. The fractured and faulted rocks,
especially those of volcanic origin, were subjected to intense alteration
and modification by warm chemical-laden ground waters that percolated through the fractures when these rocks were buried at great depths
beneath the ground surface. As these chemically active fluids percolated
through the rocks, they deposited calcite, quartz, and pyrite within
fractures, forming the veins we see today.

Monterey Formation. Perhaps the most distinctive rocks at Point
Año Nuevo are the light-gray to white, thinly bedded mudstones that
are present at the north and south points and east of the Año Nuevo
thrust fault. These conspicuously layered rocks, typical of Monterey
Formation siliceous (quartz-rich) mudstones, were formed by the deposition of clays and silts and silts mixed with siliceous skeletal remains of
millions of one-celled organisms. The skeletons of diatoms, radiolarians, and silicoflagellates that existed in the former sea, settled as a thick
ooze on the ocean floor in water 150 to 450 m deep. As these sediments
were buried deeper and deeper, the ooze compacted, skeletons were
crushed, and the sedimentary materials were pressed closer and closer
together. Under increased pressure and temperature, the initially soft
ooze became altered into the hard, compact, silica-rich mudstones
exposed at the point. Interbedded with these quartz-rich mudstones are
thin lenses and beds of an extremely hard, black rock called chert or
flint. Chert was formed in these rocks when part of the quartz in the

Highly fractured, altered, and weathered volcanic rocks within the Vaqueros formation exposed along the south shore of Año Nuevo Point. Fractures are filled with veins of silica and pyrite. (G. Weber)

rock went into solution in the subsurface water that percolated through the rocks. This quartz precipitated from solution under changed environmental conditions to form the nodules and beds of chert that characterize the Monterey Formation at Point Año Nuevo.

The Monterey Formation is a widespread rock unit in the California Coast Ranges, but the presence of well-developed chert lenses is not common to all areas and is typical only of areas of the Monterey Formation that were once buried deeply. While chert is common at Point Año Nuevo, chert has not formed in the Monterey Formation of the Santa Cruz Mountains. This group of rocks at the Point appears to be closely related to the Monterey Formation found in the Coast Ranges of Carmel and Monterey about 13 to 15 million years ago and has subsequently been moved over 100 km to the northwest along the San Gregorio fault zone.

The presence of chert in the Monterey Formation at Point Año Nuevo was of great importance to the Ohlone Indians who seasonally inhabited the Point for thousands of years. Because of its conchoidal fracture pattern, chert can be pressure-flaked and made into arrowheads, spear points, scrapers, and other tools. Much of the pure chert that was usable for tool-making was apparently obtained from the beach, rather than quarried from the outcrops in the seacliff, for the beach chert is of higher quality. Tools made from this chert have been found in the eastern Coast Ranges and in the Great Valley of California; and obsidian spear points from the eastern Sierras have been found in the middens at Año Nuevo. This indicates that a far-ranging trade had developed between the Ohlones and inland tribes.

Because of its high content of organic material, the Monterey Formation has been one of the primary source rocks for petroleum in the extensive Tertiary sedimentary basins of California (e.g., Los Angeles Basin, southern San Joaquin Valley). During the transformation of siliceous oozes into this rock, the organic soft parts of microscopic animals were compacted and underwent destructive distillation, forming hydrocarbons (oil and natural gas). Hydrocarbon formation from the non-skeletal remains of billions of diatoms, radiolarians, and similar organisms, is one of the most significant features of the geologic history of coastal California. Although formed in the mudstone units, the petroleum has mostly migrated out of these rocks under pressure and has accumulated in other more porous rock units. This process is reflected by the widespread presence of bitumen in rocks, occasional oil seeps, and scattered outcrops of oil-saturated sands in the Santa Cruz Mountains.

At Point Año Nuevo the presence of the Monterey Formation, the Vaqueros Formation, and a small anticline prompted Richfield Corporation to drill an exploratory oil well near the edge of the dune field about 300 m north of the south shore. The well was drilled to a depth of 900 m, penetrating 30 m of oil-saturated sandstones at a depth of 90 m. However, the oil was too viscous to flow into the well bore and was considered nonproductive using the techniques available at that time. The total volume of potentially recoverable oil, and the extent of the field are not known but are undoubtedly very small.

Santa Cruz Mudstone. Although not exposed at the point, Santa Cruz Mudstone is the prevalent bedrock throughout the coastal portion of northern Santa Cruz County. It is the primary source for the pebbles and cobbles found within the stream deposits on the marine terraces. This siliceous organic mudstone is similar in appearance and origin to the Monterey Formation in the Santa Cruz Mountains. The two rocks are often indistinguishable without examination of the fossils in the rocks. A striking feature of the Santa Cruz mudstone is its property of weathering into small blocks and chips and its relatively low stability in vertical cliffs. The high cliffs north of Waddell Creek, the Waddell Slide, are composed of this mudstone. The mudstone continually tumbles down the slopes, forming large talus piles at the base of the cliffs. The relatively low stability of these cliffs and the continual "rain" of debris coming down the cliff faces has presented a major problem at the Waddell slide in the construction and maintenance of the coast highway.

Monterey Formation mudstones exposed at the Point. View to east displays typical thin-medium bedded fine-grained siliceous rocks. (F. Lanting)

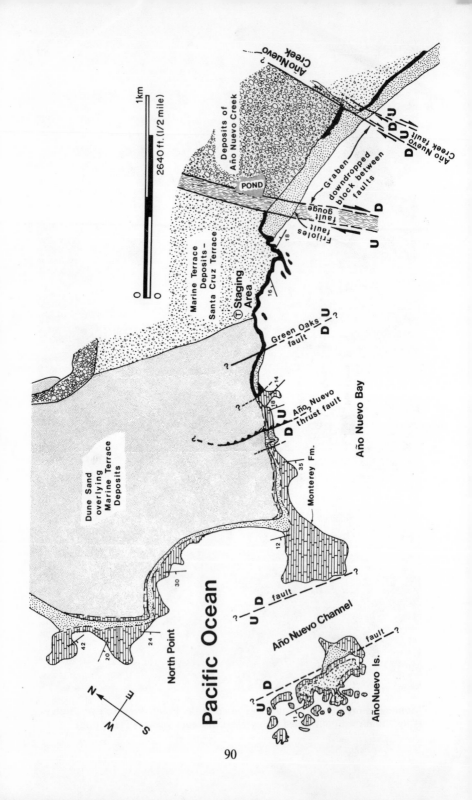

Pacific Ocean

Año Nuevo Bay

Año Nuevo Channel

AñoNuevo Is.

North Point

Dune Sand overlying Marine Terrace Deposits

Marine Terrace Deposits— Santa Cruz Terrace

Deposits of Año Nuevo Creek

POND

Graben downdropped block between faults

Frijoles fault

fault gouge

Año Nuevo Creek fault

Green Oaks fault

Año Nuevo thrust fault

Monterey Fm.

Staging Area

1km

2640 ft. (1/2 mile)

90

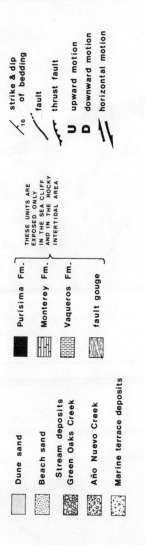

Generalized geologic map of Point Año Nuevo.

Two views of the Waddell Bluffs looking south. *Above,*1905. Note the well developed talus piles at base of the cliff that are formed in the siliceous mudstones of the Santa Cruz Mountains. (R. Arnold, U.S. Geological Survey) *Below,*1971. (K.R. Lajoie, U.S. Geological Survey)

Purisima Formation. The high vertical seacliffs along the south shore of Point Año Nuevo west of the Frijoles fault and the cliffs southeast of Año Nuevo Creek are formed in hard sandstones of the Purisima Formation. The sandstones are generally silty and yellowish-brown to dark gray in color with widely spaced layering, or bedding planes. Although the Purisima Formation is composed primarily of silty sandstones, the basal portion of this rock group consists of a dark-gray, clay-rich mudstone. This mudstone is exposed for 300 m in the sea cliff along the south shore of the Point at Cave Beach. Here, dark-gray claystone that weathers to a reddish-brown can be found overlying the Monterey quart-rich, organic mudstones at the west end of the beach. This unit is typical of other Tertiary mudstones in that it weathers deeply and rapidly, breaking up into small chips and blocks. The shape of the coastline dramatically reflects the difference is resistance to erosion of this mudstone within the Purisima Formation compared to the adjacent Monterey Formation and the sandstone of the Purisima Formation. The coast is indented in areas where the mudstone is exposed, as at Cave Beach on the south shore of Año Nuevo Point.

Two striking features of the Purisima Formation in the Año Nuevo area are the presence of concretions, or hard nodular balls, along certain beds and of well-preserved hard layers of fossil molluscs. Common features in sedimentary rocks, concretions are formed when chemicals in solution percolate through the rock to an area where they precipitate out. The rock within the concretion does not differ from the surrounding rock except for the presence of the precipitated chemicals (e.g., calcite, quartz) within the pore spaces of the rock. Chemical precipitates act as cements, welding the individual grains together and increasing the resistance of the rock to weathering and erosion. The rock is far denser and harder than surrounding rock and is exposed as near-spherical or hemispherical knoblike protrusions. The chemical cements often concentrate along certain bedding planes, probably because of differences in porosity and permeability, and they create "lines" or layers of concretions visible in the seacliffs.

The origin of the numerous layers of fossil material present in the Purisima Formation can be best understood by trying to reconstruct the environment in which the formation was deposited some 5 to 7 million years ago. At that time, Año Nuevo was part of the coastline of a shallow sea bordered by broad barrier islands and offshore sandbars. The Purisima sands and silts appear to have been deposited in broad shallow lagoons which lay behind large barrier islands, a setting probably similar to that of the broad bays and lagoons of the Texas Gulf

Contact between the fine-grained beach sand deposits and the stream deposits composed largely of mudstone pebbles and cobbles. (G. Weber)

Coast and portions of the eastern seaboard. Normal deposition in the lagoons and bays consisted of fine sands and silts, but during occasional great storms, large waves picked up vast numbers of molluscs and other animals from the ocean floor and washed them over the barriers into the lagoon, where they accumulated as a thin layer of shell debris. Many of the shells are still articulated, others broken. None are in lifelike positions. Between storms, sand, silts, and clays from river and streams were deposited in the lagoons. The differences in the sediments exposed in the cliff indicate the episodic changes in environmental conditions which affected this area during the high deposition of materials at the edge of a long-vanished sea.

Regional Geologic History

All of these older bedrock units at Año Nuevo and in the Santa Cruz Mountains represent a period of earth history that preceded the evolution of the California coastline as we know it today. Central California, 5 to 40 million years ago, was part of a series of offshore shallow marine basins in the process of filling up with sediments derived from the continental land mass lying to the east. About 35 to 40 million years ago, the present-day Santa Cruz Mountains were not mountains but part of a deep-water basin lying due west of the continental land mass at about the latitude of what is now Bakersfield. The land has since moved slowly to the northwest and been uplifted along the San Andreas fault system to its present position. In general, the geologic evolution of Año

Nuevo and the Santa Cruz Mountains has been one of slow northwest movement along the San Andreas and San Gregorio faults and slow uplift. These movements have resulted in a shoaling or decrease in the depth of the seas along the continental margins, with the eventual emergence of the area above sea level several million years ago. The elevation of the Santa Cruz mountains occurred during the last million years. These processes are continuing. Movement of the continental plates continues, and stress continues to mount until relieved by major earthquakes. The Santa Cruz Mountains continue to move northwestward and to rise ever-so-slowly at a rate of about 20 cm/1000 years.

Fault Zones

Much of the geological complexity of the California Coast Ranges, the Santa Cruz Mountains, and Point Año Nuevo is related to the presence of large active fault zones. The Coast Ranges of central California are bisected by the boundary between two large plates of the earth's crust, tens of kilometers in thickness, that slowly and continuously grind past each other along a great break, or series of breaks in the crust, known as the San Andreas fault system. This system is very complex and composed of an incompletely understood group of related active fault zones that include the San Andreas, Calaveras, Hayward, Zayante, and San Gregorio fault zones. Earthquakes occur along these zones, instantly releasing years of stress accumulted by the continuing movement of the plates.

Point Año Nuevo lies astride one of these large active fault zones, the San Gregorio fault, which branches off the San Andreas Fault at Bolinas Lagoon, north of San Francisco, and extends at least as far south as Point Sur, south of Monterey. Recent geologic studies suggest that the San Gregorio fault zone may extend farther to the southeast and connect with the Hosgri fault that lies offshore from the San Luis Obispo County coastline. This probable continuation of the San Gregorio system, and its connection with the Hosgri fault, make it the second largest fault zone in California.

Except for a 5-km segment at Seal Cove north of Half Moon Bay, and a 32-km segment between San Gregorio Creek and Point Año Nuevo, the San Gregorio fault zone is not exposed on land but lies below the sea on the continental shelf. At Año Nuevo, exceptionally well-exposed faults within this major fault zone are present in the sea cliff along the south shore of the point.

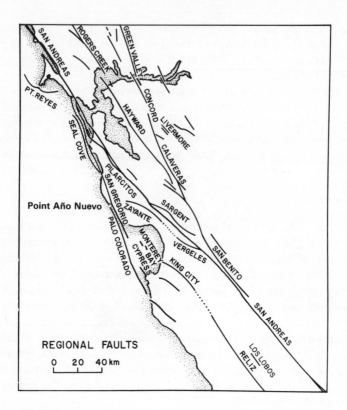

Map of active faults in the San Francisco Bay area.

The San Gregorio fault zone, like all major fault zones, does not consist of a single line of breakage but rather of a number of individual related faults, which have experienced repeated episodes of movement and surface breakage during the past 15 million years. At Point Año Nuevo the fault zone is 2.6 to 3.2 km wide, extending from the base of the Santa Cruz Mountains to the middle of the channel between the point and the island. Within this zone are at least 7 and possibly 8 distinct faults or zones along which movement has occurred. Since all of these faults clearly offset or break the sedimentary deposits of the Santa Cruz Marine terrace, we conclude that these faults must have been active within the past 105,000 years.

along the south shore just below the small reservoir. Here the fault truncates a group of nearly flat stream deposits and juxtaposes them with crushed Purisima Formation. The stream deposits can be traced in the sea cliff from their contact with the Frijoles fault southeastward to the mouth of Año Nuevo Creek. They consist of pebble conglomerates and interbedded silts and clays derived from Año Nuevo Creek when it was flowing at a higher level 8,000 to 10,000 years ago. The age of the stream deposits was determined by radiocarbon dating of the numerous bits of charcoal in these deposits. The charcoal was probably derived from trees burned in naturally occurring forest fires in the Santa Cruz Mountains and then later incorporated into the stream sediment.

Since the Frijoles fault clearly truncates and offsets these stream deposits of Año Nuevo Creek the fault must have experienced movement since the deposition of the youngest sediment about 8,000 years ago. The Frijoles fault is easily observed in the sea cliff as a 75 to 90 m wide zone of crushed and broken rocks formed during countless earthquakes. This zone of crushed and sheared rock is particularly wide and well developed along the Frijoles fault, and it is characterized by landslides and rapid sea cliff retreat. The rock within the zone of shearing was originally identical to the hard Purisima Formation sandstone that forms the seacliffs west of the fault. Shearing and breakage has reduced dramatically the strength of these rocks and their resistance to erosion.

The Frijoles fault is readily traceable to the northwest as a linear trough or swale across the Santa Cruz terrace surface within which lies the small freshwater reservoir. This swale and the steep northeast facing slope (fault scarp) that lie along the Frijoles fault have resulted from slow uplift of the area southwest of the fault and a lowering of the area to the northeast. The northeast-facing scarp formed over the past 100,000 years. It was initially a low vertical cliff, but weathering and erosion have altered it into a low gentle slope.

The other primary fault trace, the Coastways fault, lies southeast of the reserve and is not visible in the sea cliff. It lies at the base of the Santa Cruz Mountains and forms the boundary between the high rugged tree-covered mountains and the low rolling grassland and terrace terrain. Although the movement in this fault is also predominantly right-lateral strike slip, the relatively higher elevation of the mountains compared to the coastal strip indicates that vertical movements along this fault have caused the Santa Cruz Mountains northeast of the fault, to be uplifted relative to the area to the southwest. The area lying between these two primary faults is sinking slowly to form a graben.

This shallow depression is filling in slowly with sediment from small streams draining the Santa Cruz Mountains, especially the 8,000 to 10,000-year-old deposits of Año Nuevo Creek.

Although numerous other active faults are present at Point Año Nuevo, most of them are poorly exposed. For example, the Año Nuevo Creek fault, Green Oaks fault, and several others are not readily observable since they are covered by landslides or heavy brush. In contrast, the Año Nuevo thrust fault is a striking, obvious, and active fault exposed in the sea cliff about 450 m east of the point. Contrary to the normal pattern of right lateral horizontal movement, this fault exhibits vertical movement resulting from compression. The 105,000-year-old wave-cut platform of the Santa Cruz terrace is vertically displaced 5.1 m, with the displacement resulting from about 6.6 m of compressional movement, and with the northeastern block (composed of Monterey Formation) being pushed out and over the terrace deposits in a south-westerly direction. The fault is readily visible as a zone of relatively coarse, crushed, and broken rock, or as thin layers of extremely clayey material (fault gouge) along the plane of movement. Detailed studies of this exposure indicate that this fault has experienced 9 episodes of vertical movement during the past 105,000 years and that the most

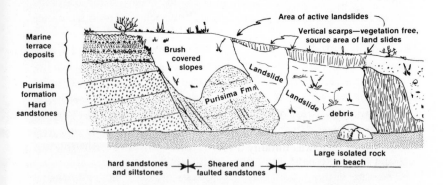

Where visible in the sea cliff, the Frijoles fault is a 90 m wide zone of intensely crushed and broken rock (fault gouge). The rock has been crushed by countless episodes of movement along the fault and is extremely weak. Hence the rocks erode rapidly in the surf zone and landslides commonly form in the crushed rock in the cliff face. The zone of most recent movement lies along the east side of the gouge zone where the 10,000 year-old deposits of Año Nuevo Creek are deformed by recent fault movement. Large masses of uncrushed rock (knockers) are often present within the crushed rock of the fault zone. The large isolated rock in the beach appears to have originated in this fashion.

recent movement occurred within the past 6,000 years. However, this fault is a minor secondary fault within the San Gregorio fault zone and moves infrequently, about once every 9,000 to 12,000 years.

In summary, the San Gregorio fault zone is one of the most striking and well-exposed geologic features of Point Año Nuevo. It is one of the few areas in California, or anywhere else, in which the geologic relationships and features associated with both large and small active faults are so well exposed and clearly visible. Many of these features, such as fault gouge zones, fault scarps, and evidence of recent fault movement are textbook examples of the results of an important ongoing geologic process that has shaped the landscape over the past 15 to 30 million of much of California, especially the coast of California from Humboldt Bay to the Mexican border.

COASTAL PROCESSES

The coastal and marine processes that formed the rocks and marine terraces at Point Año Nuevo are still going on today. Erosion, deposition, beach growth, and decay are exceedingly rapid the effects of which can be seen in periods of months or weeks, or occasionally on a daily basis.

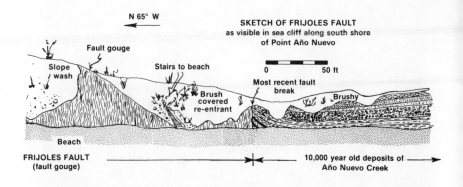

Bedded 10,000-year-old sediments of Año Nuevo Creek translocated and deformed by the Frijoles fault. To the left of the vertical fault break lie crushed Purisima Formation sandstones.

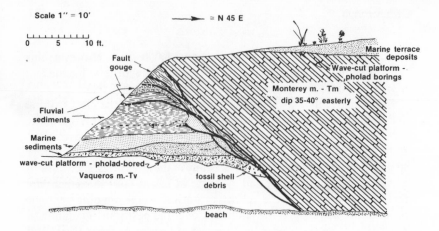

Scale 1″ = 10′

≅ N 45 E

0   5   10 ft.

Fault gouge

Fluvial sediments

Marine sediments

wave-cut platform - pholad-bored

Vaqueros m.-Tv

fossil shell debris

beach

Marine terrace deposits

Wave-cut platform - pholad borings

Monterey m. - Tm
dip 35-40° easterly

Generalized diagram of Año Nuevo thrust fault.

Año Nuevo thrust fault in sea cliff along south shore of point. Ladder stands on wave-cut platform west of the fault. East of the fault, light colored Monterey Formation siliceous mudstones are tilted to the east. Fault has a minimum of 17 feet of vertical displacement and is marked by zones of crushed and broken rock. Marine terrace sediments west of fault record evidence of 9 episodes of faulting, each associated with moderate sized earthquakes. (G. Weber)

102

Cliff Retreat

The most striking of these coastal processes is the slow but inexorable erosion of the sea cliffs by waves. Every year erosion destroys valuable beachfront property and homes along the west coast of the United States. Waves, particularly the large storm waves up to 7 to 12 m high that are associated with extra-tropical winter storms, smash incessantly against the sea cliffs, slowly eroding them at the base. Waves slowly abrade the seacliff with sand, cobbles, and small boulders that they hurl against the cliff face with great force. The weight of the water itself is also an important factor. A large wave collapsing against a rocky headland or sea cliff forces water at exceedingly high pressure into cracks in the rock, thereby breaking out small and large pieces of rock. The importance of this process (hydraulic plucking) can be appreciated if one considers that a 10-foot breaking wave can generate pressures of 1,200 lbs/in^2 for about 0.01 second in small fractures.

The effects of wave impact vary from place to place depending upon the type of exposed rock. Relatively soft unfractured rocks, such as the 10,000-year-old stream deposits of Año Nuevo Creek, are affected most severely by the process of abrasion. The hard and fractured older rocks along the south shore of the point (Monterey, Purisima, and Vaqueros formations), although affected by abrasion, are eroded most rapidly by hydraulic plucking. The sea caves and arches in the Monterey Formation along the south shore are all formed along large fractures that have been etched out and enlarged by wave erosion. Nearly all small channels in the intertidal platform are reentrants in the sea cliffs, arches, or bridges. Often the general shape of the coastline in all rocky shorelines is controlled by the presence of joints or faults, large or small.

Despite some spectacular features, coastal erosion at any one spot along the coastline is not constant. The process of wave erosion alters the base of the cliff slowly, eventually undermining and causing the upper portion of the cliff to collapse suddenly. The rates at which cliffs retreat are calculated as average rates per year. However, averages can be misleading. A cliff may not retreat one centimeter for 10 years, and then during a big storm 5 m may disappear overnight. Once again, it is the human scale vs. geological time that determines if the process is perceived as episodic or constant.

The incremental and sudden nature of sea cliff retreat presents severe hazards to casual seaside visitors. High vertical sea cliffs should be approached with caution. Each year people are killed or severely injured in San Mateo and Santa Cruz counties from a variety of

Oblique aerial photograph of south shore showing major sea cove collapse of April 27, 1971. (G. Weber)

mishaps resulting from sea cliff collapse. These include being struck by falling rock or falling off the sea cliff because of small landslides near the top of the cliff.

Along the top of the high sea cliffs at Año Nuevo, several hundred meters west of the reservoir and the Frijoles Fault exposure, a rusted barbed-wire fence isolates an area of recent coastal retreat. In April 1971, brussel sprouts were growing on the terrace, and a narrow path along the cliff edge led out to the point. On the morning of April 21st, about 1/4 acre of the sprout field collapsed into what must have been a huge sea cave. The entire area fell in one large chunk, as if stamped out with a giant cookie cutter. The 1/4 acre of brussel sprouts, undisturbed, continued to grow on the terrace surface lying 12 m below its previous position. During the following 5 years wave erosion removed the collapsed portion, leaving a large semicircular cove in the sea cliff.

Beaches

Most casual visitors to beaches think of them as broad, light-colored, essentially permanent masses of small rock fragments or sand, that lie at the interface between land and sea. In reality, beaches are dynamic, ever-changing, ephemeral masses of sediment, composed of an almost infinite variety of particles of different sizes and materials. The Año Nuevo beaches are no exception and consist of a mixture of fine- to coarse-grained sand (particles 0.03 to 2 mm in diameter), with pebbles, cobbles and boulders up to a meter in diameter. Beach sediment in San Mateo and Santa Cruz counties is derived from both cliff erosion and from the small coastal streams and rivers draining the Santa Cruz Mountains. There is no indication that any of the beach sediment has been derived from San Francisco Bay, or from areas lying north of the Golden Gate, or even from the Half Moon Bay area.

Año Nuevo has two large, long beaches, one lying along the north shore of the point (North Beach) and one lying south of the point and extending to the mouth of Waddell Creek (South Beach). Smaller beaches are present between the north and south points (Bight Beach), on the east side of the island (Island Beach) and along the south side of the point. All of these beaches exhibit seasonal fluctuations in beach-sediment movement. The dominant pattern of sediment movement depends upon wave conditions. During winter and spring, large extratropical storms in the western Pacific generate large waves which are closely spaced. These waves of great height and relatively short wavelength contain large amounts of energy which, on impact, rapidly erode beaches. Finer-grained beach sediment (sand) is winnowed from the beach and moved offshore, where it accumulates in long ridges or offshore bars parallel to the beach front. Shoal areas above these bars can often be recognized along the south and north beaches as areas far offshore where the waves first break. Usually, the waves reform after this initial break and continue toward the shore, where they break again, sometimes reforming one more time before finally collapsing on the beach. Under the impact of these large high-energy waves the beach erodes to cobbles and boulders and is often reduced to several meters in width. If the beaches become too thin during winter storms, the seacliff lying behind the beach will be subjected to wave erosion and the shoreline will be driven back.

During summer and fall, the character of the waves changes to relatively small waves with low wave height and long wave length. These waves contain far less energy than the large, closely spaced winter storm waves; they simply pick up sand lying in the offshore bars and carry it onto the beach. This process builds the beach back up again. A summer beach is typically hundreds of meters wide with a surface of sand lying on top of cobbles and boulders. Thus each year beaches undergo a pattern of sand loss and thinning in winter, and rebuilding and widening in summer.

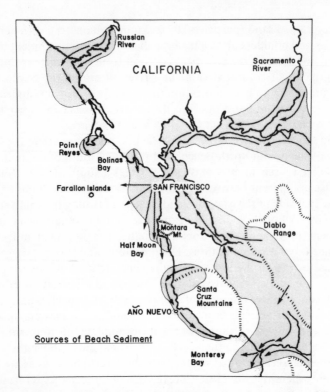

Sources for beach sediment in central California. Based on studies of "heavy" (dense) minerals found in beach sands. Indications are that the sediment in the Año Nuevo beaches is all locally derived from small coastal drainages south of Half Moon Bay, principally Pescadero, San Gregorio, Pomponio, and Gazos Creeks. (Modified from Yancey and Lee)

Littoral Drift

Seasonal onshore and offshore movement of beach sediment is only part of the story. Beach sands also move parallel to the shore. When individual sand particles are washed up on the beach face they are moved at an angle to the beach face. When carried back down the beach face by backwash the grains move perpendicularly to the shoreline. Thus, sediments are moved laterally along the beach. The continued uprush and backwash of water with each wave results in a net transport of beach sediment parallel to the beach. Each particle can be envisioned as travelling a complex zig-zag path up and down the beach face, eventually moving laterally over time. Lateral movement of the water

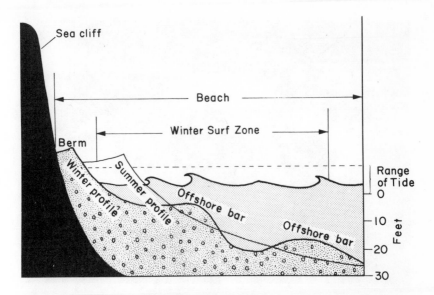

Seasonal changes in beach profile. Winter beaches are thinned by storm waves with most sand being deposited offshore in bars. Summer waves move the sand back onshore forming a broad beach and removing the offshore bars. (After Bascom, 1963)

along the beach face is referred to as the longshore current, and the lateral movement of the beach sediment is called the longshore or littoral drift.

Although not readily apparent, except in areas like the mouth of the Santa Cruz Yacht Harbor, the total volume of sand in the littoral drift is very large. The volume of sand moving past a given point in San Mateo and Santa Cruz counties can vary from 100,000 to 300,000 cubic yards per year. Beaches may be thought of as "rivers of sand" moving slowly along the edge of the continent, moving offshore in winter and back onshore in summer. Although individual particles move in an erratic, zig-zag fashion along the beach, the net movement is continuous from northwest to southeast unless interrupted by natural barriers such as headlands, points, reefs, or by artificial barriers such as breakwaters, jetties, or groins. The existence of "natural" beaches is governed by the presence of major headlands or points along the coastline that protrude perpendicularly to the direction of sediment movement. The north beach at Año Nuevo and the beach north of Franklin Point are examples of beaches formed behind major headlands.

Typical winter and summer beaches; South Beach at Point Año Nuevo. View to southeast. *Above,* Summer beach (September 1975); *Below,* Winter beach (February 1977). The amount of cliff erosion can readily be estimated from changes in the position of large rock in the beach face and Waddell's wharf remnant. (G. Weber)

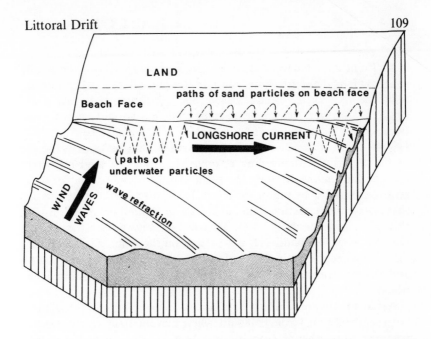

When waves approach shoreline obliquely they refract (bend) so as to become subparallel to the shoreline. A longshore current is set into motion in the surf zone where the waves break. Sand grains move in erratic curved or zig-zag paths both on the beach face and in the surf zone. The swash or uprush of water from breaking wave on the beach face is at an angle to the beach face—with a longshore component of movement. Backwash is perpendicular to beach face. This motion—up the beach at an angle, down the beach perpendicular—results in littoral drift of sediment with a net movement of sand parallel to the shore.

Sand in the littoral drift is derived from cliff erosion and from small coastal streams north of Point Año Nuevo. Where does it eventually go? The longshore drift of sand continues along the rocky north coast of Santa Cruz County, with only minor amounts of sand being lost to the offshore areas. The sediment eventually moves past the city of Santa Cruz, with some of it accumulating on the broad south county beaches. Sediment movement continues southward until it reaches the head of the Monterey Submarine Canyon at Moss Landing. The sandy sediment is carried down the steep canyon in turbid, sediment-saturated flows at the base of the water column and deposited on the deep ocean floor. The sediment moving along South Beach at Point Año Nuevo this year may be deposited in a few years in the deep ocean floor in 3,000 to 3,600 m of water, 150 km from shore. This sand is lost forever from the littoral drift.

At Point Año Nuevo, North Beach, South Beach, and the small beaches along the south shore, all follow the normal seasonal pattern of sediment movement. South Beach best illustrates these seasonal changes. However, the simple onshore-offshore seasonal pattern does not apply to Bight Beach and the beach on the island. These beaches exhibit slightly different patterns of movement that are of importance to the elephant seal breeding colony. Movement of sand into and through the channel between the point and the island is complex and largely controlled by minor variations in the direction of wave attack that affects the refraction (bending) of waves around the island. Bight Beach is characterized by wide stretches of sand during the winter months, when elephant seals are present on the point. Similarly, the main island beach lies in the lee of the island and moves north or south and waxes or wanes in response to complex wave refraction around the island.

Aerial photos show clearly that the waves bend around the island, entering the channel from the south, where they intersect with the waves coming into the channel from the northwest. It is the complexity of the seas created by these intersecting, refracted wave trains, along with the rapid currents through the shallow channel, that make Año Nuevo channel so hazardous to navigation. The island beach is caught between these two wave patterns; the refracted waves that enter the channel from the south tend to move sand toward the north, while the waves entering from the north tend to push the sand on the beach toward the south. This beach is in a position of "dynamic equilibrium" and reacts rapidly to changes in the dominant wave direction. During the winter months the island beach widens, becomes longer, and shifts southward in response to the dominant wave direction from the northwest and west-northwest. At this time refracted waves from the southwest are small, and their effect on beach size and position is minor. During the summer months the direction of the dominant swell and of the waves shifts toward the south and southwest. The size of the refracted waves entering the channel from the south at this time are larger than the waves entering the channel from the north. This causes the southeastern end of the beach to erode slowly, and the entire beach moves slightly northward. The annual change in size, and the movement pattern on the beach, are of great importance to the elephant seal colony. The major part of the colony breeds on this beach at a time when the beach is largest.

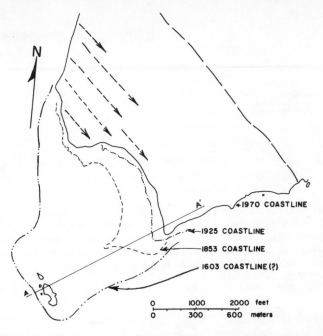

Coastal erosion and shoreline changes at Point Año Nuevo: 1603-1970. (The 1603 shoreline is speculative and based on the observations of Sebastián Vizcaíno in 1603. The 1853 shoreline is from the initial coastal survey of the U.S. Coast and Geodetic Survey, while the 1925 shoreline is taken from a map of the dune field by Theodore Hoover, T.S. Barnes, and H.S. Bryant. The 1970 shoreline was taken from the 1970 U.S.G.S. topographic map.)

Recent Erosional Changes

During the past 360 years, wave erosion has dramatically changed the shape of Point Año Nuevo; a sequence of events has begun that may result in the stabilization of the active dune field and an acceleration of cliff erosion rates south of Point Año Nuevo. The shape of the shoreline in 1853, 1925, and 1970 is in each case well documented and based on a detailed survey. Our estimate of the 1603 shoreline is based on the journal of Sebastián Vizcaíno, who sailed past the point on January 3, 1603. Stanger (1966) notes: "There is nothing either on the map ... or ... journal to indicate that he [Viscaíno] noted an island off the point ..." Thus, it is logical to make the tentative conclusion that at that time the Point extended southwest at least as far as where the island is now located. At some time before 1798, the channel must have been cut, for the island is shown on the map of Peter Amador (Stanger, 1966).

The period between 1603 and 1970 is characterized by exceedingly high erosion rates, with the shoreline retreat of the point averaging between 2.7 and 3.0 m per year. This rapid retreat was the result of

111

Sequential changes in the shape of Point Año Nuevo and their effect on the dune field, littoral drift, and cliff erosion. A. Probable appearance of Point Año Nuevo in 1603. A broad beach lies north of the Point, trapped by the northwest trending reef of what is at present Año Nuevo Island. This beach is the source of the sand in the dune field. South beach is thin and the cliffs are seasonally subjected to wave erosion.

B. By the mid 1700s Año Nuevo channel had started to form with the erosion most probably occurring along the south side of the Point. North beach is still wide, the dune field active, and South beach thin.

C. After the formation of the channel in the late 1700s the point changes rapidly. By 1830-1850 the channel is 300 to 400 m wide and North beach has thinned dramatically. At the same time South beach has widened due to the influx of sand moving through the channel. The seacliff behind South beach is no longer seasonally subjected to erosion.

D. By 1890 the last set of barchan dunes has formed along the north shore. From this time forward there is insufficient sand to allow for the formation of barchan dunes. South beach is broad and protects the cliff from wave erosion.

E. 1980. The dune field is almost completely stabilized by a combination of an increase of vegetation due to a raised water table and a lack of sand because of the destruction of North beach. By the mid 1970s South beach had thinned to its prechannel condition and the sea cliff behind the beach was once again subjected to seasonal wall erosion.

between 2.7 and 3.0 m per year. This rapid retreat was the result of erosion of soft marine terrace deposits that lay in the surf zone at the point. At present, only hard, resistant Monterey Formation mudstones are exposed in the surf zone at both the north and south points. Hence, recent erosion rates have slowed dramatically to less than 15 cm per year. This change in the nature of the rocks exposed to wave attack at the point is a natural consequence of the 1° seaward tilt of the marine terrace. In time, wave erosion encounters the hard bedrock underlying the soft terrace deposits. Much of this change has occurred recently, for the channel was only about 450 m wide before the mid-1800s, and the island and point were connected by a wide sand spit at low tide.

In the past 5 years there has been another major change in sea cliff erosion rates along the south beach. For the past 112 years, the cliff behind South Beach has not been subjected to wave erosion because of the wide beach that acted as a buffer to wave attack. A low broken piling that was found at the northern end of South Beach in 1974 was apparently one of the original pilings of Waddell's Wharf, constructed in 1864 for loading lumber on ships. In 1974 this piling stood about 90 cm from the base of the cliff, with the tip about 30 cm above the beach. The proximity of this piling to the cliff face suggests that it was the first one driven into the beach and that originally it was placed within 90 cm of the cliff face. During the winter of 1976-77, South Beach was so thinned that storm waves impinged on the cliff and eroded it rapidly. The sea cliff retreated approximately 3.3 m directly behind the piling, and the old wharf piling became a reference point for measuring sea cliff retreat. During the following winter the cliff retreated another 2.1 m. In the summer of 1978 the piling was located 6.3 m from the sea cliff, and it protruded 1.5 m out of the sand. The 1978-79 winter brought less erosion and cliff retreat, only 60 cm. On December 21, 1979, one of the first large storms of the 1979-80 season tore the piling out of the beach, destroying the valuable reference point for measuring sea cliff erosion. Other reference points had been emplaced the previous year, and the sea cliff retreat was measured as 1.5 to 2.1 m during the 1979-80 winter season. Thus, the observational record tells us that there was no erosion of the sea cliff from 1864 to 1976 and there was 7.5 m of cliff retreat from 1976 to 1980. Why has the erosion rate increased so dramatically after at least 112 years of negligible erosion?

The last of three interrelated recent changes at Point Año Nuevo is the stabilization of the active dune field. The 300-350 acre (about 130 hectare) dune field at Point Año Nuevo is typical of coastal dune fields and consists of fine- to medium-grained sand derived from a windward

The last remaining piling from Waddell's wharf originally built in 1864. *Above,* Position of wharf piling on June 16, 1977. Piling is about 1 meter from the base of the cliff. This is thought to be approximately the same position it had in respect to the sea cliff in 1864 when the wharf was constructed. *Below,* Position on March 26, 1978 after the cliff erosion caused by two storm seasons. The piling is about 5 m from the base of the cliff. (G. Weber)

beach. Along the north shore of Point Año Nuevo beach sands are winnowed by the prevailing northwesterly winds, and the finer-grained sands are carried up onto the low terrace above the beach. The dunes move slowly to the southeast across the point and cascade off the cliff along the south shore, returning the sand to the littoral zone. Sand in the dune field is actually part of the littoral drift; its presence on land is temporary.

Coastal dune fields form in any area where the shoreline trends at a severe angle to the dominant winds, as at Point Año Nuevo. The largest and best-developed dune fields form where the angle between the dominant winds and the shore are greatest, where the shoreline is long, and where a prominent headland or "reef" can act as an effective barrier to sand movement. The existence of a coastal dune field requires the presence of a broad upwind beach from which the sand can be winnowed by the prevailing winds. A dune field will die if the sediment source, the beach sand, disappears.

At present, the dune field at Año Nuevo is almost entirely stabilized and few areas of active dune movement exist. Moving dunes present today consist of small, irregular masses of sand having no distinct shape. The original barchanoid (crescent-shaped) dunes have either blown off the cliff or have been partially stabilized by encroaching dune vegetation. Two barchan dunes were largely destroyed by sand quarrying operations in the 1950s that were initiated to build Highway 1 (Cooper, 1967). Longitudinal dunes, largely stabilized by beach strawberry, sea rocket, bush lupine, and ice plant are the common dune forms on the northwest half of the point.

The active dunes were far more extensive in the recent past than they are today. Aerial photographs reveal that the sand supply available to the north shore beach had already begun to decrease before 1925. The northern half of the point at that time consisted of longitudinal dunes, because insufficient sand was available to allow for the formation of barchanoid transverse dunes like those present on the southern half of the point. At some time between 1941 and 1956 the rate of consolidation of the vegetative cover in the dune field increased enormously. There are two distinctively different processes controlling the changes in the dune field at Point Año Nuevo: a decrease in the supply of sediment available along the north beach, and the rapid colonization and stabilization of the existing dune field by vegetation.

The dune field at Point Año Nuevo is probably 3,000 to 6,000 years old. This age is based on a C^{14} age determination of 2,800 $\pm$ 300 years

B.P. of a willow root from a peat bed at the base of an exposed dune, and on a 6,000 year B.P. date based on organic material from an interdune pond. The sea level 6,000 years or more ago, was much lower than at present and the coastline was too far to the west for a coastal dune field to form at the present location. Thus the decline in the activity of the dune field appears to be a rather recent event.

Analysis of sequential aerial photographs and studies by W.S. Cooper in the 1920s indicate that between 1925 and 1968, the dunes that eluded stabilization were moving across the point at a rate of 13 to 25 m per year. Extrapolating the rate of dune movement backward in time, it appears that the last set of barchanoid transverse dunes (No. 4 and No. 5 of Cooper, 1967) must have formed along the north shore in the late 1800s, probably between 1860 and 1890. At that time, the amount of sand present on the north shore beach must have decreased significantly; this reduction of sand has continued to the present. Using an average rate of movement of 15 to 17 m per year, we extrapolate that the Año Nuevo Point dune field will probably be entirely stabilized by the year 2000.

The rapid spread of vegetation and the shrinkage of active dune areas is unique in California (Cooper, 1967). Part of this development is directly related to a raising of the water table in the dune field. Since the 1940s, specialty crops requiring irrigation have been cultivated on the flat terrace surface inland (northeast) from the dune field. The excess water sinks into the ground and moves seaward in the terrace deposits, forming a perched water table above the wave-cut platform. The elevated water table in the dune field has enabled the vegetation to flourish. Year-round springs and seeps in the cliff face at the point provide additional evidence of a higher water table. Local residents claim that the seeps and springs are a recent development and did not form until after the widespread use of irrigation in the area.

Since the sand for the dune field is derived from the beach along the north shore, the decrease in the size and activity of the dune field is related to a decrease in the size of the wide beach that must have existed along the north shore before the late 1800s. The decrease in the amount of sand on North Beach is probably related to the erosional opening of the channel that separates the point from the island. The development of the channel also appears to be directly responsible for the sequence of events that has led to the rapid erosion along South Beach.

Before the creation of the channel, sand moving along North Beach as littoral drift was trapped by the groinlike reef that angles northwest

**Vertical aerial photographs of Point Año Nuevo showing dune field changes
between March 1941** *(above)* **and July 1974** *(facing page)***: major elements of
a marine terrace: the relationship of wave-cut platform to the overlying terrace
deposits, the relationship of shoreline angle to sea level, and how old sea cliff
rapidly changes its shape.** (K.R. Lajois)

from Año Nuevo Island. When the channel opened, the length of the receptive shoreline decreased, and sand in the littoral drift no longer migrated around the point (what is now Año Nuevo Island). As a result, sediment no longer backed up to widen North Beach; it merely moved through the channel. As the width of the channel increased, greater amounts of sand moved through the channel to southern beaches and North Beach thinned. For a time, these southern beaches were far larger than normal. By the late 1800s, North Beach had become so reduced that insufficient sand was available to maintain the dune fields.

For a while, there was sufficient littoral drift through the channel, and sufficient sediment derived from rapid erosion at the point, to supply an abnormally large amount of sand to the south shore and South Beach. However, between 1945 and 1955, South Beach began to thin. In 1976, the beach thinned enough to allow the waves to erode the sea cliffs.

In summary, the formation of Año Nuevo channel brought about the destruction of the beach that fed the dune field. Bereft of its source of sand and invaded by vegetation, the dune fields began to stabilize. Meanwhile, sand carried through the channel for 250 years had built up South Beach to abnormal proportions. Only recently has the volume of sand in the littoral drift diminished to pre-channel-formation levels, causing this beach to thin and reestablishing the normal coastal equilibrium—one of moderate to rapid erosion and cliff retreat.

This sequence of events calls our attention again to the difference between human perception of physical changes and the geologic time scale. European settlers came to coastal California in the mid-1700s. Since that time, South Beach at Año Nuevo has been wide and deep, protecting the cliffs from erosion. It is apparent now that this broad beach was an abnormality—a once in a "geologic lifetime" event—that existed for only about 200 years. The shoreline has returned to a more common equilibrium for this coast: a broad summer beach, thinning in winter, with moderate to high rates of cliff retreat. This pattern existed for thousands of years before the late 1700s and probably will continue until the beginning of the next major change in sea level. Events of this sort should provide a great deal of "food for thought" for those who characterize natural processes from data based on only a few years of observations.

References

Bascom, W. 1964. *Waves and Beaches, the Dynamics of the Ocean Surface.* Doubleday and Co., Garden City, N.Y.

Bradley, W.C., and Griggs, G.B. 1976. Form, genesis, and deformation of Central California wave-cut platforms, *Geological Society of America Bull.* 87, 433-449.

Byers, H.R. 1930. Summer sea fogs of the Central California coast. *University of California Publications in Geography,* 3, 291-328.

Cooper, W.S. 1967. Coastal dunes of California. *Geological Society of America, Mem.* 104.

Gilliam, H. 1966. *Weather of the San Francisco Bay Region.* University of California Press, Berkeley.

Patton, C.P. 1956. Climatology of Summer Fogs in the San Francisco Bay Area. *University of California Publications in Geography,* 10, 5.

Rantz, S.E. 1971. Mean annual precipitation and precipitation-depth-duration frequency data for the San Francisco Bay region California: U.S. Geol. Survey, open-file report.

Silver, E.A., and Normark, W.R., eds., 1978. San Gregorio-Hosgri fault zone, California. Special Report 137, California Division of Mines and Geology, Sacramento, California.

Stanger, F.N. 1966. A short history of Año Nuevo in San Mateo County, California. Prepared for State Division of Beaches and Parks, Sacramento, California.

Tinsley, J.C., III. 1972. Sea cliff erosion as a measure of coastal degradation, San Mateo County, California. Unpublished student research project, Department of Geology, Stanford University.

Weber, G.E., Lajoie, K.R., and Griggs, G.B. 1979. Field Trip Guide—Coastal Tectonics and Coastal Geologic Hazards in Santa Cruz and San Mateo Counties, California. Field trip guide for the 75th Annual Meeting of Geological Society of America.

3

LAND PLANTS

Stephanie Kaza

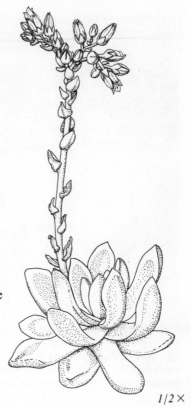

1/2 ×

Live-forever, *Dudleya farinosa.*

T HE LAND PLANTS at Punta del Año Nuevo face harsh and changing conditions throughout much of the year. Yet they are exquisitely beautiful in their struggle to survive and reproduce. These organisms are both hardy and delicate as they cope with the changing environment.

Perhaps the most strenuous influence on plant survival is the prevailing offshore wind, which sometimes blows up to 50-60 mph across the mainland. The year-round wind carries sand and salt spray which also affect the plants. The powerful winds buffet small bushes and herbs, leaving them torn and ragged after rough winter storms. As large stretches of sand dunes migrate south across the point, plants are alternately buried and exposed. The land plants at Año Nuevo are beautifully adapted to survive under the shifting conditions in this coastal habitat.

Both the island and the point are open, exposed areas subject to intense solar radiation on non-windy days. Physical conditions are similar to those of chaparral communities: poor soil, extensive sun, and low summer rainfall. However, the coastal strand differs from chaparral areas in humidity and moisture levels due to summer fogs (see chapter 2).

Point Año Nuevo is distinguished from other parts of the central coast by the presence of extensive ground water, often as high as 1 meter

Año Nuevo Point juts out from the central coastline, catching the offshore winds and the littoral drift. The Santa Cruz mountains rise above the coastal marine terraces in this southeast view from the point. (F. Lanting)

below the surface in summer. This is due primarily to the seepage of irrigation water from nearby agricultural fields. Until recently the open fields on the point were cultivated in brussels sprouts; an artificial irrigation pond was maintained for this purpose and is still in existence.

Despite the high winds and winter storms, the overall climate is mild and temperate at Año Nuevo. Although spring is the peak of the reproductive year, the growing season is long—virtually the entire year—with some species in flower every month.

PLANT ASSOCIATIONS

The plants at Año Nuevo State Reserve exist in groups or associations according to the physical and biological conditions in specific areas. There is some species overlap between habitats, but the landscape is visually distinct in each of these areas with a particular grouping of dominant plants. These major habitat areas are: the closed cone pine forest, the riparian area, the open fields, the freshwater pond, the cliffs and cliff seeps, and the sand dunes.

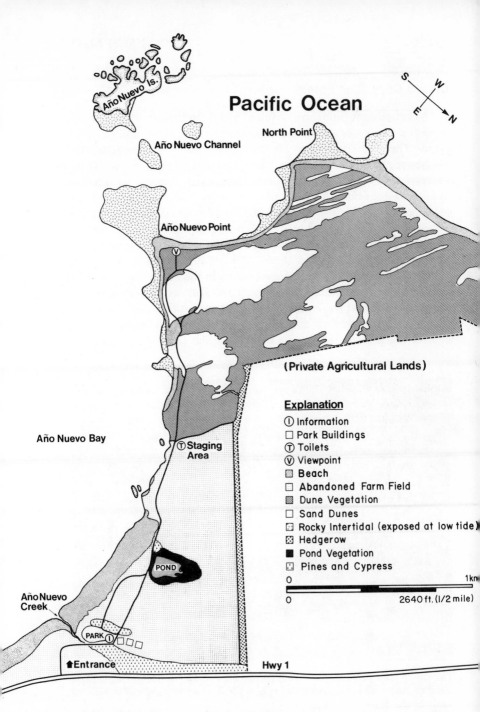

Pacific Ocean

Año Nuevo Is.

Año Nuevo Channel

North Point

Año Nuevo Point

S W E N

(Private Agricultural Lands)

Año Nuevo Bay

Staging Area

Explanation

ⓘ Information
▢ Park Buildings
Ⓣ Toilets
Ⓥ Viewpoint
▨ Beach
▢ Abandoned Farm Field
▨ Dune Vegetation
▢ Sand Dunes
▨ Rocky Intertidal (exposed at low tide)
▨ Hedgerow
■ Pond Vegetation
▨ Pines and Cypress

0   1km
0   2640 ft. (1/2 mile)

POND

Año Nuevo Creek

PARK ⓘ ▢ ▢ ▢

⬆ Entrance

Hwy 1

Vegetation distribution and landmarks at Point Año Nuevo.

Closed Cone Pine Forest

The closed cone pine forest is found mainly to the east of Highway 1, though a few pines are now growing near the southwest edge of the pond. The primary species are Monterey pine (*Pinus radiata*) and knobcone pine (*Pinus attenuata*) and their natural hybrids here. Other evergreens in this association include Douglas fir (*Pseudotsuga menzie-sii*), coast redwood (*Sequoia sempervirens*), and the coast live oak (*Quercus agrifolia*). The term "closed cone" refers to the fact that the cones of these pines remain closed for several years after maturation, opening later and dispersing the seeds. Both the Monterey pine and the knobcone pine are adapted to the periodic fires characteristic of the central California coast; these cones open in the heat of fire, allowing the species to reseed after a fire. This section of closed cone pine forest is a remnant of what was once a widespread pine forest along the coast. Monterey pines are now distributed only in scattered spots along the central coast, from Santa Cruz County to San Luis Obispo County.

The closed cone pine forest east of Highway One across from Año Nuevo State Reserve. Some pines are also growing near the freshwater pond and in isolated spots in the dunes. (F. Lanting)

Riparian Area

Alongside New Year's Creek, or Año Nuevo Creek, by the entrance road to the State Reserve, the vegetation is lush and tangled, especially during the spring bloom. Some riparian plants associate here with species from other nearby plant communities. Red or Oregon alder (*Alnus oregona*) and California buckeye (*Aesculus californica*) form a canopy of dense foilage, and willows (*Salix* sp.) fill in the understory with a thicket of branches. California bay laurel (*Umbellularia californica*), coffee berry (*Rhamnus californica*), coast live oak (*Quercus agrifolia*), and mugwort (*Artemisia douglasiana*) also live here in this moist corridor, along with numerous small herbs and perennial wildflowers.

Three of these stream trees provided major food resources for the Ohlone Indians that lived in the area. The nuts of the bay laurel were roasted and eaten whole; and the large seeds of the toxic buckeye were used to stupefy fish in the streams, thus facilitating fishing. These buckeye seeds were a source of food along with coast live oak acorns. Both seeds required a lengthy process of leaching to remove the tannic acid. Today's distribution of both of these plants was probably affected by the geographical pattern of Native American use. Buckeye trees are frequently found near Indian kitchen midden mounds.

Where the creek empties out on the south beach, pools of freshwater that last into the spring support a small community of marsh plants. Cattail (*Typha* spp.) forms a thick cover of shoots in the wetter areas directly below the entrance bridge along New Year's Creek Road. As the winter-flooded stream recedes in the spring, the bright yellow flowers of cinquefoil (*Potentilla egedii*) dominate the moist flat land north of the creek. Occasional sea rocket plants (*Cakile maritima*) take root here and there according to the quixotic shifts in seasonal ground moisture.

Around some of the old Steele family buildings and the top of the creek canyon are several small stands of Monterey cypress (*Cupressus macrocarpa*). This tree, like the Monterey pine, is found in only a few places along the central California coast. It is also a remnant from past evolutionary dominance and is less successful in its present habitat. This tree takes on odd windblown shapes in response to the direction of the prevailing winds, giving it a gnarled and weatherbeaten character symbolic of the rugged coast.

Año Nuevo Creek, looking south down the canyon to the ocean. Cattails, stinging nettles, and cinquefoil dominate the vegetation at the mouth of the creek, though a wide variety of field and riparian plants exists along the creek banks. (F. Lanting)

Open Fields

The open fields at Año Nuevo State Reserve were once under agricultural cultivation for brussels sprouts. Since 1971 they have been allowed to revert to a natural state in accord with State Reserve management guidelines. Pioneer species and fast colonizers have now invaded the area in the first stages of succession. Most of these plants are annuals with easy and efficient means of seed dispersal. They germinate quickly, reach early maturation, and produce an abundance of seeds. In the open and exposed habitat of the point, field plants generally have smaller leaves and lighter-colored foliage than forest plants. The most common species in the abandoned farm fields are field mustard (*Brassica campestris*), wild radish (*Raphanus sativus*), cobweb and sow thistles (*Circium occidentale* and *Sonchus oleraceous*), wild oats (*Avena* sp.), and poison hemlock (*Conium maculatum*). In spring the fields are aglow with the bright yellow of mustard flowers and the white and lavender of wild radish plants. These pioneers and the other field species provide protection and humus for development of the slower growing perennials which follow in the pattern of ecological succession.

In places throughout the fields, especially near the pond and toward the edge of the dunes, these fast-growing herbs have already been replaced by woody shrubs. Here the landscape begins to take on the appearance of a coastal scrub community dominated by bushes with some lower-growing perennials. In places the thick clumps of coyote bush *(Baccharis pilularis)* and lizard tail or seaside golden yarrow

(Eriophyllum staechadifolium) are penetrable only by small rabbits and field mice. Poison oak *(Toxicodendron diversilobum)* and California blackberry *(Rubus ursinus)* grow as vines over the bushy foliage. Along the disturbed trail edges, English plantain *(Plantago lanceolata)* and hairy cat's-ear *(Hypochoeris radicata)* survive well in the compacted soil, filling in the ground layer of vegetation.

The bright flowers or conspicuous seeds of other coastal scrub flowering plants punctuate the dense bushy growth in random patterns, adding color and texture to the field community. Figwort (*Scrophularia californica*) and dock (*Rumex crassus*) stand about a meter tall with long stalks of abundant seeds present in fall and winter. Though uncommon, the large, beautiful yellow flowers of Hooker's primrose (*Oenothera hookeri*) are striking in appearance and stature. The white flowers of yarrow (*Achillea millefolium*) and pearly everlasting (*Anaphalis margaritacea*) contrast with the red Indian paintbrush (*Castilleja latifolia*) and the bright orange California poppy (*Eschscholzia califor-*

The open fields at Año Nuevo were once cultivated farm land. Since 1971 they have been overgrown by native and alien coastal scrub species. The first invaders are the fast-growing annuals which are now well established in most of the field. In many areas ecological succession is further advanced, and bushes and shrubs dominate the landscape. (F. Lanting)

nica). Two species of buckwheat, coast buckwheat (*Eriogonum latifolium*) and California buckwheat (*Eriogonum fasciculatum*), spread seeds from spherical blossom clusters on tall stalks. The less abundant blue flowers of the seaside daisy (*Erigeron glaucus*), the yellow-flowered live-forever (*Dudleya farinosa*), and orange-blossomed fiddleneck (*Amsinckia spectabilis*) are also found in this open field area.

It is likely that the next stage in ecological succession beyond the growth of woody shrubs and bushes will include the appearance of taller growth forms such as conifers. Already half a dozen Douglas fir seedlings have reached 1-2 meters in height in the area of the field near the parking lot. At least that many small Monterey cypresses are also gaining a foothold here. Near the irrigation pond there are several young Monterey pines that have grown up since the field has been abandoned. In time it is possible that these longer-lived species will come to dominate the former farm field area, though the pressures of wind and salt spray may retard this successional pattern.

Fields such as this abandoned farm area may have been maintained by the Ohlone Indians for the purpose of food gathering by regular brush burnings. It is known that the Indians burned fields to facilitate small mammal hunting and to clear the underbrush for ease in collecting acorns, the main food staple in their diet. These burns also had the ecological effect of retarding succession and maintaining the native bunch grasses which supplied seeds for most villages. After several years of successional growth in which grasses were gradually superseded by other chaparral plants, the shrublands were burned and the pattern begun again. Since the time when the Ohlones utilized the natural fire ecology of the central California coast habitat, most of the native grasses have been replaced by alien species brought over from Europe. This has occurred throughout their entire range. These non-natives are more resistant to the impact of grazing animals and have been more successful than the native grasses in the competition for survival. The landscape we see today may be visually similar to that in the days of the Ohlone, but it is ecologically distinct.

Freshwater Pond

The freshwater pond forms a unique habitat for many of the animals at Año Nuevo because of the generally available supply of water. Vegetation around the pond and along the trail near the pond is dense and brushy, providing thick cover for birds and small vertebrates. This habitat is somewhat distinct from the rest of the open field, though

California bulrushes, or tules, are the most conspicuous plants in the pond. Their dense growth provides cover for resident and migrant bird species visiting the pond. (F. Lanting)

many of the same colonizing plants exist here. Like the plant association in the open field, this one is relatively recent. Plant distribution is changing from year to year and is affected by the steady succession of colonizers in the open field. This habitat is also strongly influenced by the water level of the pond which has varied from almost empty during the drought of 1976-1977 to overflowing in heavy winters (especially 1980). Freshwater species directly dependent on this wet habitat fluctuate in abundance with the availability of water.

The freshwater pond supports several sedges and rushes as well as smaller surface- or edge-dwelling plants. The tall California bulrush,* or tule *(Scirpus californicus)*, is the predominant sedge and is usually found with its roots submerged. Species of *Carex* are also present. Salt rush *(Juncus leseurii)* forms knee-high clumps along the moist bank. Pond plants provide cover for resident and migrant water birds, some of whom rest in the thicket of stems. Insect-eating birds and dragonflies are also drawn to this area to feed on insect life associated with the pond. The Ohlone people used long-stemmed tules for making small boats; other species were used in basketry and weaving.

In contrast to the lush green stands of water plants in the pond itself, the trail along the pond and the perimeter embankment are characterized by hardy colonizers capable of withstanding dry conditions. Bushes of Douglas' nightshade *(Solanum douglasii)* and poison oak intermingle with coyote bush. The thorny trailing vines of California blackberry

*The common name *bulrush* is misleading as this plant is a sedge, not a rush. Many botanists prefer the less confusing synonym *tule*.

most often associate with coyote bush rather than lupine or nightshade, suggesting a higher tolerance level for overgrowth in coyote bush. Several thistles and the warty-leaved ox-tongue *(Picris echioides)* have sprung up along the trampled edge of the path with the sturdy English plantain. In the midst of this ticket of dense foliage, the maroon flowers or seed stalks of California bee plant *(Scrophularia californica)* are well camouflaged. Poison hemlock *(Conium maculatum)*, with its white umbel flowers and lacy fern-like leaves, is also common along this trail and around the pond.

The one major stand of pine trees in the Reserve itself creates a small shady spot on the west edge of the pond. Though young, these trees are growing rapidly and producing viable seeds. Several pine seedlings have become established in the near vicinity, and it seems likely that more of these trees will take hold as succession progresses in the abandoned farm field.

Cliffs and Cliff Seeps

The coastal sea cliffs are the least stable of the plant habitats at Año Nuevo next to the exposed sand dunes. These areas are subject to harsh winds, salt spray, and the direct impact of winter waves. In heavy storm years the ocean waves slam against the marine terrace cliffs, biting huge chunks out of the toe of the cliffs, undercutting the field soils above and causing major slumps. Cliff vegetation is either buried in the rubble or persists on the surface of the slide, reestablishing roots as the rock mass settles.

The high water table at Año Nuevo has created an unusual feature along the cliff areas. Where water has percolated to the seacliff edge and seeped out in specific areas, microhabitats support a variety of plants usually associated with stream or freshwater communities. In this somewhat anomalous situation, freshwater horsetails (*Equisetum telmateia*) and monkey flower (*Mimulus guttatus*) exist against a backdrop of ocean spray. Cinquefoil (*Potentilla egedii*) and brass buttons (*Cotula coronopifolia*) both grow in these cliff seep microcommunities though one is typical of freshwater conditions, the other of brackish water.

Throughout the south-, west-, and north-facing cliffs of Año Nuevo Reserve, vegetation is representative of the adjacent horizontal communities. Coyote bush, lizard tail, nightshade, and blackberry form brush thickets that provide some cover for low-growing perennials such as pearly everlasting, plantain, and hairy cat's-ear. Occasional clumps of cattails *(Typhy* spp.*)* or pampas grass interrupt the otherwise low growth pattern of the colonized cliffs. Crabgrass (*Digitaria* sp.), salt

On the inland side of the pond, the vegetation is dense and tangled. Even in winter the bare branches of willow and low-growing annuals create an almost impenetrable thicket. (F. Lanting)

Because of the groundwater runoff through the dunes, horsetails and iceplant are neighbors here in an unusual association of freshwater and coastal strand plants. (F. Lanting)

grass (*Distichlis spicata*), and European beach grass (*Ammophila arenaria*) spread rapidly along exposed surface areas, helping to stabilize loose sand or rock substrates.

In this seacliff habitat, vegetation diversity and distribution may shift rapidly from year to year according to the immediate physical conditions. Individual seep areas have collapsed and recolonized over the past 10 years, usually showing a predominance of 2 to 3 species rather than a well-developed, diverse plant community typical of a more stable environment. The wide range of plant assemblages in these cliff and cliff seep habitats is an indication of the diverse conditions available for settling and the random dispersal of seeds.

Sand Dunes

The shifting dunes along the windblown point are the most dramatic and challenging habitat for plant species at Año Nuevo. With the recent high water table, vegetation cover has increased steadily, indicating a trend toward total dune stabilization. Several major dunefields have moved entirely off the edge of the point, and other dunes continue to progress southward. Slower-moving areas are now grown over by dune colonizing plants and few areas remain bare.

Dune stabilization through the pattern of succession changes constantly from season to season and year to year. Depending on wind activity, a single dune may move 5-10 meters in several months, completely altering the landscape in the area, burying existing vegetation and exposing new areas as it moves on. As certain plant species germinate on the dunes, they in turn alter the environment, creating protected microhabitats for further growth. Root systems bind the sand in place, and dropping foliage forms a small layer of soil beneath the plant. Underneath the shade of the colonizing plant, temperatures are cooler and moisture levels higher. In this area of decreased exposure to sun and wind, new seedlings have an increased chance for survival. The balance between plant stabilization and dune movement is dynamic, shifting constantly according to wind activity and water availability. Possibly because of an apparent decrease in the amount of sand in the littoral drift system (see chapter 2) and certainly because of the increase in ground water, vegetation spread now appears to be gaining over sand movement.

The succession pattern in the dunes is marked by fairly specific stages, characterized by species adapted to the physical conditions available at the time. The first species to invade a barren area are called "pioneer

Año Nuevo Point, looking northwest. The dunes closest to the point are now overgrown with vegetation though some dunefields remain bare and continue to move across the peninsula from the northwest. (F. Lanting)

A single dune may move through an area that once was flat, altering the topography in a matter of days or weeks during windy seasons. (F. Lanting)

plants." These plants use many of the same strategies as the annuals that have invaded the abandoned farm field. They mature rapidly, investing most of their energy budget in reproduction. They flower quickly and over a long period of time, allowing the production of a large number of seeds. These seeds are generally small and easily dispersed by wind or animal carriers. Some pioneer plant flowers have become so modified that they have no petals; this further facilitates seed dispersal. Pioneer species on the dunes survive vigorously on resources available in this harsh environment. They need only a small amount of soil nutrients to grow to reproductive maturity.

These first invading plants insure their own survival against the moving sand masses by immobilizing the sand immediately around them with extensive fibrous root systems (e.g., European beach grass, *Ammophila arenaria*) or with a long fleshy tap root (e.g., yellow sand verbena, *Abronia latifolia*). Beach strawberry (*Fragaria chiloensis*) and beach morning glory (*Convolvulus soldanella*) send out long runners over the surface of the sand which hold the sand in place while extending vegetative growth. All of the growth forms are low and survive the force of frequent strong winds. Beach bur (*Franseria chamissonis*) and yellow sand verbena grow especially close to the ground. Sea rocket (*Cakile maritima*) forms small rounded clumps, blocking the sand movement behind each plant in a temporary mini-dune.

Many of these pioneer species have succulent leaves, an adaptation that retains moisture against the evaporative forces of the wind. Sea rocket, though similar in flower to wild radish, has noticeably succulent foliage. Yellow sand verbena and ice plant or sea fig (*Carpobrotus chilense*) are succulents as well, storing water in their thick leaves to sustain the plants through harsh colonizing conditions.

The extensive fibrous roots of European beach grass, *Ammophila arenaria* (above), lie somewhat exposed here as the sand dune continues to move. Runners of beach strawberry, *Fragaria chiloensis,* (left) act to stabilize moving sand in the first stages of dune succession. (F. Lanting)

The two parts of the sea rocket pod provide two strategies for reproductive survival: the lower, heavier segment remains attached to the parent, eventually dropping to the ground nearby, while the upper, lighter segment blows away for wider dispersal. (F. Lanting)

Sea rocket is a particularly successful dune colonizer. Its adaptive features have been studied in some detail by Barbour et al. (1973). Since rain water percolates rapidly through sandy soil, the ground surface is usually dry to a depth of 2.5 cm and unsuitable for seedling establishment. Sea rocket seeds germinate 5-10 cm below the surface, relying on accumulated rainfall rather than slight surface moisture. The seeds are adapted to withstand high salinities, as in the ocean. They are not killed by exposure to salt conditions but merely inhibited from germinating until rainwater leaches the seeds clean. This ability to survive saline conditions is useful in seed dispersal. The sea rocket seed pod forms in two parts: the heavier segment remains attached to the parent plant, while the lighter half is blown away. The light segment can float on sea water for up to 11 days and still germinate once washed clean. The heavier segment drops to the ground near the parent plant in a protected microhabitat suitable for germination. Through this double method of seed dispersal, sea rocket has been able to extend its range from the Queen Charlotte Islands in British Columbia to Cedros Island off Baja California, reaching approximately 3000 km in 40 years.

As pioneer plants become well established on the dry, moving sand, new microhabitat conditions are created at the surface and other species are able to gain a foothold. Accumulated organic matter forms a minimal soil layer that can support larger plants such as lizard tail and buckwheat. Yarrow, figwort, and dune goldenrod (*Solidago spathulata*) spread through the dunes from already established areas in the dunes and out in the abandoned farm field. In this intermediate stage of succession, beach sagewort (*Artemisia pycnocephala*) and mock heather (*Haplopappus ericoides*) may grow a meter tall. Here and there, in isolated pockets, the delicate beach primrose (*Camissonia cheiranthifolia*) with its small yellow flowers can be found growing in the protection of the other stabilizing plants. Species that are less able to withstand sand burial and dry conditions from strong winds gradually become established, forming a more stable sand dune community that further retards sand movement.

As organic matter accumulates from plants of this intermediate stage of succession, the soil is enriched, water retention is improved, and the microhabitat becomes a more favorable place for germination. Large species such as bush lupine (*Lupinus arboreus*) and willow (*Salix lasiolepis*) exist in these stabilized areas, along with coyote bush (*Baccharis pilularis*). In late spring and early summer the abundant yellow lupine flowers create an orgy of color and odor, marking this season a highlight of the year.

Dune succession is initiated by the pioneer plants such as sea rocket that gain a small foothold in the moving sand (upper left). Beach strawberry, sand verbena, and other low-growing species bind the sand in place, forming a microhabitat for the establishment of larger species (upper right). Over time, a once-moving sand dune will be almost totally covered with vegetation (lower left). Eventually larger growth forms will succeed these pioneers as they have in parts of the north point area (lower right). (F. Lanting)

The flowers of the gorgeous yellow bush lupine reach a peak in abundance in June and July, blanketing parts of Año Nuevo with lush color and a sweet odor. (F. Lanting)

Coyote bush most often occurs in a bush form *(Baccharis pilularis consanguinea)* (left) but in the dunes and parts of the open fields at Año Nuevo, a prostrate form is dominant *(B. pilularis pilularis)* (right). This low-growth form is more successful under the pressure of extreme winds common along the coast almost year-round. (F. Lanting)

In the windblown environment of Año Nuevo, coyote bush has adopted a prostrate form (*B. pilularis,* ssp. *pilularis*) that contributes to its success as a dune stabilizer. Coyote bush can flower over an extended period of time and produce an abundance of seeds for insured survival. If the trunk is broken off, new plants will sprout from the roots. This species is one of the hardiest colonizers of both dune and grassland communities.

In areas where the sand has been fairly well stabilized, large stands of willow or bush lupine dominate the landscape. This is not yet a coastal strand climax community, for most areas have not been settled long enough to display a well developed species diversity like that of portions of the strand along Highway 1. As dune soils are so easily disturbed, pioneer species are sometimes found growing amongst more established plants. Plant distributions vary within the different dune habitats of Año Nuevo and may be quite distinct from those of dune succession patterns elsewhere along the coast (Gordon, 1974).

The largest number of species at Año Nuevo Point is found in the scoured interdune area (Szyjewicz and Rosner, 1978). This area was radically disturbed in the 1950's when sand was removed to construct Highway 1. The bare ground is coarse-grained, pebbly soil in contrast with the fine sand in neighboring dune areas and the humus in stable inland areas. Succession patterns have been altered with this impact, permitting rapid establishment of vegetation. Both pioneer species (such as sea rocket) and species of the stable dune area (lupine and coyote bush) are present, but plants of the intermediate successional stage are most abundant. Additional disturbance from human foot traffic and Park vehicles has encouraged the growth of weedy species such as hairy cat's-ear, dock, *Plantago* spp., and clover *(Trifolium* spp.).

The inland dune area is the most stable community at Año Nuevo Point. Here the vegetation grows in dense masses characteristic of later stages in dune succession. Willow and lupine are common, mixed in with lizard tail, nightshade, buckwheat, and coyote bush. Some poison oak has spread into the area, and one Monterey pine has been observed (Szyjewicz and Rosner, 1978). It is likely that these species will come to dominate the inland dunes area in the future, marking a further stabilization of the shifting dune habitat at Año Nuevo.

DUNE ADAPTATIONS

Plants in the dunes must survive the harsh conditions of extreme wind, sun, and salt spray as well as poor soil and disturbance from visiting animals. Such physical constraints provide selection pressure for species whose physical, physiological, and metabolic characteristics are suited for survival in this environment. A whole range of strategies is used by dune plants in this struggle with the elements.

The strong winds, predominantly from the northwest, batter the dune vegetation on the point and island off-and-on throughout the year. They are especially strong during winter storms, sometimes reaching wind speeds of over 50 mph. The extreme winds affect the plants directly, causing mechanical injury through breakage and leaf loss. The wind also blows the unstable sands around, exposing individual root systems and burying foliage and stems of other plants. The sand particles themselves inflict further damage on the plants through abrasion. The small leaf size and low-growth forms in most dune species help minimize wind damage.

During the long dry season from May to October, dune plants may be exposed to long periods of intense sun, though heavy fogs provide some relief. Water loss is minimized by individual adapations that reduce the evaporating surface of the leaves. Some plants have a waxy cuticle on the leaves and stem (willow, coyote bush); some are covered with small hairs as protection (buckwheat, yellow sand verbena). Much of the foliage is a light green or silvery shade due to pigmentation or the presence of wax or hairs (beach sagewort, lizard tail). This reduces the effect of intense solar radiation by reflecting some of the light. In some plants, the leaves orient vertically during the summer so that the plant receives the intense sunlight at an angle instead of directly (mock heather, willow). Others simply drop leaves, or the leaves curl up reducing exposure during drought periods (willow, dune goldenrod, beach pea). Further adaptations include sunken stomates on the leaves and wide spacing of plants, perhaps in response to low water supply.

Many dune plants (iceplant, live-forever) have succulent, fleshy stems and leaves that enable them to store water for long periods under dry conditions. Various root systems utilize the small amounts of water that are available, either through a long tap root (e.g., sand verbena) reaching down to deep sources of water, or via shallow root systems that capture the surface moisture from a light rainfall, heavy dew or fog. Some species are able to extract moisture from the sand in very low amounts through the existence of a high diffusion pressure gradient within their root cells.

The succulent iceplant *(Carpobrotus chilense)* **extends across the dunes, storing water and stabilizing exposed land surface.** (F. Lanting)

Dune soils are particularly poor in nutrients as well as moisture. Organic matter is minimal, and there is little to support a soil community of bacteria and other microorganisms. Dunes are composed of almost pure sand; there are very few clay particles to retain water or nutrient ions. The soil salt content is relatively low because rainwater percolates through the sand quickly, leaving the surface dry to a depth of 30 cm or more. Aside from adaptations for retaining water described above, dune plants actually benefit from the low levels of nitrogen. High nitrogen levels generally encourage the development of larger, softer leaves with thinner cuticles and fewer hairs. Such characteristics would sustain increased mechanical injury in the harsh winds and sand of the dune environment. Low levels of nitrogen prevent such leaf development, thereby increasing dune plant tolerance to strenuous physical conditions.

Salt spray has a very strong impact on dune vegetation. The amount of salt suspended in the air correlates with the wind speed and distance from the ocean. Salt water droplets become airborn at wind speeds over 13.8 knots or 7 meters per second (Munk, 1947) when whitecaps are formed on the ocean. It is the bursting foam that actually shoots the salt water droplets into the air. Next to the wind, salt spray is the most limiting factor governing establishment of plant species in the dunes. Vegetation zonation and successional patterns depend on both wind exposure and salt tolerance to a large extent.

A study by Rosner (1978) at Point Año Nuevo showed a salt spray profile that reflects the topography of the land and a correlation with wind strength. Salt levels in the strand area closest to shore were actually very low, as were the relative wind speeds. This is explained by the presence of large stands of willows which direct the winds off the ocean upward upon reaching land. While there is great turbulence overhead, it is less windy close to ground and the saltwater droplets tend to remain in suspension. As the airborne salt is carried farther inland, the less turbulent air allows it to settle out. Highest salt spray was recorded at both the foredunes and the hinddunes, with lower readings in the scoured interdune area. The steep uphill slope of each of the dune masses catches the wind most directly and the most salt is deposited here. Farther inland where the effect of the wind is less severe, salt deposition is lower. This study showed that the two major factors determining the amount of salt spray affecting an area are the distance from the ocean and the degree of protection from the wind by plants and topographic features (Rosner, 1978).

Dune plants cope with high levels of salt in several ways. Higher concentrations of dissolved salts in the tissues can be balanced by an increased water level in thickened fleshy leaves or stems. A plant is actually physiologically "dry" under salty conditions, for it has difficulty pulling in necessary moisture against the osmotic gradient. To compensate for this condition, halophytes or "salt-loving" plants have the ability to increase their own internal concentration of salts to a higher level than the surrounding environment; under this gradient, the plants are able to absorb necessary water through the cell membranes. Succulence is one adaptation for achieving this ionic balance.

Leaf adaptations that reduce water loss also often reduce salt intake. Waxy cuticles, thick hair cover, and fewer stomata and veins per unit of surface area as compared with that of inland species, are some of the mechanisms used to reduce the impact of salt spray in dune plants.

Salt ions enter dune plants primarily through the exposed aerial parts; little is absorbed through the roots underground. The main points of entry are places of mechanical injury. The chloride ions, rather than the sodium or potassium ions, cause necrosis in the plant cells. If the chloride ions are not diluted through stored water in succulents or secreted through special salt glands or hairs, they are translocated through the plant to the tops of the leaves and twigs. The chloride ions collect at these points until eventually the cells die and these parts of the plant break off. This frequent abcission is the major cause of asymmetrical growth and conspicuous canopy angles in many of the dune plants. At Año Nuevo, this is especially noticeable in the willow stands. Salt deposition is heaviest on the windward side of the plant and chloride ions are generally translocated to this area rather than the leeward side.

The long tap root of sand verbena is sometimes exposed as the dunes shift. This root is one dune plant adaptation for reaching deep-level sources of water. (F. Lanting)

Most of the necrosis is then on the windward side, creating a sharp angle that reflects the intensity of the wind and salt spray in the area. This canopy shape is also maintained through salt spray, for branches that shoot up above the average canopy height accumulate excess chloride ions and cannot survive. Wind and salt spray operate to create a uniform canopy appearance in the dunes.

The dune plants at Año Nuevo must also survive the effects of the transient populations of animals and humans that migrate through the area annually. Fall and spring bird migrations bring large numbers of shorebirds and other species to the area (see chapter 4) to forage on the dune seeds and shoots. Of much greater significance is the increasing northern elephant seal population (*Mirounga angustirostris*) which inhabits the area from December through March each year. Over 400 seals, weighing 40 to 2,500 kg, traversed the coastal strand area in 1980 during social activities related to reproduction. Dune vegetation, especially iceplant and other low-growing forms, is severely trampled in certain areas. Trampling is further increased by the large number of human visitors who come to the area to see the elephant seals on guided interpretative tours. In 1978-79, over 60,000 people walked over a prescribed trail, widening the path in some areas and creating new paths in others (according to the daily location of the seals).

Trampling causes compaction, altering the soil's capacity for water penetration and affecting the temperature below the surface. Trampling also causes direct mechanical damage to plants through the screwing action of human heels and shoes and the removal of taller vegetation by

Trail-edge vegetation is subject to trampling by a visiting school group led through the dunes by a University of California (Santa Cruz) student intern. (F. Lanting)

vehicle tires. Szyjewicz and Rosner (1978) found that the number of species declined in the disturbed area, but the remaining species thrived under the reduced competition. Since the first users of a trail inflict the greatest damage, it is likely that new paths at Año Nuevo will have the strongest effect on dune vegetation. Plants along existing trails will probably not suffer much more damage from trampling over future years.

Some species are well adapted to survive trampling for they maintain only leaf and stem vegetation during periods of trampling stress, and form flowers and seeds during times of low disturbance (spring through fall). Plants under trampling stress are generally shorter in height and many grow up at acute angles to the ground, reducing some of the impact of direct trampling pressure. A relatively narrow band of vegetation along the trail is affected: some of these plants are tolerant to the effects of treading, and others die off, but sometimes new species come to invade the trampled areas. Though elephant seal impact is actually more extensive than human impact, it is not quite so constant over single areas and so appears to inflict less long-term damage to the vegetation.

The individual species within each of the habitats at Point Año Nuevo have various strategies for surviving the harsh conditions of this exposed area. Some of these plants have been used by the early Ohlone Indian settlements for food and medicine; some have continued to serve pharmacological purposes for American inhabitants through the 1800s.

In the following section, the most common plant species at Point Año Nuevo are described in detail with reference to botanical features and human use. They are listed by primary habitat areas, though some species are found in several plant locations (see Appendix).

Specific medicinal or nutritional uses listed here are anecdotal in origin and may or may not be reliable either in safety or usefulness. The reader should bear this in mind if considering the use of any of these plants.

COMMON PLANT SPECIES
Illustrations by Fran Ciesla

Riparian Area

Monterey Cypress, *Cupressus macrocarpa* ("cupressus," classical name for cypress). Family Cupressaceae. The monterey cypress has one of the most restricted ranges of any tree in California. It is found only in a few places along the Monterey Peninsula and Point Lobos and up the California coast past Santa Cruz, though here it is not native. Its dense foliage provides a good windbreak and usually reflects the patterns of the predominant winds. The small cones can be recognized by the 6-8 pairs of shield-shaped scales.

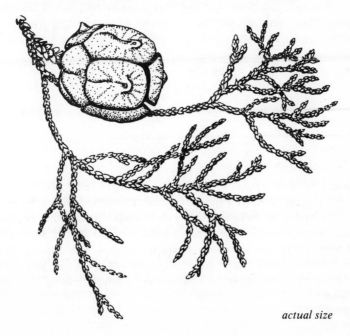

actual size

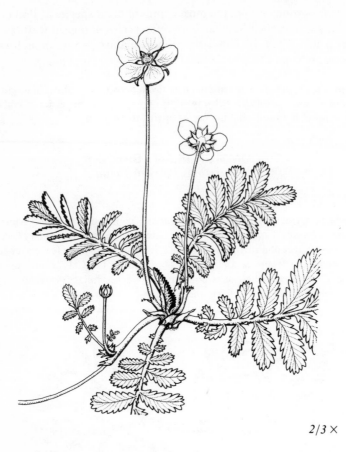

2/3 ×

Cinquefoil, *Potentilla egedii* (from "potens" meaning powerful, because of its supposed medicinal powers). Family Rosaceae; relatives include beach strawberry, roses, and many fruit trees. The leaves of cinquefoil, with their serrated margins, closely resemble those of beach strawberry but are pinnately compound with 6-12 leaflets; strawberry leaves always grow with 3 leaflets in a clover shape. Cinquefoil flowers are bright yellow with five simple petals and sepals. The plant spreads by means of vegetative runners, colonizing easily in a moist area.

Cattail, *Typha* sp. (the ancient Greek name). Family Typhaceae, the cattail family. Cattails are marsh plants with shoots of 6-10 flat, light-green leaves. The flowering stalk is a brown cylinder on a stout peduncle, full of downy seeds. The male half of the flower produces pollen at the top of the stem while the ovules mature on the lower half of the spike. Many parts of the cattail are edible under a variety of preparations. The roots contain a core of pure starch and can be eaten boiled or roasted like potatoes or dried and then ground into flour. The young shoots are good raw or steamed. The mature leaves are useful for weaving mats. The downy flowering stalk was used for bedding material by early native Indians and Americans. Even the pollen was harvested and added to bread for nutritional enrichment (Clarke, 1977). Marsh waterfowl also use these plants for food resources, foraging on the root stocks and underground stems.

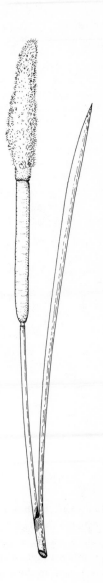

2/9 ✕

Open Fields

2/3 ×

Wild Radish, *Raphanus sativus* (Greek "raphonos" means quick appearing, from the plant's rapid seed germination). Family Brassicaceae; relatives include wild mustard, sea rocket, cauliflower, broccoli. Annual or perennial. This plant, like mustard, is a rapid invader and is very common in open fields. Its flowers are four-petaled, in the shape of a cross, and may be white, yellow, pink, or purple. Wild radish originated in China and was cultivated extensively in Egypt. It grows abundantly in the Mediterranean area where the climate is similar to that of California (Clarke, 1977). The leaves may be used in salads or soups, and the seed pods can be added to salads if gathered while still green (Clarke, 1977). Both the seed pods and the long white roots have a spicy taste similar to cultivated radish but often stronger.

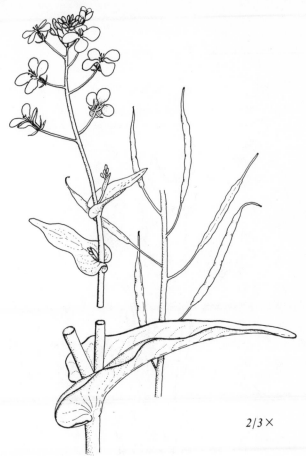

2/3 ×

Field Mustard, *Brassica campestris* (Latin "brassica" means cabbage). Family Brassicaceae; relatives include cabbage, broccoli, cauliflower—all *Brassica* spp. Other crucifers are wild radish, sea rocket, and watercress. Annual. This plant is one of the most common in the abandoned farm field. It invades open areas easily and spreads quickly. The four-petaled flowers are bright yellow and arranged in the shape of a cross. Field mustard is an excellent source of vitamins A, B_1, B_2, and C. The buds may be eaten as wild broccoli; the flowers may be used in soups if added at the last minute and in salads as a useful digestive aid. Native Americans ate the seeds parched and ground into meal for seed cakes and ate the greens raw or cooked. A medicinal plaster can be made from the ground seeds that may bring relief to aching joints or chest colds. A syrup made from fresh leaf juice with honey and lemon may soothe a cough or help recover a lost voice (Buchanan).

2/3 ×

California Poppy, *Eschscholzia californica* (named after Dr. J.F. Eschscholtz, 1793-1831, the surgeon and naturalist with Russian expeditions to the Pacific coast in 1816, 1824). Family Papaveraceae; related to other poppies. Perennial along the coast. This bright orange flower with silver green foliage is the California state wildflower. Its leaves or dried roots may be useful for toothache pain (Murphy, 1959). It is considered poisonous to grazing stock.

1/3 ×

English Plantain, *Plantago lanceolata* (Latin "planta" means footprint, after the plant's habit of springing up in disturbed or walked-on areas). Family Plantaginaceae, the plantain family. Perennial. Plantain leaves are distinctive for their prominent longitudinal ribs; the small flowers are borne at the top of the stem in a dense cluster. Plantain seeds are coated with a mucilage that makes them adhere easily to passing animals who act as seed dispersal agents. Young plantain leaves are good in salads; older leaves may be eaten cooked. The leaves can also be steeped to make a tea. The raw seeds with their mucilaginous coats may be soaked in water and taken for a laxative (Clarke, 1977). If parched, roasted, and ground into a meal, the seeds can be used for birdseed or made into a mush or added to cornmeal and soups (Buchanan). Poultices of crushed leaves may be useful in soothing insect stings, nettle stings, cuts, and other skin irritations (Buchanan). Native Americans called this plant "White Man's Foot" because it grew wherever white men set foot (Clarke, 1977).

3/4 ×

Cobweb Thistle, *Circium occidentale* (Greek "kirsion" is a kind of thistle). Family Asteraceae; relatives include yarrow, beach burr, goldenrod, coyote bush, and sunflower. This rose purple flower, with a mass of white fibers resembling cobwebs on the prickles below, prefers coastal dunes and grassy slopes. Another thistle at Año Nuevo, bull thistle (*Circium vulgare*) has large purple blossoms but lacks the white fibers. A familiar relative is the commercial artichoke, whose bud is eaten before the flower opens.

1/6×

Curly Dock, *Rumex crispus* (Latin "rumex," ancient name for dock). Family Polygonaceae; relatives include the buckwheats. This plant is becoming more and more common in the open fields. It is conspicuous in the summer and fall because of its tall rust-colored stalks bearing hundreds of polygon-shaped rust or brown seeds. These seeds have polygon-shaped wings that catch the wind and glide effectively, propelling them farther than wingless seeds. The long and thin leaves are high in vitamins A and C, iron, and chlorophyll. All species of *Rumex* are edible and used by some for medicinal purposes. *R. crispus* leaves can be eaten raw or simmered in several changes of water to remove the unpleasant taste. Dock seeds may be ground for seed cakes or used as a substitute for buckwheat flour. The largest roots and stems can be cooked like potatoes or asparagus. The fresh leaves can be applied for relief of rashes, stings, infection, and burns (Buchanan) or applied to a boil to bring the infection to a head (Krochmal and Krochmal, 1973). The leaves are high in vitamin C content and have served as an antidote to scurvy.

2/3×

Seaside Daisy, *Erigeron glaucus* (Greek "eri" means early, and "geron" means old man, the old name of an early-flowering plant with wooly hairs). Family Asteraceae; relatives include coyote bush, sunflowers, asters, and daisies. Perennial, blooms April-August. This daisy, with pale violet to lavender ray flowers, is common along coastal bluffs and beaches. It is adapted to tolerate salt spray with its fleshy stem and thickened leaves. The flower produces an abundance of seeds that are easily distributed by wind.

2/3 ×

Poison Oak, *Toxicodendron diversilobum* (former genus name *Rhus* from the Greek "rhous," ancient name for sumac). Family Anacardiaceae, sumac family; relatives include cashews and mangos. This plant is marked by 3-lobed compound leaves that turn red in the summer and fall. It can be distinguished from the 3-lobed leaf of California blackberry by the absence of thorns. In winter the woody stems can be recognized by the light brown color and small remaining buds. The leaves, stems, roots, and berries of this plant may produce a skin irritation of varying degrees from contact with the oils of the plant. Breathing of poison oak smoke from burning or ingestion of plant parts may cause a severe internal reaction. Poison oak was apparently less irritating to the Native Americans. They are said to have eaten small pieces of leaf regularly each spring to prevent ill effects the rest of the year. The leaves were also used to cover bulbs while baking or to wrap loaves of acorn meal bread during cooking. This dilute ingestion of oils may have further stimulated the necessary antibody production for external protection. The slender stems were used as the warp in woven baskets, and the juice from the plant produced a strong black dye which was used in staining basketry materials.

3/5 ×

Poison Hemlock, *Conium maculatum* (Greek "konas" means to whirl about, a
symptom of vertigo associated with death from this plant; Latin "maculatum"
means spotted, referring to the purple spots on the stem). Family Umbelliferae;
relatives include carrots, parsnip, dill, anise, Queen Anne's lace. Biennial. This
plant, with tall stalks and lacy fernlike leaves and delicate white flowers, is the
source of the famous poisonous tea that Socrates drank on his deathbed. It
invades open places, particularly where there is some moisture. Poison hemlock
seeds are efficiently dispersed through a shot-put mechanism that throws them
out into passing wind currents. All parts of this plant contain a volatile, alkaloid
oil which is extremely poisonous. Small children have suffered toxic effects
from using the hollow stems for toy whistles. In small doses hemlock acts as a
sedative and has been used as an antidote for strychnine poisoning and tetanus.
Overdose causes paralysis, loss of muscular control and convulsions, though the
mind remains clear and unaffected until death.

2/3×

Monterey Pine, *Pinus radiata* ("pinus," Latin for pine). Family Pinaceae; relatives include other pines. This pine is found in only a few spots along the California coast from Santa Cruz County to San Luis Obispo County. At Año Nuevo, it grows near the irrigation pond in a small area. Needles grow in bundles of 3s and the cones are generally closed. This species and the knob-cone pine are adapted for surviving frequent fires with cones which open under heat and seeds which can withstand scorched soil. On a warm day, these cones can be heard crackling and popping as they open and release their seeds. As the fastest growing species of over 90 pines, this tree has been imported as a timber producer into Australia, New Zealand, Chile, South Africa, and Spain (Metcalf, 1959). Native Americans obtained the seeds from the cones by roasting them over a fire or starting a small fire at the base of a tree. The seeds were then eaten whole or crushed into a meal.

Irrigation Pond

California Bulrush, or Tule, *Scirpus californicus.* Family Cyperaceae, the sedges. Perennial. Tules are the most conspicuous plants at the pond. As a sedge, it has edges on the stalks and may grow 2-3 meters tall. The dense stems provide cover for pond animals and the seeds are eaten by red-winged blackbirds and other songbirds. The sweet roots may be eaten raw, baked, or cooked in mush (Kirk, 1970); dried and ground, they make a fine white flour. Native Americans made cakes of the pollen, and used the stems and long leaves for weaving beds and roofing materials. The seeds are nutritious whole or ground into meal for flour or mush.

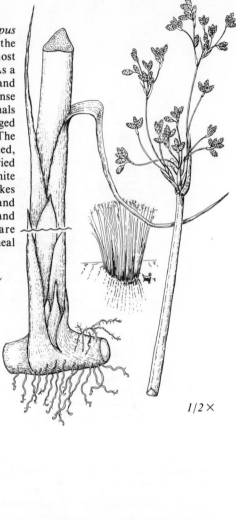

1/2×

1/2×

Rush, *Juncus spp.* (Latin for rush, possibly from "jungere," to bind). Family Juncaceae, the rushes. Perennial. These plants are common in wetland areas along the California coast. As a rush, it has a round stem with flower parts below the top of the stalk. It grows along the edge of the pond and other moist areas of the Reserve.

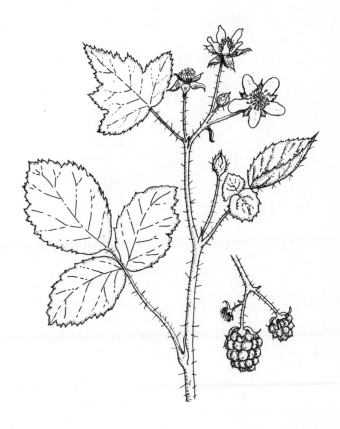

3/4 ×

California Blackberry, *Rubus ursinus* (Latin for bramble, related to "ruber" which means red). Family Rosaceae; relatives include roses, apple, peach, plum and strawberry. This thorny vine, common throughout California, grows primarily near the irrigation pond at Año Nuevo. Its 3-lobed compound leaf resembles poison oak but is distinguished by the presence of stiff sharp hairs. The berry is edible, though the plants at Año Neuvo are relatively unproductive. The fresh or dried leaves can be brewed to make a tea; tea from the roots may serve as a remedy for diarrhea (Clarke, 1977). Native Americans dried the berries to preserve them, and then soaked them in water when needed for use.

3/4 ×

Douglas' Nightshade, *Solanum douglasii* (Latin "solamen" means quieting, because of the narcotic properties of some species). Family Solanaceae; relatives include tobacco, tomato, potato, pepper, and Jimson weed. Perennial. This plant can be recognized by its small, white, tomato-like flowers. Nightshade leaves and green fruit are highly toxic, though the ripe berry may be eaten if cooked. Alkaloid poisoning from nightshade results in intestinal distress and/or nervous disorder sometimes leading to death. Nightshade occurs in small patches throughout the dunes as well as along the irrigation pond where it associates with California blackberry. Blue witch *(S. umbelliferum)* is another species of nightshade found at Año Nuevo. Its somewhat larger flowers are blue and the leaves are darker green.

Cliff Seeps

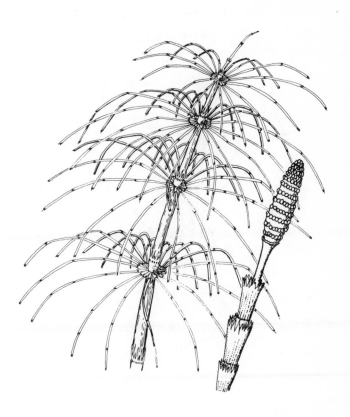

2/3 ×

Horsetail, *Equisetum telmateia* (Latin "equus" means horse and "seta" means bristle). Family Equisetaceae, the horsetails or scouring rushes. This single genus is the only representative of a once large and dominant group of primitive plants. Horsetails reproduce by spores from terminal spore cones rather than flowers. The whorled pattern of needlelike stems is characteristic of sterile stalks: naked stems are often fertile and spore-producing. The inner pulp can be eaten raw and the outer silicious stem is useful for scouring out camping pots or polishing hardwood. Horsetails are poisonous to some livestock but not to humans.

2/3 ×

Monkey Flower, *Mimulus guttatus* (from Latin *mimus* (comic actor or mime) +
ulus (little one), because of the resemblance of the flower to a grinning mask).
Family Scrophulariaceae; relatives include figwort, foxglove, and penstemon.
Monkey flower is not generally common in the harsh coastal scrub habitat, but
it grows at Año Nuevo where freshwater is present, both along the cliff seeps and
occasionally in low wet spots among the dunes. The two-lipped flower is yellow
with brown to maroon dots along the throat. The leaves and stems may be eaten
raw in salads though they may have a slightly bitter taste. Native Americans
applied crushed leaves and stems as a poultice for rope burns and wounds
(Sweet, 1962).

Sand Dunes—Pioneer Plants

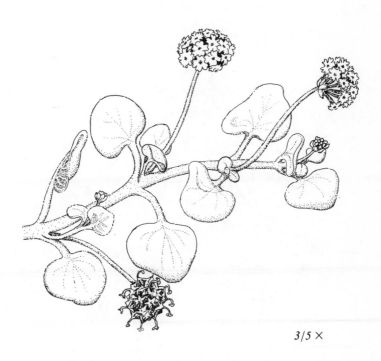

3/5 ×

Yellow Sand Verbena, *Abronia latifolia* (Greek "abros" means graceful). Family Nyctaginaceae, the four-o'clock family. Perennial, blooms February-November. This plant is one of the first to colonize moving sand dunes. Its thick fleshy taproot is adapted for finding water below an unstable surface environment. Minute glandular hairs cover the succulent plant and exude a sticky substance to which sand grains adhere, doubling the weight of the plant and providing it with stronger protection against the wind. The exposed parts of the plant, the leaves and flowers, connect under the sand by spreading branches up to 10 feet long. Each blossom of the bright yellow, globular flower head is actually a modified calyx, not a corolla of true petals. Beach Sand Verbena *(A. umbellata)* is a pink-flowering species also found at Año Nuevo. *Abronia* flowers are noted for their exceptionally sweet fragrance.

3/5 ×

Beach Bur or Silver Beachweed, *Franseria chamissonis* (for Antonio Franseri, Spanish physician and botanist). Family Asteraceae; relatives include yarrow, thistle, goldenrod, coyote bush, and mock heather. Perennial. As a pioneer plant, beach bur is prevalent on the more seaward side of active and stable sand areas. It is the dominant plant on the island, forming thick mats over most of the sandy areas. The silver foliage is an adaptation that reflects the intense solar radiation characteristic of the dune environment. Flowers are borne in dense clusters on stalks, the male flowers at the end of the stalk, the female flowers maturing below into spiny bur seeds.

4/5 ×

Sea Fig or Iceplant, *Carpobrotus chilense* (formerly *Mesembryanthemum chilense*). Family Aizoaceae. Perennial, blooms April-October. This plant is native to the Southern Hemisphere, especially in Chile and South Africa. It has been employed as a drought-resistant plant along roadsides, useful in preventing erosion. An extensive root system helps to stabilize moving sand. The seed vessel opens only during wet weather, facilitating survival. The leaves and stems may be eaten fresh in salads and can be used as a substitute for cucumbers in making pickles (Clarke, 1977). They are less palatable cooked, as the succulent plants quickly grow mushy. The fruit is also edible (Kirk, 1970), and the flower buds are consumed by small animals.

1/2 ×

European Sea Rocket, *Cakile maritima* (old Arabic name). Family Brassica-ceae; relatives include radish mustard, cabbage, broccoli, and cauliflower. Annual, blooms April-October. Sea rocket is one of the hardiest pioneer plants colonizing the dunes. Its 4-petaled flower is very similar to that of wild radish, but the foliage is succulent, an adaptation to dune conditions. The low-lying growth accumulates small amounts of sand around it, forming isolated humps of vegetation. Sea rocket is especially adapted for seed dispersal. Sea rocket leaves or young shoots may be eaten raw in salads or boiled like spinach (Clarke, 1977).

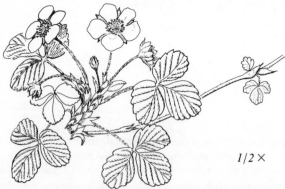

1/2 ×

Beach Strawberry, *Fragaria chiloensis* (Latin "fragum" means fragrant). Fam-ily Rosaceae; relatives include roses, peach, plum, blackberry, apple, and toyon. Perennial. This low-growing plant has a compound leaf of three serrated lobes and a 5-petaled white flower. It reproduces vegetatively by bright red runners. According to Cooper (1967) the most abundant growth of beach strawberry outside of Alaska is found at Año Nuevo. The berries are a good source of B and C vitamins; Native Americans dried them for future use. The leaves may be dried or used for tea; a tea made from the root may cure diarrhea and increase urine flow (Krochmal and Krochmal, 1973).

1/2 ×

European Beach Grass, *Ammophila arenaria* (Greek "ammos" means sand, "philos" means loving). Family Graminae, the grasses. Perennial (in comparison with most grasses which are annuals), blooms April-October. This sand colonizer has been introduced from the shores of the Mediterranean Sea. Its fibrous root system makes it an excellent sand binder. The plants produce underground stems or rhizomes growing out in all directions and sending shoots up at regular intervals from the parent plant.

Sand Dunes—Intermediate Stages of Succession

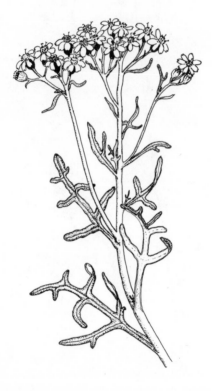

3/5×

Lizard Tail, *Eriophyllum staechadifolium* (Greek "erion," meaning wool, and "phyllon" meaning leaf, refer to the wooly herbage). Family Asteraceae; relatives include yarrow, mock heather, coyote bush, and sunflower. Perennial. This plant is abundant in the open fields as well as the dunes area and can be recognized by its dense bright yellow flower head resembling yarrow. The plant forms waist-high bush cover in association with many different combinations of species. Lizard tail seeds are heavier than some wind-blown seeds and are dispersed by a shot-put mechanism that carries them into passing wind currents.

3/5 ×

Yarrow, *Achillea millefolium* (named in honor of Achilles). Family Asteraceae; relatives include mock heather, goldenrod, thistle, coyote bush, and pearly everlasting. Perennial. Yarrow is found in the open field area as well as the sand dunes. It can be recognized by its fernlike delicate leaves and dense white flower head. The spreading underground root stalks make it a strong colonizer against moving sand. Yarrow has been introduced from Europe. It is said that Achilles used a species of *Achillea* to treat the wounds of his warriors. The leaves are reported to stop bleeding and a poultice helps heal surface inflammation (Sweet, 1962). The plant contains the drug achilleine, sometimes used to suppress menses. A tea from the whole dry plant may be used for blood tonic and stomachache, for headaches, for breaking a fever by increasing perspiration, and for stimulating urine flow (Krochmal and Krochmal, 1973). A tea from the root may relieve gas pains and hiccoughs, and a bit of the root applied to the gum may ease a toothache.

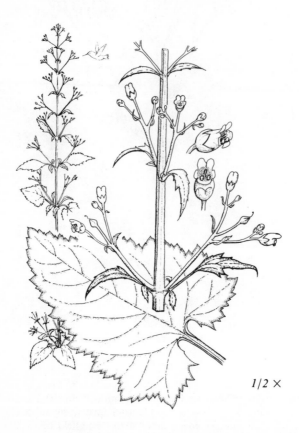

1/2 ×

Figwort or California Bee Plant, *Scrophularia californica* (from "scrophula," since the roots of some species were supposed to cure this disease). Family Scrophulariaceae; relatives include monkey flower, foxglove, penstemon, and owl's clover. Perennial. This plant is characterized by 4-angled stems and opposite leaves, and by very small dark red flowers on a tall stalk. Nectar dripping from the flowers attracts bees and hummingbirds. This plant survives well in many different habitats and is found near a number of different species in both the open field area and the sand dunes.

3/5 ×   3/5 ×

California Buckwheat, *Eriogonum fasciculatum* (left) and **Coast Buckwheat,** *Eriogonum latifolium* (right) (Greek "erion" means wool, "gonu" means knee or joint for some species which are hairy at the nodes). Family Polygonaceae, buckwheat family; relatives include rhubarb, beet pickleweed, dock. Perennial, blooms June-October. The pink and white flower heads of these plants are borne on naked stems, with the leaves found basally near the ground. The flowers have no actual petals. The seeds are polygon-shaped like dock, with wings for effective wind dispersal. Buckwheat flowers are favored by bees and are a source of distinctive honey. This plant is found in the open fields as well as in the stable inland and hinddune sand. It helps to maintain dune stability by an extensive root system and a thick bush ground cover. The stems and roots may be boiled for a tea to treat bladder trouble (Sweet, 1962). A tea from the flowers may be used as an eyewash and for high blood pressure and bronchial ailments. Native Americans are thought to have made a decoction from the leaves for relief of headache and stomach pains (Sweet, 1962).

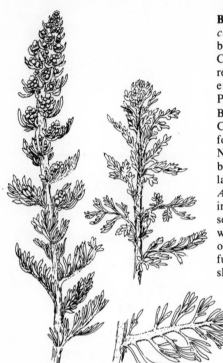

2/3 ×

Beach Sagewort, *Artemisia pycno-cephala* (named after Artemisia, botanist and medical researcher in Caria, Greece). Family Asteraceae; relatives include yarrow, mock heather, lizard tail, and coyote bush. Perennial, blooms May-October. Both this species and its close relative, California Sagebrush *(A. californica)* found in the abandoned fields at Año Nuevo, have silvery green foliage, but beach sagewort is more velvety and lacks the sage-like odor of most *Artemisias*. It is found on the more inland portions of stable sand. The seeds are edible and may be eaten whole or pounded into a meal with other seeds to make pinole. An infusion from the leaves is said to relieve skin irritations and wounds.

2/3 ×

Mock Heather, *Haplopappus ericoides* (Greek "haploos" means simple, and "pappos," the Greek word for grandfather, refers to the pappus, a downy tuft that crowns the ovary or fruit in some seed plants). Family Asteraceae; relatives include coyote bush, beach sagewort, and yarrow. Perennial, blooms late summer.
This plant is marked by its comparatively dark, very small needle-like leaves and small yellow flowers. It is common in the interdune and rear-dune areas, but near the point is found only along the interpretive trail.

3/5 ×

Dune Goldenrod, *Solidago spathulata* (Latin "solidus," to make whole, from its reputed medicinal value). Family Asteraceae; relatives include coyote bush, sunflower, dandelion, yarrow, and lizard tail. Perennial. This plant can be recognized by its bright yellow flower clusters and lance-shaped leaves on a one-meter stalk. The dried leaves and flowers can be used for a tea or as a source for yellow dye (Sweet, 1962). An antiseptic lotion may be made by boiling the stems and leaves, an antiseptic powder by drying the mature leaves (Kirk, 1970). According to *Pharmacopeia,* goldenrod is an astringent causing tissues to contract and stop bleeding, and also a diaphoretic, increasing perspiration.

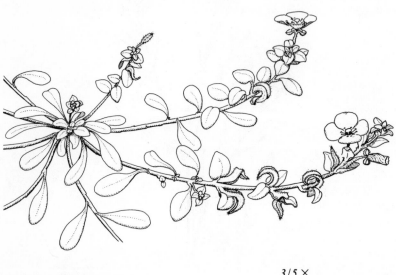

3/5 ×

Beach Primrose, *Camissonia cheiranthifolia* (formerly *Oenothera cheiranthifo-lia*). Family Onagraceae, evening primrose family; relatives include fuchsia, Hooker's primrose, and *Clarkia.* Perennial, blooms April-July, some all-year round. This small, low-growing plant is inconspicuous except for its small yellow flowers. It can tolerate only slightly moving sand, so it is usually found isolated on the seaward sides of active and stable sand. The small root can be pounded up and applied wet to sores to reduce inflammation (Murphy, 1959).

Sand Dunes—Climax Vegetation

Coyote Bush, *Baccharis pilularis* (named after the Greek god Bacchus, god of wine and pleasure). Family Asteraceae; relatives include yarrow, thistle, dandelion, mock heather, and lizard tail. This species, found on windswept dunes and headlands along the coast, grows in dense, prostrate mats in comparison with the variety *B. p. consanguinea,* a tall rounded shrub more commonly found in less exposed habitats. *Baccharis* is dioecious—having male and female flowers on separate plants. It begins to bloom in the late summer, generating abundant windblown seeds throughout the fall and winter, but it can also reproduce vegetatively from broken roots or cuttings. *Baccharis* is common at Año Nuevo throughout the stabilized dune area and abandoned fields.

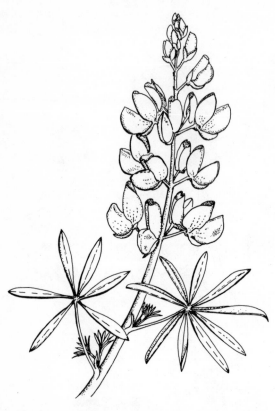

2/3 ×

Bush Lupine, *Lupinus arboreus* (Latin for "lupus," meaning wolf, because of an old mistaken idea that lupines rob the soil of nutrients). Family Fabaceae; pea family; relatives include peas, beans, sweet peas, vetch, and clover. Perennial, blooms April-July, some throughout the year. This large bush is common in the stablized dune areas and can be recognized by its star-shaped compound leaves and long stalks of yellow pea-like flowers. Contrary to the old legend, nitrogen is fixed in these plants by the bacteria that grow in nodules on the roots, actually replenishing the surrounding soil. Lupine seeds develop in a pea-shaped pod that later dries and splits, the two halves twisting to pop the seeds out. These seeds contain alkaloids that are especially poisonous to stock animals, causing convulsions and liver damage.

2/3 ×

Arroyo Willow, *Salix lasiolepis.* Family Salicaceae, the willow family; relatives include aspen and poplar. This large tree/bush is dominant throughout the stabilized dune areas of Año Nuevo. Its seedlings have a hard time establishing themselves in shifting sands, but the lateral roots send out shoots in vegetative growth. Even the shoots tend to be successful only on the leeward side of the plant where they are out of the wind and salt spray. The plants are dioecious like coyote bush, with male and female flowers on separate individuals. The yellow flowers have no petals and grow out of the soft "pussy willows." Many of the willow leaves are dotted with red galls formed where *Pontania pacifica* wasps lay eggs. The Ohlone tribes used willow stakes and branches for the structure of their thatched houses. They obtained red and brown dyes from willow bark for their basket weaving, and made a tea from the bark to relieve the aches and pains. The active pain-relieving chemical in willow is the same as in aspirin, acetylsalicylic acid, and can be tasted clearly in the stems. Ohlone people also used willow for netting fish, for making whistles and clappers, and for hot rock lifters. The inner bark was made into a kind of rope, and the bitter inner bark was sometimes eaten raw as an emergency food.

7/8 ×

Indian Paintbrush, *Castilleja latifolia* (after Castilleja, a Spanish botanist).
Family Scrophulariaceae; relatives include figwort, monkey flower, foxglove,
and owl's clover. Perennial. This low-growing plant is conspicuous for its red
bracts, one of the few red flowers in the Año Nuevo area. A tea from the flowers
is said to be a love medicine (Murphy, 1959).

1/2 ×

Hooker's Primrose, *Oenothera hookeri* (Greek meaning wine-scenting—once an unknown relative of this plant was used for that purpose). Family Onagraceae; relatives include fuchsia, *Clarkia,* and beach primrose. Biennial. These plants have an unmistakably grand yellow flower on a one-meter stem. They grow in isolated patches at Año Nuevo, though they are quite common along the coast highway. The root is said to be good when cooked in early spring; during other seasons it has a peppery taste (Kirk, 1970).

References

Barbour, M.G., Craig, R.B., Drysdale, F.R., and Ghiselin, M.T. 1973. *Coastal Ecology: Bodega Head.* University of California Press, Berkeley, California.

Buchanan, B. Common native edible plants and medicinal weeds—wilderness nutrition and survival notes. Santa Cruz, California.

Ciesla, F. 1980. On drawing plants for publication. University of California, Santa Cruz, senior thesis.

Clarke, C.B. 1977. *Edible and Useful Plants of California.* University of California Press, Berkeley, California.

Cooper, W.S. 1967. *Coastal Dunes of California.* Geological Society of California, Inc. Boulder, Colorado.

Kirk, D. 1970. *Wild Edible Plants of the Western United States.* Naturegraph Publishers, Healdsburg, California.

Krochomal, A. and Krochmal, C. 1973. *A Guide to the Medicinal Plants of the United States.* Quadrangle, New York Times Book Company, New York.

Lepage, W.F. 1967. Some observations on campground trampling and ground cover responses. U.S. Forest Service Research Paper NE. 68, 1-11.

Metcalf, W. 1959. *Native Trees of the San Francisco Bay Region.* University of California Press, Berkeley, California.

Munk, W.H. 1947. A critical wind speed for air-sea boundary processes. *Jour. Marine Research, 6:203-218.*

Munz, P.A. 1959. *A California Flora.* University of California Press, Berkeley, Calif.

Murphy, E. 1959. *Indian Uses of Native Plants.* Mendocino County Historical Society, Fort Bragg, California.

Sweet, M. 1961. *Common Edible and Useful Plants of the West.* Naturegraph Publishers, Healdsburg, California.

Szyjewicz, E., and Rosner, N. 1978. A multifactorial study of the vegetative processes of the Año Nuevo region. University of California, Santa Cruz senior thesis.

Thomas, J.H. 1961. *Flora of the Santa Cruz Mountains.* Stanford University Press, Stanford, California.

4

Marine Plants

Judith E. Hansen

A MID THE RICH BIOTA of the Año Nuevo region are the marine plants. They are the primary producers, initiating or contributing to nearly every marine food web. Like the green plants on land, the marine algae can "trap" light energy and convert it to chemical energy through the process of photosynthesis. They are marvelous little factories which harness sunlight as an energy source to drive life processes such as growth and reproduction.

In addition, the marine flora contribute a substrate, shelter, and protection to a myriad of marine animals. They also act as mechanical buffers, dampening the turbulent and eroding effects produced by the continual pounding of the powerful surf.

The algae conventionally fall into two categories: the phytoplankton (microscopic, free-floating cells or colonies) and the macro-algae, or "seaweeds." The phytoplankton are "forage of the open sea," grazed by fish as well as by microscopic animals such as copepods. When certain phytoplankton population explosions occur they form "red tides," common along our coast during the summer. These immense populations can be deleterious to other organisms by consuming too much of the oxygen within an area or by producing compounds toxic to other organisms. Collectively, microscopic marine plants are major primary producers and are affected to some degree by all the factors which influence seaweeds. However, because they are microscopic in size and will not be seen as individuals by the visitor, they will not be treated in further detail here.

The seaweeds are conspicuous either during a low tide, attached to rocks and other substrates in the intertidal, or when cast ashore, sometimes in great masses, serving as shelter for thousands of beach animals. Ultimately, the beach-cast seaweeds decompose into the primary nutrients required by all photosynthetic plants. During the processes of decomposition by bacteria, fungi, and animals, aromatic hydrocarbons are also released, filling the air with the exhilarating smells characteristic of the seashore.

The macro-algae to be considered here are of four types: the blue-greens (Division Cyanophyta), the greens (Division Chlorophyta), the browns (Division Phaeophyta), and the reds (Division Rhodophyta). In addition, surfgrass (*Phyllospadix*) a flowering plant, is a large component of the marine flora at Año Nuevo. For the reader interested in the species of Año Nuevo, a field checklist of the marine flora is included in the Appendix.

Zonation and Characteristic Seaweed Assemblages

The marine plants live in a diverse range of intertidal habitats. They are by no means restricted to rocks, sand, and mud, but also live on other plants, on animals, embedded in shells, or attached to nearly any substantial piece of free-floating material (flotsam) or stationary structure (e.g., pilings). In this chapter I will discuss only the dominant or characteristic species of these habitats.

Seaweeds tend to occur in zones within the intertidal habitats which are established by the direct or indirect influence of tidal action. The length of exposure to the air during low tide may be the primary critical

TIDAL CYCLE

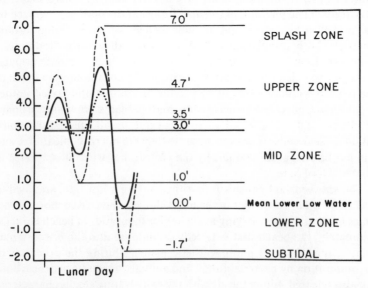

___ Mean Tidal Cycle
---- Spring Tide
..... Neap Tide

factor controlling zonation or more specificially the successful reproduction and colonization of algae. The effects and influences associated
with exposure: temperature, rainfall, drying, wind, and salinity may be
secondary. The biotic effects of interspecific algal competition may also
influence algal distribution and zonation.

The zones commonly recognized at Año Nuevo are referred to as the
splash, upper, mid, and low zones. They can be clearly identified or
difficult to delimit, depending upon the slope of the shore, exposure,
and surf action, which vary seasonally.

Splash Zone

At Point Año Nuevo and the more protected area to the south, the
splash zone is clearly defined as the cliff bluffs and the layered rocks of
cream-colored chert near the Point Año Nuevo sign. A comparable
zone exists on the island. The splash zone habitats are above 1.6 m in
elevation and are wet only a few days in each month for a brief period.
Otherwise these habitats receive saltwater splash during high tides and
strong winds. The cliff bluffs are especially susceptible to freshwater
runoff and erosion. Here the primary colonizer is the ubiquitous green
alga *Enteromorpha*, seemingly able to colonize any disturbed environment in the upper zones. It is even found in the seeps among the mosses
and other cliff dwelling land plants.

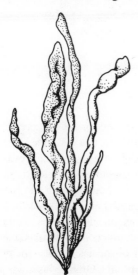

Enteromorpha intestinalis   2/3×

Bangia vermicularis   1×

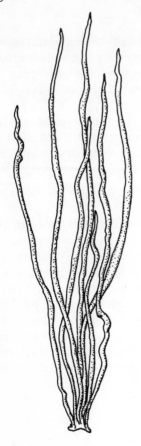

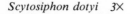

Scytosiphon dotyi   3×   *Porphyra pseudolanceolata*   1/2×

An assemblage of tiny algal species occupies the cracks and crevices of the chert rock formations. Most characteristic from a distance are the bands of blue-green algae, which are blackish in appearance, resembling wet feltpads. They are colonies of microscopic tapering filaments, simple in structure like all blue-green algae. Associated with the blue-greens is the hair-like red alga *Bangia vermicularis* and the tiny tubular brown alga *Scytosiphon dotyi*. The assemblage on the island is similar, but also includes the red alga *Porphyra pseudolanceolata,* which covers the flat tops of the rocks. This tissuepaper-like species is only one cell thick and the males and females are separate plants. On hot days, whole plants dry out to the point of cracking when touched. Perhaps this species doesn't colonize the tops of rocks on the mainland because they are continually disturbed. *Porphyra* heads the list of the world's edible algae and forms the base of Japan's billion-dollar nori industry.

High Zone

Just below the 1.6 m tide level, the substratum is submerged every 10 to 23 hours. This zone is typified by the flat, layered rocks just below the Point Año Nuevo sign. At the very top fringe of this zone the small, forked rockweed, *Pelvetiopsis limitata*, occurs. The rockweeds are brown algae, even though they appear olive green. They characteristically have forked branches usually with inflated tips that contain the eggs and sperms. The fertilized eggs can easily be seen if one opens the tips of a rockweed from the piles of beach-cast weed.

Pelvetia fastigiata
1/3×

Pelvetiopsis limitata 2/3×

Below the upper fringe of this zone, the substrate is covered and uncovered by the tides twice a day. Here the largest plants are two other rockweeds: the slender, twig-like *Pelvetia fastigiata* and the broad, flat *Fucus distichus. Fucus* eggs produce a chemical attractive to sperms, which also attracts a protozoan that feeds on the eggs! Another brown alga, *Analipus*, typical of this zone, resembles a slender, shaggy bottle-brush with a tightly interwoven golden-brown holdfast. The erect portion disappears during winter, leaving only the holdfast which produces new erect portions the following spring.

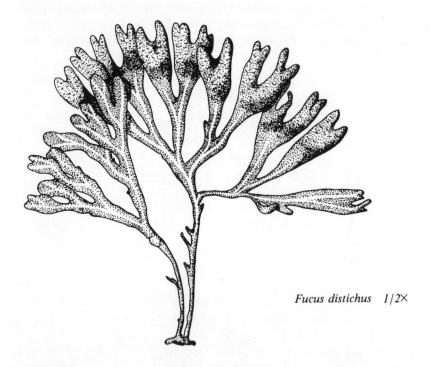

Fucus distichus   1/2×

The most common red alga of this zone and of most similar central and northern California habitats is *Gigartina papillata*. As the name describes, the surface of the female is covered with papillae, but that of the male is smooth. The life history of this species puzzled phycologists until it was demonstrated that the separate and common plant resembling a reddish tarspot, *Petrocelis middendorffii,* produced spores which germinate into the upright male and female *Gigartina* plants (Polanshek and West, 1977). The wiry red alga *Endocladia muricata,* which

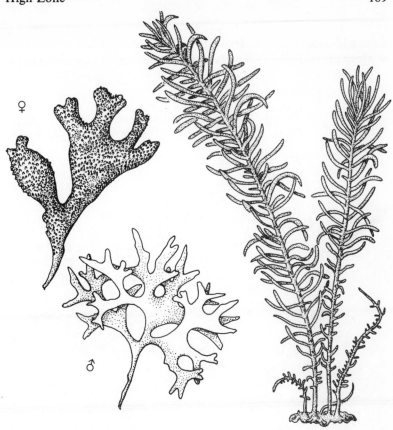

Gigartina papillata 2/3×   *Analipus japonicus* 3/4×

resembles a branched "brillo" pad, occurs much less frequently but is typical of this zone. When reproductively mature, the females are decorated with tiny golden yellow spheres.

Common on this rock substrate throughout the year are the bright green cushions of *Cladophora columbiana,* looking more like moss than algae. Sometimes they are obscured by sand, as grains have a tendency to accumulate between the branches. Another green alga in the sand surrounding the upper zone rocks, is the long (up to 1m), stringy *Chaetomorpha linum.* When the plants become especially long, the individual cells resemble a delicate string of tiny green beads.

The upper zone is most susceptible to disturbance due to trampling because it is exposed a good deal of the time. However, the many crevices and channels among these rocks act as catch basins for drift

algae and danger spots to tramplers. Many casual observers will attest
to stepping off rocks into such accumulations up to one meter deep.

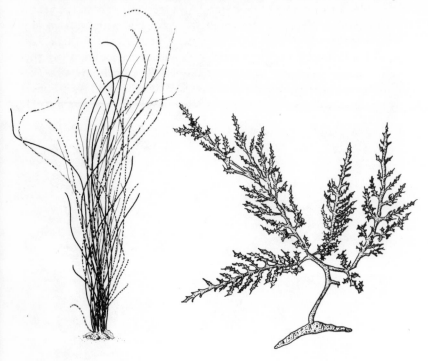

Chaetomorpha linum   1/2×   *Gigartina canaliculata*   2/3×

Mid Zone

The upper fringe of the mid zone lies somewhere near the 1m mark.
Those plants living above this level are exposed more than one-half the
time and those below are submerged more than one-half the time. The
gently sloping terrain of the Año Nuevo area forms an expansive mid
zone. The tidal influences and accompanying fluctuations in environmental factors are within the tolerance ranges of the myriad of species
that contribute to the complex communities of this zone. Some species
such as *Iridaea flaccida* occur only within the mid zone. This large,
leaflike red alga is bright green in color owing to the predominance of
the green plant pigment chlorophyll and the paucity of the red pigments, phycobilins, of the red algae. This species exhibits a typical

spring burst of growth followed by a peak summer growing period. Another red alga typical of this zone is *Gigartina canaliculata,* which resembles a tiny clump of pine trees. Also seen throughout the year is *Gastroclonium coulteri.* Its cylindrical branches with inflated tips sometimes appear to have a greenish tinge, though it is a red alga. This plant is a favorite home for worms; its branches may be stuck together with mucous secretions from these animals. The steel-gray alga *Porphyra perforata* can cover large expanses of this zone and is as slippery as any ice-covered pond. The plants are quite elastic, yet they are only one cell thick!

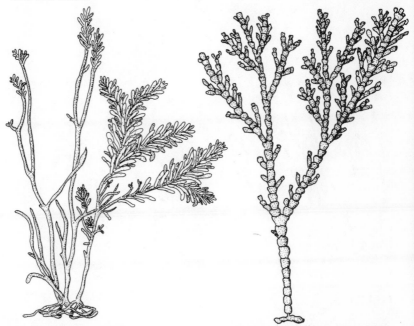

Gastroclonium coulteri   1/2×   *Corallina vancouveriensis*   3/4×

Unique among the red algae are the corallines. The members of this family, whether crustose or erect and branching, are impregnated with calcium carbonate compounds and may look like sessile, segmented animals, or if crustose, like pink rocks. The erect corallines consist of calcified segments with uncalcified kneelike joints between, allowing for flexibility. When tiny white bumps appear on the surface and/or sides of the calcified segments this indicates that the plants are reproductively mature. *Corallina* with its thin cylindrical segments, and

Bossiella with flat or butterfly-shaped segments are common to this zone. Parts of Año Nuevo Island are covered with pure stands of these corallines. When the plants break off and wash to shore they bleach in the sun to white skeletons. In Britain and France the sparkling white beaches made up of these coralline algal skeletons are mined and used as soil additives.

A red alga quite evident at the upper parts of this zone is *Halosaccion glandiforme,* which resembles the hollow fingers of a rubber glove. The blades stand erect at low tide, partially filled with water. When squeezed, they squirt tiny jets of seawater out of pinpoint holes.

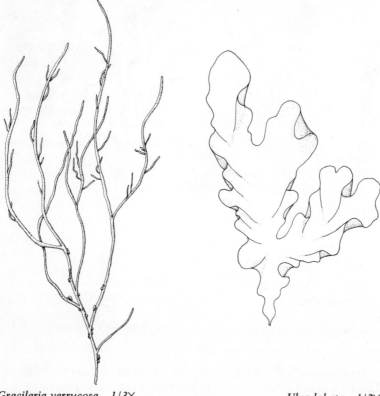

Gracilaria verrucosa   1/3×   *Ulva lobata*   1/2×

The cylindrical, stringy red alga *Gracilaria* grows only in the sand in the lower reaches of the mid zone. Tufts of long, red branches emerge from the sand like wilting bouquets. This edible plant is also a source of agar, that is commercially extracted for industrial use (foods, biomedical products, cosmetics). This seaweed is farmed extensively in Taiwan both for food and industrial applications (Hansen and Packard, in press). At the base of the *Gracilaria* plant, buried deep in the sand, the close observer will find one of the few true algal parasites, *Gracilariophila*. These parasites dot the lower parts of the host and resemble tiny white pin cushions.

Another apparent sand inhabitant is the leaflike brown alga *Phaeostrophion*. Upon investigation one will see that it is merely attached to sand-covered rocks, apparently highly tolerant or requiring sand movement and cover.

Ever present is the ubiquitous green alga *Ulva*. In appearance it is the sea's closest approximation to lettuce, though it is not particularly tasty. A number of species occur at Año Nuevo, some broad and lobed, some slender, and some long and twisted. They are all characteristically bright grass-green and are obvious from long distances even on the dreariest of foggy days.

Two abundant species of red algae, that somewhat resemble one another, occupy the lower parts of this zone. *Callithamnion pikeanum* drapes the vertical faces of rocks and is surprisingly soft in texture (like fluffy felt). *Rhodomela larix* occupies the top parts of nearly every rock at these levels and is stiff and wiry to the touch. Its short branches wind around the long slender axis in a spiral pattern. These plants often appear muddy brown when covered with diatoms, and at times they house droves of yellow amphipods and mucous-secreting worms.

A fuzzy area exists between the mid and low zone at about +0.3 m. This is the highest level that is exposed only once each day; the maximum single submergence is no longer than 12 hours. Only a few tenths of a meter lower, plants may be submerged one to one and one-half days without exposure. This fuzzy zone is recognized as the break between *Iridaea flaccida* (bright green) above and *I. cordata* below. The large blades of *I. cordata* resemble *I. flaccida* in form but range from purple or maroon to reddish-brown in color. When underwater the immature blades are a tantalizing iridescent blue, thus its name—*Iridaea*.

Low Zone

Just below this fuzzy area, at 0.0 m (mean lower low water; MLLW) is the most conspicuous and well-marked break in the intertidal flora. Few species occurring above the 0.0 tide level exist below this level. It is well-marked not by an alga, but by a flowering plant, the surfgrass *Phyllospadix*. The long, thin leaves of surfgrass grow from rhizomatous

roots that cling tenaciously to the flat substrate. This plant is a conspicuous component of the flora at this tide level. With close investigation,
seed pods can be observed toward the base of the plant. Surfgrass also
spreads quite successfully by vegetative reproduction.

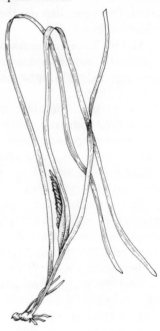

Rhodomela larix 1/2×   *Phyllospadix torreyi* 1/4×

From the high to the low zone, there is an obvious transition from the
brownish reds and greens to the dominant maroon and bright red algae
below. Deeper into the low zone (below -0.3 m) surfgrass populations
give way to flourishing *I. cordata* populations. The blades of *I. cordata*
from this Point Año Nuevo population are significantly larger than
blades from surrounding central California populations during certain
times of the year. The large crop is correlated with the peak seal
populations on Año Nuevo Island and the associated peak in
ammonium-nitrogen in the surrounding water. This correlation suggests that enrichment derived from seal excrement enhances *Iridaea*
production, much the same as nitrogen additives fertilize land crops. *I.
cordata* growth is initiated in early spring coincident with increasing
light levels. Peak growth rates occur in summer along with reproductive

maturation. The blades then begin to senesce and decay during autumn and are finally torn loose by strong winter surf action (Hansen, 1976).

Other red algae in the low zone are *Hymenena flabelligera* resembling a bright-red branched fan, the intricate *Plocamium cartilagineum* that looks like interwoven lace, and the ever-present corallines. The bright pink blades of *Halymenia schizymenioides*, so slippery to the touch, are ephemeral winter visitors. The small feathery-red branches of *Pterosiphonia dendroidea* emerge conspicuously from sand-covered rocks, and on the most exposed rocks are the maroon, spiny *Gigartina corymbifera* blades about the shape and size of ping pong paddles.

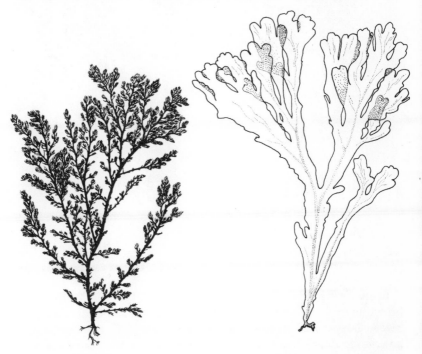

Plocamium cartilagineum   1/2×   *Hymenena flabelligera*   1/2×

While wading in the low zone, one quickly becomes entangled in the masses of ropelike feather-boa kelp (*Egregia menziesii*). These plants can reach well over 7 m in length. Bobbing to and fro with each wave at Point Año Nuevo are the fanlike blades of the kelp *Laminaria dentigera,* while only 1 km south this species is replaced by large populations of the thin, belt-like *L. sinclairii*. Curiously, both species occur together on the island.

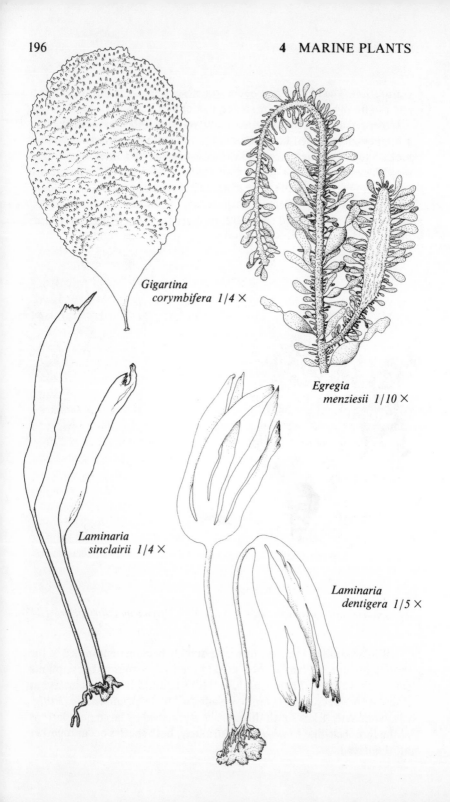

Gigartina corymbifera 1/4 ×

Egregia menziesii 1/10 ×

Laminaria sinclairii 1/4 ×

Laminaria dentigera 1/5 ×

Ecology of the Marine Plants

The Año Nuevo region supports a marvelously diverse assemblage of marine plants. However, it is not necessarily this diversity that makes the area so unique and attractive to the marine botanist. It is the overall algal biomass, the massive drift accumulations and size of the individual plants that overwhelms one's scientific curiousity. Quantitative studies show that the seal populations have a complex and positive influence on the algae in the immediate Año Nuevo region.

A host of physical, chemical, and biological factors control the distribution, reproduction, and growth of marine algae. All of these factors are either directly or indirectly influenced by the tides. The tides at Año Nuevo, like those for all of the Pacific coast of North America, are irregular and semidiurnal (see chap. 2). During spring and summer the low tides occur in the cool early mornings and the plants suffer little effect from exposure. Most intertidal plants have evolved metabolic processes which protect them from the conditions of exposure. These adaptations involve mucous secretion and extreme tolerance to dessication. Other less tolerant species exist only as an understory, protected by the covering of moist, more tolerant plants. If low tide occurs during daylight hours, as it does in the autumn and summer, the plants are exposed to the prolonged heat of sunlight that promotes water loss and increases the surface salinity by evaporation. The high winds at Año Nuevo enhance these effects, particularly dessication. The fog, common in the mornings, acts as a buffer to sunlight during low tides.

Another relatively recent low tide influence on the plants appears in hipboots (the casual onlooker), or shiny black neoprene suits (in pursuit of the abalone), and in tennis shoes with bucket and pronged trowel in hand (the clammer). The "trampling effect" can be compared to walking through a botanical garden without paths. This has had disastrous effects on the southern California intertidal flora, but *so far,* there is little similar evidence in the more lush northern intertidal areas. The destructive effect is not exactly unidirectional, as many have experienced after stepping on some of the most slippery types of seaweed (*Iridaea* and *Porphyra*). Many an early morning at Point Año Nuevo, I have witnessed what appears to be amateurs on an ice rink.

When the tide is in or high, the algae are submerged in seawater and are protected against most of the atmospheric and land-derived factors. However, the seawater filters light, the primary requirement for photosynthesis, to a varying degree depending upon the clarity of the water. During winter and early spring the water is usually clear, but during spring, summer, and early autumn it can be quite turbid due to phyto-plankton blooms, decaying beach-cast seaweed, and excretions from seals. Seawater selectively filters out red light just below the surface (one of the wavelengths used by all green plants). It is only the blue and green light that reaches any depth in the sea. Some of the algae, notably the reds and browns, have evolved special accessory pigments that can "trap" the blue and green light during photosynthesis. Thus they are able to live deeper in the water column than are most of the green algae.

Seaweeds, like land plants, require nutrients for growth. On land when the soil becomes depleted, it can be supplemented with fertilizers. In the sea, the required nutrients, most notably nitrogen and phospho-rus, are dissolved in the seawater bathing the plants, which thus con-stantly receive a fresh supply of nutrients depending upon the water motion and currents. Nutrients such as nitrate and phosphate are supplied during upwelling (see chapter 2). At Año Nuevo, upwelling occurs commonly in spring and winter when strong north winds blow continually for two or more days. Ammonium-N, organo-phosphate compounds, vitamins and amino acids are derived through processes of regeneration. Such plant nutrients are released continually into the water when plants and animals die and decay. This is especially evident as the beach-cast seaweed decomposes. The excreted products of the intertidal invertebrates, fishes, birds, and especially the numerous seals, are high in nitrogen and phosphorus and are important "fertilizers" for the marine plants.

Marine plants require constant water motion to replenish the supply of nutrients, oxygen, and carbon dioxide. In most cases this require-ment is amply fulfilled by surf action where fresh, highly aerated seawater is always available. At certain times the intertidal plants are subjected to strong currents and violent surf action due to storms. To cope with such water motion, the majority of algae that lie on the open coast have evolved strong holdfasts. These basal organs, either crustose or tendril-like, are molded to the rock surface, held by their own adhesive and can usually weather all but the strongest surf. The most highly developed holdfasts are those of the kelps (brown algae) which form dense beds in the slightly protected areas at the northern end of Año Nuevo Island. During the winter, storm waves tug at these giant marine plants (up to 16 m in length), finally dislodging the rocks they are attached to! The battered remnants of three or four species of kelp, still attached to their rocks, litter the beach after storms. Usually, kelp beds help prevent erosion of the shoreline by buffering waves during high tide and storms. Not so at Año Nuevo. The kelp with their attached rocks, and also the millions of cobbles concentrated at Point Año Nuevo, are tossed against the fragile cliffs and *enhance* erosion.

These mobile rocks and cobbles roll about dislodging plants and animals from the substrate and exposing new bare surfaces for colonization by plants which are reproducing at that particular time. Some "weedy" plants such as the bright green genera *Ulva* and *Enteromorpha* and the thin, papery red alga *Porphyra* are among the first to appear on any denuded surface. These green and reddish-gray patches often appear as tiny islands among the uniformly colored established communities. It is on these denuded surfaces that biological competition among species is especially active. Soon more robust species begin to colonize and grow, eventually outcompeting the original colonizers by forcing the holdfasts off or by shading them.

As primary energy producers, the algae occupy a key position in marine food webs. These plants are constantly subject to grazing by herbivorous animals. Numerous species of animals, primarily snails, chitons, and kelp crabs graze the surface of the seaweeds (see chapter 5). One well-known gastropod, the abalone, feeds mainly on drift (free-floating) seaweed. Many of the beach animals feed on the accumulations of beach-cast seaweed which is always present though most abundant from late summer through winter. Another group of grazers are the herbivorous fishes.

The phytoplankton, on the other hand, are eaten by filter-feeding animals, e.g., barnacles, clams, zooplankters. The epiphytic (living on another plant) and benthic microscopic algae (e.g., diatoms) are consumed by detrital feeders and animals that feed by scraping surfaces.

Seaweed Growth Strategies

The marine plants as a whole are in a constant state of flux exhibiting the myriad of life history events: germination, growth, maturation, reproduction (both sexual and asexual), senescence, and decomposition. Among the diverse algal types are short-lived ephemerals that "bloom" predictably at specific times of the year, e.g., the thin brown blade *Phaeostrophion* and slippery, red *Halymenia*. There are also annuals which grow, reproduce, and senesce in one year, e.g., the bull-kelp, *Nereocystis*. And there are perennials, e.g., the commercially important carrageenophyte *Iridaea*, the gnarly, bush-like *Cystoseira*, and the fan-like kelp *Laminaria*. Some of the seemingly short-lived plants can be quite deceiving. They produce a conspicuous, upright portion that soon dies leaving a small, healthy holdfast tightly attached

to the rock. The plant remains in this form until conditions become
favorable once again for production of the upright portion (e.g., the
brown bottle-brush *Analipus*).

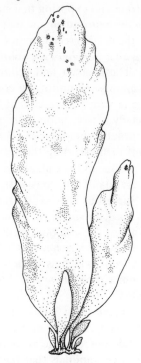

Iridaea cordata   1/3×

Ecology of the Red Seaweed Iridaea

The majority of algal species exhibit fluctuations associated with the
changing seasons or other cyclic events. These fluctuations are influenced
or triggered by a number of environmental factors such as the amount
of light (irradiance), daylength, seawater temperature, nutrients, dessication, and grazing. Some of these physical and chemical factors have
been measured at Año Nuevo.

The amount of light reaching the surface of the water, in conjunction
with daylength, is a critical factor as it is necessary for photosynthesis
and is associated with stimulation of initial plant growth. Studies on the
red alga *Iridaea cordata* (Hansen, 1977) and on many other species
worldwide have shown that the spring burst of growth is associated with

the near tripling of light that occurs between winter and spring. Irradiance remains at a high level, with intermittent depressions due to fog, throughout the spring and summer when algal crops reach a peak and then slowly decline in autumn.

Solar Radiation

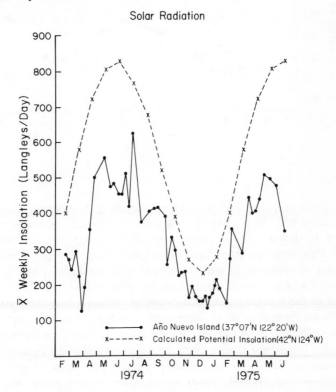

On the other hand, marine plants experience mild seawater temperature fluctuations compared to those at the same latitude on the Atlantic coast. Seawater temperature at Año Nuevo changes little during winter and spring and probably is not an important factor in promoting the annual spring algal bloom. However, the warmer summer and autumn temperatures are associated with peak algal standing crops and subsequent senescence and die-back.

Fluctuations in the primary plant nutrients are of special interest at Año Nuevo because of the unique contribution derived from seal-excreted products. The regenerated ammonium-nitrogen (NH_4-N) is a good indicator of the seal excreta (Hansen, J.C., 1971). The unusually

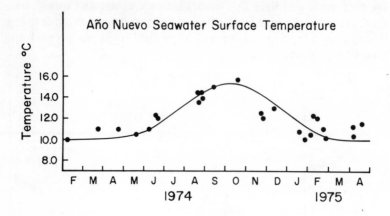

Año Nuevo Seawater Surface Temperature

high levels of NH_4-N in the waters surrounding Año Nuevo Island are associated with the peak seal populations on the island, and with storms which wash the island of its excreta and guano deposits. Further, the peak algal standing crops, and more specifically those of the red alga *Iridaea,* are associated with both peak seal populations and NH_4-N levels. The Año Nuevo algal crops are greater than those at Pigeon Point to the north, and the *Iridaea* plants are larger than those studied at Pigeon Point or south at Davenport Landing and Scotts Creek. This is not surprising in light of recent laboratory results on nitrogen uptake kinetics. It has been demonstrated that *Iridaea* and other algae preferably take up NH_4-N in the presence of other nitrogenous compounds (e.g., NO_3-N), (Hansen, 1980). In addition, *Iridaea* plants have the capability of utilizing much greater NH_4-H concentrations than are usually found in the near-shore zone or open ocean outside of the Año Nuevo area. When NH_4-N is low (winter, spring, and early summer), there is apparently adequate NO_3-N and PO_4-P available for growth from upwelled waters. This evidence suggests that through a complex system of biological and chemical events at Año Nuevo the top carnivores (seals) enhance the food web by enriching seawater that is then used by the primary producers (the algae). This phenomenon makes Año Nuevo an ideal field "laboratory" for studying the processes and implications of natural enrichment in marine systems.

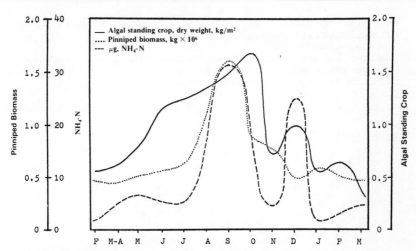

NH₄-N, pinniped biomass, and algal standing crops from the lower zone at Año Nuevo Point. (Hansen, J.C., 1972)

References

Abbott, I.A., and Dawson, E.Y. 1978. *How To Know the Seaweeds.* Revised Ed., W.C. Brown Co., Dubuque, Iowa.

Abbott, I.A., and Hollenberg, G.J. 1976. *Marine Algae of California.* Stanford University Press, Stanford, California.

Doty, M.S. 1946. Critical tide factors that are correlated with the vertical distribution of marine algae and other organisms along the Pacific Coast. Ecology, 27:315-28.

Doty, M.S., and Archer, J.G. 1950. An experimental test of the tide factor hypothesis. American Journal Bot., 37:458-64.

Chapman, A.R.O. 1973. A critique of prevailing attitudes towards the control of seaweed zonation on the seashore. Bot. mar., 16:80-82.

Hansen, J.C. 1972. Marine algal nutrient regeneration: The enrichment of the water surrounding Año Nuevo Island, California by pinnipeds. M.A. Thesis, Fresno State College.

Hansen, J.E. 1976. Population biology of *Iridaea cordata* (Rhodophyta: Gigartinaceae). Ph.D. Thesis, University of California, Santa Cruz.

Hansen, J.E. 1977. Ecology and natural history of *Iridaea cordata* (Gigartinales; Rhodophyta) Growth. J. Phycol., 13:395-402.

Hansen, J.E. 1980. Physiological considerations in the mariculture of red algae. In: Abbott, I.A., Foster, M., and Ecklund, L., eds. *Pacific Seaweed Aquaculture.* California Sea Grant College Program, UCSD, La Jolla, CA. 80-92.

Hansen, J.E., and Doyle, W.T. 1976. Ecology and natural history of *Iridaea cordata* (Rhodophyta:Gigartinaceae): Population Structure. J. Phycol., 12:273-78.

Hansen, J.E., and Packard, J.E. Mariculture of Red Seaweeds. Special Publ. Univ. of Calif. Sea Grant Program, S10, La Jolla, Calif. In press.

Polanshek, A., and West, J.A. 1977 Culture and hybridization studies on *Gigartina papillata* (C. Ag.) J. Ag. (Rhodophyta). J. Phycol., 13:141-49.

Ricketts, E.F., and Calvin, J. 1962. *Between Pacific Tides.* 3rd. Ed. revised by J.W. Hedgpeth, Stanford Univ. Press, Stanford, Calif.

Smith, G.M. 1969. *Marine Algae of the Monterey Peninsula.* Stanford University Press, 2nd ed., incorporating the 1966 Supplement by G.J. Hollenberg and I.A. Abbott. Stanford, Calif.

Stephenson, T.A., and Stephenson, A. 1949. The universal features of zonation between the tidemarks on rocky coasts. J. Ecol., 37:11-41.

Yonge, C.M. 1949. *The Sea Shore.* Collins London.

Acorn barnacles
(Sharon Hobson)

5

INTERTIDAL INVERTEBRATES

John S. Pearse

THE ROCKY SHORES of central California are blessed with unusually favorable conditions for intertidal life. At Año Nuevo, with its wide variety of habitats and substrates, intertidal animals are especially diverse and numerous. Invertebrates, in particular, flourish in stunning variety and abundance. Patches of barnacles, mussels, tube worms, and anemones blend with the numerous red, brown, and green algas* to create a cornucopia of colors, textures, and shapes. Closer inspection reveals myriads of delicate, colorful or cryptic animals among the rocks, algal fronds, and tide pools. Each visit yields surprises as one discovers new animal forms and behaviors.

Intertidal animals, by definition, live between the high and low tide levels where they are alternately totally submerged in seawater and fully exposed to air. Most are marine forms with special modifications enabling them to live periodically exposed to air. Impermeable shells

---

* The plural form of the word *alga* is either *algae* or *algas* (but never *algaes*!). I prefer *algas* because it avoids bothersome grammatical confusion and error and because it follows the continual evolution in English (e.g., *plantae* to *plants, laminariae* to *laminarians, formulae* to *formulas, hydrae* to *hydras, amoebae* to *amebas, antennae* to *antennas, vertebrae* to *vertebras.*)

help prevent excessive drying. Many animals also conserve moisture by living in protective holes, in crevices, or among algas, or by covering themselves with sand and shells. Physiological adaptations compensate metabolically for the rapid salinity and temperature changes experienced with the daily changing tides.

When submerged, intertidal animals often are awash in waves breaking over them, sometimes with great force, but they have means of finding and firmly keeping their places. Even plants are in danger of being swept away, particularly during storms. On the other hand, the waves bring in the inorganic nutrients that support the high plant production in the intertidal (see chapter 4), and these plants are used as food and habitat by many of the animals. The waves also bring planktonic plants, animals, and detritus to the intertidal, providing food for the many suspension-feeding animals. Equally important, the constant motion of the waves maintains high oxygen concentrations in the water and washes away and dilutes the poisonous metabolic wastes produced by all the life in the area.

The moderate climate along the coast of central California is the main reason the intertidal life here is among the most luxuriant in the world. Sea temperatures are remarkably constant for a temperate latitude; they fluctuate seasonally only from about 10-12°C in the winter and spring to about 15-17°C in the summer and fall. This is in contrast to comparable latitudes on Atlantic shores where temperatures range from near freezing in the winter to well over 20°C in the summer. Cool fog banks shroud the central California coast in the summer, while the moderating influence of the sea maintains pleasant coastal air temperatures in the winter. Even the tidal pattern along the central California coast favors intertidal life. The extreme low tides during the spring and summer occur in the early morning hours when there is little chance of the animals being "baked" during unusual days of warm sunshine. It is only during the cooler fall and winter months that the extreme low tides occur in the midafternoon.

As Año Nuevo is situated in the center of the central California coastline, it is not surprising that its shores are cloaked with a rich variety of intertidal life. Furthermore, there is an unusual range of habitats at Año Nuevo. A wide stretch of layered shale of the Monterey Formation extends offshore, providing extensive rocky substrate for attachment by plants and animals. Mud, sand, and cobble deposited in the lee of Año Nuevo Island and offshore reefs contain a surprising assemblage of burrowing animals. Beach wrack thrown up from winter storms serves as a microhabitat for still other organisms. It is this combination of climate and other physical conditions that makes the intertidal community at Año Nuevo unique along the central coast of California.

Año Nuevo Island and Point Año Nuevo cloaked under an offshore fog bank during late summer. (R. Buchsbaum)

PATTERNS OF DISTRIBUTION

Looking out over the rocky intertidal at low tide, one can often distinguish several broad bands or zones of life running more or less parallel to the shoreline. These zones can be seen most clearly along the southern shore of Año Nuevo where steep cliffs plunge into Año Nuevo Bay. On closer examination, these apparently clear boundaries often fade, and delineation of the zones is not easy. Conspicuous species of plants and animals that occur at different tidal levels are often convenient to use as marker species. However, conditions are different from place to place, and the abundance and location of these species may vary to some degree. Despite such limitations, several zones can be distinguished on most rocky shores of central California, and these have been described by Ricketts, Calvin, and Hedgpeth (1968) as zones 1, 2, 3, and 4, or the "splash," "high," "mid," and "low" zones.

1. The Splash Zone

Most of the splash zone at Point Año Nuevo is obliterated by sand, but it can be seen along the cliff faces on the south shore. The zone receives wind-blown spray from the waves and is submerged only by the highest tides or when there are high seas and exceptionally large waves. For many consecutive days most of the zone is fully exposed to air and films of evaporated seawater coat the rocks. In some places freshwater seeps from the surrounding land and dribbles over the splash zone rocks. The area experiences extremes of both temperature and salinity.

Some blue-green algas and some lichens thrive under these seemingly harsh conditions and are found on splash zone rocks around the world. The blue-green algas give the rocks a distinctive blackish coloration. The fauna contains a mixture of terrestrial and marine animals, including mites, centipedes, springtails, and midges. Among the most noticeble splash zone animals at Año Nuevo are wood lice, *Porcellio scaber,* and rock lice, *Ligia pallasii,* which scurry about among the crevices and graze on the thin films of plants on the rocks. Rock lice, found on rocky shores all over the world, are restricted to the narrow splash zone; they drown when submerged, but dry quickly and die when placed in more terrestrial environments.

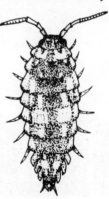

Rock louse,
Ligia pallasii
(Sharon Hobson)

Large periwinkles, *Littorina keenae,* also are seen on the rocks of the splash zone. These marine snails produce mucus that dries and seals their shells to the rocks. Thus securely attached, the snails can retract far into their shells and remain inactive for many days. When the rocks are moistened by waves, the animals awaken and begin to feed by scraping algal films from the rocks. Their hard teeth remove both the algas and some of the rocky surface; in some places populations of periwinkles remove one or more centimeters of rock surface every 10-20 years.

Large periwinkles, *Littorina keenae,* **in the splash zone.** (R. Buchsbaum)

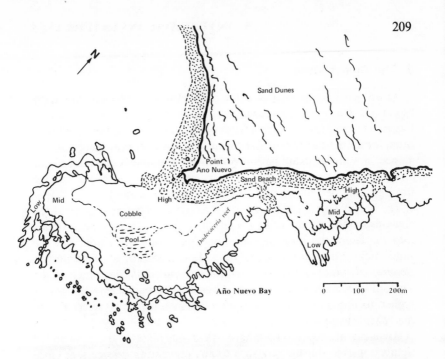

Map of the intertidal region at Point Año Nuevo exposed on a -30 cm (-1 foot) low tide showing the high, mid, and low zones.

Zonation on isolated intertidal rocks on the south shore of Point Año Nuevo. Scattered white acorn barnacles mark the high zone, clumps of stalked barnacles show the mid zone, and dark clusters of algas indicate the low zone. (F. Lanting)

2. The High Zone

At Point Año Nuevo most of the rocks closest to the shore are in the high zone. This zone, between about 75 and 150 cm (2.5 to 5 feet) above the mean lower low tide level, is exposed daily during the tidal cycle, often for more than 12 hours at a time. The rocks appear barren at first glance, but closer examination reveals an abundance of small plants and animals. These organisms are particularly well adapted to survive through long periods of exposure to air, sun, and rainfall.

The higher portion of this zone is marked by scattered clumps of red algas, especially the tissuelike *Porphyra perforata,* the papillated *Gigartina papillata,* the scouring-pad-like *Endocladia muricata,* and the small rockweed, *Pelvetiopsis limitata.* Two species of acorn barnacles, *Balanus glandula* and the smaller *Chthalamus dalli,* dot much of the rock surface, often with nearly solid barnacle-to-barnacle cover, so this higher portion of the high zone is sometimes whitish and is referred to as the "barnacle zone."

Barnacles are covered with hard calcareous plates that can be pulled tightly together during exposure to air, preventing dessication. Once submerged, the animals open their plates and catch drifting bits of plankton and detritus with their bristly legs. The animals are cemented to the rocks and remain in the same spot all their adult lives. Like most other crustaceans, barnacles transfer sperms by copulation, and this may be a special problem for completely sessile adults. Barnacles "solve" this problem in several ways. First, the planktonic barnacle larvas preferentially settle next to other barnacles, often resulting in clumps of barnacles on the rocks, all close together. Second, most barnacles are hermaphroditic, so any animal can copulate with any other animal nearby. Finally, each barnacle has an exceptionally long, wormlike penis, and astute observers sometimes see barnacle penises snaking their way over the rocks in search of other barnacles.

In the lower portions of the high zone, clumps of sea mussels, *Mytilus californianus,* are often common, especially along cracks that hold moisture. These bivalve molluscs attach themselves to the rocky substrate with strong threads that provide security against the force of waves.

Growing among the mussels and along the cracks are sand tube worms, *Phragmatopoma californica,* and stalked barnacles, *Pollicipes polymerus.* The polychete worms with delicate purple tentacles build intricate tubes of sand grains stuck together with a protein cement.

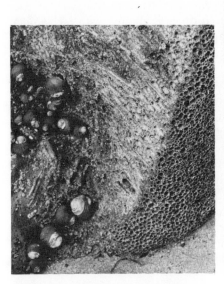

Portion of sand tube worm aggregation. Open ends of tubes *(on right)*
and broken section of aggregation *(in
center)*. Black turban snails cluster on
rocks at base of aggregation *(in lower
left)*. (F. Lanting)

High zone rock cluster of
stalked barnacles surrounded
by small acorn barnacles and
limpets. (F. Lanting)

Elegant sea anemone clone *(Anthopleura elegantissima)* at low tide. All the
animals are partly closed and partially covered with sand. (F. Lanting)

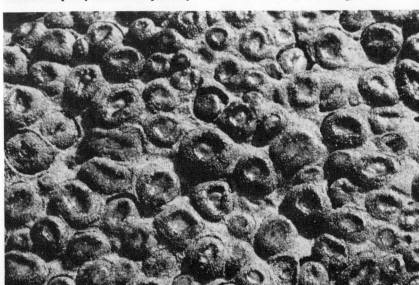

Often the worms settle and grow together, spacing their tubes evenly to form massive reefs with a honeycomb-like structure. Stalked barnacles also often settle close together to form large clumps, with each animal extending above the surrounding mussels and algas on a tough flexible stalk. The inside of the stalk contains the ovary, which is said to be delicious in a chowder.

Elegant sea anemones, *Anthopleura elegantissima,* are also common residents of the high zone. These small animals, 3-5 cm in diameter, cover their bodies with sand and shell fragments, reducing moisture loss. They reproduce by dividing, and clones of the asexually produced individuals often cover large areas in lower portions of the high zone, growing over and smothering other animals such as barnacles. Different clones, each with distinctively patterned, identical individuals, compete for space, and individuals from different clones actually fight when they come in contact. Adjacent clones maintain discrete borders with a bare zone one centimeter or more wide between them. Perceptive observers sometimes find anemones of two clones fighting across this "no-man's land" with special swollen white tentacles loaded with stinging cells.

All of these animals are sedentary or sessile and depend mainly on food brought to them by the waves. Barnacles, mussels, and sand tube worms feed on small particles of food, especially small zooplankton, while the sea anemones snare quite large morsels as well with the sticky and poisonous stinging cells of their tentacles. In addition, the elegant sea anemones obtain nourishment from single-celled brownish algas growing symbiotically in their tissues. In this cooperative relationship, the algas provide some food to the anemones, mainly carbohydrates, while the anemones protect the algas from dessication and supply them with inorganic nutrients. The anemones are very responsive to the light needs of their algas. They open in the morning, like flowers, apparently to "sun" their algas, and they often close during midday protecting their symbionts from too much light.

The main grazing animals in the high zone include limpets *(Collisella digitalis* and *C. scabra),* black turban snails *(Tegula funebralis),* small periwinkle snails *(Littorina scutulata),* and chitons *(Nuttallina californica).* Many of the turban snails have limpets on their shells, such as *Collisella asmi,* that graze on the algas growing on the snails' shells, and horned slipper shells, *Crepidula adunca,* that use the snails as a base from which they suspension-feed. During the periods of low tides the rock limpets clamp down tightly on the rocks to avoid dessication, while the periwinkles and turban snails nestle in crevices and among the

The limpet *Collisella scabra* in its "home scar." (C. Cardwell)

The chiton *Nuttallina californica* nestled among acorn barnacles in the lower portion of the high zone. (C. Cardwell)

This predatory snail, *Acanthina spirata,* feeds on barnacles by prying open the barnacle's shell and rasping out the flesh with its radula. (R. Buchsbaum)

mussels and sea anemones. Some of the limpets, especially *Collisella scabra,* carve depressions in the rocks with their teeth, and their shells fit snugly in these "home scars." During moist nights, or when covered by high tides, the limpets and snails leave their resting places to scrape microscopic algas from the rocks. The grazing pressure on these algas is intense; within weeks after limpets and snails are experimentally removed, the barren-appearing rocks become lush and green from unhampered algal growth.

There are few major predators in the high zone. Shore birds, especially Black Oystercatchers, *Haematopus bachmani,* pick over the area during low tides and take a toll of limpets, snails, mussels, worms, and crustaceans living among the algas and rocks. Two species of snails, *Acanthina spirata* and *Nucella emarginata,* also feed mainly on barnacles and mussels in the high zone and are fairly common at Año Nuevo.

Physical factors, however, account for most of the mortality of animals in the high zone. Low tides occasionally coincide with warm sunny days, and the intense heat and dessication kill those sea anemones, barnacles, and mussels which occupy sites too far away from protected moist places. Prolonged rainstorms during low tides also may kill some animals which are unable to tolerate freshwater. More dramatically, winter storms roll boulders and toss about logs that crush many animals. Such unpredictable events periodically clear large areas of rocky surface that can be recolonized by newly recruited barnacles, mussels, and tube worms. Consequently, the high zone is an exceptionally dynamic area with continual population flux, and populations of plants and animals rarely become dense enough to compete directly for space.

3. The Mid Zone

The animals of the mid zone, between the mean lower low tide level and about 75 cm above that level, are not so heavily influenced by physical factors as are those of the high zone. Most of the mid zone is exposed to air at least once each day, but never for periods longer than 5 or 6 hours. Severe stress from sun or rain during low tides is rare, allowing the community to develop greater complexity with more biological interactions. The mid zone is the center of the intertidal region and most of its inhabitants are quite specialized to live here; relatively few species of the mid zone are found either on the land above or in the sea below the intertidal region. This area is the widest of the 4 zones at Año Nuevo and forms a broad band that stretches over halfway across the intertidal.

At Año Nuevo the mid zone is characterized by a dense cover of red algas. Diagnostic here and elsewhere along the rocky shores of central California is the large greenish red alga *Iridaea flaccida* growing throughout the mid zone and mixed with many other species of red algas, forming a slippery mat of plant cover. Nestled among the algas is a rich assortment of animal species. Suspension-feeding sessile animals include barnacles, sand tube worms, mussels, and sea anemones such as those found in the high zone. Sometimes the mussels or sand tube worms form such dense clumps that they replace the algal cover. There are few bare places on the rocks of the mid zone, and competition for space is intense.

In the mid zone, solitary individuals of elegant sea anemones, *Anthopleura elegantissima,* tend to grow quite large, reaching 15 cm or more in diameter. Although highly variable, the oral disk of these animals is usually pale yellowish brown, and it has distinct lines radiating from the mouth like the spokes of a wheel. Solitary giant green anemones, *Anthopleura xanthogrammica,* with solid-colored oral disks, also can attain large sizes, and these magnificent animals often live crowded in large pools or hanging from under ledges in the mid zone. In addition to zooplankton and detritus, they feed on mussels and other large animals that are torn loose from the rocks by waves. Skeptics who stick their fingers into the mouths of these animals should not be surprised when they feel large mussel shells inside.

Mid zone rocky outcrop covered with mid-zone algas, including sheetlike *Iridaea flaccida* **characteristic of the area.** (F. Lanting)

Large solitary elegant sea anemone, *Anthopleura elegantissima.* **Another species,** *A. artemisia,* **is in the lower right corner of the picture.** (R. Buchsbaum)

Giant green anemone, *Anthopleura xanthogrammica.* (R. Buchsbaum)

Like the elegant sea anemones, giant green anemones contain numerous symbiotic algal cells. These cells are yellow-brown in color, and the deep bluish-green color of the anemones is *not* directly due to the algal cells inside. Rather, the anemones themselves produce the green pigments in response to bright sunshine. Animals far back under ledges or in dark caves produce little pigment and contain few algal cells, and these are usually very pale. The green animal pigment probably serves to protect the algas from too much light, illustrating further the exquisite symbiotic interaction between these anemones and their algal cells.

Another sea anemone which adds variety to the mid zone is the small solitary orange, pink, or gray *Anthopleura artemisia* found scattered about in small holes and cracks. In addition, reddish or greenish brooding sea anemones, *Epiactis prolifera,* are often found attached to algas and rocks with their young held in a special fold around the body for closer parental protection. The brooding anemones are hermaphroditic, and each parent and its brooded young have identical color patterns, suggesting self-fertilization.

Other sedentary animals that depend on wave action for most of their food resources include several species of polychete worms. The burrowing tentaculate worm *Cirriformia spirabrancha* lives among the sand and gravel between the rocks, waving myriads of greenish-white feeding tentacles above the sand. White calcareous tubes of the pretty little fan worms *Serpula vermicularis* twist among the rocks and end with a whorl of red tentacles. But most spectacular at Point Año Nuevo are the calcareous mounds formed by tiny black worms, *Dodecaceria fewkesi.* These worms are suspension feeders, similar to sand tube worms, but rather than building fragile sand tubes they secrete hard calcium carbonate to build their homes. They divide asexually, and as the worms increase in number, the calcareous structure they jointly produce increases in size. Small patches of *Dodecaceria* are common all along the California coastline. But the massive structures at Año Nuevo, up to several meters in diameter, are unique and add substantially to local topography. Their large size may be related to the presence of the numerous seals and sea lions, because the tiny worms may benefit by feeding on the wastes and associated bacteria produced by these mammals.

Grazers that scrape algas off the rocks in the mid zone include the ubiquitous limpets *(Collisella digitalis, C. pelta, C. scabra, and Notoacmea scutum)* which are scattered over the rocks among the sessile plants and animals. Black and brown turban snails *(Tegula funebralis* and *T. brunnea)* cluster along cracks and ledges in massive numbers. An

assortment of chitons crowd these rock surfaces as well, including the
tiny *Cyanoplax dentiens,* the delicately lined *Tonicella lineata,* the
bristly *Mopalia muscosa,* and the large shiny black *Katharina tunicata.*

Calcareous mounds formed by tiny polychete worms, *Dodecaceria fewkesi.*
**Each mound is secreted by a colony of hundreds to thousands of worms
produced asexually.** (C. Cardwell)

Many other animals feed on the larger algas and are often found on or
among the plants. Kelp isopods, *Idothea stenops,* which look like
grotesque flattened pillbugs, and kelp crabs, *Pugettia producta,* both
feed on large kelps to which they cling with grasping clawlike legs. Other
crabs are more oportunistic feeders and eat a variety of plant and
animal debris brought to the shore by waves. These include large red
rock crabs, *Cancer antennarius,* and lined shore crabs, *Pachygrapsus
crassipes,* as well as hermit crabs, *Pagurus* spp., which use snail shells as
homes.

Kelp isopod, *Idothea stenops,* grasping a piece of feather-boa kelp. (R. Buchsbaum)

A shy little hermit crab *Pagurus hirsutiusculus* living in a worn *Tegula* shell. (R. Buchsbaum)

Snail's-eye view of a lined shore crab, *Pachygrapsus crassipes.* (R. Buchsbaum)

Many intertidal animals are selective carnivores, feeding on specific prey in the mid zone. Long slimy ribbon worms (phylum Nemertea), such as the white, snotlike *Amphiporus imparispinosus* and the purple and yellow *Paranemertes peregrina* slither among the algas in search of small polychetes. Most of the polychetes themselves are voracious predators, including the startling mussel worms, *Nereis vexillosa,* which reach lengths of more than 20 cm. Other predators include drilling snails (*Acanthina* spp., *Nucella* spp., *Ocenebra* spp.), tidepool fishes, and the exquisite sea slugs, many with color patterns precisely matching those of their sponge, bryozoan, or tunicate prey.

But probably the most important predators in the mid zone are the predaceous sea stars, especially ochre sea stars, *Pisaster ochraceus,* and the smaller six-rayed brooding sea stars, *Leptasterias* spp. These sea stars feed on chitons, snails, and limpets, and prevent such animals from limiting the algal cover. They also feed on barnacles and mussels and keep these sessile animals from overgrowing large areas to the exclusion of other plants and animals.

The sea star *Pisaster ochraceus* **is among the most voracious predators in the mid zone. Stalked barnacles,** *Pollicipes polymerus,* **are seen among the mussels,** *Mytilus californianus.* **Large acorn barnacles** *Tetraclita rubescens* **are also common.** (R. Buchsbaum)

A mussel worm *Nereis vexillosa,* common among the algas and rocks of the mid zone. *(R. Buchsbaum)*

Sea slug *Hermissenda crassicornis* is a gastropod without a shell. Like *Hermissenda,* most sea slugs are beautifully colored. (R. Buchsbaum)

4. The Low Zone

Bright green surf grasses *(Phyllospadix* spp.) conveniently mark the beginning of the low zone. Large straplike brown algas, particularly the oar kelps *(Laminaria* spp.) and feather-boa kelps *(Egregia menziesii)* are conspicuous in the low zone, growing among the surf grasses and the ubiquitous red algas. The low zone is essentially just a small extension of the shallow subtidal region, and nearly all the plants and animals found there also occur at greater depths. It offers the non-diver the chance to glimpse first hand the dazzling diversity of life found in the shallow waters just off the shores of central California.

The low zone extends from the mean lower tide level (zero tide level) to as far out as the tide ever goes. The maximum drop in water level along the shores of central California is about 60 cm (2 feet) below zero tide level, occurring each year in June and December. Usually the tide does not drop below the zero tide level more often than a few days every other week near the time of the new and full moon, and then it usually exposes the low zone for only a few hours. It is well worth the trouble to come to the shore during a really low tide, and to do this one must consult a tide level chart or a newspaper to get the correct times. The plants and animals in this low zone are seldom stressed by exposure to the air, and a rich and complex community of both plants and sessile animals can develop with intense competition occurring among them for places to become established and grow.

The low zone particular favors encrusting animals that feed on small particles in the water and need to filter large volumes of water to obtain enough food. The multitude of filter-feeding sponges, bryozoans, and tunicates in a bewildering array of colors, shapes, and textures makes the low zone a spectacular experience for anyone prowling among the rocks and plants. Delicate hydroids and arborescent bryozoans often grow in profusion among the red, pink, yellow, and tan mounds of sponges and slippery colonial tunicates. Orange solitary corals *(Balano-phyllia elegans),* orange or pink solitary anemones *(Anthopleura arte-misia),* pink, red, or violet jewel anemones *(Corynactis californica),* and translucent lightbulb tunicates *(Clavelina huntsmani)* dot vertical faces and the undersurfaces of ledges. Fragile white calcareous tubes of the colonial polychete worms *Salmacina tribranchiata,* looking like tangles of bleached shredded wheat, also are conspicuous under ledges and in small caves.

Several species of limpets, snails, and chitons graze on the plants growing on the low zone rocks. Dunce-cap limpets, *Acmaea mitra,* are

Low zone rocks at Año Nuevo covered with surf grass *Phyllospadix scouleri* **and feather-boa kelps** *Egregia menziesii.* (F. Lanting)

Jewel anemones, *Corynactis californica,* **add delicate color under ledges in the low zone.** (R. Buchsbaum)

characteristic of the low zone, living mainly on encrusting coralline algas. Other limpets also are specialized to live on particular species of low zone plants; seaweed limpets, *Notoacmea insessa,* are usually found on the fronds of feather-boa kelps, *Egregia menziesii,* while the tiny narrow limpets *Notoacmea paleacea* just fit the narrow blades of surf grasses.

Sometimes the channels and pools of the low zone contain numerous purple sea urchins, *Strongylocentrotus purpuratus,* each living in a small depression in the rock. The animals excavate the holes themselves, picking the rock away with their living, movable spines and teeth. They remain in their holes most of their lives and snare wave-borne pieces of algas with their long sticky tentaclelike tube feet. Like sea stars, sea urchins also use their tube feet to move along the bottom when they leave their holes. Larger, mainly subtidal red sea urchins, *Strongylocentrotus franciscanus,* also are occasionally found in the channels between the low zone rocks. Like purple sea urchins, they are mainly sedentary animals that catch drifting pieces of algas for food, but rather than live in protective holes, they depend more on their long spines for defense.

Several sea stars are major predators in the low zone and shallow subtidal, and they are often found at Año Nuevo. Magnificent, large sunflower stars, *Pycnopodia helianthoides,* prowl the area in search of snails, abalones, and sea urchins, which they engulf whole. These prey have well-developed defenses against sunflower stars; they all flee when near the stars, the snails and abalones nearly galloping. In addition, the sea urchins use poisonous little pincers (pedicellarias) and their spines to hold off attacking sea stars. Nevertheless, sunflower stars with snails and sea urchins in their stomachs are found frequently enough to show that these defenses are often futile.

Blood stars, *Henricia leviuscula,* and the slippery leather stars, *Dermasterias imbricata,* with a distinctive garlicky odor, are more subtle predators. Blood stars feed on sponges, while leather stars prey on sponges, tunicates, anemones, corals, and sea urchins. Both sea stars evert their stomachs over their prey and slowly digest it away. The sedentary prey must depend on rapid recruitment, growth, and regeneration, or the production of toxic chemicals, for defense.

The enormous variety of omnivorous crabs and shrimps, of predaceous snails, slugs, and fishes, and of other animals of the low zone provide endless opportunities for natural history studies. Even for the casual visitor, however, observations of all of these animals combine to give an unforgettable impression of luxuriance.

Sunflower star *Pycnopodia helianthoides,* **a major predator of the low zone.** (R. Buchsbaum)

Sea urchins *(Strongylocentrotus purpuratus)* **in a tide pool.** (R. Buchsbaum)

Beach Wrack

Many subtidal plants and animals wash ashore on the sandy beaches above the rocky intertidal at Año Nuevo. When large ocean swells sweep around Año Nuevo Island they pick up sick or unattached animals and plants from the shallow sea floor and carry them onto the beaches. Judging from the material on the beaches, the powerful winter storms must rip out many healthy plants and animals as well. Large numbers of dead and dying giant gumboot chitons *(Cryptochiton stelleri)*, top shells *(Astraea gibberosa)*, and rock crabs *(Cancer antennarius)* are common sights on the Año Nuevo beaches in the winter. And a variety of shells, including white butterfly-shaped internal plates of gumboot chitons, can be found among the beach debris. The subtidal populations of these animals must be enormous.

The great piles of wrack consist mainly of kelps and other plants. Kelp flies, *Coelopa vanduzeei,* and beach hoppers, *Orchestoidea* spp., rapidly colonize these piles and aid in their decomposition. Or, much of the wrack can be buried under sand to decompose anaerobically into petroleumlike material that oozes out of the sand releasing strong-smelling vapors of methane and other hydrocarbons. The rich aromas of rotting and fermenting seaweeds combine with the odors of the urine and feces produced by the pinnipeds on nearby Año Nuevo Island to create a most distinctive odor along this stretch of coastline.

By-the-wind sailors *Velella velella* **cast up on the beach. These delicate animals live floating on the sea surface far offshore, but they are occasionally blown ashore, often in enormous numbers, by onshore winds.** (R. Buchsbaum)

A pile of beach wrack at Año Nuevo containing a variety of intertidal and subtidal algas. (F. Lanting)

Beach hoppers, *Orchestoidea spp.,* live in burrows in the beach sand and feed on organic debris. (R. Buchsbaum)

DIVERSITY OF INTERTIDAL LIFE

Compared to other sites along the central California coast, the intertidal zone at Año Nuevo is nearly unique for its variety of invertebrates, as shown by a study of intertidal communities along the coast of Central California in 1971-73.*

The study focused on two sites at Año Nuevo: one at the tip of Point Año Nuevo and the other to the east, facing into Año Nuevo Bay. At the first site, extreme low tides expose some 8 hectares (20 acres), almost all at the mid zone tidal level. Much of the exposed area is an unconsolidated field of boulders and cobbles in a matrix of sand and mud. Such an intertidal habitat is unusual for the open coast and may be the result of the partial protection from waves afforded by Año Nuevo Island and adjacent offshore reefs. The high zone of the area is a small series of rocky outcrops right at the tip of Point Año Nuevo. There is usually an unstable sand beach landward of these outcrops, and periodically sand accumulates and covers most of the high zone rocks. Seaward to the west, beyond nearly 200 meters of cobble and muddy sand, are more rocky outcrops of tilted layers of cherty Monterey shale with plants and animals characteristic of the mid zone. Beyond this, at the edge of the water at low tide, are stands of surf grasses, oar kelps, and other species marking the low zone.

The second study site was chosen approximately 350 meters east of the tip of Point Año Nuevo. With a southern exposure into Año Nuevo Bay, there is considerable protection from the northwest swells of the winter storms. Layers of Monterey shale are tilted and broken to form ridges more or less perpendicular to the shore. The topography is extremely rugged with many ledges, pools, and cracks. The high, mid, and low zones grade one into the other as the shelf gradually drops below the surface of the sea. Several high rocky outcrops form a ridge in the high zone, and landward of the high zone is a sandy beach, which is washed by the waves during periods of high tide.

Over 300 species of invertebrates were recorded at the Año Nuevo sites during the 2-year study (see Appendix for complete list). Considerably more species were found at the Año Nuevo Bay site than at the Point, even though the Bay site covered much less area. No particular group of animals seemed especially favored at the Bay site; rather a few

---

* The study was done by students at the University of California, Santa Cruz, and was supported by grants from the Janss Foundation and the U.S. Department of Commerce, Sea Grant Program.

more species in each group were present there. We do not know why this smaller and apparently more homogeneous site supports a greater diversity of animals than the Point. The Bay site is more protected from the onslaught of the winter waves, and there are fewer loose boulders for the waves to toss around, so more complex communities with more species may be able to develop there. In addition, the extremely rugged topography provides numerous nooks and crannies for intertidal life, and discourages human visitors from exploring the area. The Point, by contrast, attracts regular influxes of clam diggers, abalone pickers, and tidepool observers who swarm over much of the area when it is exposed each month at low tide. The Bay site may simply be less trampled than the Point site, and the intertidal community there may be more diverse and complex under the less disturbed conditions.

Many of the species found at Año Nuevo were relatively rare, both in comparison with the rest of the coast and in frequency of observation at Año Nuevo. About one-third of the animals noted at Año Nuevo were found only once during the entire 2-year study. This is a much higher frequency of rare species than found at other sites along the central California coast and is a main component of the unique character of Año Nuevo. One has a better chance of finding a rare species here than at most other places.

On the other hand, about 40 species found at Año Nuevo were common and conspicuous. Most of these species are resident year-round and can be seen easily by anyone looking for them. They are also common along the Santa Cruz and San Mateo coastlines and are among the most familiar intertidal animals on the entire central California coast. They are the species the novice should learn first as an entry into recognition of the main intertidal animals at Año Nuevo; most of these species have been mentioned in this chapter.

Of the 10 sites studied between Soquel Point on Monterey Bay and Pigeon Point north of Año Nuevo, the 2 sites at Año Nuevo had the largest number of invertebrate species. This unique diversity of animals may be due to several factors. The presence of large numbers of seals and sea lions on and around Año Nuevo Island certainly distinguishes this area from the others. These pinnipeds add substantial amounts of organic material (urine, feces, carcasses) to the surrounding waters. Some of this material may be used directly as food by animals such as sponges, tube worms, and tunicates that feed on tiny organic particles and bacteria. Soluble nutrients, including ammonia, probably enhance algal growth (see chapter 4), and this increased plant production may provide food and habitat for more kinds of animals.

However, the main factors that probably account for the high number of species at Año Nuevo are the peculiar geology and geography of the area. The hard, layered outcrops of cherty Monterey shale are unique and provide an exceptional topography full of pools and crevices. While the coast north and south of Año Nuevo receives the full force of oncoming ocean storms, impact on the intertidal region at Año Nuevo is buffered by Año Nuevo Island and the surrounding subtidal reefs. The area has a mixture of both exposed and semiprotected

	Porifera	Cnidaria	Annelida	Mollusca	Arthropoda	Echinodermata	Tunicata	Site Total
Pigeon Point: north side	13	9	15	68	33	11	8	157
Pigeon Point: south side	17	13	15	81	37	14	11	188
Point Año Nuevo	**16**	**14**	**32**	**81**	**41**	**11**	**18**	**213**
Año Nuevo Bay	**18**	**17**	**39**	**96**	**37**	**18**	**19**	**241**
Scott Creek	15	15	17	64	24	10	10	155
Davenport Landing	12	16	23	68	29	9	12	169
Natural Bridges	16	12	15	53	25	5	11	137
Santa Cruz: Almar St.	12	8	15	50	25	4	5	119
Point Santa Cruz	13	18	19	50	25	5	11	141
Soquel Point	1	9	24	64	26	8	6	138
Phylum Total	**30**	**26**	**73**	**157**	**73**	**25**	**28**	**412**

Total number of species of major invertebrate phyla found at the sites studied during 1971-1973 along the Santa Cruz and San Mateo County coastlines. The sites are arranged in latitudinal order from north to south. The Soquel Point site was in the area of a domestic sewage outfall since discontinued.

habitats, and the fauna reflects this heterogeneity. In addition, the life at Año Nuevo benefits from the moderating influences of the sea. Often a curtain of fog lying just offshore of Davenport and Scott Creek hides Año Nuevo within its folds.

Many of the animals at Año Nuevo are characteristic of open exposed shores. These include subtidal animals that survive and thrive in intertidal areas with adequate wave splash at low tide, such as solitary corals *(Balanophyllia elegans)*, octocorals *(Clavularia* sp.), jewel anemones *(Corynactis californica)*, red abalones *(Haliotis rufescens)*, decorator crabs *(Loxorhynchus crispatus)*, leather stars *(Dermasterias imbricata)*, red sea urchins *(Strongylocentrotus franciscanus)*, and white calcareous tunicates *(Didemnum carnulentum)*. Other species are strictly intertidal but require open exposed conditions. The shiny black chiton, *Katharina tunicata,* is one such species that is common at Año Nuevo.

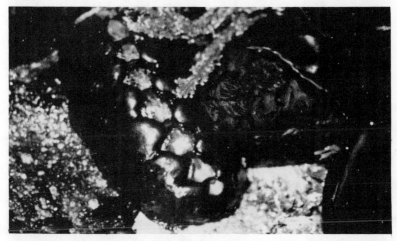

The black chiton *Katharina tunicata* **is an animal found mainly on open exposed rocky shores.** (R. Buchsbaum)

Animals more characteristic of protected shores and embayments usually find shelter by burrowing in soft or loose material. Since Año Nuevo Island and the surrounding rocky reefs break some of the force of the incoming waves, the sediment load in the water settles and forms banks of unconsolidated cobbles, rocks, sand, and mud, such as the extensive cobble region off the tip of Point Año Nuevo. Such banks of rocks, sand, and mud, although quite different from typical mudflats, do provide suitable habitat for some typical mudflat animals. Scurrying about these areas are drab little mudflat crabs, *Hemigrapsus oregonensis;* and nestled and burrowing among the rocks are occasional nemerteans *(Cerebratulus californiensis)* and lugworms *(Abarenicola claparedii).* The most curious inhabitant, however, is the fat innkeeper *(Urechis caupo),* which is characteristic of the most protected and

Solitary coral, *Balanophyllia elegans,* can withdraw into a stony cup for protection. (R. Buchsbaum)

The leather star, *Dermasterias imbricata,* feeds on sponges and anemones in the low zone of open exposed coasts. (R. Buchsbaum)

gooiest mudflats such as those in Elkhorn Slough and Tomales Bay. The pink, sausage-shaped worm (some say, resembling a penis) pumps water through its burrow and traps tiny food particles in a mucous net which it eats. It is an innkeeper to several animals that share its burrow, including a scale worm, a clam, a crab, and a fish; usually only one individual of each species lives with a worm, and it seems likely that all have fascinating mutualistic interactions in their little microcosm.

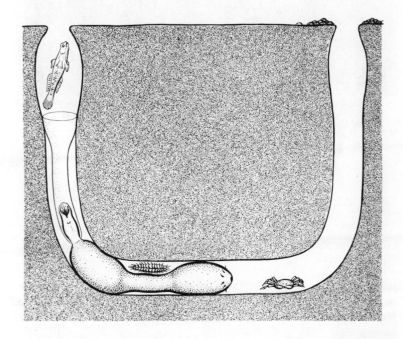

The "innkeeper," *Urechis caupo,* an echiuroid worm with its commensals: an annelid worm, a crab, and a fish. (From *Basic Ecology,* by R. and M. Buchsbaum. Based on Fisher and MacGinitie). ×½

HUMAN USE OF THE INTERTIDAL ZONE

The cobble region off Point Año Nuevo is of particular interest to human visitors because of the abundance of clams, especially cockles *(Protothaca staminea),* nestled among the cobbles and loose rocks. At present people are restricted from the area during elephant seal breeding season, but at other times hordes of people visit at low tide to dig trenches and pits in search of tasty bivalves. The continual disturbance

Red abalone, *Haliotis rufescens,* **is a favorite food of both people and sea otters.**
(R. Buchsbaum)

provides numerous new surfaces for plants and animals to settle and
begin growth, and it may even enhance the diversity of the area.
However, it probably inhibits the development of a mature biological
community.

Abalone pickers find more interest in the lowest regions of the
intertidal between Point Año Nuevo and Año Nuevo Island. These
people in wet suits or waders search under ledges along tidal channels
for red abalones, which, although predominantly subtidal, occur inter-
tidally along open exposed coasts. The number of these large limpetlike
snails in the intertidal is now quite low, and virtually all of them live
deep in cracks and crevices. Only a few decades ago many of the
abalones lived in the open on low intertidal rocks, sometimes in such
great numbers that they formed a shell-to-shell cover which excluded
other sessile animals and many of the algas. Since then, nearly all the
animals within sight and easy reach of people have been collected and
turned into abalone steaks.

Two centuries ago and before, most abalones almost certainly lived deep in crevices and under ledges as they do today. The coastal people of that time, like people today, collected and ate the abalones of the intertidal as indicated by the abalone shells in the prehistoric middens at Año Nuevo and elsewhere along the California coast. Moreover, two centuries ago sea otters also were abundant along the shores of Año Nuevo. Predation by these animals and by people undoubtedly restricted the abalone populations to crevices, as they are now along the Monterey coastline where sea otters thrive. With the decline of the native people and the sea otters during the last century (see chapter 1), the abalones were freed of their major predators, and the abalone populations were able to expand into the open to cover large areas of the California coast.

During recent decades, as more people learned to appreciate the taste of abalones, people again became the major predator of abalones, and almost all the easily accessible abalones have been harvested from the central California coastline. When the expanding population of sea otters returns to Año Nuevo, as it certainly will if not restricted by people, the abalone population of the intertidal will be much as before, with little trace of the brief abalone population explosion that occurred in the absence of the sea otters. Subtidal populations of abalones also are being reduced back to prehistoric levels by fishing. It appears to be a race between people and sea otters to see who can collect most of the abalones that are in the open before the abalone populations are once again fully restricted to inaccessible cracks and crevices. At Año Nuevo, at least, people have won already in the intertidal.

With the developing environmental awareness of the past several decades, human use of the intertidal has been increasingly esthetic. People simply enjoy seeing the bizarre and beautiful life of the intertidal. At Año Nuevo the exquisite variety of intertidal animals and plants combines with the sounds of the waves and pinnipeds, and the most distinctive odors, to attract a diverse assortment of people at every low tide. As the Año Nuevo State Reserve becomes more widely known, many more people will visit. Such use, if carefully exercised, will not mar the unique diversity of the intertidal life at Año Nuevo, and the area will continue to be enjoyed by countless future visitors.

References

Barbour, M.G., R.B Craig, F.R. Drysdale, and M.T. Ghiselin (1973) *Coastal Ecology—Bodega Head.* University of California Press.

Buchsbaum, R. (1976) *Animals Without Backbones.* 2nd ed., revised and updated. University of Chicago Press.

Carefoot, T. (1977) *Pacific Seashores.* University of Washington Press.

Hedgpeth, J.W. (1962) *Introduction to Seashore Life of the San Francisco Bay Region and the Coast of Northern California.* University of California Press.

Morris, R.H., D.P. Abbott, and E.C. Haderlie (1980) *Intertidal Invertebrates of California.* Stanford University Press.

Ricketts, E.F. and Calvin, J. (1968) *Between Pacific Tides.* 4th ed., revised by J.W. Hedgpeth. Stanford University Press.

Smith, R.I. and Carlton, J.T., eds. (1975) *Light's Manual: Intertidal Invertebrates of the Central California Coast.* 3rd ed. University of California Press.

Stephenson, T.A. and Stephenson, A. (1972) *Life Between Tidemarks on Rocky Shores.* W.H. Freeman & Co.

A **kelp crab,** *Pugettia producta,* **feeds on kelp and provides a surface for acorn barnacles to grow.** (R. Buchsbaum)

6

BIRDS

W. Breck Tyler
and
Kenneth T. Briggs

Marbled Godwit

A RICH AND DIVERSE avifauna inhabits Año Nuevo State Reserve; some 225 species of birds use this area during the year. These include 50 different seabirds, 30 shorebird species, 40 kinds of marsh birds and waterfowl, 15-20 raptors, and nearly 100 species of landbirds. More than 50 of these species reside here throughout the year; the remainder are present seasonally as visitors or passers-through.

A variety of factors contribute to the diversity of birdlife at Año Nuevo Reserve. One of the most important is its geographic location near the midpoint of the California coast. This central location places the Reserve within the seasonal ranges of faunal groups from both the north and the south.

Many of the species observed here use the Pacific flyway during their annual migration. Each spring these transients move through the Año Nuevo region on their long journey from tropical wintering grounds to breeding sites in the far north. They pass through again in autumn on the return trip. Disoriented vagrants from the eastern United States occasionally turn up at Año Nuevo coming up or down the wrong coast.

Among the shore and seabirds, migrants preferring cool waters stop and spend the winter along the central California coast. These locally wintering populations become larger and more diverse during years when weather in Canada and Alaska is unusually harsh. Another group of birds visits annually in late summer and fall. Having completed nesting activities at their Mexican colonies, these birds disperse northward to enjoy the balmy autumn weather of the central California coast. In some years very unusual tropical wanderers appear at the Reserve.

237

Several geographic features help attract birds (especially seabirds) to the Año Nuevo region. To the south is Monterey Bay with its deep underwater canyon. The bay is rich in food resources, including fishes and squids, and affords shelter from offshore storms. Monterey Bay also marks the limit of the ranges of many northern and southern species. North of Año Nuevo lie San Francisco Bay and the Farallon Islands. The bay provides marsh, mudflat, and sheltered marine habitats. The Farallones support the largest seabird breeding colony on the Pacific coast south of Alaska. Año Nuevo Reserve, lying between these features, and possessing small areas of many of these types of habitats, draws birds from the entire central coast region.

Año Nuevo Reserve is located in an area of California where a variety of habitat types exist close together. Coniferous forests, agricultural fields and orchards, brushy canyons and chaparral-covered slopes, river bottoms, and freshwater marshes all may be found within 10 km of Año Nuevo Point. A few kilometers to the east lie the Santa Cruz Mountains. Much of this range is covered by coniferous forest, mostly coast redwoods, but areas of oak woodland and foothill chaparral are also present. Near sea level, much of the available land is used for pasture and row crops. Scattered patches of unused land are covered by low brush and chaparral. Rain-driven mountain streams, such as Pescadero Creek to the north, and Scott and Waddell Creeks to the south, form fresh- and brackish-water marshes as they reach the sea. Each habitat supports its own characteristic species of the regional avifauna, and many of these birds find their way to Año Nuevo Reserve.

The specific geographic characteristics of the Reserve contribute to avian diversity and abundance. Año Nuevo Point projects 3 km westward, perpendicular to the mainland coast (see map p. 125). Prominent peninsulas like Point Arena, Año Nuevo, and Point Pinos concentrate landbirds before and after long overwater flights and provide sheltered waters on which seabirds rest and feed. The small offshore island at Año Nuevo offers a sanctuary where shy, colonial, and solitary seabirds and shorebirds nest and roost. The island acts as a shield against the turbulence of the open ocean, and the channel which separates island from mainland provides quiet waters for resting and foraging waterbirds. Because access from the mainland is limited, egging and disruption of nesting by other forms of "peopollution" have been minimized. The sad history of destruction of seabird colonies by human disturbance and introduction of predators (cats, rats, and goats) on islands like the Farallones and the California Channel Islands has thus been minimal at Año Nuevo Island.

THE ORNITHOLOGICAL RECORD

Early explorers of coastal California were undoubtedly cognizant of the Año Nuevo region by the early 17th century, but there is no record that they stopped here to explore and reprovision as they did at the Farallones. The specter of a foundering galleon driving upon such a treacherous shore was sufficient reason to stand well off from the coast at latitude 37° North.

A few records of the avian inhabitants of the mainland do exist. We know that the once-numerous California Condor plied the rising thermal of the Año Nuevo coast in post-Gold-Rush days. The first scientific descriptions of these now perilously endangered giants were based on observations of birds feeding on whale carcasses on Monterey Bay beaches. We know also that the Short-tailed Albatross was once common in the waters of the region. Today, the total world population of these North Pacific wanderers numbers less than 100 individuals.

Little attention was given to Año Nuevo's vertebrate fauna until the last few years of the 19th century. Professor Stark of Stanford University visited Año Nuevo Island with a bulky, glass-negative camera to document the island's flora and its pinniped inhabitants. G. Dallas Hanna and John Rowley of the California Academy of Sciences worked on Año Nuevo Island in the 1920's; their observations included notes on Western Gulls and other current inhabitants.

It was not until 1942 that a regional overview of the avifauna near Año Nuevo was produced. In that year Robert T. Orr published his extensive observations of land and marsh birds from the Big Basin region of the Santa Cruz Mountains, including Pescadero Marsh, the Waddell Creek watershed, and Año Nuevo Point. Later, in 1961, he teamed up with Thomas Poulter to begin a long series of investigations of the pinnipeds on Año Nuevo Island. Orr observed the birdlife on many of his visits; his notes form the only substantive historical record of this avifauna. He noted the effects of burgeoning pinniped populations and the introduced brush rabbits on the vegetation of the island. In the years since he began his observations, about half the greenery has disappeared, and with it the last of the breeding populations of two of the island's birds, Killdeer and White-crowned Sparrow.

Since the summer of 1972 censuses of both island and mainland birdlife have been undertaken. In addition, recent banding and color-marking of nesting Western Gulls and shorebirds on Año Nuevo Island has added information on the dispersal of local birds. Amateur ornithologists working on the mainland have contributed further information toward interpreting the natural history of the region's avifauna.

HABITATS

The major habitats available to birds, and the varied features of these areas, determine the kinds and numbers of birds at Año Nuevo. These include a freshwater pond surrounded by reeds and dense willow thickets that covers one hectare and is 1 to 4 meters deep (depth varies with season and rainfall). The pond area is seasonally very productive, supplying food for a wide variety of waterfowl, waders, and landbirds. Many resident landbirds also choose nest sites in the pondside foliage.

Beyond the pond, abandoned agricultural lands stretch in all directions. Fields that only 10 years ago supported symmetrical rows of brussels sprouts are now being reclaimed by native wild plants through the process of ecological succession (see chap. 3). Large flocks of rather drab-plumaged seed-eaters forage in these open areas. The fields also support an extensive rodent population, which is fed upon by an unusually large and diverse number of raptorial predators. The fields are bordered by hedgerows of Monterey cypresses that provide protection from both wind and predators.

West of the old sprout fields are large expanses of sand dunes separated by areas of coast chaparral. Though small streams and depressions fill with water during winter, this habitat is dry and harsh throughout most of the year. Continually shifting sand renders the area virtually barren of avian food resources. But such harshness provides a degree of security for those species hardy enough to survive there; the thick brush is nearly impenetrable to would-be predators. A small fauna of omnivorous landbirds inhabits the chaparral, and during wet seasons insectivorous species forage in the safety of the willows. A few cryptically colored shorebirds actually nest on the dunes. Preservation of the dune habitat at Año Nuevo is critical in light of the toll that human disturbance (i.e., dune buggies, trampling, etc.) is taking on similar areas elsewhere in California.

The Reserve includes several kilometers of ocean shoreline. This coastline supplies renewable food resources for numerous seabirds and shorebirds. Bird watching along the shores of Año Nuevo is correspondingly very rewarding. Most of the Reserve's shoreline consists of sand and pebble beach. The beachline affords usable, open bird habitat throughout the year, but feeding conditions vary with season and tide level. The high winds and surf which accompany winter storm activity provide a temporary resource of great importance. Loosened kelp, trash, and driftwood brought seaward by rain-swollen streams are cast ashore by high seas. Flotsam and debris alter the original beach habitat

The black-and-white striped head pattern of adult White-crowned sparrows contrasts with the brown and tan crown markings of juveniles. These birds first nest at age one. (F. Lanting)

Below, **Marsh Hawk, male.** These commonly seen raptors are sexually dichromatic; males are basically pale gray, females are streaky brown. Birds of both sexes exhibit a white rump. (F. Lanting)

by providing breeding and hiding places for various invertebrate prey species.

Sheer cliffs and small rocky islets border much of the Reserve's coastline. These areas provide little in the way of food for birds, but they are important as roosting and nesting sites that are secure from land-based predators and disturbance.

Immediately seaward of the beach is the shallow intertidal zone. The productivity of this zone determines the size of the bird population that can be supported locally. The Año Nuevo coastline includes many different intertidal habitats and a correspondingly diverse intertidal fauna (see chap. 5). This rich intertidal life in turn supports a substantial and varied population of seabirds and shorebirds.

The open waters of the Pacific Ocean are another habitat rich in avifauna. Elsewhere along the coast, landbased observers will see only seabirds such as gulls, cormorants, and ducks—species that either return to shore each day or rarely stray beyond the surf zone. But from Año Nuevo Point one can see pelagic seabirds as well. Waters off the Año Nuevo coast overlie the continental shelf and are relatively shallow (less than 200 m). Most oceanic seabirds spend their time at sea over these productive shallow waters. Near Año Nuevo Reserve the shelf is relatively narrow, extending only 25 km offshore. Seabirds are therefore likely to be concentrated nearer the coastline at this point and more clearly visible from land.

There are many ways of describing the avifauna of Año Nuevo Reserve. The species can be grouped by habitat or according to food requirements. Still another approach is to run through the list taxonomically, according to evolutionary relationships.

, There is, however, another approach. To the vertebrate biologist the single most striking feature of the fauna of Año Nuevo Reserve is its *seasonality*. How the animals behave, where they are found and in what numbers, even how they look, are all governed by the seasons. The dependence of birds upon the physical characteristics of their surroundings and the strikingly seasonal nature of these physical properties make this approach to the study of birdlife at Año Nuevo particularly appropriate.

THE SPRING: March Through Late May

The new year begins for birds in spring. Until March, the birds of Año Nuevo Reserve pursue their wintering routine, usually gathering in flocks to exploit limited food resources. They expend a good deal of time and energy trying to be comfortable in less-than-comfortable weather and pay little or no attention to the upcoming business of reproduction. Some may change a set of old, worn-out feathers for new ones. With the coming of spring, the physical environment changes and so do the birds.

Shifting winter storm winds give way in spring to steady northwesterlies. These winds generally blow parallel to the coast and promote the upwelling of deeper, cold waters, bringing nutrients to the surface for a surge of phytoplankton productivity. As winter rains abate, the upturn in productivity at sea is matched on land by the rapid growth of foliage and shoots, and the flowering of terrestrial plants. As freshwater pools and moist soil are warmed by the increasingly strong spring sun, insects and other invertebrates hatch and begin to multiply. The total effect is a rapid increase in both marine and terrestrial biological production that means more food for birds, be they herbivores, insectivores, or planktivores.

At the same time, day length increases, contributing to the flush of productivity and providing more hours for feeding. This is the season when the heavy food requirements of nesting and rearing of young can best be met. The pituitary gland of individual birds reacts to increasing day-length by initiating a series of neuroendocrine changes in the body. The gonads—the testes or ovaries—enlarge and begin mass production of the hormones that help to determine behavior in coming weeks. With these changes in the physical environment and in bird physiology, pair formation is initiated in those species that breed at Año Nuevo, and migration is cued in those birds that do not.

Freshwater Pond

In springtime the Año Nuevo pond is full of water and bustling with birdlife. Migrating ducks and warblers, as well as numerous local nesters, focus their activities at this freshwater habitat.

Many species of waterfowl require areas of freshwater for rest and forage during their long migration. Increasing human disturbance through landfill and water pollution has effectively eliminated many such areas in coastal California. This may explain why Año Nuevo pond, despite its small size, attracts such a wide variety of ducks.

A majority of visiting waterfowl are the "puddle" or "dabbling" ducks (Family Anatidae) which feed from the surface by "tipping up," heads underwater and tails pointed skyward. The males are brightly colored and easily identified. The duller brown females are more difficult to distinguish, but recognition by color and size of the wing patch (speculum) is possible. Mallards and Pintails are frequent visitors, and wigeons, teals (especially Greenwinged and Cinnamon Teals) and Gadwalls appear on the pond as well. Another pond species, the Shoveler, uses its spoon-shaped bill to stir up and strain bottom-dwelling invertebrates and plants.

In flight, Pintails are easily distinguished from other pond ducks by their long, pointed tail feathers. (F. Lanting)

Many insectivorous land birds winter south of the United States-Mexican border, then fly north to Canada and Alaska to nest. They raise their young amid the rich summer insect hatch typical of northern latitudes. Such migrants move across the United States in waves, usually following one of several loosely defined paths known as flyways. Birds travel through California via the Pacific flyway.

Members of many different landbird families appear at Año Nuevo each spring. The best represented among these are the warblers and flycatchers, but vireos, thrushes, orioles, and others pass through as well. The highly colorful warblers are most conspicuous among these migrants. Males exhibit bold plumage patterns and bright colors (especially yellow); the females are only slightly less gaudy. The Wilson's Warbler and Yellow Warbler occur most frequently, but any of about 20 additional species of these active insectivores can appear during the

The green-headed male Shoveler and his mottled brown mate forage together in shallow pond waters. (F. Lanting)

spring. Some of these are rare vagrants from the eastern United States which turn up here when their usually reliable navigation faculties fail. Common migrants representing other landbird families include Western and Traill's Flycatchers, Western Wood Peewee, Warbling Vireo, Swainson's Thrush, and Northern (Bullock's) Oriole.

The shiny black male Red-Winged Blackbird with his bright red and yellow epaulettes is one of the more visible and certainly the most audible of the pondside nesters. Male birds arrive at Año Nuevo in February and immediately stake out breeding territories by means of aggressive postures, displays, vocalizations, even physical confrontation. A few weeks later the first waves of streaky-brown females arrive. Males perched conspicuously atop tall branches advertise for prospective mates by singing a raucous metalic melody. In low-density colonies Red-wing Blackbirds form monogamous nesting pairs, but where prime nesting spots are scarce, a female may choose to share a good territory with other females and join in a polygynous relationship.

Another pondside dweller, best located by his bubbling call, is the Long-billed Marsh Wren. Though they are year-round residents, marsh wrens are most noticeable during nesting season when the territorial

Male Red-winged Blackbirds are territorial and aggressive toward other males during spring and summer but join in mixed-sex foraging flocks in autumn and winter.

males become highly vocal. Each year marsh wren pairs build a series of 2-5 nests low to the ground and near the water, all but one of which are unused "dummies."

Hummingbirds often go undetected amid the springtime buzzing of dragonflies and bees. Measuring less than 8 cm and weighing just 4-6 gm, these are the only birds capable of hovering without the aid of wind; they can actually fly in any direction, even backward. In most seasons, hummingbirds are noticeable only as they feed on the nectar of red and yellow blossoms. But in spring the males perform elaborate aerial courtship displays distinctive to each species. Local birds swoop acrobatically in a pendulum motion, slowly rise to 30 m or more, then dive abruptly to within a few cm of a female, sounding a loud "pop" or "vreep" as they apply the brakes. Males are marked by the presence of a throat patch or gorget which flashes brilliant, iridescent red when struck by sunlight.

Two hummingbird species are common in the Reserve during spring. Anna's Hummingbird, the only hummingbird whose range falls almost entirely within the United States, is a resident along the central coast throughout the year. The green-backed male is the only North American hummer with a true song; he often voices his squeaky notes from a conspicuous perch. Allen's Hummingbirds arrive from Mexico in late February and remain here through summer to nest. The rufous-backed males are particularly visible as they swoop about in courtship displays.

Males of both species aggressively defend nesting and feeding areas against intruders of all sizes.

Fields

Above the open fields around the pond several species forage by "hawking," or flycatching on the wing. These are the swallows and swifts, two unrelated groups that have developed nearly identical feeding habits through the process of convergent evolution. Swallows are the agile, slim-winged creatures that sail low over fields or ponds. Four species of swallows arrive at the Reserve each spring: first the Tree Swallows, then Barn and Cliff Swallows, and finally Violet-green Swallows. Barn and Cliff Swallows both nest within the Reserve, constructing homes of mud and feathers under eaves of buildings on both the island and mainland. Unlike most landbirds, swallows nest in colonies in which brothers and sisters hatched the previous year assist parents in raising chicks.

Swifts forage high above the ground, where they feed by flying through swarms of tiny insects, large mouths agape. They are distinguished from swallows by their jerky, stiff-winged flight pattern (they appear to beat each wing alternately). At Año Nuevo, Black Swifts and White-throated Swifts occur near seacliffs and over the pond.

The tall grass and brush of the Reserve's open areas provide cover for substantial populations of sparrows, finches and other members of the finch family (Fringillidae). Members of this largest of North American bird families occur in a wide range of habitats and exhibit a variety of physical characteristics, but all are equipped with thick, conical beaks for cracking seeds. Field-dwelling finches of the central coast are marked by rather drab plumages. Singing territorial males are most visible, especially the clear-breasted White-crowned Sparrow and heavily streaked Song Sparrow. Reddish House Finches and pale Savannah Sparrows also raise broods in this brushy habitat.

Chaparral and Dunes

For denizens of the chaparral, willows, and other dune vegetation, spring is a season of plenty in a usually harsh environment. The best representative of this habitat is a bird native to California and found nowhere else, the Wrentit. Light chocolate in color, with decurved beak and long tail, this bird is best located by a distinctive call that sounds like a ping-pong ball coming to rest. Other common residents of this habitat include goldfinches, towhees, bushtits, and Bewick's Wrens.

Nesting season at Año Nuevo Reserve. *Upper left,* **Mud nests at a Cliff Swallow colony;** *upper right,* **nestling Barn Swallows;** *lower left,* **Tree Swallow, adult;** *lower right,* **Black Swifts nest in cliff crevices inaccessible to predators.** (F. Lanting)

Shoreline

Migrant shorebirds appear on beaches throughout the Reserve but seem to prefer those near Año Nuevo Point. Flocks of turnstones, sandpipers, and plovers search beaches and rocks for food while awaiting the internal signal to begin their long northward flights. Some go no farther than Oregon or Washington, while others continue to the Alaskan North Slope before breeding. While still at Año Nuevo many species undergo a pre-nuptial molt, exchanging worn-out feathers of the drab winter plumage for more striking breeding dress.

Shorebirds increase in number in late April and early May; then suddenly they are gone. A few youngsters remain behind as do a few adults whose age or body condition preclude the dangerous trip. Many of these will not see the return of their kind in the fall.

Spring migration at Año Nuevo. *Above,* shorebirds congregate on sandy beaches before departure; *below,* Brants often pass near the Reserve as they journey northward to Alaskan nest sites. (F. Lanting)

249

The wealth of migrant shorebirds and landbirds is of interest not only to human birdwatchers but to avian ones as well—specifically the raptorial predators, the hawks and falcons. The Peregrine Falcon, fastest flyer of all birds, once nested commonly on remote cliffs of the California coast. A few pairs still do so, but reduction of habitat, pesticide buildups in the food chain, and the theft of eggs and young by falconers have made this species rare and endangered in California. Currently these sleek, long-winged hunters appear only in spring and fall, as they follow their food sources to and from safer breeding sites in the far north. The Peregrine Falcon and the slightly smaller Merlin can be seen at Año Nuevo raising clouds of shorebirds from the beach or harassing landbird flocks in open fields.

A group of smallish hawks specially adapted for preying on birds are the accipiters. Light-bodied and broad-winged, they are capable of foraging even in dense brush and woodland, flying low over willows and other vegetation in search of small feathered prey. The Cooper's Hawk and the nearly identical though smaller Sharp-shinned Hawk are residents of the central coast. A few individuals of each species reside near Año Nuevo all year, but additional individuals may arrive during migration.

Island and Ocean

Many of the seabird species observed along the central coast are migratory. Some of these, such as the loons and grebes, form aggregations in early spring and then move northward en masse. The large streamlined loons dive to moderate depths (10-30 m) in search of prey which they spear with their bills. A few individuals winter at this latitude, but the vast majority appear only during migration. From March through June, tens of thousands of loons head north over open waters west of Año Nuevo Island. Most of these are Arctic Loons, but Common and Red-throated Loons pass by as well. The smaller and stockier grebes are more often seen in clumps than in lines. Flocks of up to 50-100 Western or Eared Grebes often rest "head-under-wing" in Año Nuevo Channel.

Spring is also the time of greatest abundance of Black Brant in the Año Nuevo region. As the only true saltwater geese, Brant require sheltered, tidal inlets with eelgrass, their principal food, during the long trek from Mexico to Alaskan nesting areas. Due to human dredging, filling, and hunting in the last few decades, only a few such sanctuaries remain on the California coast. The coves of Año Nuevo are often

Loons, such as this Red-throated, are rather nondescript in winter plumage. They molt into dramatic breeding dress by May, at which time they are more easily identified. (F. Lanting)

Eared Grebes dive for fish in fresh and salt waters of the Reserve. Often gathering into flocks, Eared Grebes are much more numerous than the similar Horned Grebes. (F. Lanting)

Brants are small, marine geese that stop to feed on eelgrass (*Zostera* sp.) in Año Nuevo channel. (F. Lanting)

Small, thin-billed Pelagic Cormorants *(left and center)* **usually frequent sheer cliffs, while the larger Brant's Cormorant** *(right)* **prefers flat nearshore rocks.** (F. Lanting)

visited by transient Brant in spring, and some birds may even remain all year, though not to breed.

Cormorants, a group of long-necked birds that also feed underwater, pursue nesting activities in the Año Nuevo area in spring. The smaller of the two locally breeding species, the Pelagic Cormorant, builds its solitary nest on inaccessible narrow ledges of vertical sea cliffs and lays 2 eggs. The larger Brandt's Cormorant prefers open and level nesting areas such as flat offshore rocks, where dense colonies form. The distance between nests in such colonies is often just 2 cormorant body-lengths, and the opportunities for robbing neighbors of nest materials are great.

Seven or more species of gulls migrate through the area each spring, but since most of them winter here as well, they will be discussed later in this chapter. An exception is the small Bonaparte's Gull. Each April and May flocks of 50-100 individuals appear along the coast on their way to Canadian nesting areas. Often these petite gulls settle in newly plowed fields and follow farm machinery as it exposes insects, mice, and lizards. Most gulls repair northward in spring to breed on maritime coasts in Alaska, Canada, and the Pacific Northwest. Only the Western Gull remains behind to nest and rear young on Año Nuevo Island.

Western Gulls are the most numerous and conspicuous of Año Nuevo's breeding seabirds. Some birds begin to pair up and maintain territories as early as mid-winter. There seems to be strong selective pressure to act selfishly with respect to food and roosting places during the non-breeding months (about August through March). As a result, it often takes many weeks of cautious posturing, vocal displays, mutual preening, and other courtship activities before two solitary, mutually aggressive adults begin to act as a cohesive breeding pair. Courtship is followed in April by establishment of nesting territories, from which each breeding pair will drive all intruders. Año Nuevo Island has supported 70 to 110 such territories each year since 1972, and the population appears to be growing. By the first week of May most of the nests are built, and a few nests contain eggs—usually 3 to a clutch. Both Western Gull parents share incubation duties. The "off-duty" parent hunts for food around the island, on the mainland shore, or out at sea, while the "on-duty" parent sits on the nest with the eggs.

THE SUMMER: June through August

By June most visiting birds have departed this area for nesting sites elsewhere. Those residents who remain spend the summer raising

Bonaparte's Gull, adult. The black head is characteristic only of adult birds during breeding season; juveniles and all wintertime birds exhibit white heads with a dark spot on each side. (F. Lanting)

The Western Gull is the only species of gull that breeds along the coast of central California; as such, these are the only gulls found regularly in the Reserve during summer. (F. Lanting)

youngsters. Timing of nesting, the number of chicks per brood, and the number of clutches (or broods) per season vary by species and with the availability of food. For birds that nest locally, summer is a season of intense activity. Breeding adults are subjected to the strain of raising youngsters while also sustaining themselves.

An average day on the central coast finds a calm, foggy morning, followed by clear afternoon skies and harsh northwest winds (up to 20-40 km/hr). These gusty winds maintain a high level of productivity at sea by promoting the upwelling of cold, nutrient-laden waters. In fact, yearly lows in sea surface temperature and annual highs in commercial fisheries' catches are recorded during this season. It is probable that more prey biomass is also available to fish-eating birds.

This productivity at sea is not matched in terrestrial habitats. As one windy, rainless day follows another, the Reserve is marked by parched fields and dry, cracked soil. The spring bloom normally provides adequate food supplies for most birds through June but as summer passes they must often compete for dwindling food resources.

Freshwater Pond

Though most of the Reserve is quite dry throughout the summer, the pond provides a dependable supply of freshwater, and therefore continues to be a primary focus of avian activity. Common residents of the pond area include American Coots, Pied-billed Grebes, Ruddy Ducks, American Bitterns, Black Phoebes, and Yellowthroats.

American Coots reside at the pond throughout the year, but are best observed during the summer. These well known black and white birds are not ducks; their closest relatives are the marsh-dwelling rails. Distinctive adaptations include chickenlike beaks for feeding on aquatic grasses, and elongate lobed toes which allow them to walk easily on soft mud or dive to moderate depths in search of food. Dominant birds aggressively patrol prime feeding spots, sometimes even stealing grasses from the mouths of surfacing foragers.

Another inhabitant of Año Nuevo pond that is duck-shaped and has a chickenlike beak is the Pied-billed Grebe. A plain brown body and white beak with a black band are the distinguishing features of a breeding adult bird. Unlike most North American grebes, they are solitary and prefer freshwater year-round. These unobtrusive birds frequently dive, then seem to vanish among the reeds.

The only common duck-shaped bird on the pond during summer which actually is a duck is the diminutive Ruddy Duck. The plumage is

These Downy Marsh Hawk
youngsters have begun to develop their flight feathers, but it
will be 6-8 weeks before they are
able to fly. (F. Lanting)

The familiar American Coot feeds on
aquatic and pondside vegetation. Lobed
rather than webbed toes distinguish these
birds from ducks. (F. Lanting)

drab during most of the year, but breeding males develop a rich russet
attire complemented by a brilliant blue bill. Ruddy Ducks breed at
several coastal lagoons near Año Nuevo, and it is likely that a few birds
nest at the Reserve's pond. These birds are strong divers, preferring to
forage on plant material.

One must arrive at dawn to see the elusive American Bittern. Though
large, this bird is so cryptically colored as to defy detection. A bittern
skulking slowly along the pond margin is difficult enough to discern,
but once frightened it will freeze and completely disappear against the
background foliage. These sneaky waders visit the pond in search of
small reptiles, crustaceans and fishes.

The Black Phoebe (a fly-catcher) and the Northern Yellow-throat (a warbler) are insectivores that reside along the central coast throughout the year. Both species nest within the Reserve and can often be observed near the pond. Resplendent in a black and white plumage, the Black Phoebe is by far the easier of the two birds to locate. Between flycatching for-ays, solitary individuals sit on conspicuous low perches and flick their long tails. They forage every-where in the Reserve, even on the island, but generally are found near water.

Black Phoebe

During nesting season, the black-masked male Yellowthroat sings a clear "witchety, witchety, witchety" song of territoriality. He and his maskless mate are more timid in other seasons, but they can be spotted just above ground level in thick vegetation (usually near water) as they flit about in search of small insects.

Fields and Hedgerows

The tall grass and low brush of the open fields support and shelter a large number of bird families. By mid-summer all but the latest broods of youngsters have fledged, and juveniles of many species accompany their parents during the first forays into unfamiliar habitats. Barn Swallows begin to lead their young on exploratory feeding excursions in June. Though fully able to fly, the young swallows are incapable of catching their own food for several weeks after leaving the nest. The adults manage to keep the brood together, leaving the youngsters temporarily in open areas or on low perches and bringing insects to ever-waiting mouths. It may take half an hour or more for the parents, working alternately or in tandem, to feed their hungry brood. By July youngsters are on their own, and by late August most Barn and Cliff Swallows depart the area for warmer southern climes.

As parental chores conclude and territorial impulses relax, many field-dwelling species begin to congregate in flocks. These are not pre-migration assemblages, but feeding groups whch are loosely main-

tained until the next breeding season. This tendency is most widespread
among resident ground-dwelling species such as meadowlarks, doves,
and quail.

Flocks of California's state bird, the California Quail, frequent the
Reserve's brushy areas, especially the hedgerows along the northern
border. Groups of pint-sized fledglings, struggling to keep up with their
parents, are a common sight in late summer. Male sentries watch over
groups of feeding birds; the three-note alarm call (the second note is
accented) rings across the fields on still days. If frightened, quail rely on
their powerful legs for escaping on the ground before using their short,
stubby wings.

Western Meadowlarks have vibrant yellow breasts marked with
black 'V's, but are uncannily adept at keeping their plain, brown-
streaked backs toward would-be observers. If flushed, the diagnostic
stubby, white-bordered tail becomes visible. These birds are common
throughout the Reserve's open fields, where they subsist on a wide
variety of plant and animal food.

**The loud, gurgling, flutelike song of the Western Meadowlark is one of the
Reserve's most familiar bird calls.** (F. Lanting)

The strong winds typical of clear midsummer afternoons restrict most landbird activity but assist the foraging efforts of large hawks. One group of large hawks, the buteos, have broad wings and tails to ride updrafts of air caused by sea winds deflecting off coastal cliffs or by temperature differentials (thermals). This soaring flight pattern uses only minimal energy, a critical consideration for a heavy-bodied bird which must spend long hours in flight in order to forage effectively. Buteos (sometimes called "buzzards" or "chicken hawks") are often condemned as pirates of domestic poultry; in truth they play an important role in controlling rodent populations and other agricultural pests.

The Red-tailed Hawk is by far the predominant buteo in this region. Body coloration is variable, but the broad rufous-colored tail is characteristic of adult birds (juveniles have brown tails). At Año Nuevo Red-tailed Hawks often perch atop power poles or tall pines on foggy mornings. Sunny afternoons find them overhead foraging for small mammalian prey throughout the Reserve.

Less than half the size of a Red-tailed Hawk, the American Kestrel (formerly called Sparrow Hawk) is another common resident of Año Nuevo. These small falcons are active predators on insects and small rodents. Kestrels are found in open areas throughout the Reserve, resting atop all types of perches or hovering (often within 10 m of the ground) as they search for food.

Another small carnivore, the less common Loggerhead Shrike, perches on low fence posts in the Reserve. Shrikes are not related to hawks, but instead are uniquely adapted song birds (Order Passeriformes). Shrikes are infamous for impaling their prey on sharp thorns or barbed-wire (hence their nickname "butcherbird"), but this behavior is not often observed.

American Kestrel. These small falcons are characterized by intricate face patterns and bright plumages; males exhibit blue wingtops, females have rufous ones.

The hooked beak and black mask distinguish the predatory Loggerhead Shrike from the similarly colored Mockingbird (F. Lanting)

California Thrashers (like Mockingbirds) have complex, ventriloquial songs.

The California Thrasher is a common inhabitant of the Reserve's vegetation. They are most often seen perched in low brush or racing along dune paths on long legs. They have characteristic sharply down-curved beaks which are used to find insects in leaf debris and soft soil. Related to mockingbirds (Family Mimidae), thrashers are talented mimics. It is not unusual to hear a half dozen different calls from a single bird.

Because woodland habitat is limited, few woodpecker species are resident in the Reserve. An exception is the Common Flicker, an omnivorous ground feeder. The local "red-shafted" race can be recognized in flight by salmon-colored underwings and a large white rump patch. At Año Nuevo small flocks of flickers (under 10 birds) roam brushy areas, particularly along the Reserve's northern border.

Dunes and Shorelines

Few birds spend much time in the harsh sand dune region near Año Nuevo Point. It is somewhat surprising to find two shorebird species actually nesting there. Recent censuses (1978-79) indicate that 5-10 pairs of Snowy Plovers and 1-3 pairs of Killdeers make up the Reserve's mainland shorebird nesting population. Nesting activities probably commence in late April and May, with youngsters fledging by late June.

Snowy Plovers set the standard for protective cryptic coloration among small shorebirds. In the dunes, nests, eggs, and brooding parents are nearly invisible against the sand. (F. Lanting)

Visitors are advised to tread carefully or even avoid remote dune areas during this season. Adult Snowy Plovers, their eggs and young, are so cryptically colored that nests are very difficult to detect. Adults remain motionless on the nest until danger is imminent, then attempt to lure the intruder elsewhere by feigning injury (Killdeers also exhibit this behavior).

Except during breeding season, Killdeer are highly visible; when raising their young they are far more wary. The two black neck bands, bright rufous tail, and loud "kill-dee" call are unmistakable. Generally they prefer wet grasslands over shorelines. In the Reserve, small numbers are most often seen near dune puddles and the freshwater pond. Killdeers formerly nested on Año Nuevo Island.

Summer is a peaceful season along Año Nuevo's mainland shorelines. Except for gulls from the island and occasional non-breeding stragglers, the beaches are deserted. Local cormorants and gulls forage in channel waters with very little competition.

Island and Ocean

The only seabirds who visit the Reserve with any regularity are the terns which nest 50 km to the southeast at Elkhorn Slough. Caspian Terns and Forster's Terns travel north to forage off the point, most frequently after nesting is finished. Terns are adept at capturing near-surface prey by aerial plunge-diving in clear water. At a distance Caspian Terns may be mistaken for gulls because they are large,

The gull-like Caspian Tern is this region's most common large tern during summer. (F. Lanting)

heavy-bodied, and lack forked tails. Up close, the black cap and heavy blood-red beak distinguish them as terns.

While the mainland shores are quiet, those of Año Nuevo Island are bustling with activity. Four species of seabirds are busy raising the season's broods: Western Gulls, Pelagic Cormorants, Pigeon Guillemots, and Black Oystercatchers. The Pigeon Guillemot belongs to the Alcidae, a family whose members generally resort to land only for nesting and breeding and remain at sea for most of the year. Guillemots exhibit the fishing habits of other members of the family, flying underwater with their short, powerful wings and using their webbed feet as rudders. Thirty to 40 pairs of Pigeon Guillemots have nested on Año Nuevo Island each year since 1971. These birds first appear in the area in spring (winter activities and range are unknown). They may have already formed mated pairs at sea, for often they appear on the island in twos, fours, and other even-numbered combinations. Pigeon Guillemots prefer small cracks and ledges on well-protected cliffs for nest sites, laying their 1- or 2-egg clutches in May.

Guillemots exhibit an interesting cycle of breeding colony attendance during nesting season. At the start of the breeding season, adults return to the colony at night, and leave for sea about sunrise. As the season progresses, they arrive earlier in the evening and depart later in the morning. Eventually, as incubation begins, birds are present at all times.

Young guillemots remain in the nest until they are fully feathered and weigh about as much as the adults. They then leap into the surf below, apparently well before they are capable of flight, and join one or both of their parents. The young remain with a parent for several weeks, fed and protected as their flight feathers grow in and their ability to find food develops.

Though over 20 species of shorebirds have been observed at Año Nuevo Island, only one, the Black Oystercatcher, currently breeds

262

Nesting seabirds of
Año Nuevo Island. (F. Lanting)

Pelagic Cormorant with nest and 2-egg
clutch.

Pigeon Guillemot, adult.

Brooding adult Black Oystercatcher.

Adult Western Gull incubating eggs. (F. Lanting)

there. Each spring and summer, fewer than 10 pairs build secluded nests and raise young on the rocky island shelves flanking the island. We know few details of local nesting patterns, partly because the birds' excessive shyness render them difficult to study. Though inconspicuous and not present in large numbers, oystercatchers may be seen foraging along rocky mainland shores outside of the breeding season. The black body with long red beak and pink legs and eye create a clown-like appearance which is unmistakable and unforgetable. The stout beak is used to pry open mussels, scallops and other shellfish and to chisel limpets off rock faces.

Fish-eating birds find summer a season of high food availability. Baitfish and squid stocks support local breeding birds, but also sustain an enormous population of oceanic visitors. Foremost among these visitors are the shearwaters—gull-sized members of a pelagic group called "tubenoses" (Order Procellariiformes) a reference to the presence of tube-like nasal sheaths atop the upper mandible. Each year millions of these open-ocean travelers migrate from southern hemisphere nesting areas in Australia, New Zealand and South America to spend their "winter" along the North American coast. Most abundant at this latitude is the Sooty Shearwater. Pink-footed, New Zealand, Short-tailed and other shearwaters are also recorded annually.

Shearwaters are powerful fliers, alternating stiff flapping strokes with gliding, characteristically flying low to the water, not rising more than five meters above the wave tops. Also skilled at underwater flight, they prey on small baitfishes, squids, and the larger planktonic invertebrates.

Human fishermen often scan the horizon for telltale wheels or gyres of actively fishing shearwaters and gulls to indicate the presence of food for the larger, commercially valuable fishes they themselves seek.

From May until September, the waters of the central coast may be literally blackened by enormous flocks of shearwaters, primarily Sooties. Single flocks, which may number hundreds of thousands of individuals, can stretch for many kilometers along the coast. Occasionally, when prey move close to shore, clouds of birds may be seen just beyond the surfline. Such large numbers of birds consume enormous amounts of food; more than 50,000 metric tons of fishes, squids, and crustaceans may be eaten annually. For comparison, this figure represents about as much biomass as is harvested annually by all commercial squid and anchovy boats in California.

Sooty Shearwaters. Dense aggregations of these oceanic travelers occur along the California coast each summer. Flocks numbering into the hundreds of thousands of individuals are not unusual. (F. Lanting)

THE FALL MIGRATION: Late August through November

Autumn is the most exciting season for birdwatching at Año Nuevo Reserve. Tropical breeders dispersing northward, migrants passing through, and early winter visitors all contribute to an annual peak in avian density. Each subsequent wave of migrants offers a new opportunity to see rare or unusual shorebirds, seabirds, and landbirds.

Between the high winds of summer and the storms of winter, autumn brings a period of calm, warm weather. The warmest air and sea surface temperatures occur in this season. Autumn is characterized by slack winds and warm, clear surface water. These conditions sometimes attract subtropical seabirds such as pelicans and frigatebirds to central coast waters. With dispersal of the young, the day-in, day-out strain on breeding adults gives way to a recovery period of fattening-up and, for some, a change of plumage. This respite is brief, and local residents are soon forced to compete with incoming migrants for available food. Once summer winds abate and days become hot, landbird activity is restricted to the cooler hours of dawn and dusk and is concentrated near the little remaining freshwater. In wet years, early rainfall relief may arrive in October or November. Early storms make the Reserve more habitable for terrestrial species and litter beaches with kelp and debris for foraging shorebirds.

Though the earliest migrants usually reach Año Nuevo by late September, the timing of fall migration is unpredictable. How birds nesting in Boreal and Arctic zones know the proper time to depart northern climes is still unclear. Weather patterns seem to fluctuate too rapidly to provide reliable cues. Instead, the autumnal decrease in daylength appears to be of paramount importance in initiating migration. Fall migration is more protracted than spring migration, and its pace is far more leisurely. Birds who rushed north in spring seeking prime nest sites gradually work their way south again, stopping often to feed. When food is located, migrants may stay for days or even weeks until the source is exhausted. Fall migration routes are correspondingly less direct, and migrants are often more widespread than in spring.

Freshwater Pond

The first arrivals are usually detected at the freshwater pond. Except for Ruddy Ducks the pond has been barren of waterfowl since spring. One group of ducks that annually appear in the Reserve during autumn are the "bay ducks." These are diving ducks who generally inhabit deep

As with all bay ducks, the male Greater Scaup sports a brighter plumage than his rather drab mate. (F. Lanting)

water areas such as protected salt water bays and large freshwater lakes. Male bay ducks are more strikingly plumaged than females, but lack the bright colors of puddle ducks. Among these, Buffleheads, Greater and Lesser Scaup, Canvasbacks and Ring-necked Ducks appear on the pond at Año Nuevo.

During fall migration eastern vagrants often appear at the Reserve. These tiny warblers, sparrows, and other passerines may get started in the wrong direction on their annual southward trek, heading southwest instead of southeast from the muskeg and broad-leafed forests of Canada. This mistake in navigation, termed "mirror-image vagrancy," may be caused by changes in prevailing wind directions as the young leave the area of birth. These rarities combined with "normal" western migrant populations make the central California coast the scene of great surges of migratory activity.

Though most migrant landbird sightings take place at the pond, migrants who are lost and tired can turn up in brushy areas throughout the Reserve and even on the island. For example, migrant kingbirds are regular autumn visitors in open fields. Kingbirds are blackbird-sized flycatchers recognized by their yellow breasts and erect posture. Records exist for the Western, Cassin's, and the rare Tropical Kingbird. A more common fall flycatcher preferring open habitat is the Say's Phoebe. Say's Phoebes closely resemble Black Phoebes (described earlier) in habits, but they are brown, with pale rust-colored bellies. These birds may spend the winter along the coast.

Fields and Dunes

Peak numbers of Marsh Hawks and White-tailed Kites occur in autumn when local populations are augmented by migrant birds. These sleek, agile predators of the open field are year-round residents of the Reserve. Marsh Hawks are most often seen floating lazily low over fields and marshes, long wings held in a dihedral (forming a "V") in the manner of vultures. These birds foraging for small birds and rodents represent one of Año Nuevo's most familiar sights.

White-tailed Kite.

Only a few decades ago White-tailed Kites were classified as rare by many authorities. Recent surges in Kite populations have been attributed to increased habitat afforded by agriculture and irrigation. Kites are considered non-migratory, but definite influxes of these birds into the Reserve have occurred in recent autumns. A visitor to Año Nuevo may see several Kites on any given day, but on a day in October 1974, 24 Kites were observed roosting in a single Monterey pine! These beautiful white-plumaged birds often hover 10-20 m overhead as they search for small rodents. Kites are so often associated with this behavior that the habit of hovering with wings held high is often referred to as "kiting."

Shorelines

Beginning in August, the vanguard of shorebird migrants arrives on central California coast beaches. These front runners are usually adults who have departed from nesting areas days or even weeks earlier than their young. In September and October the beaches and rocks of Año Nuevo harbor hundreds of these little bits of feathers and energy. Some stay the winter, but most pass on in a few hours or days.

Shorebirds are present in largest numbers at about the autumnal equinox, when the productivity of the waters close to Año Nuevo reaches a second annual high point. Nutrient enrichment due to the fecal wastes of thousands of California sea lions contributes to this late summer bloom of plant activity. At the time of the first autumn storms great quantities of kelp and other benthic algae are cast ashore on the Reserve's beaches. It is this food base that attracts kelp flies, beach hoppers, and other invertebrates, which in turn attract the migrating shorebirds.

The numerically predominant shorebirds at Año Nuevo during fall migration are the marine forms—those species that prefer seashores over estuaries or lagoons. Sanderlings, Black Turnstones, Marbled Godwits, Willets, and Black-bellied Plovers are the most common representatives of this group. Coastal visits by shorebirds typical of freshwater habitats are an interesting feature of fall migration. One conspicuous visitor is the largest western shorebird—the Long-billed Curlew. Somewhat larger than the similarly plumaged godwit, curlews are easily identified by their exceedingly long (16 cm or more) decurved beaks. Curlews generally prefer pastures and mud flats, but birds returning southward from Canada may drop in at Año Nuevo.

The stocky, short-necked plovers, with small stout beaks and large eyes, also pass through Año Nuevo during fall migration. The American Golden Plover is the premier migrant among shorebirds, travelling 20,000 km each year. The majority of Golden Plovers follow other flyways, but a few occur at Año Nuevo along with the similar and more common Black-bellied Plovers. A small cousin, the Semipalmated Plover, is another regular fall migrant here.

Dunlin, Western Sandpipers, and Least Sandpipers are common in the fall on Reserve beaches and also abundant at neighboring estuaries. All three species occur in small flocks foraging with other shorebirds. The more solitary Spotted Sandpiper is recognized even in spotless winter plumage by its odd habit of continually bobbing up and down. Slightly rarer species such as Baird's and Pectoral Sandpipers have

Autumn shorebird scenes at Point Año Nuevo. *Above,* a Black Turnstone and a Marbled Godwit contest a crab dinner. *Below,* a Dunlin flock in migration. (F. Lanting)

appeared regularly in recent years. Nineteen Pectorals were observed near Año Nuevo Point in September 1978! That same fall the very rare Buff-breasted Sandpiper and ultra-rare Ruff (a native of Eurasia) were sighted at the Reserve for the first time.

One group of shorebirds, the phalaropes, spend much of their time on the water, often well out to sea. These birds have lobed toes, more efficient for swimming. Phalaropes forage along shorelines with other shorebirds, but more often they "dip" for small near-surface prey in shallow or clear water, sometimes stirring them up by creating small whirlpools. At Año Nuevo they frequent beaches, the pond, and even small rain puddles. Three phalarope species occur along the central coast each fall: the Northern in August and September, the rare Wilson's during autumn, and the Red in late fall and winter.

This Red Phalarope exhibits the "gray" winter plumage. Phalaropes are sea-going sandpipers that sometimes forage on beaches and shallow pools at Año Nuevo. (F. Lanting)

Over time these various shorebirds have diverged in form and behavior: adaptations that enabled them to minimize competition for food. Beak and leg length may limit foraging habitat and determine food preference. The smallest forms, Least Sandpipers and Snowy and Semi-palmated Plovers, specialize in feeding among the drift and on rock platforms above the surf. Their stubby bills and legs are suited for shallow probing and surface invertebrate foraging. The next larger "peeps," such as Sanderlings, and Sandpipers, probe for invertebrates at the water's edge. Larger waders, such as curlews and godwits, have longer bills and legs, which permit them to probe deep in soft mud or wade to chest depth (20 cm or more). Each species of sandpiper feeds on whatever prey items are available within their restricted band of mud-flat, sand, or rock habitat. Species which are most similar in feeding strategy usually arrive at different times, minimizing competitive pressure for food resources.

Ocean and Island

One of the unique visitors to Año Nuevo is the beautifully colored Harlequin Duck. The frequent sightings of Harlequin Ducks in the tidepools and surf near the mainland shore represent something of an ornithological mystery. The majority of sightings occur in later summer and autumn, but records exist for all seasons. The paradox is that Harlequins are known to breed only along the banks of high-mountain torrents and Arctic shores. Since no nest records exist for Santa Cruz Mountain streams, the presence of birds in breeding plumage is certainly puzzling. These birds could simply be non-breeders, but the possibility of local nesting should not be dismissed. Gaudily-painted male birds have been observed near the Reserve more often than the plainer females.

Seabirds nesting in warm, southern latitudes conclude their nesting activities earlier in the year than do breeders at higher latitudes. The warm water conditions of early fall enable many of these more tropical species to disperse northward as far as Año Nuevo. The most abundant of these travelers are Elegant Terns, Manx Shearwaters, Heermann's Gulls, Xantus' Murrelets, and the endangered Brown Pelicans. For many, central California is about the northern limit of post-breeding dispersal.

The most familiar of these southern imports is the Brown Pelican. As recently as 1959, pelicans nested as far north as Carmel Bay, but subsequent changes in weather patterns, fluctuations in availability of anchovies (the primary nesting season prey) and pesticide-related egg-shell thinning have greatly reduced the California breeding population. Currently, fewer than 1,000 birds nest on islands off southern California, though several tens of thousands nest in Mexican waters. Brown Pelicans reach central coast shores by late July. White-headed, grayish-bodied adults arrive somewhat earlier than do the brown-bodied, white-

Brown Pelican, adult. Pelicans forage for small near-surface fishes by plunge-diving in clear water. (F. Lanting)

Large numbers of Brown Pelicans and Heermann's Gulls from colonies in Mexico, travel north to the central California coast each autumn to feed on anchovies and other baitfish. (F. Lanting)

bellied juveniles. They feed on small schooling fishes which are caught by aerial plunge-diving in clear waters. Pelicans forage along shores throughout the Reserve, most frequently in the channel, but prefer the more protected island for roosting. Peak numbers of pelicans are present at Año Nuevo from mid-August to mid-November, and most birds depart the region by January.

As pelicans move north they are usually accompanied by small, dark-bodied Heermann's Gulls. Adult Heermann's with contrasting black bodies, white heads, and red beaks are probably the easiest gulls to identify. Though adequate fishermen in their own right, these gulls often subsist on the scraps left over from pelican foraging.

In some years the autumn oceanic (warm-water) period is more prolonged. This is the time for some avian surprises. In the autumns of 1973, 1974, and 1979, sightings of Magnificent Frigatebrids and Blue-footed Boobies were not frequent along the central coast. In 1975, a Red-billed Tropicbird was seen on Monterey Bay. In mid-January, 1975 (not really autumn proper but an uncharacteristic period of calm seas and airs and elevated temperatures) two Little Gulls were spotted on the same day, one at Año Nuevo Island and one at Zmudowski State Beach on Monterey Bay. These unusual Little Gull records, among the first few for California, may well have been of birds that were fooled by unseasonable weather into dispersing north from Atlantic Mexico.

Virtually all the migratory seabird species which use the Pacific Flyway appear at Año Nuevo at one time or another. In terms of total numbers, the majority of individuals of all these species merely pass through this region, en route to southern latitudes. Among species that enter the region *only* during migration (the "pure" transient species) the following are the most common: Sabine's Gulls, Common and Arctic Terns, and the three jaegers—Pomarine, Parasitic and Long-tailed. During fall of 1974 all but the Long-tailed Jaeger made landfalls at Año Nuevo.

Jaegers are oceanic pirates who live by harassing other seabirds and forcing them to disgorge recently eaten fish and squid. These long-winged birds are such swift and agile fliers that even the fastest gulls and terns have trouble escaping them. The Parasitic Jaeger is the species usually seen from shore.

Long narrow wings, slender bodies and beaks, and forked tails give terns a light, airy appearance in flight: this distinguishes them from the bulkier gulls. Terns are agile fliers and adept at plunge-diving for fish. Two species which occur regularly are the nearly identical Common and Arctic terns. Arctic Terns set the standard for long distance migrants;

they travel 20-25,000 km between Arctic nesting grounds and Antarctic wintering areas twice each year. Common Terns generally travel nearer the coast then do Arctic Terns.

Autumn on Año Nuevo draws to a close in late November with departure of the last migrants. The first cold blasts of winter storms—born in the great weathermakers of the North Pacific, the Bering Sea and the Gulf of Alaska—hurry the last of the migrants south to warmer climes. Island and mainland beaches host only the few Sanderlings, Willets and others hardy enough to stand the winter. Gone are the ones that have been selected to risk a thousand or more additional kilometers of migratory flight rather than deal with even so moderate a winter as that at Año Nuevo Reserve.

THE WINTER: December through February

The first storms of winter buffet the California coast by early December. Heavy rains soak the thirsty landscape and large waves pound the Reserve's shores. Winters are wet in this region; 50 cm of rain may fall at Año Nuevo and perhaps 5 times that amount on the nearby mountains. The replenishment of the water table brings about the restoration of many terrestrial habitats valuable to landbirds. Dune field depressions filled with standing water attract shorebirds and other foragers. When storm activity is particularly fierce offshore, pelagic seabirds seeking the shelter of the coast often make landfalls at the Reserve.

By mid-December wintering species are present and their daily routines of feeding, socializing, preening and roosting are established. On Año Nuevo Island, young Western Gulls must compete for the first time with other Western Gulls of all age classes and with socially-dominant Glaucous-winged Gulls, newly-arrived from breeding sites in the north. Many of the young disperse to the mainland to seek out fish docks, garbage dumps, and other supplies of nourishment. Some stand the test of competition and hold their own on the island's beaches through the first winter and beyond. A number fail at the rigorous process of competition and perish.

Pond and Forest

The wintertime bird populations at Año Nuevo Pond are not as diverse as those found during migration, but total numbers of birds may be higher. In addition to the resident species, various seabirds may be present, especially during storm activity. Divers such as Eared and

Horned Grebes, Buffleheads and other sea ducks are frequent visitors. Various gull species come to the pond to bathe in the fresh water.

The stands of Monterey Pine which border the east side of the Reserve, and their accompanying understory, are too dry for heavy bird use in most seasons. But during wet winters numerous visitors from inland habitats may forage here. Among these are a few montaine nesting species such as the Yellow-bellied Sapsucker and Ruby-crowned Kinglet whose annual altitudinal migrations bring them to the central coast.

Restricted to the damp redwood environment in dry seasons, inhabitants of the nearby Santa Cruz Mountains travel more widely during the rainy season. One familiar visitor to Año Nuevo is the Dark-eyed (Oregon) Junco. Small bands of these tame, ground-dwelling finches search cleared ground for seeds, especially during light rains. Members of feeding assemblages maintain contact with each other by means of soft but audible "chips."

Two members of the thrush family also stray from redwood forest floors to visit the Reserve—the Hermit Thrush and the Varied Thrush. Thrushes are noted for sweet, melodious songs; the clear voices of these two species echo through woodlands on quiet winter mornings. Robin flocks also appear at Año Nuevo, most frequently roosting in treetops. Other forest-dwellers that visit the Reserve to feed include Acorn Woodpeckers, Brown Creepers, and several species of nuthatches, chickadees and jays.

The soft plant shoots plus the insect fauna of rain-softened topsoil support large numbers of wintering sparrows. White-crowned, Golden-crowned, and Song Sparrows form the bulk of the Reserve's winter population, but smaller numbers of Savannah, Lincoln's, and Fox Sparrows overwinter as well.

The winter sparrow population consists partly of resident birds (some White-crowned, Song, and Savannah Sparrows) and partly of visiting migrants (some White-crowned, Song, and Savannah, plus all Golden-crowned and Lincoln's Sparrows). Competition for food and cover is keen on both intraspecific and interspecific levels. Migratory individuals are at a distinct competitive disadvantage because they are less familiar with the terrain. Resident birds know from experience which areas are predator-free and food-rich. Some migrants seek to decrease this disadvantage by returning to the same wintering grounds each year. Even so, the toll is high, especially among juvenile birds; annual mortality levels of 50% are the norm for migratory species.

Owls are not common at Año Nuevo Reserve in most seasons since most prefer to forage in open country, then return to woodlands to roost. But during winter, migratory Short-eared Owls are regular visitors along the coast. Less nocturnal than many owls, Short-eared owls forage for small mammals among the sand dunes during early morning hours. Resident owls in the Reserve are most often seen at dusk near the buildings at the entrance; these include the Great Horned Owl and Barn Owl.

Most migratory insectivores find winter at Año Nuevo too harsh, but this is not the case with the Yellow-rumped Warbler. Nesting in high mountain conifers, Yellow-rumped (formerly Audubon's) Warblers migrate downslope and arrive on coastal lowlands in late autumn. Drab wintertime birds retain the basic warbler features but lack definitive spring plumage patterns except for the distinct yellow rump. Winter flocks of up to 50 or more individuals forage near freshwater using willows for cover.

Shoreline and Dunes

Along the central coast, the year's highest and lowest tides occur during the winter. Shoreline habitats are totally submerged by these seasonal high tides,. but subsequent low tides expose large areas of rocky intertidal, including much of the channel. These areas are normally free of predator pressure; as such they provide unusually productive foraging for a wide variety of waterbirds.

Wintering shorebirds are less diverse than those passing through during migration, but of those species present, numbers are fairly high. Most are hardy marine species who prefer the rugged open coast habitat. As is true for fall migrants, body size and beak characteristics offer more reliable cues for identification than the plain winter plumage patterns.

Among the more visible shorebirds are three large (over 30 cm) species, each with a characteristic beak. These species probe for invertebrates in soft sand or forage amid beachcast kelp. Most numerous are the Marbled Godwits, with their long, slightly upcurving, bi-colored beaks. On occasion a few Whimbrels associate with the godwit flocks, and can be distinguished by their distinctly down-curved beaks and striped head pattern. The gray-backed Willet with its shorter, straight beak exhibits an unmistakable black and white underwing pattern in flight and often sings loud plaintive calls when flushed.

A number of shorebird species are equipped with short beaks less effective for sand probing (turnstones, Wandering Tattler, Surfbird). They forage instead in beach-cast kelp and in rocky intertidal areas exposed during low tides. One species, the Black Turnstone, is ubiquitous along shorelines throughout the Reserve. Two of its habits stand apart from those of other shorebirds in the Reserve: they like to feed on elephant seal milk and peck at open wounds and blood of injured seals!

The numerically predominant winter shorebird at Año Nuevo is the Sanderling. These active sandpipers scurry about sandy beaches foraging in the wake of receding waves. Small groups feed in wet sand dune areas of the Reserve on some occasions.

The hoards of winter shorebirds spend the daylight hours roaming the Reserve's shorelines in search of food, but many return nightly to Año Nuevo Island to rest. The spectacle of several hundred shorebirds of 10 or more species congregated in a single sheltered island cove is a regular early morning phenomenon. Several species occur in greater numbers on the island than are ever recorded at the adjacent mainland. Flocks of Black Oystercatchers, tightly huddled against the blasts of winter storms, may number 90 to 100 individuals. One small northern shorebird, the Rock Sandpiper, has yet to be recorded on the Reserve's mainland shore, but it occurs regularly on the island.

Low winter tides also attract occasional long-legged waders to Año Nuevo. Large herons and egrets silently stalk tidepool fishes in the clear waters of the shallow channel. Small flocks of Snowy Egrets (maximum 30, but usually fewer than 5) and solitary Great Blue Herons are the most frequent visitors. Another fishing bird partial to clear channel waters is the Belted Kingfisher. Kingfishers hover or sit atop mid-channel poles while locating near-surface schooling fishes which they capture by plunge-diving in the manner of terns.

The group which probably exerts the greatest impact on the intertidal zone are the gulls. Gulls are both numerous and diverse at Año Nuevo Reserve during the winter months. Thirteen species have been recorded since 1972, 6 to 8 of which may be relatively common along the Reserve's shores. All of these except Western and Heermann's Gulls nest at northerly or inland breeding sites. Peak numbers occur daily near sunrise and sunset when 2,000 or more gulls may roost on mainland and island shores. Counts are lower during daylight when birds are foraging offshore. The numerically predominant gull species during winter are the large-bodied Western, Herring, and Glaucous-winged, and the smaller and more scarce California, Mew, and Heermann's Gulls. Five other gull species appear irregularly: Glaucous, Bonaparte's, Ring-billed, and Thayer's Gulls and Black-legged Kittiwakes.

Winter shorebirds at Año Nuevo Reserve. *Upper left,* a four-species foraging block; *upper right,* Sanderlings, masters of perpetual motion; *lower left,* Whimbrel at lunchtime (note the decurved beak); *lower right,* the ubiquitous Black Turnstone. (F. Lanting)

Tidepool waders. *Left,* **Great Blue Herons visit the Reserve from inland colonies. Despite their gangly, long-legged build, these herons nest and roost in the tops of tall trees.** *Right,* **Año Nuevo Channel is the best place to find foraging Snowy Egrets. Snowys can be told from other egrets by their black beaks and black legs with yellow feet. (F. Lanting)**

Several winters of observations at Año Nuevo have brought to light some interesting facets of winter society in gulls. In general, the large-bodied Western, Glaucous-winged, and Herring Gulls dominate at food sources that are both concentrated in space and nutritionally desirable. This includes such things as beachcast dead fish and the placentae and carcasses of elephant seals. Smaller gulls tend to be more specialized in a dietary sense and often exploit offshore fishing grounds (e.g., Heermann's Gull, Black-legged Kittiwake), forage along shorelines for tidal invertebrates, or follow behind farmers' plows (Mew and Bonaparte's Gulls, for example). None of these dietary categories are the exclusive domain of any one species; indeed, all species overlap when food is abundant. But in general, if food is concentrated, desirable and defensible, large birds will dominate in numbers; if it is spread out and in small units (like plankton), small gulls will be dominant. It is not that small gulls do not try to feed on concentrated food sources, but rather that the larger gulls prevent them from doing so.

Surf Scoter, male. Our most abundant sea-going duck is part of the subarctic nesting fauna. Molluscs and other invertebrates are taken by diving. (R. Branson)

Wintering gulls practice habitat partitioning in a manner similar to that employed by migrant shorebirds. Herring Gulls, which are very abundant at times in winter, are obviously interested in the food resources of the seal rookery at pupping time, but the larger Glaucous-wing and Western Gulls aggressively deny them access to food. As a result, Herring Gulls seldom forage on Año Nuevo Island and only return each night to roost. By day, they are found scattered along the mainland coast foraging among intertidal rocks, on sandy beaches, and at nearby garbage dumps.

Open Ocean Waters

The waters of Año Nuevo channel support small winter populations of marine waterfowl and other diving birds. Scoters, goldeneyes, loons, grebes, and a few alcids forage in sheltered channel waters, and in surf zones and quiet coves of adjacent shorelines.

Floating flocks or "rafts" of scoters are a familiar winter sight along this coast. Scoters nest in northern Canada and Alaska, then winter on coastal waters south to Mexico. Though sluggish in flight, scoters are skilled divers that eat primarily bottom-dwelling molluscs. Adult male

birds are black in coloration, females and juveniles dark brown. Surf
Scoters are the most numerous sea ducks in central coast waters,
White-winged Scoters are second, and Black Scoters are rare.

Red-breasted Mergansers nest on freshwater in northern Canada,
but a few (apparently non-breeding) birds appear in the coves of Año
Nuevo Island throughout the year. Rusty-headed female birds are
recorded about ten times more frequently than the green-headed males.
Mergansers are diving birds that catch fish in their long thin beaks
equipped with serrated edges.

Winter storms often drive pelagic seabirds in close to shore. Species
which most frequently appear at Año Nuevo include the Black-legged
Kittiwake (a gull), Northern Fulmar (a cousin of the shearwaters), and
several alcids. Kittiwakes and fulmars breed on cliffs in southern Alaska
and winter at sea from British Columbia to Baja, Mexico. Both species
are invasionary; this means that in some years numerous birds appear
along the central coast, while in other years, few or none do so. This
periodic presence and absence probably reflects geographic variability
of optimal food and environmental conditions (such as sea surface
temperature gradients or fronts).

Northern Fulmars are stocky, stubby-winged tubenoses who make
their living at sea as scavengers. In mid-January of 1974 a flurry of bird
activity was noted at the buoy southwest of Año Nuevo Island at dusk,
but identification was impossible in the fading light. An early-morning
census the following day revealed hundreds of fulmars paddling uncon-
cernedly about the larger inlets and coves of the island. They were
apparently heavily-laden with food, for no amount of human, pinniped,
or bird activity would cause them to flush. By evening, not one
remained.

The term "alcids" refers collectively to the murres, puffins, guillemots, murrelets and auklets, all members of the Auk family (Alcidae).
These heavy-bodied birds are awkward on land and in flight but are
expert divers. They have been called the northern hemisphere equival-
ent of the penguins. These gregarious seabirds generally prefer offshore
waters; their occurrence at Año Nuevo is irregular. Ten species of alcids
have been sighted on central coast waters, and six of these breed within
100 km of the Reserve.

The most abundant alcid locally, the Common Murre, is also the
largest (35 cm). In the middle of the last century nearly half a million
murres nested on the cliffs of the Farallon Islands, but the activities of
eggers supplying gold-rush era San Francisco markets practically decimated the colony. Now protected, the colony has recovered and cur-

Above, **Common Murres are California's dominant nesting seabird. Colonies are very dense and foraging at sea is often done in groups** *(below).* (W.B. Tyler)

rently numbers several tens of thousands. Murres from this colony forage in waters near Año Nuevo and can sometimes be seen beyond the surfline. More often, murres are seen when they come ashore with feathers coated by oil. Surface-resting species such as murres are exceptionally vulnerable to oil-spill pollution.

Another alcid found at Año Nuevo, the small Marbled Murrelet, was successful in concealing the location of its nests from biologists until as late as 1974. It was in fact the only North American breeding species for which a nest remained undiscovered. In early August of that year, a tree surgeon working in Big Basin Redwoods State Park in the Santa Cruz Mountains discovered a Marbled Murrelet nest, *with young*, 60 meters up in a Douglas fir tree! This finally confirmed conjecture by several local ornithologists that summertime sightings of adults and newly-fledged young at the mouths of coastal streams in Santa Cruz and San Mateo Counties indicated local nesting.

PERSPECTIVE

The story of Año Nuevo's birdlife that we have presented is the one we see today. But the situation is by no means static. The picture was quite different 500, even 50 years ago; and we should expect comparable change over the next 10, 20, or 100 years. Diversity and distribution of species in the avian community are affected both by the ongoing changes of the physical and biological environment and by the often more abrupt changes related to human activities. We have some idea of the more recent dynamics of the bird populations at Año Nuevo as they have been influenced by historical events and human activity along the central California coast.

The earliest human inhabitants in this area were the aboriginal Indians. These people and their descendants, the Ohlones, captured and ate flightless ducks and other birds as part of their regular diet, but they were not wasteful and their impact on the bird populations was probably small. At this time the moist and rich environment supported an abundance of terrestrial avifauna. As the island was most likely a peninsula of the mainland, seabirds probably nested on the more predator-free outlying rocks.

As the ocean's eroding action separated Año Nuevo Island from the continent near the end of the 16th century, small seabird colonies may have become established here. But with the extensive activities of 18th century sealers these colonies were probably disturbed. As marine mammal populations were reduced to uneconomical levels, the island was abandoned and the rookeries were left in peace. Though grazing cattle were introduced on the mainland, avian habitat disturbance was probably too small to endanger landbird populations.

The seabird colonies at Año Nuevo were spared disruption by Gold Rush eggers because of their small size. But with the construction of the island lighthouse in the 1870s, the resident birds were subject to nearly constant disturbance for the next 75 years. On the mainland, cattle grazing continued, certainly affecting the native plant communities but probably disrupting terrestrial birdlife to only a minor degree. As the human population of California skyrocketed, however, increasing numbers of visitors appeared at central coast beaches. This appears to have been sufficient impact to affect declines in sensitive species such as Peregrine Falcons, California Condors, and Bald Eagles.

After the light tower facilities were abandoned in 1948, the island again reverted to a wild state, and seabirds, seals, and plants reclaimed deserted shores. However, seabird colonies remained small as the island was visited off and on by abalone divers and curious tourists. Landbird nesting populations increased with the growth in island vegetation. On the mainland a change in land usage from grazing to row-crop cultivation caused a major impact on terrestrial bird populations. Chaparral-dwelling species disappeared with their habitat, and they were replaced by less sensitive open field species.

With state protection of the island and Point Año Nuevo in the 1960's the area began the period of relative tranquility which it currently enjoys. Island seabird colonies have slowly grown each year. But with ballooning seal numbers, and expansion of the introduced brush rabbit population, island vegetation has been reduced and along with it, the number of visiting landbirds (except swallows). As the mainland returns to a natural brush community, more chaparral species may return to replace birds of the open field habitat.

The future of the avian community of Año Nuevo State Reserve is difficult to foresee, but it looks promising. Protected areas for migratory and resident wild bird populations continue to grow in importance as development pressure takes a toll on other wild coastal areas. It is here that the true value of the Reserve lies. Though the reserve contains few specific features that are not found elsewhere on the coast, it does represent many diverse coastal habitats in a single area. People visiting the reserve can see all of the dominant species of land, shore, and marine birds found from Big Sur to Eureka, in addition to a large number of birds visiting from nesting areas in Mexico, Alaska, and interior and eastern United States.

Future alterations to habitats at Año Nuevo State Reserve from impacts of management, protection, and natural processes like erosion, will reshape some of the familiar bird communities or replace them altogether. These changes remind us constantly of the close relationship of organisms with the structures and processes that make up their living environment.

References

Bent, A.C. 1964. *Life Histories of North American Nuthatches, Wrens, Thrashers, and Their Allies.* Dover Publications, New York, N.Y.

Bent, A.C. 1965. *Life Histories of North American Blackbirds, Orioles, Tanagers, and Their Allies.* Dover Publications, New York, NY.

Burch, S.E. 1979. *The Natural History of the Shorebirds of Año Nuevo State Reserve.* Unpublished thesis. University of California, Santa Cruz, Santa Cruz, Calif.

Davis, J. and Baldridge, A. 1980. *The Bird Year, A Book for Birders.* The Boxwood Press, Pacific Grove, Calif.

McCaskie, G. and P. DeBenedictis. 1966. *Annotated Field List; Birds of Northern California.* Golden Gate Audubon Society, Berkeley, Calif.

Orr, R.S. 1942. Birds of the Big Basin Region of California. *American Midlands Naturalist.* 27 (2): 273-337.

Peterson, R.T. 1961. *A Field Guide to Western Birds.* Houghton Mifflin Co., Boston, Mass.

Robbins, C.S., Brunn, B. and H.S. Zim. 1966. *A Guide to Field Identification; Birds of North America.* Golden Press, New York, N.Y.

Small, A. 1974. *The Birds of California.* Winchester Press, New York, N.Y.

7

Mammals

Burney J. Le Boeuf

L ESS THAN 200 years ago, the Año Nuevo region supported num-erous and diverse mammals both on land and in the sea. The abundance of fur-bearing and oil-rich marine mammals was important in attracting Spanish explorers, Americans, and other foreigners to this area, while at the same time the ferocity of some terrestrial carnivores repelled and made life difficult and dangerous for these pioneers. In time, wholesale exploitation of animals and human intolerance of animal competitors brought about drastic changes in the animal life of the area.

In this chapter, I shall resist the temptation to enumerate all of the mammals that can be found in the region. Instead, I shall focus on one terrestrial mammal, the grizzly bear, which dominated the land for such a long time, and also several marine mammals, especially the seals, which have a long history of being the most visible and in many ways the most important animal occupants of the coastline and Año Nuevo Island.

Our Sturdy Golden Bears

Before the arrival of Spanish explorers and missionaries, the grizzly bear, *Ursus horribilis,* was the most formidable terrestrial mammal in the environs of the Año Nuevo region and throughout most of Califor-nia. These large, fierce carnivores thoroughly dominated the lowlands and all of their inhabitants, including the Indians. The Ohlone, lacking weapons adequate to defend themselves against such an awesome foe, feared and avoided this animal as no other. Stone-age bows and arrows were no match for a grizzly bear that weighed up to 400 kg, stood over 2 m high high, had great physical strength, sharp canines, and long curved claws. The bear could outrun a man and even climb a tree after him.

287

Grizzly bears were once common in the Año Nuevo region. (C. Jonkel).

Although the Ohlones tried to avoid grizzly bears, it is a paradoxical coincidence that they used similar feeding strategies which brought them together at various times of the year. Grizzlies, like humans, are omnivores. And the California bear ate an impressive variety of foods: assorted berries, roots, honey, acorns, nuts, various grasses and especially clover, wild oats, wood-boring larvas, grubs, frogs, lizards, gophers, field mice, ground squirrels, fish, elk and deer, whale carcasses and other carrion, and after the Europeans arrived, domestic livestock and cultivated plants (Tevis and Storer, 1955). Like the Ohlone, grizzlies were opportunistic and nomadic, anticipating seasonal food sources. They did not wander the wild and rich land in random fashion but rather timed their movements to coincide with natural harvests. Thus, the two competitors were most likely to meet beneath oak trees during the acorn season, in a verdant clover field in spring, or along streams and creeks during the annual salmon and steelhead runs. The Indians almost always came out second best in confrontations, and many of them were killed. Early explorers noted that many Indians were maimed and lacerated and bore scars from previous bear injuries.

In contrast to the black bear, found at higher elevations, the grizzly bear was an object of extreme fear and respect in the Ohlone culture. Its powers were admired and envied, while its spirit was considered an odious and sinister force. The Indians were reluctant to hunt or trap these animals except in extreme circumstances, when competition over the same food made it necessary. If grizzlies attempted to rob an accumulated cache of acorns, the Indians countered by setting fire to the grass in an attempt to drive the bears back; or they protected the cache with baited pit-traps. On the rare occasions when an individual succeeded in killing a grizzly bear, he was permitted to wear the unmistakable badge of courage and skill, a bear-claw necklace. Eating grizzly bear flesh was taboo.

One of the first Spanish observations of grizzlies was in 1602. A diarist on Viscaíno's expedition noted the large number of grizzly bears at Monterey that came to the shore to feed on whale carcasses at night (Wagner, 1929). The Spanish did not confront the animal until many years later during Portolá's overland expedition to San Francisco. Portolá's soldiers, hungry for meat, were successful in hunting and killing a few animals. Although armed with lance, broadsword, and musket, the task was difficult and required several men and several shots to kill a single bear (Teggart, 1911).

This was the beginning of the end of the bear's reign at the top of the pecking order. The Spanish soon learned that destroying grizzlies was a sure way to earn the gratitude of the Indians, and they became more proficient at it. The Indians were so delighted that someone could successfully dispute the dominance of the bears that they brought gifts to the Spanish and this facilitated the task of the missionaries (Palou, 1913).

With the missions came the practice of cattle ranching, animal husbandry, and crop cultivation. The bears developed a taste for beef, pigs, and plants growing in the fields and took this easy, abundant prey in full view of herdsmen and farmers. The bears even began to loiter near the missions, posing a constant threat to livestock, Indians, and pioneers. With this copious food supply the bears proliferated and prospered until the gold rush days.

During the early 1800s the bear population was diminished only slightly. Mission guards were ordered to shoot the animals for target practice to curtail the menace (Torchiana, 1933), and bears were captured for "entertainment." The traditional bear and bull fights, so popular in Spain, were a favorite pastime in coastal California during the Mexican period. The spectacles were held on feast days, during fiestas, and eventually every Sunday. It was a dangerous bloody sport which began with capturing the bear.

Two methods were used. In the first, several mounted vaqueros hid a slaughtered bullock in the hills. When a grizzly came upon the bait and began to eat it, the vaqueros broke from ambush and hurled their ropes at him. In the second method, the horsemen rode to a place where grizzlies congregated, chose the largest, charged him from front and rear, and then attempted to lasso him from all directions. According to Tevis and Storer (1955, pp. 145-146):

> The usual response of the grizzly was to rise on his hind legs and strike at the ropes coming at him like arrows. If he could sieze one he would pull it toward himself, paw over paw, despite strenuous resistance by the horse. And since the opposite end of the rope was attached to the saddle, the safety of the vaquero depended on the speed with which a companion could lasso one of the paws and gallop off to throw the animal down.

Vaqueros capturing a grizzly. (After Evans, 1974).

Reatas were often greased to make it difficult for the bear to grip the rawhide (Rojas, 1953). Similarly, the horse's tail was greased; for if the bear caught it, he could drag both horse and rider backward. The bear was held captive only a short time before the fight. Many of the bears that fought in Santa Cruz were captured at La Cañada de la Salud, the Waddell Creek entrance to Big Basin State Park.

The grizzly's adversary in the arena was "the lithe, thick-necked Spanish bull, sharp of horn, quick of foot, always ready for a fight, and with a charge like that of a catapult (Kingsley, 1920, p. 22)." A 20-meter leather cord tied to the hind leg of the grizzly, and attached to the forefoot of the wild Spanish bull, kept the antagonists close together in the ring and discouraged the bear from vaulting the barrier and mauling the crowd. The bull usually initiated the attack. He roared, pawed at the earth, and pranced around the ring dragging the enraged bear. Suddenly, he would charge straight at the bear with all the speed and fury he could muster and stab at the bear with his horns. The bear would spring for the neck of the bull and attempt to get a stranglehold while sinking his teeth into the bull's sensitive nose or tongue. If the bull was bitten, he bellowed horribly. "The noise was terrific and the dust rose in clouds, while the onlookers shouted as they saw that the fight was deadly and witnessed the flow of blood (Hittell, 1885, p. 638)." At this point the bear might wrench the bull's head to one side and snap his spine. If the bear failed to gain a quick stranglehold, the bull plunged his long horns into the bear's body and tossed him high into the air and then gored him to death as he lay on the ground. The grizzly usually won, the scene was always bloody and dusty, and the crowd screamed with excitement.

In reality, grizzly bears were an unquestionable hazard to the early California pioneers (and vice versa) just as they had been to the Indians. Over 50 incidents that involved bears attacking humans were reported in central California newspapers during the period, 1851-1860. The risks and consequences of an encounter with a bear to an early Californian is perhaps best summed up by the following philosophy (Anon., 1861, p. 602-603):

The risk was great, to be sure. I knew several gentlemen in California who had been horribly mutilated by these ferocious animals. One had the side of his face torn off; another had one of his arms "chawed up," as he expressed it; a third had suffered paralysis from a bite in the spine; a fourth had received eighteen wounds in a fight with one bear; and I knew of various cases in which men had been otherwise crippled for life or killed on the spot. Hence the peculiar charm of a fight with a grizzly! If you kill your bear, it is a triumph worth enjoying; if you get killed yourself, some of the newspapers will give you a friendly notice; if you get crippled for life, you carry about you a patent of courage which may be useful in case you go into politics. ... Besides, it has its effects upon the ladies. A "chawed up" man is very much admired all over the world.

With the discovery of gold, a spectacular human invasion ensued which was to change California for all concerned, men and bears. A vast stream of gold-hungry Americans flowed into California and milked the land for timber, fur, gold, and all manner of available food (Gordon, 1977). Grizzlies and the energetic and resourceful Americans could not live in close proximity, and the rising tide of human population foredoomed the future of the bears in California (Tevis and Storer, 1955).

To the American settlers, the bear menace to life and livestock was more of a real concern than it was to Spanish and Mexicans before them. The bear slaughter began in earnest and took many forms. Men slew bears in self defense and to protect their cattle and crops. Yankee ingenuity contrived log cabin traps to capture grizzlies, then later steel traps produced by local blacksmiths or manufactured in eastern states. Set guns, whaling guns, sapling pole spring traps, and strychnine-poisoned honey or tallow were used to kill grizzlies. Miners, farmers, and eventually market hunters hunted bears for meat, a rarity in pre-gold-rush days. Roast grizzly or black bear steaks were prominent features on the bill of fare in mining camp restaurants. Bear fat was used as oil; the hides were used as rugs or bedding. The greatest reduction in the once immense bear population occurred between 1849 and 1870.

The Santa Cruz mountains were among the last strongholds of the grizzly bear, which declined here rapidly between the years 1850 and 1890. Early in this period, a bear would occasionally wander into Santa Cruz searching for scraps around the slaughterhouses and terrorize everyone in the streets. The grizzly's demise in Santa Cruz County was caused primarily by the destruction of its habitat. Railroads were built, the rivers dammed, the forests cleared, and the fields cultivated. The bear ran out of places to go to avoid the encroaching wave of human civilization. By the 1870's, grizzlies were rare. A few were reported at Green Oaks ranch, apparently attracted to honey, apples, and skim milk put out for the hogs. Violent, unpredictable encounters with bears still occurred, such as the mauling and death of William Waddell near the creek which bears his name (Santa Cruz Sentinel, October 5, 1875). But these incidents grew more and more infrequent. The last grizzly bear in Santa Cruz county is thought to have been killed in 1886 (Welch, 1931).

There are no grizzly bears in all of California today. The range of *Ursus horribilis* recoiled and contracted from the advance of civilization. Today's grizzlies live at higher elevations of the Cascade mountains of Oregon, Washington, and Idaho, the Rocky Mountains of Montana, parts of Canada and Alaska. The only signs that remain of this former monarch in California are on state flags, in the names of university football teams, a few place names, and in the myths and history books about early California.

What has been the effect on the ecosystem of exterminating a top trophic level predator and putting ourselves in its place? A staggering and profound shift of balance in nature, to say the least. All of the terrestrial animal populations in the Año Nuevo region have undergone drastic changes during the last 200 years, due primarily to the changes man wrought. Deer, mice, wolves, coyotes, and mountain lions have all been affected directly or indirectly by the bear's downfall and our rise to prominence. Human impact on the lives of terrestrial mammals in the Año Nuevo region has been more significant than forest fires, earthquakes, or hurricanes. The role of humans is an essential element in understanding fluctuations in the frequency and distribution of animals that lived in the Año Nuevo region during the last 200 years and those that are living there today.

Marine Mammals

The sea mammals of Año Nuevo suffered a similar fate as the grizzly bear during the last century. In 1800, seals and whales were abundant along the entire California coast (Scammon, 1874). During the early 1800's, the exploitation of these mammals was conducted on such a grand scale that the stocks were severely depleted and species such as the Guadalupe fur seal and the northern elephant seal were virtually extinct by mid-century. Unlike the grizzly bear, the decimated populations of marine mammals recovered. These animals have come back to the Año Nuevo area, and formerly endangered species are prospering here today.

The silhouette of Año Nuevo Island is low, flat and dominated by the abandoned lighthouse keeper's house and the old light tower. The tower toppled in 1976. (B. Le Boeuf)

Año Nuevo Island lies 800 m offshore. When seen from the mainland, the island silhouette is low, flat and unimpressive. From the air, one sees a speck, an exposed conglomeration of rocks in the path of ground swells. At low tide, the island consists of less than 12 acres of layered beds of Miocene cherty shale, which slope down to the southwest. Gently graded reefs and smooth slabs of shale are on the seaward side. The island is approximately 396 m long and 259 m wide. It is only 11 m at its narrowest. There are two sandy beaches, one on each side of the island, and each is over 90 m in length. The highest parts of the island are covered by sand on which various plants grow. There is little vegetation on the southeastern part of the island, a result of animal activity.

This tiny island is the focus of virtually all seal and sea lion life in the area. The magnitude of pinniped traffic on such a small place is staggering. At least 12,000 sea lions used the island in 1968. Assuming that each animal weighed 136 kg, this represents 1,632,000 kg of sea lion flesh! A decade later, over 3,000 elephant seals averaging approximately 450 kg apiece, were counted on the island, adding another 1,350,000 kg to the biomass. The visual impact of this number of animals is as impressive as the biomass estimates.

Año Nuevo Island is the most important pinniped rookery and resting area in central and northern California. (The only other California islands that support more seals and sea lions are San Miguel and San Nicolas Islands, two considerably larger islands in southern California.) Why Año Nuevo? What is it about this tiny island that makes it so attractive to these marine mammals? Before responding to these questions, a short digression on pinniped origins is necessary.

Pinnipeds are descendants of terrestrial carnivores that entered the sea approximately 25 million years ago in search of food. Unlike whales, who began to exploit the sea earlier and hence are more adapted to the water, present-day pinnipeds still reproduce and rest on land. Perhaps this is because parturient mothers and their young are too vulnerable in the water when faced with more aquatically adapted predators such as sharks and killer whales. Though seals and sea lions breed on land, not just any land will do. The ideal landing place for Pacific coast pinnipeds are islands free of terrestrial predators such as bears, wolves, coyotes, and mountain lions. But islands are scarce along the California coast, particularly in northern California. This is the best explanation for the popularity of Año Nuevo Island; it is virtually the only island with sloping rocks and sandy beaches between Point Conception in the south and the northern border of the state. Moreover, it juts out into the sea in close proximity to the rich upwelling currents that bring cold water and nutrients from the ocean floor. Squids, popular items in the diet of most local species, are abundant in Monterey Bay. The rocky Farallones, near the mouth of San Francisco Bay, are far less hospitable and less habitable. Thus, Año Nuevo Island is a suitable and convenient place for pinnipeds to rest while feeding in the area.

Pinniped use of the Año Nuevo area is not a recent vogue but rather a long-standing tradition. Seals inhabited this region long before the sea cut an island away from the projecting peninsula. Some of the best Miocene fossils of pinnipeds on the west coast of North America come from the general Santa Cruz county region. Analysis of kitchen middens at Año Nuevo Point suggest that the coastal aborigines used local pinnipeds for food. Francisco Gali, the Spanish explorer, noted that there was a seal colony here in 1584. Although seal hunting was almost certainly conducted on the island early in the 19th century, there is no record of such activity until 1878 (U.S. Coast Guard, Año Nuevo Lighthouse Keeper's Log Books, July, 1877 to May, 1948).

At present, the island is used by four species of pinnipeds, all year-round residents: northern elephant seals, harbor seals, Steller sea lions, and California sea lions. All but the latter breed on the island. Representatives of all four species may be seen on the island at any time of year, but the number of each species, as well as the age and sex composition of those present, varies with time of year.

In describing each species in turn, I shall summarize the essential characteristics of each species, give a brief account of the vicissitudes of each population at the hands of profit-seekers, and describe the current status and distribution of each species in the world and on Año Nuevo Island in particular. By integrating these profiles, the reader should get a general idea of the kind and quantity of pinniped life he or she is likely to observe on a visit to this rookery at any time of the year.

The Northern Elephant Seal

The recovery of the northern elephant seal, *Mirounga angustirostris,* population from the oblivion of near extinction is one of the most remarkable achievements documented for any marine or terrestrial mammal. The settlement, growth, and development of the Año Nuevo colony is best understood viewed in this context.

In 1874, the whaling Captain Charles M. Scammon wrote that northern elephant seals once bred from Point Reyes just north of San

Francisco Bay to Cabo San Lazaro on the Baja California Peninsula (Scammon, 1874). He noted that they had been abundant along the entire coast during the early part of the 19th century before sealing began. Elephant seals, as well as many other Pacific coast marine mammals, were first exploited early in the 19th century. "Elephanting" went on at a great pace for about 40 years. The oil rendered from the blubber was important in industry, being considered second only to that of sperm whales. Seal oil was used in house and street lighting, for lubricating machinery, in the tanning process, and in making paint, soap, and clothing. One adult bull was reported to have brought as much as 210 gallons of oil.

A northern elephant seal bull surrounded by females and their pups trumpets a challenge to other males in the vicinity. (B. Le Boeuf)

Elephant seals were exceedingly easy prey for sealers. They were large and slow, predictable in their habits, and unafraid of humans. The slaughter was intensive and indiscriminate of sex and age. By 1860, the population was so depleted that elephant seals were no longer considered an economically feasible source of oil; by 1869, the species was considered to be virtually extinct. By 1884, no elephant seals were seen anywhere, despite the fact that several museum expeditions made thorough searches for them. However, in 1892, C.H. Townsend, on a

collecting expedition for the Smithsonian Institution, was surprised
and elated to find 8 elephant seals on a highly inaccessible, exposed
beach on Isla de Guadalupe, a volcanic island 247 km west of the Baja
California mainland. The museum collector killed 7 of the seals, even
though he realized that these animals represented "the last of an exceedingly rare species" (Townsend, 1912).

This was unquestionably the lowest point in the population's history.
Bartholomew and Hubbs (1960) estimate that there may have been as
few as 20 animals in the entire population in 1892, and probably no
more than 100. All elephant seals living today are descendants of
individuals who composed this remnant herd on Isla de Guadalupe.

The small remote colony went largely unnoticed until 1922, when the
Mexican government recognized the threat to the species and gave it
formal protected status. By this time, the Guadalupe colony had begun
to flourish. The United States government granted immunity to the
species a few years later when animals began to appear in southern
California waters.

During the present century, the elephant seal population has been
increasing logarithmically, and the animals have expanded their
breeding range from the Farallon Islands in the north to Isla Natividad
in Baja California, Mexico. Their range is almost as extensive as it was
in pre-sealing times. The map and table on p. 299 show the time and
pattern of recolonization and the number of elephant seals associated
with each of the 12 colonies in existence in 1977. The rate of increase of
the population has been extremely high since the population bottleneck
incurred during the last century. More than 80,000 elephant seals were
living in 1984, and the population is still growing.

Año Nuevo Island was colonized by immigrants from southern California islands. The development of the colony has been thoroughly
documented. From 1890 to 1948 no elephant seals were seen by U.S.
Coast Guard personnel based on the island or by California Fish and
Game deputies who visited the island periodically to census sea lions.
The first indication that the animals had returned was when Melvin
Johansen, of the Snow Museum in Oakland, observed 2 subadult males
and 2 females in late July of 1955 (Oakland Tribune, July 31, 1955). In
subsequent years, non-breeding animals continued to be observed in
increasing numbers. Breeding began on the island in 1961 with the birth
of 2 pups (Radford, Orr, and Hubbs, 1965). The number of pups born
on the island each year since that time is shown in p. 301. The pattern
of fluctuations in the number of elephant seals seen on Año Nuevo
Island during the year is called the annual cycle and can be divided into

A large crowded elephant seal rookery on the isolated oceanic island, Isla de Guadalupe. This island provided the only sanctuary for the few elephant seals that survived during the last century. By the 1970s this island was crowded and was sending off emigrants to other Mexican and California islands. (B. Le Boeuf)

four seasons: winter breeding, spring molt for females and juveniles, summer molt for males, and fall haul-out of juveniles. The number of seals censused increased each year from 1961 to 1974 (see p. 300). The winter and spring peak numbers in 1980 were more than double the peak numbers shown for 1974.

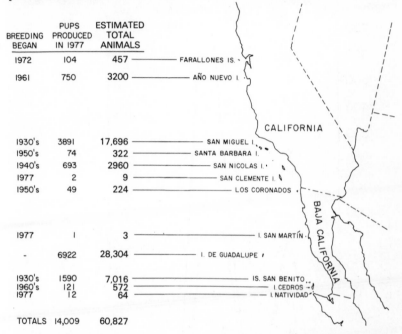

BREEDING BEGAN	PUPS PRODUCED IN 1977	ESTIMATED TOTAL ANIMALS	
1972	104	457	FARALLONES IS.
1961	750	3200	AÑO NUEVO I.
1930's	3891	17,696	SAN MIGUEL I.
1950's	74	322	SANTA BARBARA I.
1940's	693	2960	SAN NICOLAS I.
1977	2	9	SAN CLEMENTE I.
1950's	49	224	LOS CORONADOS
1977	1	3	I. SAN MARTÍN
-	6922	28,304	I. DE GUADALUPE
1930's	1590	7,016	IS. SAN BENITO
1960's	121	572	I. CEDROS
1977	12	64	I. NATIVIDAD
TOTALS	14,009	60,827	

Northern elephant seals bred on twelve islands in 1977. The figure also shows when the breeding began on each island, the number of pups produced in 1977, and the estimated colony and population size. (Adapted from Le Boeuf, 1977)

Año Nuevo Island began to get crowded with elephant seals at the peak of the breeding season during the early 1970's. These conditions made it difficult for young females to land and give birth, so some ventured to more isolated beaches. Young males were at a disadvantage in reproductive competition, so some of them also settled elsewhere. In 1972, breeding began on Southeast Farallon Island, 113 km north of Año Nuevo Island (Le Boeuf, Ainley, and Lewis, 1974). Subsequent observations showed that the majority of females giving birth on the Farallones were young animals that had been born on Año Nuevo Island. In 1975, a female gave birth on the mainland point across the

channel from the Año Nuevo and increasingly more females did so in
subsequent years (Le Boeuf and Panken, 1977).

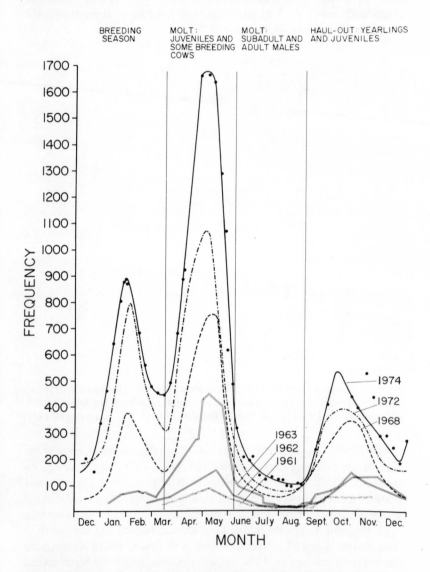

The annual cycle in total numbers of northern elephant seals on Año Nuevo
Island, 1961-1974. Note that the year can be divided into four periods.

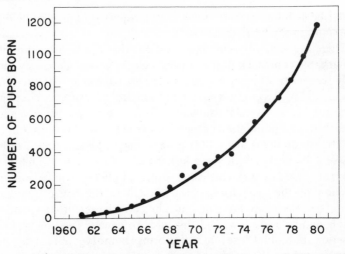

The annual production of northern elephant seal pups on Año Nuevo Island since breeding began in this century in 1961. (Data from 1961, 1962, and 1963 are from Orr and Poulter, 1965)

During the 1980 breeding season, the Año Nuevo Island rookery was more crowded than ever before. Over 2,000 adult males and females crowded together on the two breeding beaches at the peak of the season. Over 1,200 pups were born; but due to lack of space pup mortality was very high, approximately 40% of pups born. Both the new Southeast Farallon Island rookery and the Año Nuevo mainland breeding areas have continued to flourish and grow. Approximately 750 pups were born on the Año Nuevo mainland and over 400 pups were born on Southeast Farallon Island in 1984.

Because of the extensive sandy beaches available on the mainland, the elephant seals of the Año Nuevo Point breeding area have the potential to become a very large colony, far larger than that of Año Nuevo Island. Two hundred years ago a terrestrial invasion would have been a dubious strategy for a seal starting a family. Seals breeding on the mainland would have left few descendants because of the numerous terrestrial carnivores in the area who would have made a quick meal of them or their pups. With the disappearance of the grizzly bears, wolves, mountain lions, and native American Indians, the situation is just the opposite to what it used to be; the area is now exceedingly favorable for seals to settle. Not only are the predators gone but the humans in the vicinity cannot harass or in any way disturb the seals according to the Marine Mammal Protection Act of 1972. Public sentiment for protecting animals has never been greater. Given the scarcity of islands, their preferred habitat, elephant seals can be expected to proliferate on the mainland in the years to come.

There are several fascinating questions that can be asked about the remarkable comeback of the northern elephant seal. Does any species fully recover from being brought to the virtual brink of extinction (Le Boeuf, 1977)? Recovery is not simply a matter of resurgence in population number and reestablishment of breeding range. When a species goes through a population bottleneck, as did the northern elephant seal, genetic variability is lost. Many gene forms, or alleles, gained through years of natural selection are lost. Much of the loss is random and arbitrary. The few survivors who escaped a bullet or a lance bear only a fraction of the gene forms once present in the entire population. Moreover, these few survivors must breed with each other when population numbers are low, and this adds to genetic fixation or loss of genetic variability. Close inbreeding brings homozygous recessive genes together and results in inbreeding depression which may be manifested by lowered viability of the young, loss of fertility, growth anomalies, or metabolic disturbances. Inbreeding is also enhanced by the extremely polygynous breeding habits of males who mate so prodigiously and indiscriminately that father-daughter matings occur. Michael Bonnel and Robert Selander showed that elephant seals lack genetic variability as compared with other pinnipeds and terrestrial mammals (Bonnell and Selander, 1974). Analysis of 19 blood proteins revealed that 125 seals sampled were monomorphic at 24 loci, i.e., they resembled identical twins. What does this mean? Perhaps, that elephant seals have fewer metabolic options for compensating for a varying environment. They may not be able to adjust to different prey if their preferred prey becomes scarce, because they lack the appropriate enzymes to metabolize different foods. As a result, the population may not be as viable as it appears from the increasing numbers and expanding range. Population flushes are typically followed by population crashes. Will this happen to the northern elephant seal?

How many elephant seals do we want? In this decade of enlightened ecological consciousness we consider it good when a species comes back from near extinction. But the elephant seal population is growing extremely rapidly. Moreover, the recent invasion of mainland beaches will inevitably bring about serious conflicts between seals and humans over beach space in the near future. If the current growth rate continues, there will be thousands of elephant seals on the Año Nuevo mainland by 2000 and they will not remain on the state reserve. We will have to decide how many seals we want to live with in the environment. We must do this before the success story of one decade becomes a menace or cancerous growth to another.

Because of the widespread interest in the elephant seals breeding on Año Nuevo Point, and the large amount of information available on this species, the behavior of these animals is treated in detail in Chapter 8.

Harbor Seals

Harbor seals, *Phoca vitulina,* are the most elusive and wary seals observed in the area. They can be seen resting on the rocks exposed at low tides in the northern part of Año Nuevo channel near the mainland, on the rocks south of Año Nuevo Point, on the rocks lying off the northern side of the island, and on a rocky shelf south of Waddell Creek below Big Creek Lumber Company. One rarely sees a harbor seal up close. As soon as they detect a human approaching, or there is any hint of danger, they take refuge in the water. Their shyness is adaptive, for they live in close proximity to people in many parts of the northern hemisphere and humans are dangerous neighbors. Harbor seals inhabit bays, estuaries, and isolated locations along the coast, never venturing far out to sea. They are observed in small groups ranging from a few individuals to groups of about 100. Unlike most other pinnipeds, they are unusually silent.

Except for local hunters killing a few animals for their pelts, harbor seals were never hunted systematically like other Pacific coast pinnipeds. Being small animals, the potential oil yield was probably insufficient to warrant the hunting effort. Individuals are 1.5 to 1.8 m long and weigh about 113 kg. Males are slightly heavier than females. Color patterns vary from light gray to slate gray, with a variable degree of dark spotting or mottling.

Harbor seals usually haul out to rest on rocks exposed at low tide. (F. Lanting)

Two harbor seals resting on a pebble beach on Año Nuevo Island. (F. Lanting)

A harbor seal mother and pup sleeping on a pebbly beach on Año Nuevo Island. The mottled pelage of these animals makes them difficult to see against this type of rocky background. (B. Le Boeuf)

Harbor seals give birth on Año Nuevo Island or on the north end of Año Nuevo Point in late April and early May. This is somewhat earlier in the year than for populations in Alaska and later than for populations in Mexico. Females give birth to single pups. Parturition occurs on land, and shortly after birth the mother and pup swim away. Little is known about harbor seal social structure because mating occurs underwater and the shyness of the animals makes them difficult to study.

Harbor seals apparently feed in the area and thus, there appears to be little change in group composition both within the year and from year to year.

Sixty-five pups were born on Año Nuevo Island during 1976. Pup production, as well as the total local population, appears to have increased slightly over the last 10 years. The figure on this page shows that the total number of harbor seals during any year varies considerably and that the yearly variations lack a coherent pattern. The seals prefer to haul out on land early in the morning and in late afternoon during low tides. Numbers are typically highest in late July. Counts at this time have been increasing during the last decade. We counted 162 harbor seals on July 26, 1976.

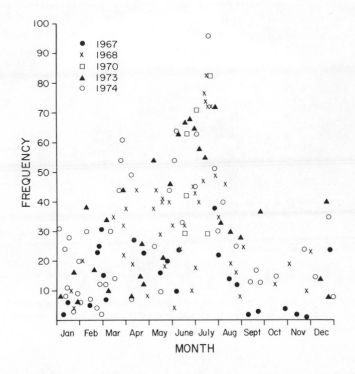

The annual cycle of harbor seals on Año Nuevo Island shows no outstanding pattern within the year or from year to year. This is because harbor seals haul out in relation to time of day and tidal conditions. One of the few consistent things in this figure is that the censuses are always highest in July.

Sea Lions

Sea lions are descendants of a bear-like ancestor and differ in many respects from the seals who derive from otter-like stock. Sea lions can be distinguished from true seals by their small external ears and their large foreflippers which are their main implements of propulsion in the water. Seals have no external ears and swim with a sculling motion of the hindflippers. Two species of sea lions frequent Año Nuevo Island: the Steller sea lion, *Eumetopias jubata,* and the California sea lion, *Zalophus californianus.* Steller sea lions breed on the island in summer. The California sea lion population is made up almost entirely of males who use the island as a resting station during their migrations up and down the coast.

Sea lions, like this Steller sea lion, have external ears. True seals do not; they have only a tiny hole in their head which usually cannot be seen because it is covered by fur. (F. Lanting)

The two species were not differentiated in early times by hunters, or later by state officials responsible for estimating the populations. Consequently, a brief history of both species together must precede the separate descriptions. Both kinds of sea lions were extremely numerous along the California coast before 1860 (Scammon, 1874). During the 1860s, when elephant seals began to get scarce, sea lions became an

Two species of sea lions frequent Año Nuevo Island and it is not difficult to tell them apart if one sees them at the same time. There are three different species in this photograph. The large, light colored animals in the center and to the right of the photograph are Steller sea lion males. The small, dark colored animals which are most numerous in this photograph are California sea lions A few elephant seals can be seen on the left hand side of the picture, some of them with California sea lions sleeping on their backs. (B. Le Boeuf)

alternate source of oil. It took 3 to 4 sea lions to yield one barrel of oil. Thus, in Scammon's words, "The number of seals slain exclusively for their oil would appear fabulous." By the late 1870s, the sea lion stock was already severely depleted and it became unprofitable to hunt them for oil. The animals that remained were killed solely for their hides, which were used to manufacture glue stock. Seal hunting on Año Nuevo Island was first mentioned in 1878:

Captain and crew of the ship *New York* landed on the island for the purpose of killing seals. Keeper Owens warned them that they would be prosecuted, but they went ahead anyway. Left and returned several days later and killed more (U.S. Coast Guard Lighthouse Keeper Log Book).

It is not clear whether these men were killing sea lions for oil or hides.

Even though the total number of sea lions of both species had already been severely reduced; and some rookeries such as Seal Rocks near San Francisco, where Steller sea lions bred, were eliminated, the Fish and Game Commission concluded in 1899 that the sea lions were too

numerous and were destructive to the fishing industry. The federal
government permitted the Commission to kill sea lions on lighthouse
reservations where many large rookeries were located. The Commission
sent two men to the Farallon Islands and two men to Año Nuevo Island.
In the Coast Guard log for Año Nuevo Island there appears the following notation for May, 1899:

Mr. George Scott arrived to kill seals with permission. Sea-lions killed one
day—21, the next day—11. Scott went to White House Rookery and killed 38
one day and 14 the next day.

Permission was revoked only 36 days after it was granted (Bonnot,
1928).

A year later, the California Commission appointed a committee to
investigate the sea lion problem. Their conclusion was that little damage
was done to fishing gear by the sea lions. Nevertheless, between 1900
and 1909, sea lions continued to be killed by commissioned deputies and
by other men without authority. Although there was no organized kill
from 1909 to 1927, some men added to their incomes by killing breeding
bulls for their genitalia or scalps. The genitalia of bulls, known in the
trade as "trimmings," were dried, powdered, and shipped to China,
where they were sold as a rejuvenating potion. Usually the whiskers
were taken at the same time and these were sold to Chinese who used
them to clean opium pipes. In addition, there was a bounty on sea lions
in Oregon and Washington state waters during the early part of this
century, and professional hunters recived up to $3 apiece for scalps. Not
satisfied with the number of scalps they collected in Oregon, these men
made illegal forays into the rookeries in California, particularly in the
Channel Islands in southern California, where they methodically decimated the male population of several rookeries. Sea lions have not been
killed in California since the 1930's except by individuals acting ille-
gally. However, systematic slaughter of these animals for domestic dog
food has occurred as recently as the 1950's in Baja California to the
south, and in Oregon, Washington, and Alaska to the north. These
actions have no doubt been partially responsible for fluctuations in the
number of sea lions seen along the coast of California.

At present it is illegal to kill, capture, or detain any sea lion in
California without a permit. There is one notable exception: a fisherman may kill any seal or sea lion which interferes with his fish-catching
operation. The fisherman alone is the sole judge and executioner. A few
permits are issued annually which permit collecting sea lions for display
purposes and for scientific investigations.

Steller Sea Lions

The Steller sea lion, *Eumetopias jubata,* is the largest of all the sea lions. The males are especially impressive when sitting on their hind flippers and basking in the sun with their eyes closed and noses pointing straight up. Males weigh about 680 to 900 kg, and they are about 3 times heavier than adult females. Males are further distinguished by a mane of coarse guard hair on the neck and shoulders. Both sexes are golden brown when dry and gray-brown when wet.

A Steller sea lion pup, its mother and an adult male sitting on the male's territory on Año Nuevo Island. (B. Le Boeuf)

The highest concentration of Steller sea lions occurs in the Aleutian Islands, southern Alaska, and the coast of British Columbia. Kenyon and Rice (1961) estimated the total population at 225,000 animals in 1959. In the early part of this century, Steller sea lions were the most abundant pinnipeds in the Channel Islands (Bonnot, 1928). This may have been a reflection of the greater decimation of California sea lions and their slower recovery. The Steller sea lion in southern California reached a peak of 2,000 in 1938. The population has steadily declined in this area since that time, and only a few individuals are there at present.

The reason for their rapid disappearance in southern California waters
is unclear. As a result, Año Nuevo Island is now the southernmost
breeding place in the species' range.

Año Nuevo Island is the largest Steller sea lion rookery in California.
Estimates of the population size ranged from 1,500 to 2,000 during the
period 1927 to 1961. These figures are not precise because pups were
either excluded from the counts (Bonnot and Ripley, 1948) or in making
the censuses the two sea lion species were not separated. Systematic
censuses of the Año Nuevo population were taken by Orr and Poulter

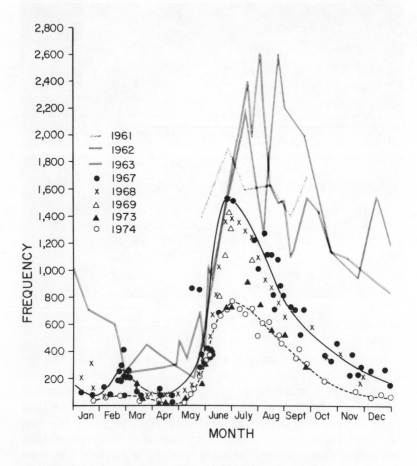

The annual cycle of Steller sea lions on Año Nuevo Island, 1961 to 1974. (Data
from 1961, 1962, and 1963 are from Orr and Poulter, 1965)

Adult male Steller sea lions defend territories on the rocks against each other. Here, three adult males converge and threaten each other at the boundaries of their respective territories. (B. Le Boeuf)

When threats do not work, males resort to overt fighting. Most fights occur early in the season. By the time females become receptive, most territorial disputes have been resolved. (B. Le Boeuf)

(1965) from 1961 to 1963 and by researchers at the University of California at Santa Cruz (especially R. Peterson, R. Gentry, and R. Gisiner) from 1967 to 1979. Recent counts are shown in the figure on page 310. It is evident that the total number of Stellers present on Año Nuevo Island, especially during the breeding season, is declining. Less than 800 animals were counted in 1974, half as many as were counted in the early 1960s and in the early part of the century. The peak number of animals present in 1979 is similar to the number observed in 1974. The cause of this decrease, like the previous decline in southern California, is unknown. The decline may be related to changes in water temperatures, as some have speculated, or may reflect what is going on in larger rookeries to the north.

Breeding occurs in June and July on sloping rocks on the seaward side of the island. Adult males appear on the breeding grounds and begin to establish territories in early May. Most territorial fights occur during the first week after the males arrive. Thereafter, threat displays at territorial boundaries usually suffice to keep male intruders from entering the territory. Pregnant females begin arriving in late May, and they group together in close contact with one another on male territories. A female gives birth to a single pup about 3 days after she arrives. Females copulate only one time about 10 days after giving birth (Orr and Poulter, 1965, 1967).

Males are highly polygynous; a few males in the colony do most of the breeding. Only males with a territory get to mate, and those males with territories located near access points to and from the water do most of the mating. Males may defend the same territories during the breeding season for up to 6 consecutive years (Gentry, 1970; R. Gisiner, personal communication).

A female nurses her pup throughout the summer between periodic feeding trips to sea. The time spent at sea feeding increases with time. The precocial pups weigh about 15 to 20 kg at birth. They are adept swimmers by the time they go to sea with their mothers in early September. About 10% of the pups born annually die on the rookery. The major cause of pup mortality is drowning.

Pups remain with their mothers in the general area for an entire year; the majority are weaned shortly before the female gives birth again a year later. Adult males move northward at the end of the breeding season and do not return to Año Nuevo until the following May (Gentry, 1970; Sandegren, 1970, 1975).

All mating occurs within the boundaries of a male's territory. Males without territories do not mate. Females mate only once a year for about 20 minutes and copulations in progress are never interrupted by other males. (F. Lanting)

A Steller sea lion female and her 2-week old pup. (F. Lanting)

California Sea Lions

California sea lions, *Zalophus californianus,* appear on Año Nuevo Island in greater numbers than any other pinniped. This is somewhat paradoxical, because they do not breed there. Most of the animals observed are males. They appear in greatest numbers in September and October, when they use the island as a resting place during their migration from southern rookeries northward in pursuit of food.

California sea lions are familar to coastal residents, as they are often seen basking on jetties or buoys. They are dark brown in color when wet and an ochre yellow or brown when dry. Males reach 2.5 m in length and weigh about 270 to 360 kg. They can be distinguised from other sea lions by a prominent sagittal crest on the head. The hair on the head-crest is usually lighter than body hair, particularly in older males. Females are usually lighter in color and weigh approximately 90 to 135 kg. It is the female of the species that we know as the circus seal; their small size relative to males makes them preferable for domestication and training purposes. They are the most common seal in zoos and oceanaria around the world.

California sea lions can also be distinguished from seals and other sea lions by their characteristic vocalization. Males bark loudly and inces-santly and can be heard several kilometers inland from Año Nuevo Island when conditions are ideal. Peterson and Bartholomew (1969) describe these calls as "brief acoustic units with sharp onsets and shallow, U-shaped dips in frequency." The spacing and duration of the barks in a series is usually constant. A typical repetition rate is 3 barks per second. During close-range social interaction, the barking rate speeds up. Barks signify a male's presence and may convey threats to another male. Females are less vocal then males, but they have a wider repertoire of sounds. Their calls are associated with aggression or interaction with pups. The forlorn, human-like wail of a female who has lost her pup stands out in sharp relief from the cacophony of male barks on a rookery.

In the water, California sea lions can be identified by their tendency to "porpoise" on the surface when swimming fast, and their habit of surfing in a wave. "Rafts" of resting sea lions, with flippers jutting out at various angles, are often seen in the water near the island.

California sea lions breed in June and July on islands in southern California, Baja California, the Gulf of California, and along the west coast of the mainland of Mexico. Smaller sub-specific populations are present on the Galapagos Islands and off the coast of Japan. During the

Año Nuevo Island is a bachelor apartment for California sea lion males migrating northward after the breeding season in Southern California. This picture was taken in mid-September, 1968. (R. Peterson)

A California sea lion male and female. Note the difference in size and color
between the sexes and the pronounced dorsal crest on the head of the male.
(B. Odell)

California sea lions can be identified in the water by their tendency to surf in
a wave (above) and their habit of "rafting" in a group with flippers jutting out
in all directions. (F. Lanting)

summer only a few animals travel as far north as Año Nuevo Island, and these tend to be sexually immature or too old to engage in reproductive activities.

The figure on this page shows the annual cycles of the total numbers of California sea lions observed on Año Nuevo Island between the period 1961 and 1974. It is evident that the peak numbers of animals occur after the close of the breeding season in the fall when males are migrating northward. The number of sea lions on the island has fluctuated greatly during the 13-year sampling period. When Orr and Poulter

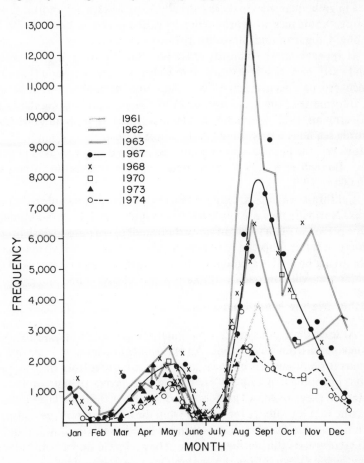

The annual cycle of California sea lions, on Año Nuevo Island, 1961 to 1974. (Data for 1961, 1962 and 1963 are from Orr and Poulter, 1965)

(1965) censused the animals from 1961 to 1964 the population was clearly increasing. The censuses taken from 1968 to 1974 indicate the opposite conclusion. Evidently the population has increased and decreased during this period. This may be a normal, natural cycle or may represent aberrancies that are human-induced. In 1979, the count was back up to 4,200 in early September. The cause of the fluctuations on Año Nuevo Island is most likely something that affects the breeding populations on the rookeries to the south. There is some evidence that human waste products such as DDT, which has been dumped into the sea in great quantities in the last decade, increases sea lion mortality and causes anomalies in reproduction (Le Boeuf and Bonnell, 1971; De Long, Gilmartin and Simpson, 1973).

It appears that the majority of sea lions taken during the last century and early part of this century were California sea lions and that their recovery has been much slower than that of Steller sea lions. No California sea lions were seen on Año Nuevo Island during the 1920s (Evermann, 1921; Evermann and Hanna, 1925). Indeed, only 941 California sea lions were counted in the whole state in 1927 (Bonnot, 1928). However, the population has recovered and is doing very well at present. Bonnell *et al.* (1978) estimated the state population to be over 50,000 in 1978.

California sea lions are not seen on the mainland coast unless they are sick. Normally they are shy creatures that are quick to avoid humans. One person in plain view can cause thousands of sea lions to dash for the safety of water. This can have catastrophic consequences when females are giving birth. These animals are not nearly as shy of humans in the water and will approach within a few feet of divers and surfers.

Other Marine Mammals

At least three other marine mammal species can be seen in the Año Nuevo area from time to time. An occasional northern fur seal, *Callorhinus ursinus,* appears on the island. Fur seals differ from the other sea lions mentioned previously in having two layers of hair or fur (in Mexico, they are known as "lobos de dos pelos"); the inner layer of fur is so fine that it insulates the animal from the cold water by preventing it from touching the skin. These animals breed in the Bering Sea and in Russian waters during the summer. They migrate down both sides of the Pacific Ocean during the winter. On the eastern side of the Pacific, they feed as far south as the waters off the coast of San Diego.

In the last two years, a few sea otters, *Enhydra lutris,* have been

Northern fur seals make an occasional appearance on Año Nuevo Island. In the photograph we see newborn pups, an adult female, and an adult male. This picture was taken on the Pribilof Islands in the Bering Sea. (R. Peterson)

A sea otter. These animals have been seen in increasing numbers near Año Nuevo Island during the last decade. (B. Le Boeuf)

observed in Año Nuevo Bay or near Año Nuevo Island, especially during the summer months. Sea otters were once abundant in the Año Nuevo region before the great sea otter hunt began in the early part of the 19th century, but they were exterminated here well before mid-century (see chapter 1). The few animals seen recently represent the migrant front that is extending the feeding range northward. In 1980, a mother and pup were observed in the area for the first time.

The California gray whale, *Eschrichtius gibbosus,* is the most frequently sighted cetacean in the area. It migrates annually from its feeding grounds in the Bering Sea to its breeding grounds in Baja California. En route, animals pass within a few kilometers of Año Nuevo Island on their way south in December and January and on their return north in February and March. The regular appearance of these whales in the sheltered breeding lagoons of Baja California, and the predictable time of their annual trek, made these whales easy prey for whalers. A booming offshore whaling industry operated at various points along the California coast during the last century, including nearby Pigeon Point (see chapter 1). The present world population is estimated at 10,000 to 13,000 animals.

Human and Animal Interactions

The human animal has effected great changes in the animal composition of the Año Nuevo area during the last 200 years. Human settlement led to the displacement of other humans, the Ohlone Indians, the dangerous grizzly bear, as well as wolves, mountain lions, and dwarf elk (Rudd, 1948). The pioneers tamed and fenced the land to provide forage for cattle, and they tilled the soil for the cultivation of plants. By any reckoning, there is no argument about which animal rules the land today.

At sea, the initial changes were similar to those brought about on land. The abundant marine mammal population in the area was decimated and for a while it's continued existence was in doubt. Unlike the terrestrial grizzly population, most marine mammal populations recovered. Some have returned quickly to the area while others are recovering very slowly. An important reason for the return of the marine mammals is that the marine environment is more foreign, formidable, and inhospitable to man than the land. It was more difficult to scour the waters and kill the remaining survivors of a species than it was to kill or displace the last bears from their habitat.

At present, when marine mammal populations are still recovering and growing, times and conditions are changed. Petroleum was discovered and is still available in greater quantities than animal fat ever was. Furlike garments can be manufactured, making it unnecessary to kill fur seals for their pelts. Today, marine mammal products do not command a high enough price to compete in the same markets they dominated in the last century. More important, there are too few animals living to begin to provide enough oil or skins for an increasingly large human market.

The human attitude towards other animals has changed too. This change works to the benefit of the marine mammals. The philosophy of the California pioneer was like that of renaissance man. Humans were considered the most important form of life; other animals were important only if they could serve or be used by us. Utility and human benefit were the key words. The renaissance ideal suited the pioneers in the last century. Surrounded by natural resources that seemed unlimited, it was natural to exploit them, especially in a time when human society was small, personal, and unindustrialized.

There are still vestiges of renaissance thinking today, but a different philosophy is emerging based on the view that life in an ecosystem is interrelated. The destruction of one form of life affects the abundance of other forms some distance removed, because many species are interrelated within a food web. If we exploit one species, its prey may increase and its predators decrease, and there may be second and third order repercussions which follow.

The morality governing human treatment of animals is also changing. In the 19th century it was perfectly acceptable to kill seals, buffalos, or pigeons for profit. It was a sporting and amusing diversion for gentlemen to while away idle moments on a Sunday afternoon shooting sea lions (Evans, 1874). Today, some marine mammals are more protected than people. The Marine Mammal Act of 1972 is one of the most protective pieces of legislation ever passed concerning the welfare of animals. People have become concerned about animal rights and animal consciousness. Marine mammals, especially the great whales, dolphins, and sea otters, seem to elicit the most protective attitude. "Save the Whales" is more than a phrase which applies to endangered cetaceans; it is an epithet which symbolizes the new attitude to animals.

It may not be long before this new morality is put to the test. As the seals, whales, and sea otters repopulate their former haunts in heavily populated California, humans will be forced into the position of determining the number of each species that will be allowed to exist. This will be necessary to avoid conflicts over space and food resources. But

SHOOTING SEA LIONS.

A sketch from Evans's book (1894) showing gentlemen shooting sea lions for sport.

animal management decisions can be extremely complicated and will certainly involve conflicting points of view. The sea otter-abalone controversy in central California is a good example. Sea otter watchers want more sea otters and no controls to sea otter growth. But sea otters eat abalones, so abalone fishermen want to reduce the sea otter population in areas where they make a livelihood. The dimension of human sentiment regarding sea otters runs from advocating killing them, to a laissez faire attitude of not laying a hand on them, to recognition of sea otters as an important asset in promoting the growth of kelp beds in which abalones and many fishes live and feed.

When we allow one animal to recover it affects the lives of others. The increasing number of elephant seals breeding in the Año Nuevo area in recent years has led to a significant increase in at least two other animal populations: white sharks and people. First, there has been a marked increase in great white shark sightings and an increase in the frequency of shark-bitten seals near Año Nuevo Island in recent years, indicating that the local shark population has grown concomitantly with the growth of the elephant seal population (Le Boeuf, Riedman, and Keyes,

1982). Great white sharks prey on elephant seals; they go where the food is. The problem is that shark attacks on humans occur most frequently near seal rookeries. Since 1955, more shark attacks on humans have occurred in the area between Point Reyes and Monterey (which encompasses the Año Neuvo and Farallon seal rookeries) than anywhere else in the world. Although we have cleared the land of dangerous wild animals lurking about, the sea is another matter.

The second consequence of the phenomenonal elephant seal growth in the area has been to attract thousands of humans to the state reserve on Año Nuevo Point. An average of 50,000 tourists per year has visited the area every winter since 1975. The impact of 100s of seals and 1,000s of people passing through the area once a year has yet to be assessed. This will surely affect the local populations of black-tailed deer, California moles, Trowbridge shrews, California myotis bats, raccoons, striped skunks, grey foxes, chipmunks, western grey squirrels, pocket gophers, deer mice, dusky footed woodrats, brush rabbits, bobcats, and coyotes. What will be the impact of seals and people on the flora, fauna, and the dunes? Human interest in the area will no doubt affect long term land use and state management arrangements and policies. By observing the seals first hand, people will become familiar with their habits and this will further affect human attitudes and understaning of these animals.

Seals attract sharks. This 15½ foot long great white shark washed ashore near Año Nuevo Point on February 3, 1977. It contained about one-third of a recently eaten 4-year-old male elephant seal. (M. Riedman)

References

Anonymous. 1861. The coast rangers: A chronicle of events in California, III-Hunting adventures. *Harper's New Monthly Magazine,* 23, 593-606.

Bartholomew, G.A., and Hubbs, C.L. 1960. Population growth and seasonal movements of the northern elephant seal, *Mirounga angustirostris. Mammalia,* 24, 313-324.

Bonnell, M.L., and Selander, R.K. 1974. Elephant seals: genetic consequences of near extinction. *Science,* 184, 908-909.

Bonnell, M.L., Le Boeuf, B.J., Pierson, M.O., Dettman, D.H., and Farrens, G.D. 1978. Summary Report 1975-1978, Marine Mammals and Seabird Surveys of the Southern California Bight Area, Volume III—Investigator's Reports, Part I. Pinnipeds. Contract AA530-CT7-36 from the Bureau of Land Management, University of California Santa Cruz, 535 pp.

Bonnot, P. 1928. The sea lions of California. *California Fish and Game,* 14, 1-16.

Bonnot, P., and Ripley, E. 1948. The California sea lion census of 1947. *California Fish and Game,* 34, 89-92.

De Long, R.L., Gilmartin, W.G., and Simpson, J.G. 1973. Premature births in California sea lions: Association with high organochlorine pollutant levels. *Science,* 181, 1168-1170.

Evans, Col. A.S. 1874. *A la California; Sketches of Life in the Golden State.* A.L. Bancroft and Co., San Francisco.

Evermann, B.W. 1921. The Año Nuevo Steller sea lion rookery. *J. Mammal.* 2, 16-19.

Evermann, B.W., and Hanna, G.D. 1925. The Steller sea lion rookery on Año Nuevo Island, in 1924. *J. Mammal.,* 6, 96-99.

Gentry, R.L. 1970. Social behavior of the Steller sea lion. Ph.D. Thesis, University of California, Santa Cruz.

Gordon, B.L. 1974. *Monterey Bay Area: Natural History and Cultural Imprints.* The Boxwood Press, Pacific Grove, California.

Hittell, T.H. 1885. *History of California,* San Francisco.

Kenyon, K.W., and Rice, D.W. 1961. Abundance and distribution of the Steller sea lion. *J. Mammal.* 42, 223-234.

Kingsley, H. 1920. Roping Grizzlies. *Overland Monthly,* 97, 22-24.

Le Boeuf, B.J. 1977. Back from extation? *Pacific Discovery,* 30, 1-9.

Le Boeuf, B.J., and Bonnell, M.L. 1971. DDT in California sea lions. *Nature,* 234, 108-110.

Le Boeuf, B.J., and Panken, K.J. 1977. Elephant seals breeding on the mainland in California. *Proceedings of the California Academy of Sciences,* 41, 267-280.

Le Boeuf, B.J., Ainley, D.G., and Lewis, T.J. 1974. Elephant seals on the Farallones: Population structure of an incipient colony. *J. Mammal.* 55, 370-385.

Le Boeuf, B.J., Riedman, M., and Keyes, R.S. 1982. Shark predation on pinnipeds in California coastal waters. *Fishery Bulletin,* 80, 891-895.

Orr, R.T., and Poulter, T.C. 1965. The pinniped population of Año Nuevo Island, California. *Proceedings of the California Academy of Sciences,* 32, 377-404.

Orr, R.T., and Poulter, T.C. 1967. Some observations on reproduction, growth, and social behavior in the Steller sea lion. *Proceedings of the California Academy of Sciences,* 35, 193-226.

Palou, F. 1913. *Francisco Palou's Life and apostolic labors of the venerable Father Junipero Serra, founder of the Franciscan missions of California.* G.W. James, Pasadena.

Peterson, R.S., and Bartholomew, G.A. 1969. Airborne vocal communication in the California sea lion, *Zalophus californianus. Animal Behavior,* 17, 17-24.

Rojas, A.R. 1953. *California Vaquero.* Academy Library Guild, Fresno, California.

Rudd, R.L. 1948. The Mammals of Santa Cruz County. MA Thesis, University of California, Berkeley, 209 pp.

Sandegren, P. 1970. Breeding and maternal behavior of the Steller sea lion (*Eumetopias jubata*) in Alaska. University of Alaska, College, M. Sc. Thesis, 138 pp.

Sandegren, F. 1975. Sexual-agonistic signaling and territoriality in the Steller sea lion. *Rapp. P. -v. Re'un. Const. int. Explor. Mer.* 169, 195-204.

Scammon, C.M. 1874. *The Marine Mammals of the Northwestern Coast of North America.* John Carmany and Sons, San Francisco.

Teggart, F.J. 1911. (Ed.). *Diary of Miguel Costanso, the Portola Expedition of 1769-1770,* University of California, Berkeley.

Tevis, T.I., and Storer, L.P., Jr. 1955. *California Grizzly,* University of California Press, Berkeley.

Torchiana, H.A.V. 1933. *Story of the Mission Santa Cruz.* P. Elder and Co., San Francisco.

Townsend, C.H. 1912. The northern elephant seal. *Zoologica,* 1, 159-173.

Wagner, Henry E. 1929. *Spanish Voyages to the Northwest Coast of America in the Sixteenth Century.* California Historical Society, San Francisco.

Welch, W.R. 1931. Game reminiscences of yesteryears. *California Fish and Game,* 17, 255-263.

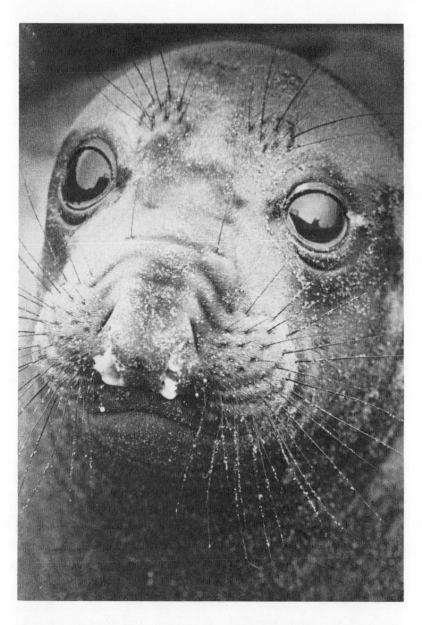

A newly weaned northern elephant seal pup or weaner. Like puppies, weaners are the cutest and most charming of all the elephant seals. Unfortunately this period in development lasts only a short time. (F. Lanting)

8

Elephant Seals

Burney J. Le Boeuf

EVERY WINTER, from December to March, northern elephant seals congregate on the sandy beaches of Año Nuevo Island and the adjacent mainland. You will not confuse these seals with any other marine mammal. Their size and improbable looks provide unique identification. Adult males are 5 meters long and weigh about 2,700 kg. At the front of the whalelike body is a whimsically designed, pendulous, elephantine, proboscis which hangs over a mouth that seems to be fixed in a permanent smile. The smile is deceptive. Bloody fights between males coincide with the sudden appearance of bulging pregnant females, a signal that the animals are here to reproduce. To a biologist, reproduction is the most important thing that this animal or any other animal does. The geneticist J.B.S. Haldane explained that to survive without reproducing is genetic death. The psychologist Frank Beach put it more succinctly, "Coito ergo sum."

To understand the behavior and biology of northern elephant seals, *Mirounga angustirostris,* bear in mind that each individual has been selected to maximize his or her reproductive success, leaving more genes in the next generation than do its competitors. This means producing as many offspring as possible that survive to reproduce, or helping relatives, with whom genes are shared, to reproduce.

All of the seals living today are descendants of ancestors who reproduced successfully, and the survivors bear the genetically based traits of these ancestors. As Michael Ghiselin says (1974, p. 41), "organisms play the game because, and only because, their ancestors did not lose." Years of evolution in varying environments has produced the present model of an elephant seal. Natural selection, as Darwin set forth in his theory of evolution, has determined what they look like, has shaped their behavior, and has even programmed their development. Virtually everything elephant seals do can be construed as an adaptation, an adjustment, an instrument, a strategy to maximize individual reproductive success. From this perspective, life is a reproductive strategy. The seal need not be conscious of this strategy, understand the principles behind it, or fathom the end result of the forces driving it to behave in a certain way. For seals and all other animals, it is the consequences of their actions that count.

It is important to emphasize that individuals do not act primarily in accordance with what is good for the colony or the species, though this was once a prevalent misunderstanding of the level at which natural selection operates. Individual elephant seals "selfishly" pursue their own aims. An individual often does something which is self-benefiting but is bad for the colony. A bull killing a pup in its path is an example. If the strongest male reproduces and this strengthens the local breeding stock, it is coincidental and secondary; the male is selected to maximize his own reproductive success, and that is the most parsimonious explanation for his behavior.

In this chapter, I attempt to explain why elephant seals behave, appear, and function the way they do. Since 1968, my students and I have conducted behavioral and population studies of elephant seals in the Año Nuevo area as well as on other rookeries in the entire breeding range from Baja California, Mexico, to central California. In 1976, the program expanded to include physiological studies under the direction of Dr. C. Leo Ortiz. The elephant seal is ideal for studying reproduction, development, the physiology of fasting, and population dynamics, the four general types of studies we have emphasized. Here I summarize our studies of reproduction, development, and fasting. Studies of population dynamics are treated briefly in chapter 7.

Some of the elephant seal's assets which facilitate study are: (1) Elephant seals are aggressive and unafraid of people. Unlike most other pinnipeds, they do not rush into the water at the appearance of a human. Indeed, they are more likely to charge the person than to flee. This trait can be used to advantage. When the seals are asleep, one can mark individuals so that they can be recognized, aged, and followed for the rest of their lives. Physiologists can collect blood and milk samples with minimal disturbance. (2) Elephant seals breed at the same time and place every year, a schedule which permits the scientist to anticipate and plan the studies. (3) The Año Nuevo rookery can be reached in less than an hour from the University of California at Santa Cruz. The animals, themselves, are large and slow moving, and since most of their reproductive activities occur on sandy beaches, one can see and follow them with ease. (4) All breeding-age animals haul out to breed on known

In order to understand the game, you have to recognize the players. Here B. Le Boeuf puts a dab of paint on the nose of a full grown bull.

The best way to mark elephant seals for the purpose of following them from day to day is a mixture of hydrogen peroxide and "Lady Clairol Ultra Blue." The mixture is used to write names on animals as they sleep or attend to something else. The hair is bleached and the marks last until the animal molts approximately six months later. (F. Lanting)

B. Le Boeuf records the vocalizations of two fighting bulls on Año Nuevo Point. (M. Alexander)

Males and females differ considerably in size and appearance. Here you see an adult female and an adult male. (F. Lanting)

islands during the breeding season. All pups are born on land. This permits one to get estimates of pup production and the number and composition of the breeding colony by censusing each rookery.

Social and Reproductive Behavior

One is more apt to understand elephant seals if their behavior is put into context with that of other mammals and vertebrates. Three general types of mating systems are observed in nature: polygyny, monogamy, and polyandry. Approximately 95% of vertebrate species studied, including virtually all mammals, are polygynous. This mating system is characterized by males competing for females, with the result that a few males do most of the breeding. Males contribute genes to the offspring and nothing else; they do not help rear the pups or act to insure their survival. Monogamy is characteristic of less than 5% of the vertebrates. It is best known in songbirds and long-lived seabirds, and is characterized by both parents sharing in the care and feeding of offspring. Polyandry is an extremely rare mating system in which the female gets help in raising the young from two or more males. A few birds, frogs, and fishes (among them the seahorse) are polyandrous.

Because polygyny is the most prevalent type of mating system found in nature, and because elephant seals exhibit an extreme form of it, these mammals are an excellent choice for the study of reproductive

behavior. Sexual dimorphism, a phenomenon associated with polygyny, is also well marked in elephant seals. In a dimorphic species the
males and females differ in size or appearance. Why is polygyny so
common? Why are elephant seals polygynous? How did they get that
way? To answer these questions, we conducted long term studies aimed
at finding out how males and females, separately, go about maximizing
their reproductive success, and why there are differences within and
between the sexes.

Elephant seals spend most of the year in the water, hauling out on
traditional rookeries once a year to breed and once a year to molt (see
chapter 7). The figure on this page shows the relative frequency distributions of juveniles, adult males, adult females, and pups observed during
the breeding season. These curves are based on data collected on Año
Nuevo Island in 1968 (Le Boeuf, 1972). Except for the frequency scale,
the pattern is similar for other rookeries or for Año Nuevo Island in
subsequent years. The breeding season is heralded by the arrival of the
adult males in early December. Most of the males that participate
prominently in breeding arrive by Christmas. Their number remains

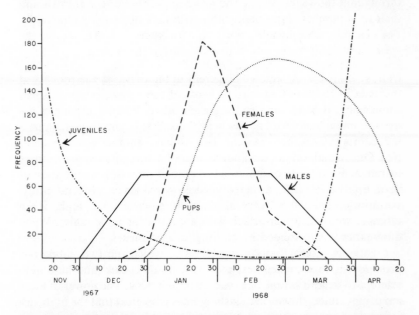

**A schematic diagram showing the number of animals in various age classes
on Año Nuevo Island during the 1968 breeding season.** (Adapted from Le
Boeuf, 1972)

fairly constant until late February, when some of them begin returning to sea. Males precede females on the rookery and most of them do not depart until all of the females are gone.

Females begin arriving about mid-December. They seek each other out and gather in harems on sandy beaches. Their number reaches a peak during the last week in January. After that time their number declines until mid-March when all of them have returned to sea. All but a few females that appear on the rookery in winter are pregnant. A pregnant female gives birth to a single pup approximately 6 days after she arrives. The most common pattern is for a female to nurse her pup daily and keep it near her for an average of 28 days. During the last 3 to 5 days of nursing, she copulates several times and gets reimpregnated. Four weeks after giving birth, 34 days after arriving, and on her last day of estrus, the female weans her pup and goes back to sea (Le Boeuf, Whiting, and Gantt, 1972). Pups remain on the rookery until they are 3 to 4 months old, at which time they go to sea (Reiter, Stinson, and Le Boeuf, 1978).

Although elephant seals are seen on rookeries like Año Nuevo Island throughout the year, the sex and age composition of the animals and their total number varies predictably with time of year (see chapter 7). For example, adult females return to Año Nuevo Island to molt in the spring and adult males return to molt during the summer.

Males. Bulls are extremely belligerent upon arrival at the rookery at the start of the breeding season. Most of their waking time is spent challenging, fighting, and chasing each other. When these males are marked individually with names, a method we have employed for years, it becomes evident that the male that displaces another is dominant to him. Once a male dominates another male, he can cause the subordinate to retreat by any one of a number of graded threats: a simple stare or "evil eye," a headlift, a stereotyped low-frequency, guttural threat vocalization emitted with the head and forequarters held high, or the ultimate weapon, direct attack with apparent intent to maim. When dominance is not decided by bluffing, a fight ensues.

Fights are violent bloody spectacles in which the two ponderous protagonists face each other, and with heads cocked and held high attempt to strike a savage bite on each other's neck. The power of these amazingly quick, downward slashing bites is so great that the blubbery exterior of the recipient undulates with the force of the impact. In addition to the vicious canine bites, which never fail to draw blood, there is a great deal of feinting, pushing, and maneuvering for position.

As soon as females arrive they gather in harems. The most dominant male in the area attempts to prevent all other males from approaching the females. Here, a male issues the typical threat vocalization in the direction of a male that is out of the picture. (B. Le Boeuf)

All elephant seals undergo a drastic molt of their hair and skin once a year. Females, like this one, molt in April. (B. Le Boeuf)

Most fights last only a few minutes, but power struggles between two imposing giants may go on for 45 minutes, leaving both the victor and the vanquished bloody and exhausted on the beach and barely able to move (Le Boeuf, 1971).

The result of all this pairwise posturing, display, and bloodshed is the establishment of a social or dominance hierarchy in the vicinity where a female harem will form. Social rank in this hierarchy determines proximity to females, with the highest ranking males positioning themselves closest to the females. The top ranking male, or alpha bull, dominates all other females on the beach and takes a position in or near the female harem. He attempts to keep all other males away from the females. Indeed, all males try to get as close to females as possible while at the same time keeping other males away. The difficulty of this task increases as social rank decreases (Le Boeuf and Peterson, 1969).

To the victor goes the spoils, and in this species males fight for the favors of the females, which are not so much given as taken. The best fighters become the highest-ranking males, and these do all or most of the mating. The division of mating privileges varies as a function of three characteristics of the female harem: the number of females in it, the number of males competing, and the location and topographic setting of the harem. Generally, when a harem contains 50 females or less, the alpha bull can prevent all other males from approaching females and he alone will monopolize mating. He may sire 50 pups in a single year.

A typical fight sequence between adult males on the periphery of a harem. The fight begins with the two males threatening each other vocally. In b the males jockey for position and feint or butt each other before exchanging blows in c and d. Note that the male on the right is marked with the name "Chub."(B. Le Boeuf)

When harem size exceeds 50 females, the alpha male becomes over-whelmed with the task of patrolling the harem. His dilemma is all too obvious. To effectively keep other males out of the harem, he must patrol incessantly. When he chases an intruder on the left, another enters on the right, and so it goes. This leaves him no time to mate. Most bulls resolve this conflict by ignoring the outer reaches of the harem and consolidating their central position with the majority of females. This is not to say that alpha doesn't make a sortie to the periphery periodically to let his subordinates know who is boss. If he picks on anyone it is usually the number 2 and number 3 bulls who ensconce themselves on the periphery and copulate when they can. Number 2 and number 3 pick on numbers 4, 5, 6 and so on down the line.

As harem size increases above 100 females to as high as 1,000, more and more bulls infiltrate into the harem and achieve a share of the mating roughly proportonal to their social rank. Defensibility or vulnerability of harems influences variance in male reproductive suc-cess. Harems located in coves in which male intruders must approach from one direction, the sea, can be defended by one bull more readily than harems located on a beach which allows males to approach from all sides.

The Point harem on Año Nuevo Island near the peak of the breeding season in 1975. The harem contains many more females than a male can defend from other males. Under these conditions several of the top ranking males remain in the harem. (B. Le Boeuf)

The monopolization of mating by a few males is confirmed by data collected on Año Nuevo Island from 1968 to 1973 (Le Boeuf, 1974). During these five years, less than one-third of the males present did all of the mating observed in the two harems on the island. In 1968, only 14 males (14% of the males present) mated with the 193 females in residence. All of them were fully grown adults. Five males did 83% of the mating. As the number of females in residence increased, the monopoly decreased. In 1973, 34% of the 185 males present did all of the mating with 470 females. The top five males did 48% of the breeding. This trend has continued to the present. In the crowded conditions that existed on the island in 1979, 50% of the males present mated with the 1200 females in residence.

Male-male competition results in a system in which copulation frequency is roughly proportional to social rank. The higher a male's social rank, the more frequently he copulates. This generalization has greatest validity when female density is low. For example, the alpha male always accounted for the majority of copulations with the 40 to 81 females present in the small Cove harem on Año Nuevo Island from 1968 to 1973. The percentage of females with whom the alpha bull copulated in those years was 73, 100, 100, 59, 100, and 100, respectively. The alpha male on the Point harem, larger and more difficult to defend, accounted for 12 to 49% of the matings observed. With the growth of the female population, the positive correlation between male social rank and mating decreased. The alpha male in a large harem may still copulate with as many females, but proportionately his share of the mating is lower.

As female number increases and more males infiltrate into the harem, it becomes more likely that a few young males will copulate. Indeed, very young males have one advantage over older larger males: they more closely resemble females. By keeping a low profile, they get overlooked by high-ranking bulls and a few of them manage to obtain a few surreptitious matings.

Some alpha bulls not only monopolize mating throughout a breeding season but return to the same location to reign again. A bull named Adrian was the alpha bull on the large Point harem at Año Nuevo Island for four consecutive years, 1971 to 1974. It is estimated that he inseminated at least 225 females. This is the most remarkable male performance we have recorded in 12 years of elephant seal watching. It is all the more impressive because most males never get a chance to mate at all. Most males die before they reach breeding age, and the majority

Copulation is what all the fighting among the males is about. This is a typical sequence. The male pins the female down with the weight of his head and neck (a), puts a foreflipper over the female's back (b) just prior to turning on his side and initiating genital contact (c). Several pelvic thrusts precede insertion which is accompanied by bending of the male's lower back (d and e). The copulating male disengages as a dominant bull advances towards him (f). (B. Le Boeuf)

of those that survive to breeding age are prevented from mating by higher-ranking bulls. For example, only 3% of the males born on Año Nuevo Island in 1964 survived to age 8. Males born in 1966 did a little better, 14% surviving to age 8. Eight years of age is the earliest time that a male can begin to compete effectively with the highest-ranking males. It is rare for a male to become an alpha male before he is 9. A male's prime is from 9 to 11.

If a male survives to breeding age, what are his chances of mating? Before answering this question it is necessary to describe the age categories of males observed during the breeding season. Males can be divided into five categories for the purpose of identification (Cox and Le Boeuf, 1977). Adults, aged 8+, include males that are fully developed; the youngest are in their prime and the oldest are past prime. Subadult (SA) males come in 4 sizes: SA4s are 7 to 8 years old and not quite fully developed; SA3s are 6 to 7 years old and just past puberty; SA2s are small, 5-year-old pubertal males, and SA1s are sexually premature 4-year-olds. All of these males are physiologically capable and psychologically willing to breed, but stronger males prevent them from doing so. A male prevents another male below him in rank from mating by keeping him away from females, by interrupting attempted copulations, and by disrupting copulations in progress. From 1968 to 1973, the percentage of males in each age category that did *not* mate was: adults 22-56%; SA4s 54-89%; SA3s 72-100%; and SA2s 97-100%. Clearly, survival to breeding age is necessary for mating, but it is not enough.

These studies on Año Nuevo Island suggest strongly that males who conquer their rivals leave more offspring than those that are conquered (one would have to determine parentage to confirm this statement). What distinguishes the winners from the losers? What attributes does a successful male possess? Obviously, many variables are involved. For example, to live to age 9 a male must successfully avoid predators like killer whales and great white sharks (Le Boeuf, Riedman, and Keyes, 1980); and he must not bear lethal genes which exert their effect before reaching prime breeding age. To compete effectively, a survivor to adulthood must have great size and fighting ability and the ability to fast throughout the breeding season. Fasting is extremely important, because those who can go without food remain on the rookery impregnating females. To fast for three months, a male must be an efficient feeder in the fall. The heavy blubber layer he carries in December provides the energy he lives on through March. Even psychological strategy is important. A male must arrive on the rookery to start the breeding season at just the right time, and he must conserve his energy. If he arrives too early, he may achieve high rank but is apt to tire out and get deposed from his lofty position before the females become receptive. If he arrives too late, he must fight too many battles to establish a social

The appearance of males give a good indication of their age. The fighting
bulls in the top figure are in their prime, 9 to 11 years of age. Note the large
nose and elaborate, corrugated, ventral neck shield, both signs of maturity.
The 5-year-old males in the middle picture are just going through puberty and
are making their first appearance on the rookery during the breeding season.
Their noses are just starting to fold over and their fighting is more playful than
serious. They are capable of inseminating females, but rarely get the chance.
In the last figure are 3-year-old male juveniles that cannot be distinguished from
females from this position. Regardless of age, they all spend a lot of time
fighting or playing at it. (B. Le Boeuf)

rank high enough to permit him to mate. Superbulls, like Adrian, arrive just early enough to establish a lofty social position, but they do not waste energy chasing other males away from the females before they can be impregnated. When the females begin to come into estrus in mid-January, the smart bulls make a final move to upgrade their social position, for that is when rank begins to count.

Now we can begin to see how natural selection acts on males to maximize their reproductive success. The potential reproductive success of any individual is very high. In one successful breeding season, a male can mate with a hundred females. What limits a male's reproductive success is gaining access to females; another larger, better fighter usually stands in the way. Thus, the winner in this reproductive game, which all play, are males who delay competition with other males until they have developed fully and are well advanced in years. Some males may attempt to mate early in development, but they achieve only minimal success at the risk of possible injury which may detract from performance during prime years. This kind of selection pressure led to the evolution of sexual dimorphism. Males have gotten larger and larger through years of selection so that at present they are 3 to 4 times larger than females. The ideal lifetime reproductive strategy of a male elephant seal is to have at least one good year, to hit the jackpot. Few males succeed. Those that do succeed belong to a very select club with stringent entrance requirements and the reproductive privileges which all males pursue. To get in, a male has to have everything going in his favor and he has to gamble. He lives a high risk life with the promise of a high gain.

Females. The reproductive success of a male is limited by the number of females with whom he mates. Females have no trouble finding a mate; nearly all adult females mate and get inseminated every breeding season. In contrast, a female's reproductive success is limited by the number of young she bears and her success in rearing them. Because the female gestates the developing fetus in her body for almost a year, she is limited to producing a maximum of about 11 pups in a lifetime. To maximize her reproductive potential a female has been selected to give birth early in life, give birth annually, and live long. Furthermore, a female can influence the quality of her offspring by selection of a mate (the father provides one-half of her pup's genotype) and by maternal investment in the pup after birth. A mother must learn to recognize her newborn and protect it from aggressive female neighbors and rampaging males. She must nurse it daily until it is weaned in a healthy condition with a good chance of surviving on its own.

Clearly, females go about maximizing their reproductive success in a different way than males. Their low reproductive potential relative to males leads us to expect a low-risk approach to life. Whereas males must gamble to have a good reproductive year, females should play it safe in order to produce a single pup every year in a long life. Nature favors females that are conservative and consistent.

Females are accosted by male suitors as soon as they emerge from the sea bearing a full-term fetus. The vigorous mating attempts of the large bulls are aversive, and females reduce the frequency of this activity by clumping together. In a group or "harem" they are protected, by the alpha bull, from the scores of suitors. Better to be pestered by one bull than by many.

Parturition takes only a few minutes from the time a nose or tail appears, to when the fetus is expelled (Le Boeuf, Whiting, and Gantt, 1972). Tail-first presentations are almost as common as head-first ones, due in part to the marine-adapted, streamlined body configuration. Immediately, the mother turns to face the pup, nuzzles it, and begins emitting pup-attraction calls in its face. The precocial pup, wobbly head up and eyes blinking in amazement, squawks periodically; and a vocal duet between mother and pup continues for several minutes after birth. This is an important time in which the mother learns to recognize her pup and, less so, the pup its mother. A social bond is formed. If mother and pup are separated before the bond is formed, reunion is unlikely and the orphan starves or is injured and dies. The major cause of pup death is the rampaging bulls, who trample pups in their paths to and from other bulls, and nursing females who bite orphans that attempt to suckle them (Le Boeuf and Briggs, 1977).

Most cows nurse only their own pups and reject all others. This lack of altruism is understandable when one considers the constraints under which this unusual mammal operates. A mother does not feed or drink during the four weeks that she nurses her pup. This is all the more astounding since the pup averages 38 kg at birth and escalates to a mean weight of 136 kg at weaning. All of this mass gain comes from mother's milk. But the mother's fat store, from which she feeds her pup and maintains herself for an average of 34 days, is limited. Whatever she gives away or allows to be stolen subtracts from her own pup's survival. Females that bite and kill orphans are acting like good mothers provid-

The typical sequence of events in an elephant seal birth. The fetus is first seen encased in the amniotic membranes (a). The latter usually rupture when the head or hindflippers begins to protrude (b). The following stages in parturition occur rapidly (c and d). A female with a young pup of her own approaches from the right and sniffs the newborn (e). The mother turns and nuzzles her pup while at the same time emitting a pup attraction call (f and g). Gulls flock to the area and devour the afterbirth (h). (Adapted from Le Boeuf, Whiting, and Gantt, 1972)

Many pups are killed on the rookery by adult bulls who run over rather than around them. (F. Lanting)

Females bite and often kill pups that are not their own. Orphans, who are starving and must steal milk to survive, are most vulnerable. (B. Le Boeuf)

ing the best for their own offspring. They are maximizing their reproductive success by protecting their genetic investment.

Rearing a pup successfully to weaning age is affected by a number of variables. One of the most important is the mother's age. Table 1 summarizes data collected on Año Nuevo Island over a 4-year period (Reiter, Panken, and Le Boeuf, 1980). It is clear that 3-year-olds, most of whom were giving birth for the first time, were the least successful. Only 20% of the females in this age group (7 of 35) weaned their pups successfully. The totals show that the weaning rate increased with advancing age and then leveled out. "Old females," 6 years of age or more, were almost twice as successful as "young females," 5 years of age or less (73% vs. 38% pups weaned).

Table 1. The percentage of females in various age categories that produced pups surviving to weaning age on Año Nuevo Island. N is in parentheses

Breeding season	Age										
	3	4	5	6	7	8	9	10	11	12	13
1976	25 (4)	65 (17)	47 (17)	100 (4)	86 (14)	100 (2)	—	—	—	—	—
1977	36 (11)	50 (10)	73 (11)	88 (8)	100 (3)	100 (15)	—	100 (1)	100 (1)	—	—
1978	0 (4)	13 (16)	0 (1)	20 (5)	30 (10)	50 (2)	30 (10)	0 (1)	100 (1)	100 (1)	100 (1)
1979	13 (16)	25 (8)	40 (10)	33 (3)	100 (1)	67 (3)	100 (3)	100 (5)	—	100 (1)	—
TOTALS	20 (35)	39 (51)	51 (39)	65 (20)	68 (28)	91 (22)	46 (13)	86 (7)	100 (2)	100 (2)	100 (1)

The social and physical environment exerts a powerful effect on the reproductive success of females of all ages by affecting pup mortality. High female and pup density correlated with high levels of female aggression and a high incidence of mother-pup separation. Storms at peak season kill pups directly, or indirectly, by increasing density and creating chaos and confusion. The adverse effect of these variables on pup mortality, and hence on female reproductive success, is inversely proportional to the mother's age. The performance of the youngest females, poor under optimal conditions, is even worse in crowded conditions and in bad weather. The performance of old females is less affected by suboptimal conditions. For example, 1978 was a bad storm year, and the reproductive success of all females was depressed, but young females incurred a much greater loss than old females.

Old females are more successful than young ones because of their size, aggressiveness, and maternal experience. Like many other mammals, female northern elephant seals give birth before they have attained full growth. Increase in total length and weight starts to plateau at around age 6, the beginning of a female's physical prime. Thus, females older than 6 years are larger than those that are less than 6 years of age.

Size advantage gives older females an important reproductive edge over younger competitors. The larger of two females usually dominates in an aggressive encounter. The dominant female secures the safest place to give birth and nurse her pup and is better able to fend off neighbors who might injure her pup. In addition, the larger a female, the larger her fat reserves and the more she has to give to her pup. The

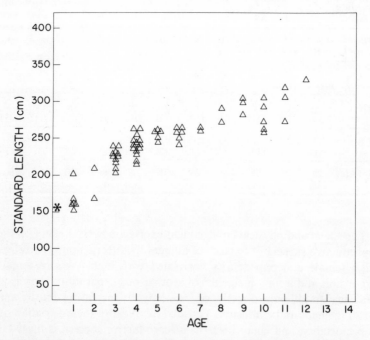

Female length (note the tail) as a function of her age. The asterisk refers to the mean standard length of 23 female pups measured at 1 month of age. (Adapted from Reiter, Panken and Le Boeuf, 1980)

Storms kill pups directly by drowning and indirectly by causing crowding, chaos, and confusion in the harem. Under these conditions pups lose their mothers and are bitten or trampled. The *top* figure shows part of the flooded and crowded Point harem on Año Nuevo Island at high tide. In the *bottom* figure high tide and high surf combine to inundate the Cove harem, driving females up against the base of the cliff. (B. Le Boeuf)

weight of a pup at weaning increases with the age and size of its mother. If the fattest are the fittest, and there is good reason to suspect so, the older females are producing pups that are more likely to survive beyond weaning age.

Maternal experience accumulates with age. Inexperienced female seals, like human females, make the poorest mothers. They commit stupid blunders which jeopardize their pup's survival. For example, one female might abandon her pup for no apparent reason, respond to the wrong pup, or fail to respond at all. Experience alone is important. Four-year-old females, who had given birth the previous year on Año Nuevo Island, weaned a higher percentage of their pups ($11/16 = 69\%$) than four-year-old females giving birth for the first time ($19/35 = 35\%$).

Older females tend to give birth earliest in the breeding season, while the youngest females are the last to give birth. This difference, plus those already mentioned, enables the older females to preempt the optimal time and place for rearing healthy pups. For example, on Año Nuevo Island during the late 1970's, late arriving young females were forced to

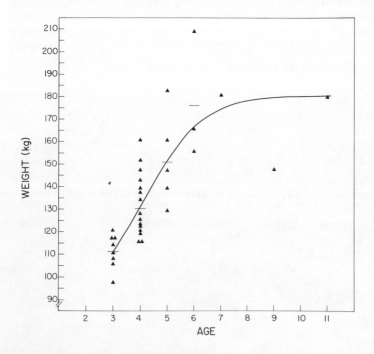

The weight of pups at weaning in relation to mother's age. Adapted from Reiter, Panken, and Le Boeuf, 1980)

give birth on the periphery of crowded harems. Being subordinate they could not force their way to a safe place in the center of the beach. Females on the periphery bore the brunt of high tides and high surf during storms, the constant harassment of courting males, and the repeated theft of their milk by itinerant orphans. As a result, young females were least successful in rearing pups to weaning age because they gave birth when it was most crowded, they were forced to give birth in an inferior location, and they lacked maternal experience.

There are additional pup-rearing advantages for females who arrive early and give birth in an optimal place. The pups of early-arriving females are weaned when the number of nursing females is at a maximum. With the departure of their mothers, these weaners are presented with an excellent opportunity to steal milk from other nursing females. Approximately 10% of them attempt to get additional nourishment in this way (Reiter et al., 1978). Pups weaned late in the breeding season do not have this option since there are few or no nursing females left on the rookery. Successful milk thieves may gain an additional 100 kg, a substantial weight advantage over "honest" weaners, who fast and lose weight daily. Perhaps because of this early inequity in physiological fitness, early-born female pups reproduce earlier in life than pups born late in the breeding season. Table 2 shows these results for females born at various times during the 1974 breeding season. By 1980, when these

Table 2. Percent primiparous births on Año Nuevo Island, the Año Nuevo Mainland, or on Southeast Farallon Island by females born at various times during the 1974 breeding season on Año Nuevo Island. N is in parenthesis

Year and age of primiparity	Early (N = 32)	Middle (N = 92)	Late (N = 47)	Total (N = 171)
1976 2 years old	—	1.1	—	0.6
1977 3 years old	15.6	7.6	8.5	9.4
1978 4 years old	21.9	13.0	10.6	14.0
1979 5 years old	—	2.2	6.4	2.9
1980 6 years old	3.1	—	—	0.6
TOTALS	40.6	23.9	25.5	27.5

females were 6 years old, 41% of the females in the early-born group had given birth as opposed to only 25% of the females in the late-born group. Two other points are worth noting: (1) the majority of females from the 1974 cohort are not represented, and there is no good evidence to assume that they died before reproducing, and (2) the column totals show that age at primiparity varied from 2 to 6, with the majority of females giving birth for the first time at age 4. These data suggest strongly that females born early during the breeding season, presumably to older, fitter mothers, produce more offspring in their lifetimes than their cohorts born later in the season.

The early-arriving female that gives birth in the center of the harem is also more apt to mate with a high-ranking adult male, i.e., a male who has demonstrated his fitness by surviving to maturity and achieving high rank. The "best" males dominate mating most thoroughly early in the breeding season. In contrast, untested, subadult males inseminate some females on the periphery of the harem. Females that produce pups sired by high-ranking adult males are more likely to leave more genes in the next generation, i.e., be more successful, than females that mate with subadult males. The reason is simply that if the female has a male pup, it will inherit some of its father's attributes. A winning male is more likely to produce winning progeny who perpetuate the genes of both the father and the mother.

When sexually accosted, all females behave in a manner which increases the probability of mating with a high ranking adult male (Cox and Le Boeuf, 1977). They reject noisily all copulatory attempts during early estrus. The female's protests signal to all nearby males that copulation is imminent. All males attempt to prevent others lower in rank from copulating. Thus, the probability that the mounting male will be interrupted by another male is a function of the mounter's social rank. The lower his rank, the higher the probability of interruption. The result is that mature males of high social rank have more time and freedom to attempt copulation, and they succeed in doing most of the mating. The female's behavior intensifies this monopoly by making it more difficult for young, subordinate males to copulate. The female gets what is best for her by the simple expedient of inciting males to fight and then mating with the winner.

The prospects of a young female elephant seal reproducing for the first time in a crowded rookery are very grim. On the one hand, selection makes it profitable to reproduce early in life so as to leave more offspring than competitors. On the other hand, the odds of being successful in a crowded rookery are extremely low, and there is reason to believe that reproductive failure early in life reduces net reproductive success in a lifetime. A female that conceives at age 2 must channel nutrients away from her own body to the developing fetus. Thus, early pregnancy may retard growth and result in a smaller adult size than that which a female might attain if initial pregnancy is delayed. How do young females resolve this dilemma? To mate or not to mate? What course of action has the most favorable reproductive consequences?

Males attempt to mount females regardless of their reproductive condition. Females cry out and attempt to escape. The commotion usually results in the mounting being displaced by a higher ranking male. (K. Parker and E. Fisher)

Young females have two options: they can move and give birth in a place where their pups are more apt to survive, if such a place is available, or they can postpone breeding to an age when they are sufficiently well developed to be more successful. The first response is one that individuals can make depending on the circumstances that prevail at the time of parturition. It calls for adaptable behavior and it is reasonable to suspect that some individuals will cope with existing conditions better than others. The second response is clearly a long term

solution that would evolve as a consequence of negative selection
pressure, i.e., if females that are genetically programmed to give birth
later in life leave more offspring in a lifetime than those giving birth
early (and failing in these early trials) then the mean age at primiparity
in a colony will increase.

One expects the first response to be used in an expanding population
and the second when the population is stable and in equilibrium. The
northern elephant seal population is still expanding at present, following the drastic reduction in numbers suffered at the hands of sealers in
the last century (Le Boeuf, 1977). Food and space have been plentiful in
the niche void during the recovery period, conditions which favor the
production and survival of offspring. In general, this is the optimal time
for females to reproduce early in life. However, during the rapid recovery some rookeries have become crowded and more competitive, and
the young females (and young males) have been the first to suffer
lowered reproductive success.

This process is well documented in a recent study of Año Nuevo
Island-born females (Reiter et al., 1980). It shows that some of them
colonized new breeding areas when their birthplace began to get
crowded. After Año Nuevo Island was colonized in 1961, the number of
pups born annually increased at such a rapid rate that by the mid 1970's,
harems were crowded with females and pups at peak season (see chapter
7). In 1972, breeding began on Southeast Farallon Island, 89 km north
of Año Nuevo Island (Le Boeuf, Ainley and Lewis, 1974). Growth was
rapid there too, so that by 1979 over 130 pups were born. In 1975, a
female gave birth on the Año Nuevo mainland, less than 1 km from the
island (Le Boeuf and Panken, 1977). Only 9 years later, in 1984, 730
females produced pups at this location. These new colonies were created
in response to crowding on Año Nuevo Island. Young females could not
land to give birth, or if they succeeded in landing, they were forced by
larger, more aggressive females to give birth in inferior locations. The
majority of the female colonizers in both new places were young individuals who had been born on Año Nuevo Island. Seventy-six percent
of the females that gave birth for the first time on Southeast Farallon
Island, between 1974 and 1978, were born on Año Nuevo Island; 87% of
those giving birth on the mainland were born on the island. Virtually all
of the original colonizers were young primiparous females, aged 3 or 4.
A few of them had given birth on the island in the previous year and
failed to wean their pups. The young females that moved were much
more successful in producing healthy weaned pups than their counter-

Females

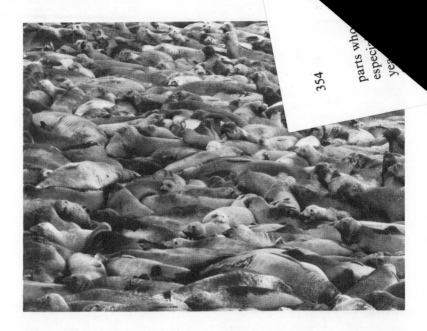

parts who
especi
ye

As Año Nuevo Island (above) has gotten increasingly crowded, young females have given birth elsewhere, such as the Año Nuevo mainland (below) (B. Le Boeuf)

remained on crowded Año Nuevo Island (Table 3). This was
lly true in bad weather years, such as 1978, and in the most recent
rs, when island harems were most crowded. The trend continued in
1980: the pup mortality rate was 36% on the island and less than 3% for
pups born on the mainland. Crowding was the big difference; the island
was crowded and the new breeding areas were not. In addition, there
were few large old dominant females present in the new areas to attack
pups or harass young mothers. Blunders from inexperience were not so
severely penalized in the new colonies.

Table 3. **The proportion and percent of young females, 5 years of age or less, that produced pups surviving to weaning age in good condition and weaned by their own mothers. Adapted from Reiter et al., 1980**

Breeding Season	Año Nuevo Island Point Harem	Southeast Farallon Is.	Año Nuevo Mainland
1976	15/42 = 47%	7/8 = 88%	0/1 = 0
1977	13/27 = 48%	7/12 = 58%	2/4 = 50%
1978	1/19 = 5%	8/17 = 47%	10/12 = 83%
1979	6/31 = 19%	not available	10/17 = 59%

If and when the elephant seal niche becomes saturated and all breeding beaches are used up, competition will be fierce everywhere. In this
context, we would expect selection to favor females that postpone
giving birth until they are in their prime years and can compete most
effectively.

The remarkable conclusion to this part of the story is that new
colonies are started by the young, reproductively repressed, harassed,
and unsuccessful individuals. The exploration of new ground is not the
result of a bold adventuresome spirit, it is something that is forced on
individuals of an age class that lose out in reproductive competition
unless they break convention. The convention in elephant seals is for
females to breed where they were born or where they bred least year.
Since young individuals of both sexes have difficulty reproducing in a
high density situation, they enhance their reproductive success by moving. The colonization process plays an important role in adaptive
radiation of a population and in the evolution of the species. Whether it
is "wise" for an individual to move or not depends on the social and
physical environment at the moment. Selection clearly favors individuals that can "read" the context quickly and accurately and act accord
ingly.

Development

Reproductive competition among elephant seals is the driving force behind individual behavior and population phenomena. The product is offspring. The most successful parents produce offspring that produce offspring themselves, and so on. Because reproduction is so important in adulthood, individuals are selected to get an early start in life and do certain things at certain times so as to maximize the probability of breeding. Success benefits the developing individual as well as its parents. Development can be viewed as the unfolding of a lifetime reproductive strategy.

The major danger for a newborn is losing its mother (Le Boeuf and Briggs, 1977). Pups with good mothers are protected from neighboring belligerent females, and they are nursed at least 2-4 times per day until weaning. Pups that are separated from their mothers are forced to attempt to suckle alien females or starve. This exposes the orphan to injury from females protecting their own pups and to the charges of the monstrous bulls, who are apparently oblivious of the pups. The major cause of death on an elephant seal rookery is the trauma-starvation syndrome which follows mother-pup separation. Circumstances which promote it are high density and anything which disturbs the tranquility of the harem and increases female aggressiveness, e.g., males fighting in the harem, or bad weather.

Most pups remain near their mothers throughout the nursing period and each one is nursed by its own mother. There are no playful interactions between pups at this time. It is too risky, and the important business is to get as much milk as possible while the supply lasts. Weaning is abrupt. The mother goes back to sea leaving her pup behind. It is unlikely that mother and offspring meet again or, if they do, they show no signs of recognizing each other.

The weaned pup finds itself in a hostile environment. Alien mothers threaten it and force it out of the harem, and young males aggressively attempt to copulate with it regardless of its sex, small size, inappropriate condition and unwillingness. Each year, a few healthy weaners are killed by adult males or females. Finding safety in numbers, most weaners gather in weaner pods, inland from the harem, where they spend the daylight hours sleeping. The majority of them fast from food and water for 8 to 12 weeks before they depart the rookery. At departure time, they have lost 25% of their weaning weight.

Some interesting exceptions to this norm occur. Approximately 10% of the weaned pups every year do not take readily to this imposed fast;

The mother assumes the nursing position and her 1-week-old pup suckles. (B. Le Boeuf)

After 4 weeks of suckling, the pup is considerably larger and its mother is noticeably smaller. This pup is about to be weaned. (B. Le Boeuf)

One of the things a weaner has to avoid is being mounted by the giant males. In their frustration to mate some males will mount weaners regardless of their sex. A few weaners are crushed and killed in this way every year at Año Nuevo. (F. Lanting)

Weaners avoid the dangers of being mounted by bulls and bitten by adult females by gathering together in weaner pods inland from the female harem. They spend most of the day sleeping and then venture out to the water's edge at sunrise and sunset. (B. Le Boeuf)

they attempt to obtain more milk. Two general strategies can be discerned. Milk thieves reenter the harem and attempt to steal milk from unwary females. The unsuccessful thief is stealthy and opportunistic. It approaches the female from the rear and nudges or bites her gently, prompting her to assume the nursing position (a nursing female often does not check to see whether the stimulus comes from her own pup). The thief displaces younger, smaller pups from the nipple without attracting attention, and does not cry out when caught in the act. When a milk thief is detected, the female attempts to bite it. Successful milk thieves persevere and may reenter the harem daily for up to 2 to 3 weeks after weaning (Reiter et al., 1978).

The second strategy is safer and more effective, if it can be arranged. A few pups are adopted and nursed by another female in addition to their own mothers. The additional fostering usually happens after they are weaned. These pups may suckle for a total of 8 weeks and are called "double-mother sucklers." When they finally stop feeding, some of them weigh almost twice as much as the average pup at weaning. One of these, momentarily detained in 1978, weighed 238 kg! Nearly every year, a few exceptionally large superweaners are observed on Año Nuevo Island as well as on other large rookeries. These animals are so bloated that their corpulence makes it difficult for them to move. Most superweaners observed are evidently double-mother sucklers.

Securing additional milk after weaning provides an excellent opportunity for an individual to obtain an advantage over others at a time when the majority of weaned pups in a cohort are fasting. The average weight loss of a fasting weaner ranges from 0.58 to 0.87 kg per day (Ortiz, Costa, and Le Boeuf, 1978). Milk thieves do not simply derive a weight advantage by putting on more fat; they obtain proteins, calcium, vitamins, and other elements from milk which are essential for muscle, tissue, and bone growth. The nursing period is an optimal time for one animal to obtain a size advantage over others because this is when the rate of individual growth is most rapid.

An interesting aspect of milk stealing is that males are most frequently involved; they try harder than females and they are more successful. Virtually all superweaners are males. In addition, two developmental processes are delayed in males which may be adaptive in permitting them to effectively mimic suckling pups and thus facilitate milk stealing. Pups molt from the original black pelage to a silver coat after weaning. The process begins later for males than females and it takes longer to complete. Similarly, the canine teeth erupt after weaning in males, and before weaning in females. To a nursing female, a one-

Two weaner milk thieves vie to suckle from a sleeping female. The female's marked pup sleeps to her right and another potential milk thief creeps up from the left. In the bottom figure the female has awakened and turned to threaten the milk thieves. (K. Parker and E. Fisher)

A super-weaner, a male weaner that has been fortunate enough to suckle from two mothers successively. This animal weighs almost twice as much as the average weaner.

month-old male pup probably looks and feels younger than a female pup of the same age. Male pups also get more from their mothers than female pups; they are nursed one full day longer than females, and they are heavier at birth and weaning. These sex differences emphasize that pups of both sexes embark on their respective and different reproductive strategies early in life (Reiter et al., 1978).

Males are selected to risk injury, when stealing milk, for the benefit of getting an edge on other males. If a male outweighs his cohorts early in life, the size advantage is likely to be maintained to adulthood, and he will have an edge in aggressive competition for inseminating females. A male either wins big or he loses completely. Males must gamble to win. The risk of injury in stealing milk is the same for females as males, but the benefits of a weight advantage are not proportional. Thus, females are more likely to maximize their reproductive success by pursuing a conservative strategy.

Sex differences are also evident in early play behavior. Young males initiate more mock fights, and interactions between males last longer than those involving two females. To a remarkable degree, males

Weaned pups first attempt to swim in tide pools, ponds of standing water, or shallows at the water's edge. They are not very good at first but are very interesting to observe.

exhibit the most prominent components of fighting in adult bulls, while females exhibit the basic elements commonly observed in quarreling adult females. Otherwise, one cannot distinguish sex in weaned pups except when the genital opening of the male is visible or by inspecting the teeth. Sex differences are notably absent in behaviors that do not influence sexual selection directly, e.g., latency in entering the water, acquisition of aquatic skills, initial exploration of the water and shoreline, time of departure from the rookery, and survival to 2 years of age.

Weaned pups begin to approach the water when they are 6 to 7 ½ weeks old. At first, their visits are restricted to sunrise and sunset and they are curious, fascinated, and afraid of the water. The first few days they simply get their bellies wet or wallow in tidepools. Their first swimming attempts are awful. They thrash about clumsily and waste a great deal of effort. However, after only a week's practice they are swimming effortlessly, right side up and upside down, floating head up or belly up, diving in a circle after their own tails, or playing chase games with each other. As novice swimmers, they remain underwater for only

362 8 ELEPHANT SEALS

a few seconds. After 2-3 weeks in the water, their dives last several
minutes. After 5 weeks, they may sleep underwater for 10-15 minutes.
They begin to explore coves and beaches removed from their birthsite.
By the time they are ready to leave the rookery, they spend more time in
the water than on land.

The majority of weaned pups leave Año Nuevo and go to sea during
the last 3 weeks in April. Departure may be timed to facilitate feeding
and to avoid predators. A coastal upwelling occurs in this area during
March and April which results in enrichment at the base of the food
chain. This phenomenon has important effects on fish populations and
may be an ideal time for young seals to feed. Recent findings also
suggest that great white sharks, a major predator on northern elephant
seals in winter, may migrate out of the area in spring (Ainley et al., 1978;
Le Boeuf et al., 1980).

Weaned pups go to sea singly and disperse northward. Many of them
feed off the coast of northern Washington and Vancouver Island in
British Columbia. They do not reappear on land again until September.
The majority of those still living return to Año Nuevo or nearby
Southeast Farallon Island. Fifty percent of the pups weaned in 1974
returned in September and survived their first 5 months at sea. Only
30% were still living at age 2, and 13% survived to age 3 (Reiter et al.,
1978).

During the first 4 weeks of life, the edge, superiority, or better luck
that one pup has over another is due primarily to its heredity and the
efforts of it's mother. After weaning, each individual must compete on
its own. Differences in size, condition, and social behavior in early
development has an important influence on reproductive competition
in adulthood. Conversely, reproductive competition in adulthood
selects for the appearance of certain behavioral and morphological
traits and sex differences in early development. Thus, the pattern of
development subserves and is shaped by reproductive competition.

Some physiological adaptations

Elephant seals accomplish some extraordinary feats in the water. For
example, they dive to great depths and remain submerged for long
periods; they regulate their temperature in cold water; and some of them
feed on animals that are as salty as seawater. These marine adaptations,
which facilitate feeding at sea, enable elephant seals to perform extraordinary feats on land. One of them—fasting for long periods—plays a
key role in reproductive competition and in the lifetime reproductive
strategy of individuals of this species.

Before considering fasting, it will be helpful to have a brief background on the general marine physiological adaptations of elephant seals. By and large, most aquatic adaptations are not newly evolved special mechanisms but rather they are the result of extending tissue or organ capacities and increasing their efficiency (Ridgeway, 1972). For example, elephant seals rely heavily on blood oxygen during prolonged dives, not on lung air. Their extraordinary capacity for blood oxygen storage is made possible by an extremely large blood volume, which is about 20% of their body weight (Ridgeway, 1972; Elsner et al., 1964; Simpson, Gilmartin, and Ridgeway, 1970); it is about 13% in humans. The thick layer of subcutaneous fat or blubber helps to insulate them from the cold water in which they make their living as well as helping to streamline their bodies for efficient swimming. The elephant seal's kidney, like that of the sea lion (Ridgeway, 1972), appears to be able to handle electrolyte loads from their ingested prey, that are as salty as the seawater. All of these adaptations—storing oxygen in blood, using fat for thermoregulation, and kidneys for concentrating salts—are not new developments. They are simply more developed in this pinniped than in terrestrial mammals, presumably in response to the specific ecological demands of the marine environment. Physiological capacity for a task varies from one species to the next. The capacity of a particular species is in part a result of the demands to which the animal is exposed in the environment in which it lives. Put another way, the animal's body limits what the animal can do, but if there is a reproductive advantage in doing something, natural selection pushes the limits of organs, tissues, and cells to their maximum. A good example of this is fasting.

Elephant seals fast completely from food and water for long periods. High-ranking adult males go without food and water for 3 months during the breeding season. Pups fast for 2-3 months after weaning. The accomplishment of female elephant seals is even more remarkable and virtually unique among mammals. A female fasts for 34 days, during which she gives birth and nurses her pup until it quadruples its birthweight!

To appreciate why these mammals fast and what is gained, we must once again think in terms of reproductive units or survival points. Female elephant seals clump together and come into estrus during an 8-week period once a year, 15 January to 15 March. This situation has what is called a high environmental potential for polygyny (Emlen and Oring, 1977). A bull that can keep all other males away from a group of females can inseminate all of them and sire many offspring, *provided* that he remains near the females night and day keeping his competitors at bay. If he has to go to sea to feed, someone else replaces him and mates in his absence. Clearly, the mating success of an alpha male is roughly proportional to his length of uninterrupted stay on land during the mating season.

Fasting while nursing provides numerous advantages to females. By not having to go to sea periodically to feed, like sea lions, an elephant seal female can gorge her pup with milk so that it develops rapidly. After only 4 weeks of nursing, the pup is sufficiently large to be weaned and live for 2-3 months without feeding. As a result, maternal investment is brief and ends abruptly, freeing the mother to prepare for future offspring. In contrast, sea lion mothers do not wean their pups until they are at least 6 months old and often not until they are over one year of age and competing for the nipple with a newborn. A fasting elephant seal remains near her pup and protects it when it is most vulnerable to injury from others in the colony. She has no need to find and recognize her own pup among hundreds of others, as sea lions must do after a feeding bout at sea. A good mother *Mirounga* simply does not let her pup out of her sight until she is done with it.

Weaned pups may fast for various reasons. First, they are not yet capable of traveling and of catching their own food. Swimming, diving, and coordination of head and eye movements must be developed while fasting because pups have no choice in the matter. They must learn to deal with the marine environment before finding food in it. Fasting may also be beneficial in that it postpones departure from the rookery until a time when prey may be most abundant and predators least abundant in the area.

Clearly, there is positive selection pressure for adult males, adult females, and weaned pups to remain on land for long periods; and ultimately the benefit is enhanced survival and reproductive success. There is rarely food or water available to marine mammals on land, so they are forced to abstain. The next question is how do they do it? What are the behavioral and physiological "enabling devices?"

To begin with, elephant seals put on a huge fat store before fasting. Adult males are at sea and presumably feeding from March to July. They molt on land in August and then return to sea to feed from September to the end of November. Adult females are at sea continuously from about mid-April to the time they arrive to give birth in winter. Pups suckle for a month before fasting. The blubber and skin of an adult male make up 50% of its weight; the blubber may be more than 15 cm thick above the shoulders of a male. Just before fasting, adult males, adult females, and weaned pups are visibly obese. Unquestionably, all individuals that fast have an enormous capacity to store fat, and they apparently have no problem getting enough to eat in order to do this.

In addition to the advantages that blubber confers on seals in the water by acting as an insulation against the cold, it serves as an energy reserve and a water source during long fasts. This is a good example of parsimony in natural selection; a modification that facilitates thermoregulation in the sea is also employed to facilitate fasting on land. The energy reserve sets a limit to the length of the fast.

Weaned pups

A recent study shows that weaned elephant seal pups are able to fast for up to 3 months by deriving necessary water and energy from the oxidation of fat stores (Ortiz et al., 1978). Weaners were investigated, instead of adults, for the simple reason that they are more manageable experimental subjects than adults. It is assumed that the mechanisms which permit weaners to fast are similar to those operating in adults.

The mass of a pup at weaning is approximately 50% adipose tissue. Approximately 10% of adipose tissue is water. Oxidation of this fat fuel results in the production of ATP and the byproducts, water and CO_2. Fat is the most productive fuel for generating ATP and water. The rate of production of ATP and water by a fasting weaner from its fat is determined by the work it performs, just as in any other vertebrate. The problem for the fasting seal is water balance. It's sole source of water is from lipid catabolism. The interesting and unique species-specific adaptations have to do with output, i.e., how the animal prevents water loss.

Surviving total water abstinence depends on the difference between the rate of metabolically generated water and obligatory water loss from evaporation and urine formation. The most significant finding of the Ortiz et al., study is that starving weaners have a low rate of water turnover. Most of the water produced is conserved. Water economy saves the day and permits the rate of metabolically generated water to equal or exceed that which is lost.

Water can be lost through respiration, cutaneous evaporation, urine production, and a few other minor ways. Respiration and urine formation probably account for about 80% of water loss. Water economy measures are operative in each category.

In order to get water from oxidation of fat, oxygen is needed. But in breathing, moisture is lost. Elephant seals minimize respiratory water

Elephant seals, especially adults, hold their breath for as long as 25 minutes while they sleep. In this way they lose less water to the environment. Animals sleeping in the water, or with just their heads in the water, are a common sight on Año Nuevo Point. (F. Lanting)

loss by modifications in breathing pattern, nasal passage structure, and in the oxygen-carrying capacity of their blood. The breathing rhythm of elephant seals is irregular or temporarily suspended (Bartholomew, 1954); periods of arrested respiration, varying from 2-3 seconds to 60 seconds or more, follow inhalation. Periods of breath-holding following exhalation last from a few minutes to more than 10 minutes, depending on the circumstances and the age of the animal. Irregular breathing occurs during sleep as well as waking. The consequences of this unusual pattern of breathing is that elephant seals, like most marine mammals, breathe infrequently but more efficiently, obtaining more oxygen from the air they breathe. This enables them to conserve water and, by cooling the air they exhale, body heat (Coulombe et al., 1965). Retention of moisture is further aided by elaborate turbinate processes in the nasal passages. These appear to function as counter-current heat exchangers that reduce respiratory water loss by condensation (Schmidt-Nielsen, Hainsworth and Murrish, 1970). In addition, elephant seals have a greater capacity for storing oxygen in their blood than do most other marine mammals (Ridgeway, 1972). Blood volume makes up a high proportion (19-20%) of their body weight, their blood has very high hemoglobin-oxygen binding capacity, and they have a high ratio of red blood cells to plasma (Simpson et al., 1970).

Urine formation in elephant seals also reflects the efficiency of minimizing water loss. Less urine needs to be formed when fat is the fuel, than when protein is used as in the case of newborn pups. Nitrogen is not given off in fat catabolism, as it is in protein catabolism. Hence less urine, the vehicle for getting rid of nitrogen, is formed. Water is further conserved by *concentrating* the small amount of urine produced for removing other wastes. Fasting weaners urinate infrequently because they have little to void. The average amount of urine formed in a fasting weaner is only 200 ml per day, about 3/4 of a cup (C.L. Ortiz and D. Costa, personal communication).

Not much is known about cutaneous evaporation because it is difficult to measure. However, cutaneous water loss would appear to be minimal in elephant seals because they have few sweat glands in their integument. Tearing and feces production are other minor avenues of water loss.

The temporal pattern and intensity of weaner behavior is also consistent with conserving water. They expend little energy and keep cool. Weaners sleep most of the day and night. Their activities, such as playful interactions among themselves and learning to swim and dive, are of low intensity and they are confined primarily to sunrise and sunset when temperatures are low. When temperatures get so low that pups run the risk of losing heat, they group together tightly for warmth. When heat stressed, they flip cool sand on their backs or enter the water.

Evidently, the combination of behavioral and physiological means for conserving metabolically generated water is sufficient to satisfy most of the physiological requirements of fasting elephant seal pups. But what about the adults? They are subject to even more demanding requirements in the face of similar environmental and nutritional

Elephant seals flip sand for a variety of reasons. One of them is to keep cool.
Animals of both sexes and all ages do it, such as the unmolted weaner above
and the adult male below. (B. Le Boeuf)

stresses. Adult females have the added burden of nursing and nurturing their pups; adult males expend considerable energy in fighting and mating.

Nursing females

Lactation is energetically expensive. In many mammals, the nursing female must double or triple her food and water consumption to sustain herself and nourish her offspring. This makes the mother elephant seal's achievement all the more remarkable. While abstaining completely from food and water, she transfers enough milk to her pup so that it gains 100 kg during only 4 weeks of suckling. Like a fasting weaner, she expends little energy by sleeping most of the time and avoiding heat stress. The same physiological mechanisms described for weaners are used to conserve water except that there is the additional problem of milk production and transfer. The nutritional link between mother and pup involves some fascinating co-adaptations.

The need to conserve water during lactation and fasting requires that nursing be efficient and of short duration. The milk must be concentrated with fuel and low in water, because water is scarce for milk

Marianne Riedman maneuvers cautiously to obtain a small sample of milk from a nursing female. A vacuum is created in the cylinder which she carries on her back. When she is able to push the suckling pup aside and cover the nipple with a funnel, a button is pressed and a momentary vacuum is created which permits her to collect a small sample of milk. The technique permits repeated sampling from the same female, but is risky and demands great patience. (K. Parker and E. Fisher)

production. In fact, elephant seal milk has a higher mean fat content (54.5%) and a lower mean water content (32.8%) than any mammal investigated (Le Boeuf and Ortiz, 1977). These figures characterize milk composition only during the last two weeks of nursing. By taking repeated milk samples from females throughout their nursing period, Reidman and Ortiz (1979) showed that milk composition changes drastically during the course of lactation. Water, which makes up 75% of the milk shortly after parturition, declines to a plateau of approximately 35% after two weeks of nursing (see figure on this page). During the same period, fat content rises from 12% to over 50%. In contrast, protein content remains relatively constant within the range of 5 to 12%.

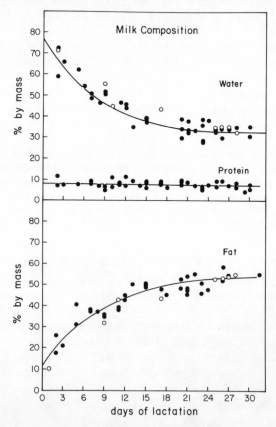

Changes in water, protein, and fat content in elephant seal milk during lactation. The closed circles represent single or multiple samples from 18 females. The open circles represent repeated samples from one individual. (Adapted from Riedman and Ortiz, 1979)

This inverse pattern of fat and water transfer is the result of changing requirements of the pup and declining capabilities of the mother. At birth, the newborn needs a lot of water; it's urine production must be high to excrete the wastes produced by carbohydrate oxidation in utero and by protein oxidation in early lactation. The newborn has no thermal insulating blubber that retards heat loss. Keeping warm necessitates a high metabolic rate and much oxygen. The pup must breathe a lot to get enough oxygen and in doing so it loses water. As it develops blubber, it reduces heat loss and it needs less water from milk since it can metabolically generate its own. The female, on the other hand, has increasingly less to give. At first, her milk is composed of a combination of free and metabolic water. As lactation proceeds, the problem of water balance in the female becomes more acute. The substitution of fat for milk water helps her to conserve water. Not only is it easier for her to give fat at this time but it is the best thing for the pup, who can now use it.

The efficiency of the nutritional pathway between mother and pup is further illustrated by the transfer of other essentials in milk. Instead of making fatty acid chains in the mammary glands as do most nursing mammals that feed, elephant seals may save energy by direct transfer of circulating blood lipids or by making only minor modifications in them. The relatively constant transfer rate of proteins and electrolytes essential for life is an adaptation which maximizes quantitative transfer given the production limitations of the female and the use-storage capacity of the pup. Caloric content of elephant seal milk, which is much higher than that of other mammals studied, is transferred in the same pattern as fat. Finally, nursing behavior is concentrated and apparently highly efficient. Mothers nurse 2 to 4 times during daylight hours every day and apparently follow a similar pattern at night.

Females can afford to give more to their pups as they get older because female size and ability to store fat increases with age (Reiter et al., 1980). The figure on this page shows that the weaning weight of pups increases as a function of mother's age, which is positively correlated with size. Part of the reason is that a female's fat reserves limit the amount of time she can spend on land, fasting and feeding her pup. Old, large females fast and feed their pups longer then young, small ones. Females that lose their pups and do not nurse or nurse infrequently, remain on the rookery longer than females that nurse their pups daily until weaning. Clearly, when the energy reserve is used up, the female is stressed and it is time to return to sea and feed. There is preliminary evidence that older females produce milk that is richer in proteins than that of younger females (Riedman and Ortiz, 1979).

The fact that female energy reserves limit the duration of fasting and of feeding pups, leads to some interesting predictions. Disturbance to nursing females causes them to be more active, and this should cause increased water loss, shortening the fasting period and reducing the amount of nutrients pups receive. At the colony level, one might expect differences in mean fasting duration of females between good and bad weather years, or between disturbed and undisturbed areas. Viewed the other way around, mean fasting duration might serve as an indicator of the degree of disturbance to a colony of females due to social or physical causes.

Adult males

The prodigious fasts of males are as impressive as those of females but for different reasons. Males expend tremendous energy in their effort to achieve high social status and to mate. At any moment they may be required to arise from a torporous resting state to all-out war with competitors. They must always be prepared to fight or flee. Success in fighting leads to the expenditure of additional energy in copulating. Since reproductive warfare on the rookery is constant, a male cannot permit himself the luxury of a long deep sleep. That would be tantamount to deserting his post and would permit copulations by competing males. Sleep among high-ranking males is more like opportunistic catnapping. The usual strategy is to sleep when others are sleeping, and to be alert and ready to prevent copulations when necessary. Obviously, males are hooked on the horns of a dilemma. Physical exertion depletes fat reserves, but a male must exert himself in order to maximize his reproductive success. Any steps a male can take to minimize physical activity without reducing reproductive success can be advantageous.

What is the relative cost of fasting to adults and pups? How many kilocalories are burned up? How much weight is lost? Who is most stressed? Are individuals more vulnerable to predators or infectious diseases at the end of a fast? These questions invite brief speculation. Appearances suggest that adults are more seriously taxed by fasting than weaners. Adults of both sexes are evidently debilitated and haggard by the end of their period of abstinence. The female that looked like a blimp when she arrived resembles a torpedo when she leaves. The mass gain of her pup, and estimates of the kilocalories it receives, indicate the magnitude of the mother's sacrifice. Ortiz and I have found that a pup that gains 100 kg during the suckling period receives at least 130 kg of whole milk. A mother that transfers that much energy probably loses 150 to 200 kg in a little more than a month..

Males appear to lose 1/3 of their mass in 3 months of fasting. They are gaunt and listless at season's end, shadows of their former selves. Many males are so exhausted that they sleep for several days after all of the females have departed. Adults would appear to be especially vulnerable to predators in this condition, and data on males support this hypothesis. The major portion of the annual mortality rate of 50% in males (Le Boeuf, 1974) occurs in spring, after the fast, as opposed to in fall, after a second brief period of molting on land. In contrast, weaners are most sprightly at the end of their fasts just before leaving the rookery. Thus, it appears that adults take their bodies much closer to the physiological limits during fasts than weaners do. This appears to be a consequence of the different advantages each gains from fasting. Fasting in weaners is in part a necessity ordained by the reproductive strategies of mothers. Fasting in adults is more directly linked to reproductive success.

In summary, the struggle for existence and reproductive competition in elephant seals begins early in life, never stops, and is conducted on several levels simultaneously. Selection for favorable variants over thousands of generations has led to the evolution of an animal which never fails to evoke superlatives: The largest seal, one of the deepest divers, capable of prodigious fasts, an animal that not only has survived near-extinction but has made a remarkable comeback; and finally, an animal that continues to teach about us life.

References

Bartholomew, G.A. 1954. Body temperatures and respiratory and heart rates in the northern elephant seal. *J. Mammal.*, 35, 211-218.

Coulombe, H.N., Ridgeway, S.H., and Evans, W.E. 1965. Respiratory water exchange in two species of porpoise. *Science,* 149, 86-88.

Cox, C.R., and Le Boeuf, B.J. 1977. Female incitation of male competition: a mechanism in sexual selection. *Amer. Natur.* 111, 317-335.

Elsner, R.W., Scholander, P.F., Craig, A.B., Diamond, E.G., Irving, L., Pilson, M., Johansen, K., and Bradstreet, E. 1964. Venous oxygen reservoir in the diving elephant seal. *Physiologist,* 7, 124.

Emlen, S.T., and Oring, L.W. 1977. Ecology, sexual selection, and the evolution of mating systems. *Science,* 197, 215-223.

Ghiselin, M.T. 1974. *The Economy of Nature and The Evolution of Sex.* University of California Press, Berkeley.

Le Boeuf, B.J. 1971. The aggression of the breeding bulls. *Natural History,* 130, 82-94.

Le Boeuf, B.J. 1972. Sexual behavior in the northern elephant seal, *Mirounga angustiro-stris. Behaviour,* 41, 1-26.

Le Boeuf, B.J. 1974. Male-male competition and reproductive success in elephant seals. *American Zoologist,* 14, 163-176.

Le Boeuf, B.J. 1977. Back from extation? *Pacific Discovery,* 30, 1-9.

Le Boeuf, B.J., Ainley, D.G., and Lewis, T.J. 1974. Elephant seals on the Farallones: Population structure of an incipient colony. *Journal of Mammalogy,* 55, 370-385.

Le Boeuf, B.J., and Briggs, K.T. 1977. The cost of living in a seal harem. *Mammalia,* 41, 167-195.

Le Boeuf, B.J., and Ortiz, C.L. 1977. Composition of elephant seal milk. *J. Mammal.,* 58, 683-685.

Le Boeuf, B.J., and Panken, K.J. 1977. Elephant seals breeding on the mainland in California. *Proc. Calif. Acad. Sci.,* 41, 267-280.

Le Boeuf, B.J., and Peterson, R.S. 1969. Social status and mating activity in elephant seals. *Science,* 163, 91-93.

Le Boeuf, B.J., Riedman, M., and Keyes, R.S. 1982. Shark predation on pinnipeds in California coastal waters. *Fishery Bulletin,* 80, 891-895.

Le Boeuf, B.J., Whiting, R.J., and Gantt, R.F. 1972. Perinatal behavior of northern elephant seal females and their young. *Behaviour,* 43, 121-156.

Ortiz, C.L., Costa, D., and Le Boeuf, B.J. 1978. Water and energy flux in elephant seal pups fasting under natural conditions. *Physiol. Zool.,* 51, 166-178.

Ridgeway, S.H. 1972. Homeostasis in the aquatic environment. Pages 590-747 *in* S.H. Ridgeway (Ed.) *Mammals of the Sea: Biology and Medicine,* Thomas, Springfield, Illinois.

Reiter, J., Panken, K.J., and Le Boeuf, B.J. 1980. Female competition and reproductive success in northern elephant seals. *Animal Behaviour* (in press).

Reiter, J., Stinson, N.L., and Le Boeuf, B.J. 1978. Northern elephant seal development: the transition from weaning to nutritional independence. *Behav. Ecol. Sociobiol.,* 3, 337-367.

Riedman, M., and Ortiz, C.L. 1979. Changes in milk composition during lactation in the northern elephant seal. *Physiol. Zool.,* 52, 240-249.

Schmidt-Nielsen, K., Hainsworth, F.R., and Murrish, D.E. 1970. Counter-current heat exchange in the respiratory passages: effect on water and heat balance. *Respiratory Physiol.,* 9, 263-276.

Simpson, J.G., Gilmartin, W.G., and Ridgeway, S.H. 1970. Blood volume and other hematologic parameters in young elephant seals *Mirounga angustirostris. Amer. J. Vet. Res.,* 31, 1449.

9

Retrospective

Burney J. Le Boeuf and Stephanie Kaza

WHENEVER one observes anything long enough and in sufficient depth, whether it is a cell, a bumblebee, or energy flow in an acre of grassland, three revelations are likely to occur: one begins to appreciate the specialness of the thing under examination, one gains a better understanding of how it works, and one perceives changes and the rate at which they occur. So it has been with our examination of Año Nuevo from multiple perspectives. We have come to appreciate that behind all of the details that characterize Año Nuevo lies a complex ecological community. We are impressed with the uniqueness of this place compared to other places along the California coast. We have identified numerous complex relationships within the Año Nuevo ecosystem which help us to understand how the place functions. With time and patience, we are beginning to appreciate the processes that bring about change in this ecosystem. We discuss each of these impressions in turn.

Special qualities. Much of the uniqueness of Año Nuevo stems from its physical environment. The geology, currents, climate, and location of Año Nuevo determine the setting in which plants and animals grow. Año Nuevo provides a variety of habitats for an unusually diverse assemblage of plants and animals. Jutting out approximately 2 km into the Pacific Ocean from the coastline, the prominent point and wide, gently sloping shelf put the area close to the California Current and to the marine upwelling that brings cold water up from the bottom of the sea. The unusual tilted and layered Monterey shale formation offshore from the point offers abundant exposed sites for the attachment and settling of a wide range of intertidal plants and animals. The substrate habitat is ever changing because the shale is extremely friable. The island is one of the few places where pinnipeds and seabirds can rest and breed along the central and northern coast of California, free from land predators. High mountains and the steep rugged topography directly

(F. Lanting)

adjacent to the coast contribute to the considerably milder microclimate of the Año Nuevo Point area relative to the rest of the nearby coastline. The benign fog protects intertidal organisms from dessication on long summer days. In contrast, the harsh winds and waves during storms wreak havoc with dune plants and elephant seal breeding colonies during winter.

These physical features distinguish Año Nuevo from other areas along the central California coast, and they determine the kind and quantity of biological communities that are present. The prominent point is a convenient stopover for birds migrating along the Pacific flyway and a repository for sand drifting down from northern rivers and streams, the latter giving rise to the unique dunefield. The low-lying, flat marine terraces at Año Nuevo, with a recent history of fault activity, affect the pattern of vegetation. Where Año Nuevo Creek deposits cover the terraces, the open field is enriched and is undergoing rapid successional transformation. The entire area from the terraces to the dunefields remains moist with groundwater throughout the year, in large part because of artificial irrigation patterns, but also because of the differential permeabilities of the underlying rock formations.

Biologically, Año Nuevo is unusual in its diversity of life forms. Rare species such as the Harlequin Duck and the San Francisco garter snake occur here. Numerous birds use the area for breeding. Because of the geographic setting and the variety of plant communities, many unusual birds pass through and feed here during migration. Marine mammals alone mark this spot as unique along the Pacific coast and in the world. The presence of five species of seals in a single locale does not occur anywhere else in the Pacific with the exception of San Miguel Island in southern California. Three species of pinnipeds breed on the tiny island. The Año Nuevo mainland is the only place in the world where northern elephant seals breed on the mainland. (The southern elephant seal, a different but related species, has one exceptional colony breeding on a continental mainland, but that is on an isolated peninsula in far off Patagonia.) Nowhere else are sea otters found in the same waters with elephant seals, Steller sea lions, and California sea lions. The opportunity for detailed, long-term scientific research on a single animal population like the northern elephant seal has yielded an exceptional data base for the social behavior of specific individuals. This sort of careful, behavioral investigation of a single species is rarely possible because of the difficulty in recognizing individuals. As a scientific laboratory, Año Nuevo offers an exceptional site and an opportunity for in-depth behavioral and biological research.

The unusual qualities of the Año Nuevo region seem to have been a lure for an unusual, exceptional, or enterprising lot of humans—people like Isaac Graham, Loren Coburn, several members of the pioneering Steele family, and Tom Poulter, to name a few. Before the Spanish arrived, one of the largest Indian settlements along the coast was located here.

Relationships. The mechanics that govern the flow of life in this region are revealed in the relationships between the various elements that compose and characterize the place. The many patterns of interaction and interdependence within the Año Nuevo ecosystem vary greatly in detail, complexity, and importance. We discuss some relationships that stand out in bold relief and which we think are important in describing this unique place and its dynamics.

(F. Lanting)

The configuration of physical variables that characterize Año Nuevo provides habitats for a variety of plants and animals, especially at primary levels of biological productivity. Increased primary productivity facilitates life at higher consumer levels in the food web. The consumer organisms that benefit indirectly from the unique physical conditions at Año Nuevo also contribute significantly to the recycling of energy in the system.

The dune area offers one example of a fluid relationship between the physical environment and biologic communities. Although the dunes keep moving with the strong northwesterly winds, vegetation stabilization has accelerated in the last few decades because of an increase in the amount of groundwater made available by agricultural irrigation. As some plants gain a foothold in specific areas, sand is bound in place and dune movement is arrested. Just when plants are beginning to thrive, wind and weather may change causing great mounds of sand to move in, smothering seedlings and halting further plant expansion. Although the vegetation is firmly rooted in some parts of the dunefield, in other areas the situation is extremely dynamic, changing from year to year, and often from week to week.

Plants and animals that benefit directly from the physical environment attract predators and scavengers and thus further enrich the area. For example, the extensive intertidal zone harbors an abundance of limpets, snails, abalones, mussels, and clams. These molluscs attract animals that feed on them such as Black Oystercatchers, sea otters, and people. Strong oceanic upwelling in offshore waters supplies nutrients for intertidal plants. The diverse marine plants provide canopy cover and food for numerous fishes and invertebrates. These in turn feed visiting sea lions and migrating birds. As the island populations of pinnipeds increase in number, free from terrestrial carnivores and major human disturbances, great white sharks which feed on them appear in the area more frequently.

Specific relationships between at least one pinniped, the elephant seal, and several bird species have been observed. Several gull species, but especially the large Western and Herring Gulls, depend on elephant seal placentas and dead pups for a major portion of their winter food. Some individuals supplement this diet with the exceptionally fatty seal milk that spills over during nursing. These gull populations have grown as the elephant seal population has increased over the past ten years. One small shorebird, the Black Turnstone, also draws on the elephant seal for food, preferring the blood from open cuts and sores. Some of these symbiotic relationships can be very subtle and not necessarily related to feeding. Many Western Gulls nest on the periphery of Steller sea lion breeding territories. One aspect of this proximal relationship is that the sea lions are provided with a distant warning system for detecting approaching predators. The gulls react to the approach of people by issuing an alarm call and flying above their nests; the sea lions have apparently learned to associate the call with the approach of

(F. Lanting)

humans or some predator which threatens the birds, and the sea lions respond by rushing to the safety of the water.

Since elephant seals began breeding on the mainland, their ponderous ramblings have taken an increasing toll on plant communities near Año Nuevo Point. Each year, as the animals fight and rumble after each other, they charge over and through vegetation. At the end of a breeding season, numerous pathways are visible through the iceplant and willows. Dune plants are trampled and damaged, and the grounds are devoid of vegetation in many areas. Seal activities, like the wind, interfere with vegetative dune stabilization. As the number of animals has increased on the mainland, the dune plants have suffered more and more seasonal damage. At present, the effect does not seem to be longlasting because each spring the area revegetates in a burst of growth and fertility. However, the long-term effects of this relatively new animal-plant interaction bear watching as the seal population continues to grow.

Many of the plants and animals that are directly dependent on the physical environment indirectly facilitate the growth and survival of other animals. The thousands of pinnipeds that use Año Nuevo Island enrich the area in a variety of ways. We've mentioned that the afterbirths and dead carcasses that decompose on the island provide food for birds, crabs, and numerous other marine organisms. In addition, the

(F. Lanting)

great quantity of nitrogen compounds from pinniped waste products accumulates on the island and mainland beaches and washes off each year with the first rains. This produces a marked increase in the ammonium-nitrogen content of the waters in the vicinity. Algal growth is promoted, enriching the intertidal zone, and providing increased food for intertidal invertebrates, small fishes, shorebirds, and eventually the seals themselves. The waters near Año Nuevo Island are a good place to fish, not in spite of the seals as fishermen used to think, but probably because of them.

In the dune and field communities, those plants drawing their nutrients and water directly from the soils serve to facilitate the growth of other plants. Where pioneer plants gain a foothold and produce organic matter, they form a microhabitat of decaying material appropriate for seed germination. Where taller shrubs of willows and lupines are well established, smaller herbs such as beach primrose benefit from canopy protection. Decomposing remnants of spring foliage support an important community from bacteria and fungi to pillbugs. These complicated nutrient-recycling relationships are extremely significant in retaining energy and biomass in the system, but little is known about them.

Humans have had a profound effect on biological relationships in the Año Nuevo ecosystem. As people have used the land for various activities, the natural plant communities have been altered extensively, affecting the animal populations that depend on them. This effect has been accomplished directly and indirectly by eradication and displacement of existing species and the introduction of new ones, by changing the actual physical environment, and by changing relationships within the ecosystem. Human activities have probably been one of the most influential factors in the evolution of coastal plant associations and changes in the landscape along the central California coast.

The earliest known human inhabitants of the Año Nuevo area, the Ohlone Indians, relied on the abundant marine and terrestrial food resources for sustenance. Some of their practices had an important impact on the kind of plants and animals that predominated. By burning the open fields regularly, the Indians inhibited the natural succession of plant communities from open field to chaparral to forest. Burning kept these areas free from invading brush and stimulated grass seed production. Seeds were more easily harvested and game animals more easily hunted in the open areas.

With the arrival of the Spanish settlers and their cattle, the native plant communities were affected once again. The sharp hooves of the heavy cattle injured, trampled, and uprooted native plant species. Euro-

(F. Lanting)

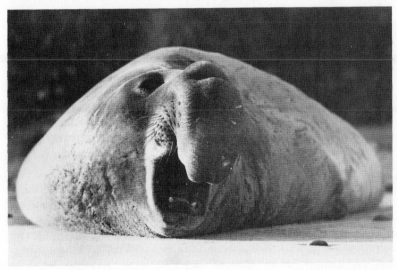

(F. Lanting)

pean annuals grasses, brought in purposely or inadvertently by the settlers, took hold in the disturbed areas and gradually replaced the native bunch grasses. This transition probably had an effect on the community of soil microorganisms as well as on the associated grassland fauna.

During this period of exploration and exploitation, entire animal populations were eradicated from the area while others were displaced from their habitat by human activities. It is difficult to assess the full impact on the ecosystem of eliminating major predators and scavengers such as the grizzly bear, the timber wolf, the sea otter, several pinniped species, and the California Condor. We can speculate that with predator pressure reduced, prey flourished; but we do not really know how extensive the change was. On the positive side, although human settlement displaced some species, it created new habitats for others. For example, the barns at Año Nuevo are now used by nesting swallows: the diversion of Whitehouse Creek, with extensive irrigation for crop cultivation, has enabled willows on the point to flourish.

At present, humans are such a commanding force in the area that simply leaving things alone causes profound changes in the biota. Currently the State Parks and Recreation Department is allowing a previously cultivated field to return to a natural state. The now grassy field is undergoing the natural process of plant succession. Coyote bush and other chaparral plants are invading the area and will certainly change the balance of both plants and animals. Small birds and rodents that subsist on seeds and insects are in turn preyed on by hawks and coyotes. As the open grassland community is invaded by brushy plants, it may become more difficult for the raptors to see and capture their prey and this may force them to seek food elsewhere. Even prey populations may decrease as bushes replace the annual grasses. These events represent initial stages of a process which may culminate in the invasion of Año Nuevo Point by coniferous trees.

Human interest in seals has changed from a relationship of exploitation to one of observation and educational study. Leaving the elephant seal population alone and giving it protected status has allowed a burgeoning rookery to develop on the island and on the mainland. The colony has grown beyond anyone's wildest expectations. Thousands of tourists, naturalists and students come to the area every winter to view these animals in their natural setting. This unusual experience is made possible by the development of an interpretive program, in which visitors are accompanied by guides trained at the University of California at Santa Cruz. Although human trampling takes some toll on the

(F. Lanting)

trailside plants, adverse impact appears to be relatively low, probably because of the strong education orientation of the interpretive program. Respect for wildlife is legally mandated in Reserve regulations and is supported as well through the attitudes of students and staff working with the public.

When we stand back and reflect on the entire Año Nuevo ecosystem, we see that all of the processes we have described are interrelated. When one animal population increases or decreases in number from whatever cause, this affects other plants or animals that it feeds on, that feed on it, or that compete with it for living space. The repercussions may continue much longer than we suspect or have the capacity to follow. The initial event may be considered trivial at the time, like the introduction of three bush rabbits on the island in 1948. The rabbits thrived and multiplied and have been eating up the vegetation on the island ever since. However, the proliferation of island rabbits comes at the expense of Killdeers and White-crowned Sparrows. These birds no longer nest on the island because the vegetative cover is no longer adequate for this purpose. With a reduction in vegetation, the eroding effect of wind and rain is increased, and this is causing the entire island to deteriorate very rapidly. Undoubtedly, the single act of introducing rabbits on the island has caused many other changes of which we are not aware.

Changes. The more we have learned about the Año Nuevo region, the more we have come to appreciate that the ecosystem is constantly in flux. Evidences of major geological changes are clearly visible and serve as reminders that the landscape is continually evolving. The shape of the land reflects the long history of marine terrace formation and also the individual faulting events that twisted rock formations in specific areas. The island is a recent formation, which probably separated from the mainland around 350 years ago. The boundaries of the island and point are eroding constantly as the relentless impact of winter waves pound against the shore. We have already described some of the substantial changes in the plant and animal communities of the Año Nuevo region, especially within recent recorded human history.

The most conspicuous changes at Año Nuevo, to the human eye, take place over the course of a year or a season or even during a single day. The beaches fill up with sand and then wash out from summer to winter. Migrating birds pass through in great flocks during fall and spring, leaving only a few species to nest and raise young in the area. The pinnipeds come and go according to their time-tested cycles. California sea lions predominate in the fall and elephant seals in the winter; harbor seals breed in the spring and Steller sea lions in the summer. Each season has its flowering plants, with the peak of growth and reproduction in most of them taking place in spring and summer. Within a single season, individual plant species succeed one another, constantly changing the floral composition of the dune and field communities.

The intertidal region shows a marked change from winter to spring, and each month the cycle of tides exposes the low zone creatures in a predictable pattern. Clamdiggers and abalone seekers follow the rhythm of the tides, which are ruled by the phases of the moon. Surfers appear with the "good" waves. Tourists, birdwatchers, and beachcombers come and go with the cycles of weather, weekends, and holidays. During a single day, fog and wind patterns are somewhat predictable, especially in summer, as are the daily habits of some of the resident animals. The small rabbits and deer are active early in the morning and at sunset; the short-eared owls replace the marsh hawks at night in search of food in the fields.

Año Nuevo is mutable; the place is constantly being transformed. Identifying the processes that induce the changes gives one added dimension of understanding. Identifying the changes, when they occur, how thay are brought about, and their effects, reveals the dynamic flow of energy within the ecosystem. These changing relationships are the heart of Año Nuevo.

The role of human beings in inducing changes in this natural system has varied considerably over the last 10,000 years. The specific orientation of cultural groups to other animals and to plants at Año Nuevo reflects a range of attitudes towards the environment. The pendulum has swung in both directions, from the living-on-the-land ethic of early native Ohlones to the period of heavy exploitation by Europeans in the 1800s, and now to the present management of part of the area as a reserve.

Unquestionably, one of the most significant influences on the future of Año Nuevo is the attitudes of humans to other animals and to plants. During the last decade, the utilitarian philosophy that predominated since the arrival of the Spaniards has come into question. In its place, an environmental awareness has emerged and attitudes have taken a distinct turn toward protection and reverence for other-than-human forms of life. This shift in values is reflected in strong federal legislation supporting greater care in managing wildlife populations as well as in restrictions on treatment of domestic and laboratory animals. According to the emerging philosophy, animals should be protected, not only from being killed or injured, but also from being harassed. Harassment may mean anything, from touching, teasing, or prodding, to inadvertent disruption of an animal's harmony and space. Even more important is the recognition that protecting endangered animals is of no avail unless the habitat in which they feed, rest, and breed is also protected. A person who shoots a sea otter or uses a group of sleeping sea lions for target practice is now apt to be viewed as a malicious, unfeeling social primitive, an object of scorn and disgust, and to be punished by the law. The law may also extend some protection to the habitats on which these animals depend for survival.

Despite the often paradoxical inconsistencies of the new ethics, the concern for animal rights and respect for animal consciousness represents a profound change in our attitude to animals other than ourselves and mirrors a change in our behavior to them.

The conditions of the State Reserve status of Año Nuevo mandate strict protection of all the living and non-living parts of the system. In the State Reserve, the protective ethic is reinforced by the visitor interpretive program, which stresses respect for the entire place and for all the members of the biological community. The strong educational orientation of the interpretive program attempts to introduce the visitor to the complexity of Año Nuevo through firsthand experience. Contact learning encourages a reexamination of cultural values as they affect wildlife and as they determine the role of human beings in the ecosystem.

What is the future of Año Nuevo? Many parts of the old land grant are being converted to homes, especially in the northern sector. Most of the southern sector remains grazing land and cultivated fields. The part of the region that we have focused on is now managed by the California State Parks system for general public use; the island is maintained as a scientific reserve for research use only. These uses of Point Año Nuevo reflect our current cultural needs and values regarding wild animals and natural environments. They very well may change in the coming years. For now, Año Nuevo represents the values of people working together, learning together, and sharing a spirit of discovery. Research and public education have been made possible through interagency cooperation. With attentive respect for the land and life of Año Nuevo, we may continue to learn about the wonders of this place and the depth of our connections with the beauty and integrity of the natural world.

(F. Lanting)

Appendix

LIST OF SPECIES

This species list reflects areas of research at Año Nuevo. Some parts of the list are more complete than others. Land invertebrates and non-vascular land plants are omitted because they have not yet been studied in detail at Año Nuevo. Some information exists for fishes, amphibians, reptiles, and land mammals, but detailed species surveys have not yet been done. For most organisms we have provided additional information regarding location found or abundance.

These references were the primary guides for listing each of the groups of species:

Marine plants: Abbott, I.A. and Hollenberg, G.J. 1976. *Marine Algae of California.* Stanford University Press, Stanford.

Land Plants: Munz, p. 1973. *A California Flora.* University of California Press, Berkeley, California

Intertidal Invertebrates: Smith, R.I. and Carlton, J.T., eds. 1975. *Light's Manual: Intertidal Invertebrates of the Central California Coast.* University of California Press, Berkeley, California.

Birds: Robbins, C.S., Bruun, B., and Zim, H.S. 1966. *Birds of North America.* Golden Press, New York.

Marine Mammals: Burt, W.H. and Grossenheider, R.P. 1964. *A Field Guide to the Mammals.* Houghton Mifflin Co., Boston.

LAND PLANTS

* = Non-native species

f = Forest
r = Riparian
o = Open Field
p = Pond
d = Dunes
c = Cliff seeps

DIVISION CALAMOPHYTA
  Order Equisitales
    Equisitaceae — **Horsetail Family**
      Equisetum telmateia — Giant horsetail (o,c)

DIVISION PTEROPHYTA
  Order Filicales — **Fern Order**
    Pteridaceae
      Pteridium aquilinum — Bracken fern (r,o)
    Aspidiaceae
      Polystichum munitum — Sword fern (r)
  Order Salviniales
    Salviniaceae
      Azolla filiculoides — Water fern (p)

DIVISION CONIFEROPHYTA — **CONE-BEARING PLANTS**
  Order Coniferales
    Cupressaceae — **Cypress Family**
      Cupressus macrocarpa — Monterey cypress (r,o)
    Pinaceae — **Pine Family**
      Pinus attenuata — Knobcone pine (f)
      P. radiata — Monterey pine (o)
      Pseudotsuga menziesii — Douglas fir (f,o,d)

DIVISION ANTHOPHYTA — **FLOWERING PLANTS**
  Class Dicotyledoneae
    Aizoaceae — **Carpet-weed Family**
      Carpobrotus chilense — Iceplant or sea fig (d,c)
    Anacardiaceae — **Sumac Family**
      Toxicodendron diversilobum — Poison oak (f,r,o,p,d)
    Apiaceae — **Carrot Family**
      Cicuta douglasii — Water hemlock (p)
      *Conium maculatum** — Poison hemlock (r,o,p)
      *Foeniculum vulgare** — Fennel (o)
      Heracleum maximum — Cow parsnip (r)
      Sanicula crassicaulis — (o)
      S. laciniata — Coast snakeroot (o,p)
    Asteraceae (Compositae) — **Sunflower Family**
      Achillea millefolium — Yarrow (o,p,d)
      Anaphalis margaritacea — Pearly everlasting (o,d)

*Anthemis cotula**	Dog fennel (r)
Artemisia californica	California sagebrush (r,o)
A. douglasiana	Mugwort (r,p)
A. pycnocephala	Beach sagewort (d)
Aster subspicatus	Aster (o,p)
Baccharis douglasii	(o)
B. pilularis	Coyote bush (r,o,p)
var. *consanguinea*	(o,d)
var. *pilularis*	Dwarf chapparal broom (d)
Cirsium occidentale	Cobweb thistle (r,o)
*C. vulgare**	Bull thistle (o)
*Conyza bonariensis**	Horseweed (o,p)
C. canadensis	(o)
*Cotula coronopifolia**	Brass buttons (p,d,c)
*Erechtites arguta**	Fireweed (d)
*E. prenanthoides**	Fireweed (p)
Erigeron glaucus	Seaside daisy (o)
Eriophyllum staechadifolium	Lizard tail or golden yarrow (r,o,p,d)
var. *artemisiaefolium*	
Franseria chamissonis	Beach bur (d)
var. *bipinnatisecta*	(d)
var. *chamissonis*	(d)
Gnaphalium chilense	Cudweed (r,o,p,d)
G. spp.	Everlastings (o,d)
Haplopappus ericoides	Mock heather (o,d)
*Hypochoeris radicata**	Hairy cat's ear (o)
Matricaria matricarioides	Pineapple weed (o)
*Picris echioides**	Prickly ox tongue (o,p)
*Senecio vulgaris**	Common groundsel (o)
Silybum marianum	Milk thistle (o)
*Sonchus asper**	Sow thistle (o)
*S. oleraceus**	Common sow thistle (o)
*S. tenerrimus**	Slender sow thistle (o,p)
Solidago occidentalis	Western goldenrod (o)
S. spathulata	Dune goldenrod (d)
*Taraxacum officinale**	Common dandelion (o)
Betulaceae	**Birch Family**
Alnus oregana	Oregon alder (r)
Boraginaceae	**Borage Family**
Amsinckia spectabilis	Fiddleneck (o,d)
Cryptantha leiocarpa	Coast Cryptantha (d)
Heliotropum curassavicum	Heliotrope (d)
Brassicaceae (Cruciferae)	**Mustard Family**
*Brassica campestris**	Field mustard (o,p)
B. sp.	
Cakile edentula spp. *californica*	California sea rocket (d)
*C. maritima**	European sea rocket (d)
Cardamine oligosperma	Few-seeded bittercress (d)
*Raphanus sativus**	Wild radish (o,p)

Caprifoliaceae
  Sambucus callicarpa
Caryophyllaceae
  *Silene gallica**
  Spergularia macrotheca
  *S. rubra**
  *Stellaria media**
Chenopodiaceae
  *Chenopodium ambrosioides**
Compositae (*See* Asteraceae)
Convolvulaceae
  *Calestegia arvensis**
  C. occidentalis
  Convolvulus soldanella
Crassulaceae
  Dudleya farinosa
Cruciferae (*See* Brassicaceae)
Curcurbitaceae
  Marah fabaceus
Fabaceae
  Lathyrus littoralis
  *Lotus corniculatus**
  Lupinus arboreus
  *Medicago hispida**
  *Melilotus indicus**
  Trifolium sp.
  *Vicia sativa**
Fagaceae
  Quercus agrifolia
Gentianaceae
  Centaurium davyi
Geraniaceae
  Erodium sp.*
  Geranium dissectum
  *G. molle**
Hippocastanaceae
  Aesculus californica
Lamiaceae
  *Marrubium vulgare**
  Satureja douglasii
  Stachys bullata
  S. rigida
    var. *quercetorum*
Linaceae
  *Linum usitassimum**
Lythraceae
  Lythrum hyssopifolia
Malvaceae
  *Malva nicaeenis**

Honeysuckle Family
  Red elderberry (r)
Pink Family
  Windmill pink (d)
  Large-flowered sand spurry (d)
  Purple sand spurry (d)
  Chickweed (o)

  Mexican tea (r)

Morning-glory Family
  Bindweed (o)
  (r)
  Beach morning glory (d)
Stonecrop Family
  Live forever (o)

Gourd Family
  Wild cucumber (r,o)
Pea Family
  Silver beach pea (d)
  Bird's foot trefoil (o)
  Bush lupine (o,p,d)
  Bur clover (o)
  (o)
  Clover (o)
  Spring vetch (r,o)
Oak Family
  Coast live oak (r)
Gentian Family
  (p,d)
Geranium Family
  Filaree (r,o)
  Cut-leaved geranium (o)
  Cranesbill (o)
Buckeye Family
  California buckeye (r)
Mint Family
  Hoarhound (o)
  Yerba buena (o)
  Wood mint (r,o)
  (r,o)

Flax Family
  Common flax (p)
Loosestrife Family
  Loosestrife (p)
Mallow Family
  Bull mallow (o)

Sidalcea malvaeflora   Checker bloom (o)
ssp. *malvaeflora*
Nyctaginaceae   **Four-O'Clock Family**
Abronia latifolia   Yellow sand verbena (d)
A. umbellata   Beach sand verbena (d)
Onagraceae   **Evening Primrose Family**
Boisduvalia densiflora   (d)
Camissonia cheiranthifolia   Beach primrose (d)
Epilobium paniculatum   Willow herb (r)
E. watsonii   San Francisco willow herb (d)
var. *franciscanum*
Oenothera hookeri   Hooker's primrose (o)
O. ovata   Suncups (o)
Oxalidaceae   **Wood-Sorrel Family**
*Oxalis pes-caprae**   Bermuda buttercup (o)
O. pilosa   (o)
Papaveraceae   **Poppy Family**
Eschscholzia californica   California poppy (o,d)
Plantaginaceae   **Plantain Family**
*Plantago coronopus**   (o)
P. hirtella   (o)
P. lanceolata   English plantain (o,p,d)
P. maritima   (r,o)
ssp. *juncoides* var. *californica*
Polemoniaceae   **Phlox**
Navarretia squarrosa   Skunkweed (d)
Polygonaceae   **Buckwheat Family**
Eriogonum latifolium   Coast buckwheat (o,d)
Polygonum punctatum   Water smartweed (o)
*Rumex acetosella**   Sheep sorrel (o)
R. crassus   Dock (0)
*R. crispus**   Curly dock (o,d)
Portulacaeae   **Purslane Family**
Montia perfoliata   Miner's lettuce (r)
Primulaceae   **Primrose Family**
*Anagallis arvensis**   Scarlet pimpernel (o)
Rhamnaceae   **Buckthorn Family**
Rhamnus californica   Coffeeberry (r)
Rosaceae   **Rose Family**
Fragaria chiloensis   Beach strawberry (d)
Potentilla egedii var. *grandis*   Cinquefoil (r,p)
Rubus parviflorus   Thimbleberry (r)
var. *velutinus*
R. ursinus   California blackberry (r,o,p,d)
Rubiaceae   **Madder Family**
Galium aparine   Bedstraw (r)
Salicaceae   **Willow Family**
Salix lasiolepis   Arroyo willow (o,p,d)

Scrophulariaceae
Castilleja latifolia var. *wightii*
Mimulus guttatus
M. moschatus
Orthocarpus faucibarbatus
   var. *albidus*
Scrophularia californica
Solanaceae
Solanum douglasii
S. umbelliferum
Urticaceae
Urtica californica
U. urens
Class Monocotyledoneae
Amaryllidaceae
Brodiaea pulchella
Cyperaceae
Carex montereyensis
C. sp.
Cyperus eragrostis
Scirpus americanus
S. californicus
S. cernuus ssp. *californicus*
Iridaceae
Sisyrinchium bellum
Juncaceae
Juncus falcatus
J. lesueurii
Liliaceae
Chlorogalum pomeridianum
Smilacina racemosa
   var. *amplexicaulis*
Poaceae
*Aira caryophyllea**
*Ammophila arenaria**
*Avena barbata**
*Briza minor**
*Bromus rigidus**
*B. rubens**
*B. mollis**
*Cortaderia selloana**
*Dactylis glomerata**
Digitaria sp.
Distichlis spicata
Elymus sp.
Festuca megalura
*F. myuros**
Hordeum brachyantherum

Figwort Family
Indian paintbrush (o,d)
Monkeyflower (d,c)
Muskflower (d)
Owl's clover (d)

Figwort or California bee plant (r,o,p,d)
Nightshade Family
Douglas nightshade (r,d)
Blue witch (d)
Nettle Family
California nettle (r)
Dwarf nettle (d)

Amaryllis Family
Blue dicks (r)
Sedge Family
Monterey sedge (o,p)
(p)
Umbrella sedge (r,p,d)
Three square (r,p)
Bullrush or Tule (c)
(c)
Iris Family
Blue-eyed grass (o)
Rush Family
Iris leaf juncus (d)
Salt rush (o,p,d,c)
Lily Family
Soaproot (o)
False Solomon's Seal (r)

Grass Family
Silvery hair grass (d)
European beach grass (d)
Wild oats (o)
Little quaking grass (o)
Ripgut (o)
Brome grass (o)
Soft chess (o)
Pampas grass (p,d)
Orchard grass (o)
Crab grass (r)
Seashore saltgrass (d,c)
Rye grass (d)
Fescue (o)
(o)
(o)

H. jubatum*   Foxtail (o)
H. leporinum*   (o)
Lolium multiflorum* Italian rye grass (o)
Phalaris tuberosa*   Canary grass (o)
Polypogon monspeliensis* Rabbit's foot grass (o,d)
Stipa sp.   Speargrass (o)
Orchidaceae   **Orchid Family**
Spiranthes romanzoffiana   Hooded lady's tresses (o)
var. *romanzoffiana*
Typhaceae   **Cattail Family**
Typha sp.   Cattail (r)

MARINE PLANTS

* = Distribution not determined; h = high tide zone; m = mid tide zone; l = low tide zone.

DIVISION CHLOROPHYTA

Bryopsis corticulans (h,m,l)
Chaetomorpha linum (h,m,l)
Cladophora columbiana (h,m)
C. microcladioides (l)
C. sakaii (l)
C. sericea (l)
C. stimpsonii*
C. sp. (h,m,l)
Codium setchellii (h,m,l)
"Collinsiella tuberculata" (h)
Endophyton ramosum*
Enteromorpha clathrata (m)
E. compressa (h,m)
E. flexuosa (h)
E. intestinalis (h)
E. linza (h,m,l)
E. sp. (h,m)
Monostroma grevillei (l)
M. zostericola*
Rhizoclonium implexum (h)
Spongomorpha coalita (h,m)
S. mertensii (l)
S. saxatalis (m)
Ulothrix pseudoflacca (h)
Ulva angusta*
U. californica*
U. expansa (m,l)
U. lactuca*
U. lobata (h,m,l)
U. rigida (h)
U. taeniata (l)
Urospora penicilliformis (h,m)

DIVISION PHAEOPHYTA

Alaria marginata (h,m,l)
Analipus japonicus (h,m)
Colpomenia peregrina (h,m)
Cylindrocarpus rugosus (h,m)
Cystosiera osmundacea (m,l)
Desmarestia latifrons*
D. ligulata (l)
Dictyoneurum californicum*

Ectocarpus parvus (l)
E. sp. (h,m,l)
Egregia menziesii (m,l)
Feldmannia cylindrica (m,l)
Fucus distichus ssp. edentatus (h,m)
Haplogloia andersonii (h,m,l)
Laminaria dentigera (m,l)
L. sinclairii (m,l)
Leathesia difformis (h)
L. nana (h)
Macrocystis integrifolia*
Nereocystis luetkeana*
Pelvetia fastigiata (h,m)
Pelvetiopsis limitata (h,m)
Petalonia fascia (l)
Phaeostrophion irregulare (h,m,l)
Postelsia palmaeformis (h)
Pterygophora californica (l)
Ralfsia pacifica (h,m,l)
Scythosiphon dotyi (h)
S. lomentaria (h)

DIVISION RHODOPHYTA

Acrochaetium porphyrae (m,l)
A. subimmersum (l)
Ahnfeltia gigartinoides (m)
A. plicata (m,l)
Amplisiphonia pacifica (m)
Antithamnionella pacifica (h)
Bangia fusco-purpurea (h,m)
Bornetia californica (m,l)
Bossiella californica*
B. chiloensis (h,m,l)
B. orbigniana ssp. orbigniana*
B. plumosa (h,m,l)
Botryoglossum farlowianum (m,l)
Calliarthron cheilosporioides (h,m,l)
C. tuberculosum (m,l)
C. sp. (h,m,l)
Callithamnion pikeanum (h,m,l)
C. rupicolum (m)
Callophyllis crenulata (l)
C. firma (l)

396

C. pinnata (l)
C. thompsonii (l)
C. violacea (l)
C. sp. (l)
Centroceras clavulatum*
Ceramium eatonianum (m,l)
Constantinea simplex (l)
Corallina officinalis var. *chilensis* (h,m,l)
C. vancouveriensis (h,m,l)
C. sp. (h,m,l)
Corallines (custose) (h,m,l)
Cryptonemia obovata (l)
C. ovalifolia (m,l)
Cryptopleura. corallinaria (h)
C. lobulifera (h,m,l)
C. violacea (h,m,l)
Cryptosiphonia woodii (h,m)
Cumagloia andersonii (h)
Delesseria decipiens (l)
Dermatolithon sp.*
Dilsea californica (m,l)
Endocladia muricata (h,m,l)
Erythrophyllum delesserioides (m,l)
Farlowia compressa (m,l)
F. conferta (m,l)
F. mollis (h,m,l)
Gastroclonium coulteri (h,m,l)
Gelidium coulteri (h,m,l)
G. purpurascens (m,l)
G. pusillum (m,l)
G. robustum (l)
Gigartina agardhii (h,m,l)
G. canaliculata (h,m,l)
G. corymbifera (m,l)
G. exasperata (m,l)
G. harveyana (m,l)
G. leptorhynchos (h,m,l)
G. papillata (h,m,l)
G. spinosa (l)
G. volans (m,l)
Gloiosiphonia verticillaris (l)
Gonimophyllum skottsbergii (l)
Gracilaria sjoestedtii (m,l)
Gracilariophila oryzoides*
Grateloupia doryphora (m,l)
Gymnogongrus leptophyllus (m,l)
G. linearis (m,l)
G. platyphyllus (l)
Halosaccion glandiforme (h,m,l)

Halymenia schizymenioides (m,l)
Herposiphonia verticillata (m,l)
Hildenbrandia occidentalis (l)
Hollenbergia subulata*
Hymenena flabelligera (m,l)
H. multiloba*
Iridaea cordata var. *splendens* (h,m,l)
I. cordata var. *cordata* (h,m,l)
I. flaccida (h,m)
I. heterocarpa (h,m)
I. lineare*
Janczewskia gardneri (m,l)
Laurencia spectabilis (h,m,l)
Lithothamnium sp.*
Melobesia marginata (m,l)
M. mediocris (m,l)
Membranoptera multiramosa*
M. weeksiae*
Mesophyllum conchatum*
Microcladia borealis (h,m,l)
M. california (l)
M. coulteri (h,m,l)
Neoagardhiella baileyi (m,l)
Neoptilota californica*
N. densa (l)
N. hypnoides*
Nienburgia andersoniana (l)
Odonthalia floccosa (m,l)
Opuntiella californica (m,l)
Petrocelis middendorffii (h,m,l)
P. sp. (h)
Petroglossum parvum (m,l)
Peyssonellia sp. (l)
Phycodrys setchellii (h,m,l)
Pikea californica (h,m,l)
P. robusta (m)
Pleonosporium squarrulosum (h,m,l)
Plocamiocolax pulvinata*
Plocamium cartilagineum (m,l)
P. violaceum (h,m,l)
Polyneura latissima (h,m,l)
Polysiphonia brodiaei*
P. hendryi (h,m,l)
P. pacifica (h,m,l)
P. paniculata (h,m,l)
P. scopulorum var. *villum* (h)
P. sp. (h,m,l)
Porphyra lanceolata*
P. occidentalis (l)

P. perforata (h,m)
P. pseudolanceolata (h)
*P. smithii**
Porphyrella gardneri (l)
Prionitis lanceolata (l)
P. lyallii (l)
Pterochondria woodii (m,l)
P. woodii (m,l)
*Pterosiphonia baileyi**
P. bipinnata (h,m,l)
P. dendroidea (h,m,l)
P. sp. (h,m,l)
Ptilota filicina (l)
*Ptilothamnionopsis lejolisea**
Rhodochorton purpureum (h,l)
Rhodoglossum affine (h,m,l)
R. californicum (h,m,l)
R. roseum (m,l)

Rhodomela larix (h,m,l)
Rhodymenia californica (l)
R. pacifica (m,l)
Schizymenia pacifica (h,m,l)
Serraticardia macmillanii (l)
Smithora naiadum (h,m,l)
Stenogramme interrupta (l)
Tenarea sp. (l)
Tiffaniella synderiae (h,m,l)
Weeksia sp.*

DIVISION CYANOPHYTA
Calothrix sp. (h)
Oscillatoria sp. (h)

DIVISION SPERMATOPHYTA
Phyllospadix scouleri (m,l)
P. torreyi (h,m,l)

The taxonomy follows Abbott and Hollenberg (1976). Algal specimens were determined by I.A. Abbott and J.E. Hansen. Voucher specimens are deposited in the Herbarium at the University of California, Santa Cruz. *Porphyra pseudolanceolata* was identified by Thomas F. Mumford.

INTERTIDAL INVERTEBRATES

* = Found only at Año Nuevo area study areas during the 1971-1973 study.
** = Found at most other study areas along Santa Cruz and San Mateo coast.

+ to++++ indicates the relative likelihood of observation in each of the three tide zones.

	High	Mid	Low
PHYLUM PORIFERA (sponges)			
Class Calcarea			
Leucandra heathi			++
Leucilla nuttingi			++++
Leucosolenia eleanor			++
Class Demospongiae			
Acarnus erithacus			++
Adocia gellindra		+	++++
Antho lithophoenix		++	++++
Aplysilla glacialis			++
A. polyraphis*			+
Axocielita originalis**			+++
Cliona celata**		+	++++
C. lobata*			+
Halichondria panicea**			++++
Haliclona sp.**		++	++++
Halisarca sp.			+
Lissodendoryx firma		++	++++
Ophlitaspongia pennata**		+	++
Paresperella psila*			+
Polymastia pachymastia			++
Suberites sp.**		+	++++
Toxadocia sp.		+	
Xestospongia vanilla			+
PHYLUM CNIDARIA			
Class Hydrozoa (hydroids)			
Abietinaria sp.			++
Aglaophenia sp.**		+	++
Campanularia sp.			++
Family Corynidae		+	++
Eudendrium sp.			++
Plumularia sp.**		+	+++
Sertularella sp.**		++	++
Sertularia sp.			++
Tubularia sp.			+++
Class Anthozoa (sea anemones & corals)			
Anthopleura artemisia**	+++	+++	+++
A. elegantissima**	++++	++++	++++

399

	High	Mid	Low
*A. xanthogrammica***	++++	++	+++
Balanophyllia elegans			+++
Clavularia sp.		+	+++
Corynactis californica			++++
*Epiactis prolifera***	++	++++	++++
Tealia coriacea			+
PHYLUM NEMERTEA (ribbon worms)			
Amphiporus formidabilis		+	+
*A. imparispinosus***		++	+
*Cerebratulus californiensis**		++	+
*Emplectonema gracile***	++		
Lineus vegetus		+	++
Micrura verrilli		+	
*Nemertopsis gracilis**	+		
*Paranemertes peregrina***	+	++	++
Tubulanus polymorphus		+	++
PHYLUM SIPUNCULA (peanut worms)			
*Phascolosoma agassizii***		++	++
Themiste dyscrita		++	++
*T. pyroides**			+
PHYLUM ECHIURA			
*Urechis caupo** (fat innkeeper)		++	+
PHYLUM ANNELIDA (segmented worms)			
Class Polychaeta			
Subclass Errantia (creepy-crawlies)			
Arabella iricolor			++
Arctonoe vittata			+
*Chrysopetalum occidentale**			+
*Drilonereis falcata**			+
Eulalia aviculiseta		+	+
*Halosydna brevisetosa***	+	++	++++
Hemipodus borealis	+	++	++
Lumbrineris erecta			+
*L. japonica**			+
L. latreilli		+	
L. tetraura			++
L. zonata		+	+
Marphysa stylobranchiata			++
*Nereis grubei***	+	++	+++
N. vexillosa	+	+	+
Ophiodromus pugettensis		+	+++
*Pareurythoe californica**			++
Perinereis monterea	+		
*Platynereis bicanaliculata***			+
*Sthenelais fusca**			+
Syllidae subfamily Eusyllinae			+
Syllidae subfamily Syllinae	+	+	++

	High	Mid	Low
Subclass Sedentaria (tube worms)			
Ampharetidae sp.*			+
Armandia brevis			+
Boccardia proboscidea			++
*Capitella capitata**			+
Chone ecaudata			+
Cirratulus cirratus			++
*Cirriformia spirabrancha***	+	+++	++
Dodecaceria fewkesi	+	++	++
*Eudistylia polymorpha**			+++
Eupomatus gracilis		+	
*Naineris dendritica***	+	+	++
*Neoamphitrite robusta**			+
Owenia collaris			+
*Phragmatopoma californica***	++++	++++	++++
*Ramex californiensis**		+	
*Sabella media**		+	
*Salmacina tribranchiata***		++	+++
*Schistocomus hiltoni**			+
*Serpula vermicularis***		+++	++
*Spinosphaera oculata**		+	
Spirorbis eximius		++	+
Spirorbis sp.			+
*Terebella californica**		+	
Tharyx multifilis		+	+
T. sp.		+	
Thelepus crispus			++
T. sp.			+
PHYLLUM MOLLUSCA			
Class Polyplacophora (chitons)			
Basiliochiton heathii			+
*Cryptochiton stelleri***		++	+++
*Cyanoplax dentiens***	++	+++	++++
C. hartwegii		+	
Katharina tunicata	+	++++	++
Lepidozona cooperi		++	++
L. mertensii			++
Mopalia ciliata		++	++
*M. hindsii***			++
M. lignosa		+	++
*M. muscosa***	++	++	+++
M. porifera			+
*Nuttallina californica***	++	++	
Placiphorella velata			+
Stenoplax heathiana			+
*Tonicella lineata***		++++	++++
Class Bivalvia (clams, mussels)			
*Adula californiensis**		++	

	High	Mid	Low
Chlamys hericius			+
*Hiatella arctica***			++
*Mactra californica**			+
Mytilimeria nuttallii			+
*Mytilus californianus***	++++	++++	
M. edulis	++		
Penitella penita		+	+++
Petricola carditoides			+
Pododesmus cepio		+	
Protothaca staminea			++

Class Gastropoda
  Cap-shaped shells (limpets)

	High	Mid	Low
Acmaea mitra		+++	++++
*Collisella asmi***	++++	++++	+
*C. digitalis***	++++	+++	+
*C. limatula***	+	++	+
C. ochracea		+	
*C. pelta***	+++	++++	+++
*C. scabra***	++++	++	+
C. strigatella	+	++	++
*Crepidula adunca***	++	+++	+++
C. nummaria		+	++
Diodora aspera		+	+++
Hipponix cranioides			++
*Lottia gigantea***		++	
*Megatebennus bimaculatus***		+	++
*Notoacmea insessa***		+	++++
*N. paleacea***		++	++++
N. persona	++		
*N. scutum***	++	+++	++
*Trimusculus reticulatus***		+	+

Class Gastropoda
  Spiral shells (snails)

	High	Mid	Low
Acanthina punctulata	+	+	+
*A. spirata***	+++	+++	+++
*Amphissa versicolor***	+	++	+++
Barleeia acuta		++	+
B. haliotiphila			+
Bittium eschrichtii	+	++	++
Calliostoma canaliculatum		+++	+++
C. ligatum		+	+++
*Ceratostoma foliatum**			+
Cerithiopsis sp.		+	
Clathromangelia interfossa			+
*Epitonium tinctum***	++	+++	++
Haliotis cracherodii		+	+++
H. rufescens			++

	High	Mid	Low
*Homalopoma luridum**			+
*Lacuna marmorata***	+	++	++
L. porrecta	+		
L. unifasciata		+	+
Lamellaria sp.*			+
*Lirularia parcipicta**		+	
L. succincta		+	
*Littorina keenae***	++	+	
*L. scutulata***	+++		
Margarites salmoneus	+	++	++
*Mitrella carinata***	++	+++	+++
Mitromorpha sp.*		+	+
Nassarius mendicus			++
*Nucella emarginata***	++	+	++
N. lamellosa			+
Ocenebra atropurpurea	+	+	
O. interfossa		+	+
O. lurida		+	++
Odostomia sp.		+	
Olivella biplicata		++	++
*Opalia montereyensis**			+
Pseudomelatoma torosa	+	+	+
*Tegula brunnea***	++	+++	+++
*T. funebralis***	++++	++++	++
T. montereyi		++	+
*Tricolia pulloides***	+	++	++
Velutina sp.			++

Class Gastropoda
No shells (slugs)

	High	Mid	Low
*Acanthodoris lutea**			+
*A. nanaimoensis**		+	
Aeolidia papillosa	+	+	
*Aldisa sanguinea**		+	
Anisodoris nobilis	+	+	++
*Archidoris montereyensis***		++	+++
Cadlina flavomaculata			+
C. luteomarginata		+	+
Cadlina modesta			++
*Coryphella trilineata***		+	++
*Diaulula sandiegensis***		++	+++
Hermissenda crassicornis		+	+
Hopkinsia rosacea		+	
*Onchidella borealis***		++	++
Precuthona divae			+
*Rostanga pulchra***		++	++
Triopha carpenteri		+	
T. maculata		++	++
Tritonia festiva			+

	High	Mid	Low
Class Cephalopoda			
Octopus sp.		++	++
PHYLUM ARTHROPODA			
Class Cirripedia (barnacles)			
*Balanus cariosus***	+	++	+
*B. crenatus***		+	+++
*B. glandula***	++++	++	++
B. nubilus			++
B. tintinnabulum			++
*Chthamalus dalli***	++++	++	++
*Pollicipes polymerus***	++	+	+
*Tetraclita rubescens***	+	++	+
Class Malacostraca			
Order Isopoda (isopods)			
Cirolana harfordi	++	++	+
*"Dynamenella" glabra**			+
Idotea aculeata		+	+
*I. fewkesi**		+	
I. montereyensis		+	+
*I. stenops***		+	++
I. urotoma	+	++	+++
*I. wosnesenskii***	+	+	+
Ligia pallasii	+		
*Synidotea pettiboneae**	+		+
Order Decapoda (shrimps, crabs)			
*Betaeus harfordi**		+	
*Cancer antennarius***	++	+++	++++
C. jordani			+
C. productus		+++	+++
Hemigrapsus nudus	+	+++	
*H. oregonensis**	++	+++	
Heptacarpus brevirostris		+	+
H. palpator		+	+
H. pictus	+	+	+
*H. taylori***		++	+++
*Lophopanopeus bellus**			+
L. leucomanus		+	+
Loxorynchus crispatus		+	++
*L. grandis**			++
*Mimulus foliatus**			+
Opisthopus transversus		+	++
*Pachycheles holosericus**			++
P. rudis		+++	+++
*P. crassipes***		++	++
*Pagurus granosimanus***	+	+++	++
*P. hirsutiusculus***	++	++	+
*P. samuelis***	+	++	+

	High	Mid	Low
Petrolisthes cinctipes	+	+++	+++
P. eriomerus		++	+++
Pugettia gracilis*			+
P. producta**	++	++++	++++
P. richii			++

PHYLUM ECHINODERMATA
  Class Asteroidea (sea stars)

	High	Mid	Low
Dermasterias imbricata	+	++++	++++
Henricia leviuscula**		++	++++
Leptasterias sp.	++	+++	++++
Patiria miniata		++++	+++
Pisaster brevispinus**		++	++++
P. ochraceus**	++	++++	++++
Pycnopodia helianthoides		+	++

  Class Ophiuroidea (brittle stars)

	High	Mid	Low
Amphiodia occidentalis		+	++
Ophiopholis aculeata			+
Ophiothrix spiculata			+++

  Class Echinoidea (sea urchins)

	High	Mid	Low
Strongylocentrotus franciscanus		+	++
S. purpuratus**		+++	+++

  Class Holothuroidea (sea cucumbers)

	High	Mid	Low
Cucumaria miniata*		+	
C. piperata			++
C. sp.*		++	++
Eupentacta quinquesemita			++
Leptosynapta sp.			+
Lissothuria nutriens		+	++
Pachythyone rubra			+

PHYLUM BRYOZOA (moss animals)

	High	Mid	Low
Crisia occidentalis		+	+++
Dendrobeania lichenoides		+	++
Eurystomella bilabiata**		+	++
Filicrisia sp.			+
Flustrellidra corniculata			+
Hippothoa hyalina			++
Scrupocellaria californica			. +
Tricellaria erecta		+	+++
T. occidentalis			++

PHYLUM CHORDATA
  Class Ascidiacea (sea squirts)

	High	Mid	Low
Aplidium californicum**			+++
Archidistoma diaphanes			++
A. psammion**		+	+++
A. ritteri		+	+++
A. sp.*			+
Ascidia ceratodes		+	
Clavelina huntsmani		+	++++

	High	Mid	Low
*Cystodytes lobatus**			+
C. sp.			+++
Didemnum carnulentum		+	++
*Distaplia occidentalis***		+	++++
*D. smithi**			+
Euherdmania claviformis			++
Perophora annectens			++
*Polyclinum planum**			+
*Pycnoclavella stanleyi**			+
Pyura haustor		+	++
Ritterella aequalisiphonis			++
R. pulchra			+
*Styela montereyensis***		++	+++
Synoicum parfustis			++
*Trididemnum opacum**			++

BIRDS

Relative Seasonal Abundance

A = Abundant, seen in very large numbers all of the time.

C = Common, seen almost every day, sometimes in large numbers.

F = Frequent, seen on most occasions.

U = Uncommon, irregularly present or hard to see.

R = Rare, seen only occasionally each year.

a = Accidental, irregular and unexpected.

Following the common name, the first grouping of letters indicates the relative seasonal abundance in the order: *Winter, Spring, Summer, Fall.*

Habitat

D = Dunes and chaparral.

F = Forest or woodland.

G = Grassland or brush.

H = Human habitations.

I = Año Nuevo Island.

O = Ocean, open water, channel, or surf.

P = Freshwater pond and surroundings.

R = Rocky coast, cliffs, and offshore rocks.

S = Sandy coast, beaches.

After the designation of relative seasonal abundance, the second grouping of letters indicates the *habitat.*

* Indicates species nesting within Año Nuevo State Reserve.

ORDER GAVIIFORMES

Family Gaviidae — **Loons**

Gavia immer — Common Loon (U,U,R,U; O)

G. arctica — Arctic Loon (C,C,R,C; O)

G. stellata — Red-throated Loon (U,U,R,U; O)

ORDER PODICIPEDI-FORMES

Family Podicipedidae — **Grebes**

Aechmophorus occidentalis — Western Grebe (C,C,U,C; O)

Podiceps grisegena — Red-necked Grebe (R,R—R; O)

P. auritus — Horned Grebe (F,U—U; O,P)

P. nigricollis — Eared Grebe (F,F—U; O,P)

Podilymbus podiceps — Pied-billed Grebe (U,U,U,U; P)

ORDER PROCELLARIIFORMES

Family Diomedeidae

Diomedea nigripes — Black-footed Albatross (—U,R,R; O)

Family Procellariidae — **Tubenoses**

Fulmarus glacialis — Northern Fulmar (U,R——; O)

Puffinus griseus — Sooty Shearwater (—U,C,C; O)

P. puffinus — Manx Shearwater (R——R; O)

ORDER PELECANIFORMES
  Family Pelecanidae   **Pelicans**
    Pelecanus erythrorhynchos   White Pelican (R——R; O)
    P. occidentalis   Brown Pelican (U,R,F,C; O)
  Family Phalacrocoracidae   **Cormorants**
    Phalacrocorax auritus   Double-crested Cormorant (U,U,U,U; R,O)
    P. penicillatus   Brandt's Cormorant (C,C,C,C; R,O)
    P. pelagicus   Pelagic Cormorant* (C,C,C,C; R,O)
  Family Fregatidae
    Fregata magnificens   Magnificent Frigatebird (———a; O)

ORDER CICONIIFORMES
  Family Ardeidae   **Herons and Bitterns**
    Ardea herodias   Great Blue Heron (U,U,U,U; R,S)
    Butorides striatus   Green Heron (— — R —; P)
    Casmerodius albus   Great Egret (R,R,R,R; R,S)
    Egretta thula   Snowy Egret (F,U,R,U; I,R,S)
    Botaurus lentiginosus   American Bittern* (U,U,U,U; P)
    Bubulcus ibis   Cattle Egret (R———; I)
    Nycticorax nycticorax   Black-crowned Night Heron (R,R,R,R; P)

ORDER ANSERIFORMES
  Family Anatidae   **Waterfowl**
    Olor columbianus   Whistling Swan (———R; O)
    Branta canadensis   Canada Goose (———R; O)
    B. bernicla   Brant (R,U,R,U; O)
    Anser albifrons   White-fronted Goose (———R; O)
    Chen caerulescens   Snow Goose (———R; O)
    Anas platyrhynchos   Mallard (U,U,U,U; P)
    A. strepera   Gadwall (R,R—R; P)
    A. acuta   Pintail (U,R—U; P,O)
    A. crecca   Green-winged Teal (R,R—R; P)
    A. cyanoptera   Cinnamon Teal (U,U—U; P)
    A. americana   American Wigeon (U,R—R; P)
    A. clypeata   Northern Shoveler (U,R—R; P)
    Aix sponsa   Wood Duck (a,a—a; P)
    Aythya americana   Redhead (R——R; P)
    A. collaris   Ring-necked Duck (R——U; P)
    A. valisineria   Canvasback (U——U; P)
    A. marila   Greater Scaup (U——U; P)
    A. affinis   Lesser Scaup (U——F; P)
    Bucephala clangula   Common Goldeneye (U,R—R; O)
    B. islandica   Barrow's Goldeneye (R——R; O)
    B. albeola   Bufflehead (F,U—U; O,P)
    Oxyura jamaicensis   Ruddy Duck (F,F,F,F; P,O)
    Histrionicus histrionicus   Harlequin Duck (U,R,R,U; O)
    Somateria spectabilis   King Eider (a,a—a; O)
    Melanitta deglandi   White-winged Scoter (F,U—U; O)
    M. perspicillata   Surf Scoter (C,C,R,C; O,P)
    M. nigra   Black Scoter (U,R—R; O)

Lophodytes cucullatus — Hooded Merganser (R,R—R; P)
Mergus serrator — Red-breasted Merganser (F,U,R,U; O)

ORDER FALCONIFORMES
Family Carthartidae — **Vultures**
Carthartes aura — Turkey Vulture (R,U,F,U; G,F)
Family Accipitridae — **Kites, Hawks, and Eagles**
Elanus leucurus — White-tailed Kite (F,U,U,F; G,D)
Accipter striatus — Sharp-shinned Hawk (U,U,R,U; F)
A. cooperii — Cooper's Hawk (U,U,R,U; F)
Circus cyaneus — Marsh Hawk* (F,F,U,F; G,D)
Buteo lagopus — Rough-legged Hawk (U,R—R; F)
B. jamaicensis — Red-tailed Hawk* (C,C,C,C; F,G)
B. lineatus — Red-shouldered Hawk (R,R—R; F)
Aquila chrysaetos — Golden Eagle (a,a—a; —)
Family Pandionidae
Pandion haliaetus — Osprey (R,U—U; S,R)
Family Falconidae — **Falcons**
Falco peregrinus — Peregrine Falcon (—R—R; G)
F. columbarius — Merlin (U,R—U; G)
F. sparverius — American Kestrel* (C,C,C,C; G)

ORDER GALLIFORMES
Family Phasianidae — **Quails, Pheasants**
Lophortyx californicus — California Quail* (F,F,F,F; G)
Phasianus colchicus — Ring-necked Pheasant (R,R,R,R; G)

ORDER GRUIFORMES — **CRANES AND ALLIES**
Family Rallidae — **Rails**
Porzana carolina — Sora (R,R,R,R; P)
Gallinula chloropus — Common Gallinule (R,R,R,R; P)
Fulica americana — American Coot* (C,C,C,C; P)

ORDER CHARADRII- — **SHOREBIRDS, GULLS, ALCIDS**
Family Haematopodidae — **Oystercatchers**
Haematopus bachmani — Black Oystercatcher* (F,U,U,F; R)
Family Charadriidae — **Plovers**
Charadrius semipalmatus — Semipalmated Plover (—R—U; S)
C. alexandrinus — Snowy Plover* (U,U,R,U; S,D)
C. vociferus — Killdeer* (F,F,R,F; D,G)
Pluvialis dominica — American Golden Plover (———R; S)
P. squatarola — Black-bellied Plover (C,F,U,C; S,R)
Family Scolopacidae — **Shorebirds**
Aphriza virgata — Surfbird (F,U,R,C; R,S)
Arenaria interpres — Ruddy Turnstone (F,U,R,F; R,S)
A. melanocephala — Black Turnstone (C,F,R,C; R,S)
Capella gallinago — Common Snipe (———R; P)
Numenius americanus — Long-billed Curlew (—R—R; S,R)
N. phaeopus — Whimbrel (F,U,R,F; R,S)
Actitis macularia — Spotted Sandpiper (R,U—U; S,R,P)

Heteroscelus incanus — Wandering Tattler (U,U,R,U; R,S)
Catoptrophorus semipalmatus — Willet (C,F,U,C; S,R)
Tringa melanoleucus — Greater Yellowlegs (R,R—R; I,R)
T. flavipes — Lesser Yellowlegs (———R; R,S)
Calidris canutus — Red Knot (U,R,R,U; S,R)
C. ptilocnemis — Rock Sandpiper (U,R—R; I,R)
C. melanotos — Pectoral Sandpiper (———R; S)
C. bairdii — Baird's Sandpiper (———R; S)
C. minutilla — Least Sandpiper (U,R—U; S,R)
C. alpina — Dunlin (U,R—U; S,R)
C. mauri — Western Sandpiper (R,R—U; S,R)
C. alba — Sanderling (C,F,U,A; S,R)
Limnodromus scolopaceus — Long-billed Dowitcher (R,R—R; S,P)
L. griseus — Short-billed Dowitcher (R,R—U; S,P)
Tryngites subruficollis — Buff-breasted Sandpiper (———a; S)
Limosa fedoa — Marbled Godwit (C,F,R,C; S,R)
Philomachus pugnax — Ruff (a———a; S)

Family Phalaropodidae — **Phalaropes**
Phalaropus fulicarius — Red Phalarope (U,R—U; O,P)
P. lobatus — Northern Phalarope (R,U—U; O,P,S)
Steganopus tricolor — Wilson's Phalarope (R,R—R; O,P,S)

Family Stercorariidae — **Jaegers, Skuas**
Stercorarius parasiticus — Parasitic Jaeger (R,R,R,U; O)
S. pomarinus — Pomarine Jaeger (—R—R; O)

Family Laridae — **Gulls, Terns**
Larus hyperboreus — Glaucous Gull (R,R—R; O)
L. glaucescens — Glaucous-winged Gull (F,U,R,U; O,S,R)
L. occidentalis — Western Gull* (C,C,C,C; O,S,R,P)
L. argentatus — Herring Gull (C,F,R,C; O,S,R)
L. thayeri — Thayer's Gull (R———; O,R,S)
L. californicus — California Gull (F,F,R,F; O,S,R)
L. delawarensis — Ring-billed Gull (R,R,R,R; S,R,O)
L. canus — Mew Gull (R—R; O,S)
L. philadelphia — Bonaparte's Gull (F,C—F; O,S,R,P)
L. heermanni — Heerman's Gull (F,R,U,C; S,R,O)
Rissa tridactyla — Black-legged Kittiwake (U,U—R; O,R,S)
Xema sabini — Sabine's Gull (—R—R; O,R,S)
Larus minutus — Little Gull (a———; O,R,S)
Sterna forsteri — Forster's Tern (R,U,F,F; O,S)
S. hirundo — Common Tern (—R—U; O,S)
S. paradisaea — Arctic Tern (—R—R; O)
S. albifrons — Least Tern (—RR—; O)
S. maxima — Royal Tern (———RR; O)
S. elegans — Elegant Tern (———RU; O,S)
S. caspia — Caspian Tern (—UUU; O,S)

Family Alcidae — **Alcids**
Uria aalge — Common Murre (R,R,U,R; O)
Cepphus columba — Pigeon Guillemot* (—U,U,U; A,O,R)
Brachyramphus marmoratus — Marbled Murrelet (R,R,U,R; O)

Endomychura hypoleuca	Xantus' Murrelet (———R; O)
Ptychoramphus aleuticus	Cassin's Auklet (R,R,R,R; O)
Cerorhinca monocerata	Rhinoceros Auklet (R,R—R; O)
Lunda cirrhata	Tufted Puffin (—R,R,R; O)

ORDER COLUMBIFORMES
Family Columbidae — Pigeons, Doves
- *Columba fasciata* — Band-tailed Pigeon (U,U,R,U; F)
- *C. livia* — Rock Dove (F,F,F,F; R,H,G)
- *Zenaida macroura* — Mourning Dove* (C,C,C,C; G)

ORDER STRIGIFORMES
Family Tytonidae — Barn Owls
- *Tyto alba* — Barn Owl (R,R,R,R; G,H,R)
Family Strigidae — Other Owls
- *Bubo virginianus* — Great Horned Owl (U,U,U,U; F)
- *Nyctea scandiaca* — Snowy Owl (a———; R)
- *Athene cunicularia* — Burrowing Owl (R,R,R,R; G)
- *Asio flammeus* — Short-eared Owl (R,U—R; D,G)

ORDER CAPRIMULGIFORMES
Family Caprimulgidae — Goatsuckers
- *Chordeiles minor* — Common Nighthawk (—R,U,R; G)

ORDER APODIFORMES
Family Apodidae — Swifts
- *Cypseloides niger* — Black Swift* (—R,U,R; G,R)
- *Aeronautes saxatalis* — White-throated Swift (R,R,U,R; G)
Family Trochilidae — Hummingbirds
- *Calypte anna* — Anna's Hummingbird* (F,F,F,F; G,D)
- *Selasphorus rufus* — Rufous Hummingbird (—U—R; G)
- *S. sasin* — Allen's Hummingbird* (U,F,U—; G)

ORDER CORACIIFORMES
Family Alcedinidae — Kingfishers
- *Megaceryle alcyon* — Belted Kingfisher (F,U,U,F; R,P)

ORDER PICIFORMES
Family Picidae — Woodpeckers
- *Colaptes auratus* — Common Flicker* (F,F,F,F; G,F,D)
- *Melanerpes formicivorus* — Acorn Woodpecker (U,U,U,U; F)
- *Sphyrapicus varius* — Yellow-bellied Sapsucker (U,U—U; F)
- *Picoides villosus* — Hairy Woodpecker (R,R,R,R; F)
- *P. pubescens* — Downy Woodpecker (R,R,R,R; F)

ORDER PASSERIFORMES
Family Tyrranidae — Flycatchers
- *Tyrannus melancholicus* — Tropical Kingbird (———a; G,D)
- *T. verticalis* — Western Kingbird (—,R—R; G)
- *T. vociferans* — Cassin's Kingbird (—a—a; G)
- *Myiarchus cinerascens* — Ash-throated Flycatcher (—R,U,R; G,P)

Sayornis nigricans — Black Phoebe* (F,F,F,F; P,D,R)
S. saya — Say's Phoebe (U,R—U; G)
Empidonax trailii — Traill's Flycatcher (—U,R,U; P)
E. difficilis — Western Flycatcher (—U,U,U; P)
Contopus sordidulus — Western Wood Pewee (—U,U,U; P)

Family Hirundinidae — **Swallows**
Tachycineta thalassina — Violet-green Swallow (—U,F,U; G,P)
Iridoprocne bicolor — Tree Swallow (—F,U,U; G,P)
Riparia riparia — Bank Swallow (—R,R—; P)
Stelgidopteryx ruficollis — Rough-winged Swallow (—R,R,R; P)
Hirundo rustica — Barn Swallow* (—F,C,F; G,P)
Petrochelidon pyrrhonota — Cliff Swallow* (—F,C,F; G,P)

Family Corvidae — **Jays, Crows**
Cyanocitta stelleri — Steller's Jay (U,U,U,U; F)
Aphelocoma coerulescens — Scrub Jay (F,F,F,F; F)
Corvus brachyrhynchos — Common Crow (U,U—U; F)
C. corax — Common Raven (U,U,U,U; G)

Family Paridae — **Chickadees, Bushtits**
Parus rufescens — Chestnut-backed Chickadee (F,F,F,F; D,F)
Psaltripus minimus — Common Bushtit* (F,F,F,F; D,G,P)

Family Chameidae — **Wrentits**
Chamaea fasciata — Wrentit* (U,U,U,U; D,G)

Family Sittidae — **Nuthatches**
Sitta canadensis — Red-breasted Nuthatch (R,R—R; F,P)
S. pygmaea — Pygmy Nuthatch (U,U,U,U; F,P)

Family Certhiidae — **Creepers**
Certhia familiaris — Brown Creeper (U,U,U,U; F,P)

Family Troglodytidae — **Wrens**
Thyromanes bewickii — Bewick's Wren (U,U,U,U; D,G)
Cistothorus palustris — Long-billed Marsh Wren* (U,U,U,U; P)

Family Mimidae — **Thrashers**
Mimus polyglottos — Mockingbird (U,U,U,U; D,G)
Toxostoma redivivum — California Thrasher* (F,F,F,F; G,D)

Family Turdidae — **Thrushes**
Turdus migratorius — American Robin (F,F,U,F; G,P)
Ixoreus naevius — Varied Thrush (U,R—R; F)
Catharus guttatus — Hermit Thrush (U,U,U,U, F,P)
C. ustulata — Swainson's Thrush (—U,U,R; P)

Family Motacillidae — **Pipits**
Anthus spinoletta — Water Pipit (U,U—U; S,G,P)

Family Sylviidae — **Kinglets, Gnatcatchers**
Regulus calendula — Ruby-crowned Kinglet (U,U—U; F,P)

Family Bombycillidae
  Bombycilla cedrorum

Waxwings
  Cedar Waxwing (R,R,R,U; F,P)

Family Laniidae
  Lanius ludovicianus

Shrikes
  Loggerhead Shrike* (U,U,U,U; G)

Family Sturnidae
  Sturnus vulgaris

Starlings
  Starling* (F,F,F,F; R,G,S)

Family Vireonidae
  Vireo huttoni
  V. gilvus

Vireos
  Hutton's Vireo (R,R,R,R; F,P)
  Warbling Vireo (—R,R,R; P)

Family Parulidae
  Vermivora peregrina
  V. celata
  Dendroica townsendi
  D. petechia
  D. tigrina
  D. coronata
  D. occidentalis
  D. pensylavanica
  D. striata
  D. parlmarum
  Seirus noveboracensis
  Geothylpis trichas
  Wilsonia pusilla
  Setophaga ruticilla

Wood Warblers
  Tennessee Warbler (———a; P)
  Orange-crowned Warbler (—U,U,U; P)
  Townsend's Warbler (U,R,R,U; F,P)
  Yellow Warbler (—U,R,U; P)
  Cape May Warbler (———a; P)
  Yellow-rumped Warbler (F,U—U; G,P)
  Hermit Warbler (——R,R; P)
  Chestnut-sided Warbler—(———a; P)
  Blackpoll Warbler (———a; P)
  Palm Warbler (———a; P)
  Northern Waterthrush (—a—a; P)
  Common Yellowthroat* (U,F,F,U; P,S)
  Wilson's Warbler (—U,U,U; P)
  American Redstart (—a—a; P)

Family Ploceidae
  Passer domesticus

Weaver Finches
  House Sparrow (U,U,U,U; G,H)

Family Icteridae
  Sturnella neglecta
  Xanthocephalus xanthocephalus
  Agelaius phoeniceus
  A. tricolor
  Euphagus cyanocephalus
  Molothrus ater
  Icterus galbula

Blackbirds, Orioles
  Western Meadowlark* (C,C,C,C; G)
  Yellow-headed Blackbird (—R—R; P)
  Red-winged Blackbird (F,F,F,F; P,S,R)
  Tricolored Blackbird (R,U—U; P)
  Brewer's Blackbird* (F,F,F,F; H,G)
  Brown-headed Cowbird* (R,U,U,U; G)
  Northern Oriole (—U,U,R; P)

Family Fringillidae
  Carpodacus purpureus
  C. mexicanus
  Cardeulis pinus
  C. tristus
  C. psaltria
  Pipilo erythrophthalmus
  P. fuscus
  Passerculus sandwichensis
  Chondestes grammacus

Finches and Sparrows
  Purple Finch (R,R,R,R; G)
  House Finch* (C,C,C,C; G,D,H)
  Pine Siskin (R,R,R,R; P)
  American Goldfinch* (F,F,F,F; G,D,P)
  Lesser Goldfinch (U,U,U,U; G,D,P)
  Rufous-sided Towhee (U,U,U,U; D,G,P)
  Brown Towhee* (F,F,F,F; G,D)
  Savannah Sparrow* (F,F,F,F; G,D,S)
  Lark Sparrow (—R,U,U; G,F)

Junco hyemalis	Dark-eyed Junco* (F,F,F,F; G,F,P)
Spizella passerina	Chipping Sparrow (—R,R,R; F,P)
Zonotricha leucophrys	White-crowned Sparrow* (C,F,F,C; G,D)
Z. atricapilla	Golden-crowned Sparrow (C,F—U; G,D)
Passerella iliaca	Fox Sparrow (U,U—U; P,G)
Melospiza lincolnii	Lincoln's Sparrow (U,U—U; G)
M. melodia	Song Sparrow* (C,C,F,F; G,P,D)

INDEX

Additional information about individual species can be found in the species list appendix, pages 389-414.

Numbers in **bold face** indicate illustrations on this page.